travel

Australia, NZ & the Pacific

Isabelle Young

LONELY PLANET PUBLICATIONS
Melbourne Oakland Paris London

Healthy Travel – Australia, NZ & the Pacific
1st edition

Published by
Lonely Planet Publications Pty Ltd ACN 005 607 983
192 Burwood Rd, Hawthorn, Victoria 3122, Australia

Lonely Planet Offices
Australia PO Box 617, Hawthorn, Victoria 3122
USA 150 Linden Street, Oakland, CA 94607
UK 10a Spring Place, London NW5 3BH
France 1 rue du Dahomey, 75011, Paris

Printed by
The Bookmaker Pty Ltd
Printed in China

Illustrations
Martin Harris & Kate Nolan

Published
February 2000

ISBN 1 86450 052 2

INTRODUCTION — 10

OVERVIEW — 13

BEFORE YOU GO — 21

Sources of Information &
  Advice 21
Immunisations 26
Malaria Prevention 32
Travel Health Insurance 40

Pretravel Checkups & Other
  Preparations 42
What to Take 45
Books 52

ON THE MOVE — 54

STAYING HEALTHY — 60

Adjustment 60
Coping with a Hot Climate 60
Footcare 63
Sun 64
Beach & Swimming Safety ..67
Insect Bite Prevention 69

Safe Food 73
Safe Drinking Water 76
Personal Hygiene 80
Sex & Travel 81
Injections & Blood
  Transfusions 82

DIET & NUTRITION — 84

HELP ... — 96

If You're Ill 96
Signs of Serious Illness 101

Common Signs &
  Symptoms 102

DIARRHOEA — 107

Avoiding Diarrhoea 108
Types of Diarrhoea 108

Dealing with Diarrhoea 112
Persistent Diarrhoea 119

FEVER & HEPATITIS — 122

Dengue Fever 122
Malaria 125

Typhoid Fever 132
Viral Hepatitis 133

COUGHS, RASHES & OTHER COMMON PROBLEMS — 138

Colds & Flu 138
Sinusitis 140
Chest Infection 140
Asthma 141
Hay Fever 142

Sore Throat 142
Glandular Fever 143
Cold Sores 144
Mouth Ulcers 144
Intestinal Worms 145

Contents

Constipation 148
Piles 149
Indigestion 150
Appendicitis 151
Kidney Stone 151
Prostate Problems 152
Insect Bites 153

Sunburn 154
Fungal Infections 156
Bacterial Infections 157
Prickly Heat 158
Dermatitis 159
Skin Infestations 162
Creeping Eruption 165

EARS, EYES & TEETH 166

Ears 166
Eyes 168

Teeth 174

HIV/AIDS & SEXUAL HEALTH 178

HIV/AIDS 178

STIs 184

RARITIES 190

Brucellosis 190
Cholera 190
Filariasis 191
Hansen's Disease 192
Meningitis 192
Tuberculosis.....................193

Diphtheria 194
Measles 195
Mumps 195
Rubella 195
Tetanus 196

MENTAL WELLBEING 197

Travellers Stress 197
Culture Shock & Travel
  Fatigue 199
Anxiety 200

Depression 202
Delirium 203
Mefloquine 203
Doing Drugs 204

WOMEN TRAVELLERS 206

Menstrual Problems 206
Menopausal Travellers 209
Bladder Infection 211

Vaginal Infections 212
Contraception 215
Pregnant Travellers 220

BABIES & CHILDREN 224

Before You Go 224
On the Move 229
Staying Healthy 231

If Your Child Falls Ill 236
After You Get Back 242

TRAVELLERS WITH SPECIAL NEEDS 243

Information Sources 244
Older Travellers 246

Diabetic Travellers 251
HIV-Positive Travellers 255

WILDERNESS HEALTH & SAFETY 257

Information Sources 258
Radios & EPIRBS 260
Emergency Rescue 260
First Aid Kit 262
Weather 263
Food & Water 263

Driving 264
Trekking 266
Cycling 269
Caving 271
Emergency Situations 272
Natural Disasters 277

CLIMATE & ALTITUDE 279

Heat 279
Cold 283

Altitude 288

WATER SAFETY 292

Surf & Currents 292
Cramps 294
Water Pollution 295
Snorkelling 295
Sea Kayaking 298

Rivers & Waterways 299
Amoebic Meningitis 301
Scuba Diving 301
Hazardous Marine Life 308

BITES & STINGS 318

Mosquitoes & Flies 318
Bees, Wasps & Ants 322
Leeches 323
Ticks 325

Spiders 327
Scorpions 331
Snakes 332
Animal Bites 339

AFTER YOU GET BACK 341

APPENDIX I – TRADITIONAL MEDICINE 345

APPENDIX II – ALTERNATIVE THERAPIES 359

APPENDIX III – BUYING & USING MEDICINES 372

APPENDIX IV – MEDICAL SERVICES 384

APPENDIX V – FIRST AID 396

GLOSSARY 414

INDEX 421

EMERGENCY RESUSCITATION 432

THE AUTHOR

ISABELLE YOUNG

Isabelle Young qualified as a doctor in Britain before deciding there must be more to life than bleeps and hospital coffee. Her travels through various parts of the world have provided her with plenty of opportunity for putting her training into practice.

MEDICAL ADVISERS

To ensure that the information included in this guide is the best available and in line with current practice, a team of expert medical advisers was on hand every step of the way.

TONY GHERARDIN
Reviewed most of the chapters for this guide

Dr Tony Gherardin is currently national Medical Director of the Travellers Medical and Vaccination Centre (TMVC) group in Australia. He is a keen traveller and has spent several years living and working as a doctor overseas. When not travelling with his family, he now spends most of his time providing travel health advice to travellers heading in all directions around the globe.

CORINNE ELSE
Help ..., Coughs, Rashes & Other Common Problems, Ears, Eyes & Teeth (Ears), Mental Wellbeing, Women Travellers, First Aid (Wound Care), Buying & Using Medicines

Dr Corinne Else spends most of her time working as a general practitioner in the UK. Every now and again she manages to take time off to travel in Africa with her husband, helping him to research and write Lonely Planet guidebooks.

CHRISTOPHER VAN TILBERG
Climate & Altitude, Water Safety, First Aid

Dr Christopher Van Tilberg specialises in wilderness and

emergency medicine. He is adventure sports editor for *Wilderness Medicine Letter* and active in mountain rescue and wilderness safety education in the US. He is the author of *Backcountry Snowboarding* and *Canyoneering*, both published by The Mountaineers Books.

JOHN MASON
Babies & Children, Buying & Using Medicines

Dr John Mason was a family physician for 13 years before becoming Clinical Director of the UK-based Preventative Healthcare Company. Part of his responsibility is to provide international travel care and advice to client company employees and their families, as well as managing their healthcare while abroad.

BRIAN MULHALL
HIV/AIDS & Sexual Health

Dr Brian Mulhall is a Clinical Senior Lecturer in the Department of Public Health and Community Medicine at the University of Sydney, Australia. He has travelled extensively and has written several texts on sex and travel. His contribution was sponsored by the New South Wales Health Department and the Commonwealth Department of Health as part of a sexual health promotion program for travellers.

LARRY & PAUL GOODYER
Medical Kit (Before You Go), Safe Drinking Water, Insect Bites (Staying Healthy)

Dr Larry Goodyer is Chief Pharmacist for Nomad Travellers Store & Medical Centre, London, UK. He is also a senior lecturer in clinical pharmacy at King's College, London. His travels in India and Australia give him the first hand experience to produce medical kits for both tropical and developing world travel. Paul Goodyer is the managing director of Nomad Travellers Store & Medical Centre. His travels over the last 20 years include trips to Africa, Asia, South America and the Middle East. Getting ill on the road due to lack of knowledge led to the concept of a travellers medical centre.

SPECIAL THANKS

Special thanks go to St John Ambulance Australia for providing the information for the Emergency Resuscitation section on the inside backcover and the World Health Organization for permission to reproduce the maps between the first two chapters.

FROM THE AUTHOR

First, a big thank you to all the medical advisers, without whom this book would not have come into existence. Thank you also to Fred Peterson MD for his helpful comments on the text of *Healthy Travel Central & South America*, many of which are incoporated in the text of this guide.

Thanks go to the following experts who contributed text to the guide: Graeme Johnson for the section on Eyes; Iain Corran for the section on Teeth; Michelle Sobel for the Diabetic Travellers section in Travellers with Special Needs; Chris Wheeler for the text on footcare and blisters (in Staying Healthy and Wilderness Health & Safety); Bernadette Saulenier for the boxed text 'Alternative First Aid for Travellers'; and Elissa Coffman for the chapter on Alternative Therapies.

Some of the information in this guide was drawn from Lonely Planet guides, including *Australia 9* (Hugh Finlay), *New Zealand 9* (Peter Turner), *Tramping in New Zealand 4* (Jim DuFresne), *Papua New Guinea 6* (Adrian Lipscomb) and *South Pacific 1* (Errol Hunt).

Many other people helped make this guide what it is through generously providing information, constructive comments and helpful suggestions. In no particular order, thanks go to Chris Banks and Patrick Honan of Melbourne Zoo for helpful information on snakes, spiders and scorpions; Moya

Tomlinson of Women's Health (London) for suggestions for the Women Travellers chapter; Dr Michael Thomas of the Blood Care Foundation and Professor Neil Boyce of the Australian Red Cross for pointers for information on blood transfusions; Dr John Putland of the Qantas Aviation Health Services Department and the British Airways Medical Service in Heathrow for providing heaps of background information on air travel for the On the Move chapter; the National Sports Information Centre (Australia) for great reference material on climatic extremes; John Nathan for helpful insights on older travellers; Roslyn Bullas of Lonely Planet's Pisces series and Susannah Farfor for suggestions for the scuba diving section; the staff at IAMAT for generously providing me with information on their organisation; Darren Elder of Lonely Planet's Cycling series for finding the time to come up with the safety tips for cyclists that appear in the Wilderness Health & Safety chapter; and Jenny Thorpe and Suzanne Harrison, travelling mothers extraordinaire, for invaluable insights into the rigours of travelling with children. Thanks also go to Leonie Mugavin for her helpful suggestions, book-acquiring abilities and moral support.

Finally, in time-honoured tradition, thank you to my partner, David Petherbridge, for his help and unfailing support throughout this project – next time we'll climb mountains instead.

FROM THE PUBLISHER ──────

Production of this book was coordinated on the editorial side by Isabelle Young. Russell Kerr and Peter Cruttenden assisted with editing and proofing; Martine Lleonart helped out with editorial checks at layout. Senior Designer Jane Hart was responsible for layout of the book, with assistance from Indra Kilfoyle. Kirsty Hough and Anne Davey of Tanami Design came up with the original design concept for this book. Thanks to Paul Piaia for the maps, Martin Harris and Kate Nolan for all the illustrations, and David Kemp for the cover.

INTRODUCTION

Lonely Planet's aim has always been to enable adventurous travellers to get out there, to explore and better understand the world. Falling ill or getting injured on your travels prevents you from getting the most out of your travelling experience, which is why we decided to produce this *Healthy Travel* series.

Travelling may expose you to health risks you would not have encountered had you stayed at home but many of these risks are avoidable with good preparation beforehand and some common-sense measures while you are away. Even if you take all the recommended precautions, there's no guarantee you won't fall ill at some stage on your travels, and it's natural to be concerned about how to cope with illness in an unfamiliar setting. Although this guide is not intended as a substitute for seeking medical help, we hope it will help alleviate those concerns by giving you enough background information to enable you to make appropriate decisions.

Some chapters in this guide are designed to be read through in their entirety; the rest are there for you to dip into if the need arises. Before you leave, we suggest you take a look at the Overview chapter, which summarises the potential health risks of travel in the region, and read the Before You Go chapter, which gives you the complete lowdown on preparing for the trip. Travel medicine is an ever-changing topic, so we've given you plenty of guidance on where to get the most up-to-date information on specific health risks before you leave.

The Staying Healthy chapter gives you detailed advice on how to avoid illness and injury on your travels – essential reading for everyone. And when you return, it's a good idea to have a quick read of the When You Get Back chapter – this gives guidance on when to get a checkup and what to look out for, as well as a discussion of that scourge of the returning traveller, post-travel blues. If you are planning on doing any wilderness activities, turn to the Wilderness Health & Safety chapter.

The rest of the chapters are there in case you need them. If you fall ill, turn to the Help ... chapter. This gives guidelines on when to seek help, as well as some the basics of looking after yourself. In this chapter we've summarised the possible causes of some common symptoms, to help you work out what you may have. Alternatively, if you think you know what the problem is, you can turn straight to the relevant chapter later in the book, or you could look up your symptom in the index (symptoms are highlighted in colour in the index to make them easier to find).

We've aimed to group diseases and other medical problems into easily identifiable categories, as reflected in the chapter names. To cater for the differing needs of a wide range of travellers, we've included chapters tailored to the needs women, babies and children and travellers with special needs, including older travellers. If something isn't in the chapter you think it should be in, it's always worth looking it up in the index.

Because accidents do happen, and help may not be as rapidly available as at home, we've included advice on basic first aid measures, including what to do in an emergency. Bear in mind, though, that first aid techniques can't be learnt just from a book. If you are going to be travelling in remote areas, it's definitely worth doing a first aid course before you go.

If you do need to buy or take medicines while you are away, read the Buying & Using Medicines appendix before you do. Always make sure you take the correct dose, and that you avoid any medicines you know you are allergic to.

We hope that the advice in this guide helps ensure you have a healthy trip; if you do encounter problems, we hope it gives you greater confidence in dealing with them.

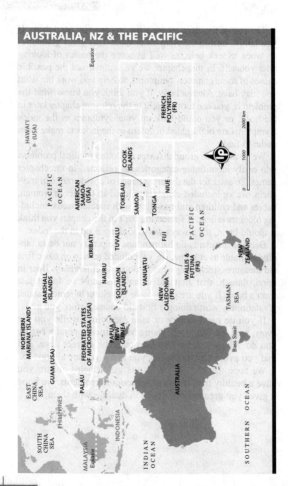

OVERVIEW

In this chapter we've summarised the main health concerns for travellers in Australia, New Zealand and the Pacific, and indicated where to look later in this guide for more details on all the issues discussed. The most important point to remember is that it's not hard to stay healthy – so long as you take some simple preventive measures.

AUSTRALIA

Although a significant proportion of Australia lies within the tropics, it's a pretty healthy place to travel around. In general, travelling in Australia won't put you at any greater risk of infectious diseases than travelling in any other developed country. It's always a good idea to make sure you are up to date with your routine immunisations (such as tetanus, p29), but you won't need any special shots.

If you are arriving in Australia from a yellow-fever infected country in South America or Africa, you will need a yellow fever vaccination certificate (p27).

Standards of health care are high here, as you might expect, but bear in mind that Australia is one of the least populated continents on earth – if you are adventuring in remote areas, medical assistance is not going to be instantly available. In this situation, it's a good idea to have some basic first-aid knowledge.

Climate

Heat (p279) and sunshine (p64) are probably the main hazards you are going to face on a trip to Australia. Much of the continent lies within the tropics, and the vast central arid region has a desert climate. The state of the ozone layer is also an important cause for concern. Although the heat is probably the most important factor to take into account, it's also worth bearing in mind that in some areas (especially highland areas), the weather can be very unpredictable. Blizzards can occur at any time of the year, including summer, in Alpine areas, and it's worth remembering that more bushwalkers die from the cold (p283) than the heat. If you are planning on doing any outdoor activities or driving in outback Australia, the Wilderness Health & Safety chapter gives guidance on a range of relevant issues.

Swimming Safety

If you're used to the gentle swells of the Mediterranean, Australian surf may hold a few surprises for you. People drown in surprising numbers off Australia's coast, so read the section on Beach & Swimming Safety on p67 as well as the Water Safety chapter before you take the plunge.

Insects & Diseases

Australia can be justifiably proud of its insects, both in terms of variety and, especially, quantity. Mosquitoes, sandflies, bush flies, horse flies and ants all make their mark on travellers in Australia – see the Bites & Stings chapter for more details.

In most of Australia, insect-borne diseases aren't the problem they are in other tropical regions. In the far north, outbreaks of mosquito-borne dengue fever (p122), currently the scourge of Asia, occur periodically and are likely to become more common; the only form of prevention is to avoid mosquito bites. Mosquitoes are also responsible for spreading Ross River fever and Barmah Forest Virus (p319; widespread, especially in the tropical north), Japanese encephalitis (p320; limited to Torres Strait Islands and Cape York) and Murray Valley encephalitis (p320; mainly in the tropical north). These are not going to be a big risk for most travellers, depending on where you are going, but it's obviously sensible to take steps to avoid mosquito bites wherever you are.

Ticks (p325) are a hazard for bushwalkers and picnickers in eastern Australia, and they can transmit tick paralysis and a type of typhus (or spotted fever), so it's worth taking steps to avoid them. Leeches (p323) are very common in most areas (apart from arid, central areas) and can be a nuisance, but they're not dangerous and don't transmit any disease.

Food, Water & Diseases

Yes, you can drink the water! You're at no more risk of diseases transmitted through food and water (p73), such as diarrhoea, food poisoning and hepatitis A, than you would be in any other developed country. Remember that food goes off quickly in the heat, so take care if you are self-catering, especially if you have no means of refrigeration.

If you are bushwalking in rural areas, you may need to purify water taken from rivers and streams before drinking, as *Giardia* (a diarrhoea-causing parasite; p120) occurs in some popular bushwalking areas.

Wildlife Hazards & Marine Creatures

Australia's wildlife is a major drawcard for travellers, but can be a potential hazard, especially if you are planning on spending time in the great outdoors. Potentially dangerous creatures include several species of venomous snakes (p332) and spiders (p327), as well as various marine creatures (p308) and, of course, crocodiles (p300). Australia's wildlife hazards tend to be much hyped (and, it must be said, much revered by Australians!), but how much they impinge on you depends on what sort of trip you are planning. If you're planning on staying in urban areas, you're probably not going to see any of these creatures, but if your itinerary includes bushwalking or swimming, you should make sure you know how to avoid contact with potentially dangerous creatures and what to do if you do get stung or bitten.

General Travel Health Issues

Some health concerns are relevant wherever you are travelling, including accident avoidance (p69), sexual health (p81) and mental wellbeing (p197). And if you want to take advantage of the plethora of alternative therapies available in Australia, we've included plenty of suggestions in the appendix on Alternative Therapies to get you started.

NEW ZEALAND

There are relatively few health concerns for travellers to New Zealand, unless you are planning on doing wilderness activities. Apart from making sure you are up to date with your tetanus shots (p29), you won't need any travel-related immunisations for New Zealand.

The sun (p64) is probably the major risk for most travellers, especially as the ozone layer is very thin over New Zealand. If you're doing any outdoor activities, you'll need to take all the usual safety precautions for wilderness activities anywhere – see the Wilderness Health & Safety chapter for more details.

The cold (p283) and unexpected severe weather changes are particular risks in New Zealand. *Giardia* (p120), an intestinal parasite that can cause diarrhoea, is found in some water sources in wilderness areas, especially in popular tramping areas, so you will need to have some means of water purifi-

Be Prepared

If you're going to remote areas of Australia, New Zealand or the Pacific islands, especially if you're going to be doing any outdoor activities, you'll need to be sure you know:

- basic precautions for staying healthy (p60)
- how to cope with climatic extremes and other environmental hazards (p279)
- basic first aid for cuts, sprains and other minor injuries (p396)
- how to treat common ailments like coughs (p140), diarrhoea (p112) and skin infections (p157)
- in malarial areas, what to do if you think you have malaria (p127)

cation (p76) with you. If you're climbing Mt Cook, you may experience problems due to the altitude (p288).

Amoebic meningitis (p301) is a potentially serious disease you can get if you put your head underwater in thermal springs in New Zealand (and elsewhere), so don't.

New Zealand only has one venomous creature: the katipo spider (p330). You'd be pretty unlucky to get into a bite situation with the katipo.

PACIFIC ISLANDS

The good news is that this isn't a particularly unhealthy region for travellers, even though it is in the tropics. Adequate medical services are available in main centres in all the islands, although services can be very limited in remote areas. For anything serious, you'll probably need to be evacuated to a centre in Hawai'i, New Zealand or Australia.

As well as being up to date with all your routine immunisations, you may need a few travel-related shots (p29). Get this organised as soon as possible – six to eight weeks before you go is the ideal time, but it's always worth getting advice on this up to the last minute.

If you are coming from a yellow-fever infected country in South America or Africa, you may need to have proof of vaccination against yellow fever – see p27 for more details.

Insects & Diseases

Mosquitoes and other biting insects are common in the Pacific islands. Dengue fever (transmitted through mosquito bites; p122) occurs in all the Pacific islands. There's no vaccine, the only prevention is to avoid mosquito bites – see p69.

Malaria (also transmitted by mosquitoes; p125) is a serious hazard to travellers, but currently only in Papua New Guinea, the Solomon Islands and Vanuatu. You'll need to get the latest recommendations on malaria prevention drugs (p34) before you go, and take precautions to avoid mosquito bites when you are there.

Mosquitoes are also responsible for transmitting filariasis (also known as elephantiasis; p191) in all the Pacific islands, although this is generally a very small risk to travellers. In rural areas of Papua New Guinea, mosquito-borne Japanese encephalitis (p320) is a potential risk.

Ticks (p325) are a hazard for trekkers in rural areas, and can transmit typhus (p327) in some areas such as Papua New Guinea, although this is not a big risk to travellers. Leeches (p323) are very common in most areas and can be a nuisance, but are not dangerous and don't transmit any disease.

Food, Water & Diseases

Infections such as diarrhoea, dysentery and hepatitis A can be transmitted through contaminated food and water (p73), and occur throughout the islands. It's worth taking some basic precautions to avoid getting ill (p60). These diseases are more of a risk in the wet season or after a natural disaster like a hurricane. Intestinal worms (p145) are common and can be a risk if you're travelling in rural areas.

Eating some species of reef fish at certain times of the year can give you ciguatera poisoning (p146). Although this isn't a big problem if you're eating fish in restaurants, make sure you get local advice on which fish to avoid if you are eating your own catch or self-catering.

Climate & Altitude

The tropical heat (p279) and sunshine (p64) are major drawcards for travellers to the Pacific islands, but be aware of their potentially hazardous effects. In highland areas, especially in Papua New Guinea, the weather can be very cold (p283) and unpredictable. You may be at risk of altitude sickness (p288) in parts of the Papua New Guinean highlands (above 2500m).

Swimming Safety

Beware the strong currents and surf of the Pacific Ocean, especially if you are used to more genteel waves. Read the section on Beach & Swimming Safety on p67 and the Water Safety chapter before you take the plunge.

Wildlife Hazards & Marine Creatures

Various creatures can be potentially dangerous, although most travellers are unlikely to come across them. Watch out for venomous snakes (p332) and spiders (p330). The waters of the Pacific ocean are home to a fantastic variety of marine life (p308), some of which is potentially harmful. Crocodiles (p300) are a danger in some waterways, especially near mangrove swamps, so get local advice on risks and take care.

Other Diseases

Going barefoot can put you at risk of parasites such as hookworm (p145) and creeping eruption (p165). Although tuberculosis (p193) is an important health issue in some areas of the Pacific (and elsewhere), as a short-term traveller your risk is very low unless you will be living in close contact with local people.

General Travel Health Issues

Some health concerns are relevant wherever you are travelling, including accident avoidance (p69), sexual health (p81) and mental wellbeing (p197).

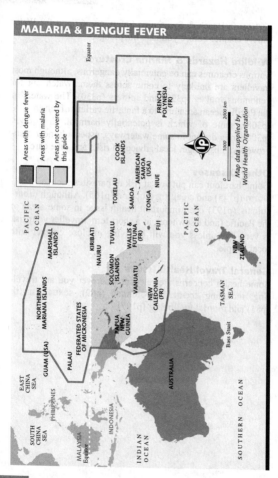

Areas with dengue fever

Areas with malaria

Areas not covered by this guide

Map data supplied by World Health Organization

0   1000   2000 km

PACIFIC OCEAN

PACIFIC OCEAN

INDIAN OCEAN

SOUTHERN OCEAN

SOUTH CHINA SEA

EAST CHINA SEA

PHILIPPINES

MALAYSIA

INDONESIA

Equator

Equator

GUAM (USA)

PALAU

NORTHERN MARIANA ISLANDS

FEDERATED STATES OF MICRONESIA

PAPUA NEW GUINEA

MARSHALL ISLANDS

NAURU

KIRIBATI

SOLOMON ISLANDS

TUVALU

TOKELAU

VANUATU

WALLIS & FUTUNA (FR)

SAMOA

AMERICAN SAMOA (USA)

COOK ISLANDS

FRENCH POLYNESIA (FR)

NEW CALEDONIA (FR)

FIJI

TONGA

NIUE

NEW ZEALAND

AUSTRALIA

TASMAN SEA

Bass Strait

BEFORE YOU GO

Wherever you're going in the Pacific region, you'll need to get a few health matters sorted before you go. There are four main chores to be ticked off: get immunisations (and health advice) for your destination; malaria prevention if you're going to a risk area; health insurance (essential for all destinations); and decide what to take in the way of a medical kit. And it's always a good idea to make sure you are as healthy as possible before you leave.

SOURCES OF INFORMATION & ADVICE

If you're looking for general or destination-specific information on travel health issues, you're spoilt for choice, especially if you have access to the internet. Good sources to try include your family doctor (although some doctors may not be as up to date with travel health recommendations as others), national and state health departments, and travel health clinics, as well as the internet.

Travel health clinics are a good option because travel medicine is their speciality, but they are often more expensive than if you go to a public health department or your usual doctor. If you would prefer to see your usual doctor, consider getting a destination-specific travel health brief from a travel health clinic which you can then take to your doctor. Many provide this service, usually for a fee, by mail, phone or fax.

If you're looking for some bedtime reading before you go, you could try some of the many publications available – we've listed a small selection under Books at the end of this chapter.

AUSTRALIA & NEW ZEALAND

As you'd expect, there are plenty of specialist clinics catering to aspiring travellers. The Travellers Medical and Vaccination Centre (The Travel Doctor) has a network of clinics in most major cities in Australia and New Zealand. Use the phone book to find your nearest clinic or check out their web site (www.tmvc.com.au). TMVC can also provide an online personalised travel health report (for a fee) via their web site.

CANADA

The Travel Medicine Program of Health Canada provides information on disease outbreaks, immunisations and general health advice for travellers, and more detailed information on tropical diseases, as well as information on travel medicine clinics. Another source of information is the Canadian Society for International Health. Contact details are as follows.

Health Canada (fax information service 613-941-3900, www.hc-sc .gc.ca/hpb/lcdc/osh).
Canadian Society for International Health (☎ 613-241-5785, fax 241-3845, www.csih.org), 1 Nicholas St, Suite 1105, Ottawa, ON K1N 7B7 Canada.

UK

General practitioners, university or college health centres, and travel medicine clinics are good sources of information and advice. Here's a selection of resources to get you started.

British Airways Travel Clinics – countrywide network of clinics (plus three in South Africa) and you don't need to be travelling on British Airways to use them. Ring ☎ 01276-685040 or check out their web site (www.britishairways.com/travelqa/fyi/health/health.html) for your nearest clinic.
Hospital for Tropical Diseases Travel Clinic (☎ 020-7388 9600), Mortimer Market Centre, Capper St, London WC1E – ring their health line ☎ 0839-337733 for recorded advice.
Liverpool School of Tropical Medicine Travel Clinic (☎ 0151-708 9393, travel health advice line ☎ 0906-708 8807), Pembroke Place, Liverpool L3 5QA – ring the health line for destination-specific advice on immunisations and other travel health issues.
Malaria Healthline (☎ 0891-600 350) – recorded information on malaria risks and avoidance from the Malaria Reference Laboratory at the London School of Hygiene & Tropical Medicine.

MASTA (Medical Advisory Services for Travellers; ☎ 020-7631 4408) at the London School of Hygiene & Tropical Medicine, Keppel St, London WC1E 7BR – no travel clinic but provides information and travel health products; ring its health line (☎ 0891-224 100) for destination-specific health information.

Nomad Travellers Store & Medical Centre (☎ 020-8889 7014, health line ☎ 09068-633414, email nomad.travstore@virgin.net), 3-4 Wellington Terrace, Turnpike Lane, London N8 0PX – it has a travel clinic (immunisations, advice etc) and sells a wide range of travel equipment, as well as health-related products.

The booklet *Health Advice for Travellers*, published by the Department of Health (☎ 0800-555 777 to order a copy), has basic advice and details of any reciprocal health care agreements for EU citizens, for example with Australia and New Zealand.

USA

The Centers for Disease Control & Prevention (CDC) in Atlanta, Georgia is the central source of information on travel health issues in the USA. You can get a travel health brief from their phone (☎ 888-232-3228) or fax (888-232-3299) information lines, and they should be able to provide you with information on travel health clinics in your area. CDC also publishes a book, *Health Information for International Travel*, but you'd probably want to be doing a few trips to make it worthwhile. Call ☎ 202-512-1800 or order it from the Superintendent of Documents, US Government Printing Office, Washington DC.

Alternatively, if you're looking for a travel health clinic near you, the following organisations will be able to provide you with a list.

American Society of Tropical Medicine & Hygiene (☎ 847-480-9592, fax 847-480-9282, www.astmh.org, 60 Revere Drive, Suite 500, Northbrook, IL 60062)

International Society of Travel Medicine (☎ 770-736-7060, www.istm.org, PO Box 871089, Stone Mountain, GA 30087)

The State Department's Citizen's Emergency Center can provide a recorded travel advisory on political and other risks of travel in specific areas. If you are in an emergency situation overseas, you can speak directly to a member of staff who can provide you with access to medical advice and assistance over the phone. The 24-hour emergency phone number is ☎ 202-647-5225 – it's a good idea to carry a record of it with you.

INTERNET RESOURCES

There's heaps of good, reliable information on travel health issues on the internet, and the great thing about it is that you can also access this information when you're on the road (so long as you can find an internet cafe). A couple of web sites are worth checking out before you look anywhere else:

CDC (**www.cdc.gov**) – the official site of the US Centers for Disease Control & Prevention, this is highly recommended. It's easily navigated and there's loads of useful information, including disease outbreak news and disease risks according to destination.

WHO (**www.who.ch**) – the official site of the World Health Organization, this is an impressive resource. For the latest health recommendations for international travel, try www.who.int/emc.

Other major sites worth checking out include:

MASTA (**www.masta.org**) – this highly recommended site of the Medical Advisory Services for Travellers (see earlier under UK) is easy to use and provides concise, readable information on all the important issues. It also has links to the Foreign and Commonwealth Office for advice on safe travel, and to the British Airways Clinics.

Medical College of Wisconsin Travelers Clinic (**www.intmed.mcw /travel.html**) – this site has good information on all the usual travel health issues, and an impressively comprehensive list of links to a variety of other travel health information sites. Browse till you drop.

Shorelands Travel Health Online (**www.tripprep.com**) – this excellent site is easy to navigate and has lots of good travel health information, as well as handy country profiles that include US State Department travel advisories.

Travel Health Information Service (**www.travelhealth.com**) – this chatty site, run by US-based Dr Stephen Blythe, is easy to navigate and has loads of good information and links.

Travellers Medical and Vaccination Centre (**www.tmvc.com.au**) – this Australian-based site has plenty of useful information, including disease outbreak news and good sections on travelling while pregnant and travel with children.

Once you start looking for more specialist health topics such as diving medicine and altitude sickness, you'll be amazed at the quality of the information you find. Some specialist resources are listed in the relevant sections later in this guide.

USEFUL ORGANISATIONS

The International Association for Medical Assistance to Travelers (IAMAT) is a nonprofit foundation that can provide you with a list of English-speaking doctors worldwide, as well as travel health information. Doctors affiliated to IAMAT charge a fixed fee. Membership is free, but the foundation welcomes a donation. For more details, check out IAMAT's web site (www.sentex.net) or, for membership inquiries, contact IAMAT as follows:

Canada
  (☎ 519-836-0102, fax 836-3412) 40 Regal Rd, Guelph, Ontario N1K 1B5
New Zealand
  PO Box 5049, Christchurch 5
Switzerland
  57 Voirets, 1212 Grand-Lancy-Geneva
USA
  (☎ 716-754-4883) 417 Center Street, Lewiston, NY 14092

MedicAlert Foundation International (☎ 1-800-432-5378, email customer_service@medicalert.org), 2323 Colorado Ave, Turlock, CA 95382-2018, USA, is a nonprofit organisation that (for a membership fee) can provide you with medical identification bracelets or tags with details of any drug allergies or important medical conditions you have, plus a call collect number for MedicAlert's 24 hour Emergency Response Center. This is worth considering if you have asthma, diabetes or severe allergy, or if you're taking steroids or blood-thinning medicine. Non-US residents can contact affiliate offices locally, including ☎ 020-7833 3034 in the UK or ☎ 08-8274 0361 in Australia, or check out MedicAlert's web site (www.medic alert.org) for a complete list.

IMMUNISATIONS

Going overseas just wouldn't be the same if you didn't have to put yourself under the needle before you go! It's mainly good news, though. If you're travelling to Australia or New Zealand, you don't need any special immunisations, although it's always a good idea to be up to date with routine immunisations such as tetanus. If you're going elsewhere in the Pacific, you will need to be up to date with your routine immunisations and, in addition, you may need a couple of travel-related immunisations.

If you're told by a tour company or an embassy that 'no immunisations are needed', take this with a pinch of salt. What they mean is that you won't be asked for any vaccination certificates when you arrive, not that no immunisations are medically recommended. Stick to your doctor's advice on this one.

TIMING

We've all been there – that last minute panic as you realise that you've forgotten to get your shots. Ideally, it's best to make an appointment with your doctor about six to eight weeks before you travel. Some courses may need to be given over several weeks (see the table later in this section for more details), and in any case it takes a week or two for full protection to develop after a booster or you finish a course. Generally, if you had a full course of an immunisation in the past, you should only need a booster injection now. You can

Do I Need a Certificate?

The answer is no – unless you are coming from a yellow fever infected country in South America or Africa. If you are, you will need a certificate proving you have been vaccinated against yellow fever before you will be allowed to enter Australia and many of the Pacific islands, but not New Zealand. Yellow fever doesn't exist in the Pacific region, but mosquitoes capable of transmitting it do (except in New Zealand). So if a traveller with yellow fever entered the region, an outbreak of the disease could occur, which is what Australia and the Pacific island nations would very much like to avoid.

Countries have different requirements for yellow fever vaccination certificates, so if you think this may be relevant for you, check it out with your doctor or a travel health clinic.

The yellow fever issue aside, it's always a good idea to have a record of your immunisations. Travellers are often given a small yellow booklet or 'International Health Card' for this purpose, but any official record will do. This way you'll know what you've had and when you're due for a top-up. Sometimes travellers are asked to produce a cholera certificate if coming from an infected area but this is unlikely in the Pacific islands and is in any case against international law.

have all your injections at the same time, if necessary, but you may want to spread them out a bit, unless you're feeling particularly masochistic.

! Don't panic if you have left it to the last minute! Immunisation schedules can be rushed if necessary and most vaccinations you'll need for the Pacific region can be given together two weeks, or even one week, before you go.

If you do get your shots late, just bear in mind that you won't be as well protected for the first week or two of your trip as you would be if you'd had them earlier.

WHICH ONES?

If you're expecting a definitive answer, you're going to be disappointed. We can certainly give you a good idea of what you're *likely* to need, but because there are lots of individual factors to take into account, you'll need to see your doctor for a definitive list. As well as your destination, your doctor will take into account the length of your trip, whether you're travelling in rural areas or sticking to resorts, which immunisations you've had in the past, any medications you're on and any allergies you have. If you have an ongoing medical condition, you will need to discuss this with your doctor, as this can affect which immunisations are suitable for you.

vaccine	full course	booster	comments
hepatitis A vaccine	single dose	booster at six to 12 months	gives good protection for at least 12 months; with booster, it protects for more than 10 years
hepatitis A immuno-globulin	single injection; needs to be given as close to travel as possible	N/A	gives protection only for a limited length of time (two to six months, depending on dose)
hepatitis B	two doses one are month apart plus a third dose six months later	three to five years	more rapid courses available if necessary
polio	three doses given at four weekly intervals	every 10 years; usually given orally	full course is usually given in childhood
tetanus, usually given with diphtheria	three doses given at four-week intervals	every 10 years	full course is usually given in childhood
typhoid	single injection or three or four oral doses	injection: every three years oral: one to five years	oral typhoid vaccine needs to be completed one week before you start malaria pills

If your immunity is lowered for some reason (for example if you're taking steroids or you're HIV-positive), some immunisations are best avoided. For more details on travelling with HIV, see the Travellers with Special Needs chapter.

Pregnant travellers and babies and children need special consideration – see the Pregnant Travellers section (p220) and the Babies & Children chapter for more details.

Routine Immunisations

Everyone should make sure they are up to date with these, which include:

- tetanus, usually given together with diphtheria
- polio
- childhood illnesses (possibly)

Travel-Related Immunisations

If you're going to any of the Pacific islands, you may need some additional shots. We've listed these in rough order of likelihood of needing them. If you want to find out more about the diseases themselves, check out the relevant section later in this book.

Hepatitis A If you're going to any of the Pacific islands, you should be protected against this common liver infection (recent figures suggest that up to 20 travellers out of every 1000 get hepatitis A). You can either have the hepatitis A vaccine, which gives good protection for at least a year (longer if you have a booster), or hepatitis A immunoglobulin, which protects you for a limited time (three to six months, depending on dose). Immunoglobulin carries a theoretical possibility of blood-borne diseases like HIV as it is a blood product, although this is a minuscule risk in most western countries. A combined hepatitis A and typhoid vaccine has recently become available, which means fewer shots for travellers.

Typhoid You may need to be protected against typhoid if you're travelling in any of the Pacific islands for longer than a couple of weeks. If you are unlucky enough to have had the old injectable typhoid vaccine, you'll know that it can make you feel pretty rough, but the new one causes few side effects. For those who would prefer to avoid an injection, there is an oral vaccine, although this can sometimes cause a stomach upset, and may not always be available.

Hepatitis B Protection against this liver infection is recommended for long-term travellers, especially if you will be living or working closely with members of the local population. Other situations in which it is usually recommended are if you're going to be working as a medic or nurse, or if needle sharing or sexual contact with a local person is a possibility at your destination. This immunisation is now given routinely in childhood in some countries, including Australia and the USA, so you may already be protected. If you need both hepatitis A and B immunisations, a combined vaccine is available.

Japanese Encephalitis This vaccination may be something you'll need to consider if you're planning a long stay in some rural areas of Papua New Guinea or the far north of Australia (mainly Torres Strait islands and Cape York). Discuss this with your doctor if you think this could be relevant.

Tuberculosis This infection is widespread in the Pacific islands, but is a small risk for travellers. You may already be protected against this, although immunisation against TB is not routinely available in the USA and some European countries. You generally won't need this unless you're going to be living with local people (for example if you're going back to visit relatives) for three months or longer.

Cholera This is not something you will need! Cholera does occasionally occur in some of the Pacific islands, but it is extremely rare in travellers. In any case, the currently available

Homoeopathic Immunisations

You may want to consider these if you've left your immunisations to the last minute – you could boost protection with a homoeopathic immunisation for a week or so until the protective effect of the injection kicks in. They may also be useful is if you can't have the conventional injections for some reason. Just bear in mind that the effectiveness of homoeopathic immunisations has not been fully explored, especially under travel conditions.

To find out more about homoeopathic immunisations, contact a registered homoeopathic practitioner or your national organisation of homoeopaths. In addition, you could try some of the publications on homoeopathic medicine listed under Books, most of which cover this topic. The UK-based Society of Homoeopaths (☎ 01604 621400, societyofhomoeopaths@ btinternet.com, 2 Artizan Rd, Northampton NN1 4HU, UK) produces a helpful leaflet *Homoeopathy and Foreign Travel*.

cholera vaccine is not recognised as necessary or effective by the World Health Organisation and is not generally recommended to travellers.

SIDE EFFECTS

Immunisations are like any other medication: they can have unwanted effects. These are generally unpleasant rather than dangerous, although occasionally serious allergic reactions can occur. There's no evidence that immunisations damage your immune system in any way.

The most common reactions are soreness around the injection site, sometimes with redness and swelling, and maybe a slight fever or a general feeling of being unwell. Tetanus, for example, commonly gives you a sore arm, while the hepatitis A vaccine can occasionally give you a fever in the evening. These reactions generally settle quickly with painkillers and rest, while an ice pack on your arm can help soothe any soreness.

!If you get more serious reactions that don't settle overnight, you should contact the doctor or clinic where you got your injections.

Very occasionally immunisations can provoke allergic reactions because of substances they may contain, such as albumin from eggs, which is why you sometimes have to stay at the clinic for observation for a little while after the injection. Allergic reactions are a possibility with any immunisation, but some (for example yellow fever) are more likely to cause this than others. These reactions are more likely if you know you are allergic to eggs or if you have multiple allergies, especially to bee stings – something you should make sure your doctor is aware of.

MALARIA PREVENTION

If you're going to Papua New Guinea, the Solomon Islands or Vanuatu, malaria is the most serious health hazard you face. Most travellers who return to Australia with malaria have acquired the infection in Papua New Guinea, and malaria is a high risk in the Solomon Islands; malaria is low to moderate risk in Vanuatu. If you're going to the Torres Strait Islands in Australia, malaria occurs in the islands adjacent to Papua New Guinea so you'll need to get reliable advice on this before you go or from a travel health clinic in mainland Australia.

!If you're going to a malarial area, take precautions to protect yourself from this potentially fatal disease.

To protect yourself from malaria, you need to:

▶ get the latest information on risks and drug resistance from a reliable information source (see following section)
▶ take suitable malaria preventive drugs or carry malaria treatment with you if appropriate – discuss this with your doctor or a travel health clinic before you go, and see later in this section

▶ take steps to avoid insect bites (see the section on Insect Bite Prevention in the Staying Healthy chapter) – this is even more important now that malarial parasites have become resistant to many commonly used antimalarial drugs

▶ make sure you know a bit about the disease before you go, including what to do if you think you have got it – see the Malaria section in the Fever & Hepatitis chapter for more information on diagnosing and treating malaria

Malarial mosquitoes are night-biters (unlike day-biting dengue mosquitoes), so take particular care to cover up at dusk and night-time. Mosquitoes breed in stagnant water, so the risk of malaria tends to be higher just after the rainy season. You're generally safe from malarial mosquitoes in highland areas of Papua New Guinea above altitudes of 2500m.

MALARIA INFORMATION SOURCES

Malaria risks and antimalarial drug resistance patterns are constantly changing, so it's important to get the most up-to-date information before you go. You've got no excuse not to – information on all aspects of malaria prevention is readily

Malaria Facts

Here are some facts to be aware of about this deservedly infamous disease:

■ malaria is a potentially fatal disease

■ malaria is becoming more common and more difficult to treat because of drug resistance

■ most cases of malaria in travellers occur in people who didn't take antimalarials or who didn't take them properly

■ most malaria deaths in travellers occur because the diagnosis is delayed or missed

■ malaria is particularly dangerous in children and pregnant women

■ malaria can be transmitted by blood transfusion and from mother to fetus

available from travel health clinics and specialist centres via phone, fax or the internet; see Sources of Information & Advice earlier in this chapter for more details. In particular, you can get reliable information from the following sources:

- CDC (www.cdc.gov/travel) – ☎ 888-232-3228 (toll free in the US)
- Malaria Healthline (UK) – ☎ 0891-600 350
- Malaria Foundation (www.malaria.org) – good source of general information on all aspects of the disease
- Travellers Medical and Vaccination Centre – www.tmvc.com.au
- WHO – www.who.ch

Because malaria prevention is such a complex and changing issue, it's best not to rely completely on advice from friends or other travellers, however well intentioned or knowledgeable they are.

MALARIA PREVENTION DRUGS

Currently, mefloquine or doxycycline are recommended if you're going to Papua New Guinea, the Solomon Islands or Vanuatu. Because of high levels of resistance in these areas, chloroquine (or chloroquine plus proguanil/Paludrine) is very much a second-best option. These recommendations may change during the lifetime of this guide, so make sure you get the latest information before you go.

As with immunisations, you'll need to get individual advice from your doctor on which antimalarial is the most suitable for you. Factors that can affect the decision include your age, any medical conditions you have, if you're pregnant, any medications you're on, any allergies you have, and what your risk of malaria is likely to be.

Antimalarials work by killing off the malarial parasites at a stage of their development before they can cause the disease; they don't prevent malarial parasites from entering your body. In recent years, there has been an inexorable rise in resistance of the malarial parasite to many of the antimalarial drugs, including chloroquine and Fansidar, making prevention and treatment of malaria a whole lot more tricky.

! Because of the possibility of resistance, your best insurance against malaria is to take measures to prevent mosquito bites, even if you are taking antimalarial drugs.

The answer to the problem of malarial resistance currently vexes whole departments of experts, but it's generally believed to lie in controlling the mosquitoes that spread the disease. There are hopes of a malarial vaccine, but there's still a long way to go before this becomes a reality.

Doses & Timing

You need to start taking malaria pills before you leave, so that they have a chance to reach maximum protective levels in your body before you arrive at your destination. It also gives any side effects a chance to show themselves so you can change medication before you go if necessary.

- It's best to start mefloquine two to three weeks before you go.
- Doxycycline needs to be started two days before you leave.
- Chloroquine (with or without proguanil) needs to be started at least one week in advance.

Make sure you are clear on what dose to take before you leave – some drugs need to be taken weekly, and some need to be taken daily, and you don't want to get it wrong.

chloroquine	500mg once weekly
proguanil	200mg once daily
mefloquine	250mg (one tablet) once weekly
doxycycline	100mg once daily

For the best protection, you need to take antimalarials regularly – try to get into a routine before you leave. Take them after food, as this makes side effects like nausea and stomach upset less likely.

Don't be tempted to stop taking your malaria pills as soon

as you leave, or you may get malaria from parasites you picked up in the last few days of your trip.

All malaria pills need to be continued for four weeks after returning home.

Side Effects & Cautions

Well, you knew there had to be some!

All antimalarial drugs cause minor side effects, but if you experience severe side effects that make you uncertain about continuing the drug, see your doctor and discuss alternatives.

Mefloquine (Lariam) Minor side effects are relatively common, and include nausea, dizziness, difficulty sleeping and

Should I take Mefloquine (Lariam)?

As you're probably aware, this controversial malaria drug has attracted quite a bit of media attention, which makes it a frequent talking point in travellers circles.

No one doubts that mefloquine is very effective at preventing malaria; the issue is side effects. Mefloquine commonly causes 'minor' side effects like nausea and diarrhoea, as do the other antimalarials, but it can also have more disturbing side effects. These range from weird dreams, dizziness and anxiety to panic attacks, depression and even fits (seizures). Some travellers claim to be permanently affected by mefloquine. Equally, a large proportion of travellers take mefloquine and have no problems.

Experts disagree on how common the disabling side effects are. Figures from studies range from one in 10,000 (about the same number as for travellers taking chloroquine and proguanil) to much higher rates (one in 140 in a recent study by the London School of Hygiene & Tropical Medicine).

Some experts point out that, purely on a statistical basis, many millions of people take mefloquine at any one time, so some people are bound to develop symptoms even though they may be totally unrelated to taking the drug. Several studies have shown that most people get used to the side effects with time.

vivid dreams, and gastrointestinal upset. More severe side effects have also been reported – see the boxed text on this page for a fuller discussion of this issue.

Mefloquine is not suitable for everyone; discuss with your doctor, but you should not take it in the following situations:

■ if you have epilepsy or have had a fit in the past
■ if you have had severe depression or other major mind problems
■ if you are on certain medicines (such as beta blockers for a heart condition)

Because of the risk of dizziness and fits, mefloquine is best avoided if you're going to be doing precision tasks like scuba diving or flying a plane, or if you are going to high altitude (it could mask signs of altitude sickness).

As a result of the controversy, the British guidelines for the use of mefloquine were thoroughly reviewed in 1997, and it was agreed that because of the risk of side effects, mefloquine should only be used when the risk of treatment-resistant malaria is high.

We suggest you find out for yourself what different people have to say about mefloquine and then make up your own mind. You can get information on mefloquine from any travel health clinic, your doctor, a pharmacist or any of the web sites listed earlier in this chapter.

For more specific information about the mefloquine issue, you could check out the Lariam Action USA web site (www.suggskelly.com/lariam), which has good links to other resources on mefloquine. Alternatively, you could try the excellent 'Lariam or not to Lariam' on www.geocities.com/TheTropics/6913/lariam.htm, which has an incredibly comprehensive list of links, including one to Roche, the manufacturer of Lariam. Lariam Action USA (☎ 510-663-5168) can also be contacted at 1563 Solano Avenue #248, Berkeley, CA 94707.

Whatever you decide, remember that malaria is a potentially fatal disease and it's vital you take precautions against it in risk areas.

Doxycycline Side effects include diarrhoea, hypersensitivity of your skin to sunlight, and vaginal thrush. It may make the oral contraceptive pill less effective, so if this is relevant to you, get advice from your doctor before you go. Doxycycline can cause irritation in your stomach, so you should always swallow it with plenty of water.

Chloroquine (Aralen) There's long experience of use of chloroquine (and proguanil), and it's a pretty safe drug if taken as recommended. Minor side effects are common and include headaches, nausea, diarrhoea, indigestion, blurred vision (temporary) and itching (especially if you're dark-skinned). Prolonged use of chloroquine (usually more than five years) can cause more serious eye problems, but this tends to be of more concern for expatriates than travellers.

! *Chloroquine isn't suitable for everyone: you shouldn't take it if you have epilepsy or are taking medication for epilepsy.*

Long-Haul Travellers

If you're planning on travelling in malarial areas for six months or more, you may be wondering what to do about malaria prevention. You've got two main options: you can either continue to take your usual malaria preventive pills or you can decide not to take them. Taking malaria pills for more than six months can work out quite expensive, and, unless you're really conscientious, it can be easy to forget to take your pills. If you do decide to stop them (discuss this with your doctor before you go), you need to be extremely vigilant about avoiding mosquito bites, and you need to be very clear about where your nearest doctor is and when to take emergency stand-by treatment. Note that you don't build up immunity to malaria with time, so you're still at risk of getting it, even if you've been in a risk area for a long time.

Proguanil (Paludrine) This drug has few side effects, but can cause mouth ulcers. Proguanil is not available in the USA, but if you wanted to take it, it is widely available in Europe and Canada.

PREGNANT WOMEN & CHILDREN

If you're going to a malarial area and you're pregnant or you're travelling with children, discuss the issue of malaria prevention with your doctor or travel health clinic as early as possible as there are some special considerations. Malaria is a much more serious disease in pregnant women and in children, and some of the more effective antimalarials are not suitable. For more details, see the Pregnant Travellers section (p220) in the Women Travellers chapter and the Babies & Children chapter.

! Travel to high risk malarial areas is generally not recommended for pregnant travellers or children.

If necessary, chloroquine (with or without proguanil) is safe in pregnancy, although you may need to take a folate supplement if you are taking proguanil. Mefloquine is best avoided in the first three months of pregnancy, although it can be taken in the final six months of pregnancy if absolutely necessary. Doxycycline is best avoided in pregnancy.

Chloroquine (with or without proguanil) is suitable for babies and children; mefloquine is best avoided in small children, although it can be taken by older children. Doses are based on weight. Doxycycline is not suitable for children under 12 years.

EMERGENCY STANDBY TREATMENT

If you are going to a high-risk malarial area where you don't have access to medical care, you need to take malaria treatment medication with you in case of emergency. You need to use a different medication from the one you used for prevention. Discuss this issue with your doctor or travel health clinic before you go. It's not just a question of popping the pills;

Malaria Diagnostic Kit

The recent development of easy to use, portable diagnostic kits for malaria has made the issue of emergency treatment much simpler. These kits (one brand is called MalaQuick) are considered to be extremely accurate. You can get them from selected travel health clinics (including TMVC in Australia and New Zealand, and Nomad Travellers Store & Medical Centre in the UK), or check out the manufacturer's web site (www .med-diagnostics.com/index.html) for more details. You can use the kits to confirm the diagnosis if you suspect you have malaria, even if you were taking preventive malaria drugs. They usually contain two tests, and you'll need to try to keep them as cool as possible, as this prolongs their life span.

you also need to be clear about when to use it and what to do if problems arise.

TRAVEL HEALTH INSURANCE

However lucky (or poor) you're feeling, it's vital you have adequate travel health insurance to cover your whole trip, usually as part of a general travel insurance covering loss of belongings, flight cancellations etc. If you have medical insurance in your home country, it may not cover you for travel in Australia, New Zealand or the Pacific islands.

! Although costs of medical care and supplies in some countries will be much lower than you may be used to, the cost of medical evacuation is always phenomenal (thousands of dollars).

Travel insurance policies are available from a variety of sources related to the travel industry, including credit or charge card companies, travel agents and travel health clinics, as well as from insurance brokers. Insurance policies vary in the details of the services they provide, so shop around to find exactly what you want. Always check the small print so you're clear on exactly what the policy covers.

Many insurance providers have a 24 hour hotline you can ring for assistance in an emergency, and they can usually provide you with names of English-speaking doctors (if necessary), arrange referral to a hospital and guarantee payment if you need to pay upfront (as is usual in most of the Pacific islands).

Most insurance policies should cover you for medical evacuation if necessary, but it's worth checking this. Some companies provide their own air transport and emergency services, while others contract it out, which is something you might want to ask about.

You will need to inform the insurance providers of any medical condition you have, as this may increase the premium you have to pay. Once you're over a certain age, usually 65 years, your premium automatically increases. Note that routine health problems and preexisting conditions (which sometimes include pregnancy) are not usually covered by travel health insurance policies.

Before committing yourself to any insurance policy, check that it covers some or all of the following:

■ the total cost of any medical or surgical treatment you might need
■ any additional costs you might incur if you were delayed by illness or injury or had to travel when injured
■ emergency evacuation – without insurance this can cost thousands of dollars, which you would need to provide up front
■ provision of safe blood supplies
■ dental treatment
■ travel while pregnant
■ adventure sports, such as trekking or scuba diving – consider getting special insurance to cover these activities if necessary (for details about insurance for diving see p302)

In the Pacific islands, you will generally have to pay cash upfront for medical treatment and be reimbursed later, so it's a good idea to have an emergency stash just in case (your insurance provider may be able to provide a guarantee of payment which may be accepted instead, but don't count on it). Always keep any receipts in case you need to present them later to be reimbursed. In Australia and New Zealand, you'll still have to pay, but will generally have more options open to you, such as credit card payments. Guarantees of payment by insurance providers will generally be accepted.

PRETRAVEL CHECKUPS & OTHER PREPARATIONS

MEDICAL CHECKUP

In some situations, this might be a good idea.

- If you're going to be away for a while or you're going to remote areas, now is the time to get any niggling problems checked out.
- If you're going to be doing something strenuous like trekking at altitude and you're on the good side of 40, it's probably a good idea to have a fitness check before you go.
- If you are going to be travelling to remote areas, you should discuss taking emergency treatment for diarrhoea or chest infections with you, which you will need to get on prescription.

If you're planning on doing any diving while you are away, remember to get a specific diving medical checkup before you go as, in theory at least, you'll need a certificate of fitness before any dive centre will let you dive.

Women Travellers

Travel can pose problems with certain forms of contraception (see p215) and hormone replacement therapy (see p209), so it's best to discuss this with your doctor before you go. Make sure you take a plentiful supply of any medications with you, in case your brand is not available locally. If you think you may need to start contraception, it's worth getting this sorted out well before you go, in case you need to try a few different options before you find one that suits you. For a summary of the main options and their pros and cons on the road, see p217.

It is possible to stop your periods temporarily (p206) if they're going to be a real nuisance (for example if you're going to be trekking in a remote area at an inappropriate moment), but it's best to discuss this with your doctor before you go. If you know you are prone to thrush (vaginal candidiasis or yeast infections) or cystitis (bladder infections), you may want to discuss taking prescription treatment for these conditions with you.

If you're planning on travelling while you're pregnant, you'll need to discuss this with your doctor as early as possible – see the section on Pregnant Travellers (p220) in the Women Travellers chapter for more information.

Babies & Children

If you are planning on travelling with babies or young children, it's sensible to discuss with your doctor tactics for dealing with common health problems you might face while you are away, as well as getting advice on immunisations and

On Record

When you're travelling, it's a good idea to keep the following information on your person at all times, in case of emergency:

- travel insurance hotline number
- serial number of your travel insurance policy
- contact details of your nearest embassy
- US State Department's Citizen's Emergency Center number (US citizens only)
- summary of any important medical conditions you have
- contact details of your doctor back home (if necessary)
- copy of prescription for any medication you take regularly
- details of any serious allergies
- blood group
- prescription for glasses or contact lenses
- if you are a diabetic, a letter from your doctor explaining why you need to carry syringes etc for customs

measures to take to stay healthy. We've covered these issues in more detail in the Before You Go section of the Babies & Children chapter later in this book.

DENTAL CHECKUP

You know it makes sense … It's definitely worth making time for this before you go, especially if you haven't been for a while. Get this organised a few weeks before you plan to go so you have got time to get any treatment done that you might need. Dental care can be hard to find on remote tropical islands, and quality can be variable elsewhere.

EYES

If you wear contact lenses, talk to your optometrist about hygiene while you're travelling, and take a plentiful supply of any cleaning solutions you use. If you wear glasses, consider taking a replacement pair, and take a copy of your prescription with you. It will be understood in any language if you need to have a replacement pair made up while you are away.

FIRST AID & SURVIVAL SKILLS COURSES

Although we include guidelines on basic first aid, including emergency resuscitation, in the First Aid appendix of this book, there is no substitute for hands-on training. Everyone should be familiar with basic first aid techniques, but it is even more important if you are going to places where you cannot rely on rapid response emergency services. If you're going to be spending time in remote areas more than a day or so away from medical help, especially if you are going to be trekking or doing other activities, you should consider doing at least a basic first aid course before you leave. Contact your local first aid organisation for details of courses available. Training in appropriate survival skills is generally offered by organisations concerned with wilderness activities such as mountaineering and trekking.

WHAT TO TAKE

What to take with you in the way of medical supplies depends on where you're going and what you're intending to do once you're there. If you are planning on going to remote areas for any length of time, you'll need to take more with you than if you are planning to stay in urban centres, where you will probably be able to get most things you are likely to need. However, it's worth having a small kit of core items with you, if only to save you the trouble of having to buy them when you're there or having to decipher instructions written in another language. If you're planning on doing any wilderness activities, you will obviously need to consider carefully what to take with you.

> If you're travelling with children, turn to the Babies & Children chapter for more guidance on what to take.

MEDICAL KIT

You can make up your own kit or you can take a prepacked kit. These come in a variety of sizes, and are widely available from travel health clinics, specialist travel equipment suppliers and first aid organisations. Taking a commercial kit is a convenient option, but shop around as some are better value than others. What many travellers do is to take a basic commercial kit and to add in some familiar remedies (conventional and complementary).

For loose medical supplies, zip-lock plastic bags and film canisters are handy. Keep the whole kit together in a waterproof container – a clear plastic box is ideal, as it's squashproof too. Medicines should be kept as cool as possible (ie in the middle of your pack) and out of direct sunlight.

!If you're allergic to any drugs (such as penicillin), it's a good idea to carry this information on you at all times. You can get engraved bracelets or tags with this information from specialist companies like MedicAlert (see Useful Organisations earlier in this chapter).

Drug Names

This is a confusing issue for everyone, medics included. All drugs have two names: a generic (official medical) name and the brand name (chosen by the manufacturer). Because brand names vary from country to country, we've used the official medical name for all drugs mentioned in this book. This may seem a bit frustrating to you if you're reading this at home, but it means that any doctor or pharmacist anywhere in the world will be able to recognise the generic name (or at least can look it up) and should be able to suggest brands available locally.

If you want to find out the generic name of a drug, look on the packet or leaflet accompanying the drug – the generic name should be there, usually in smaller type just below the brand name – or ask a pharmacist.

You'll find more information on all aspects of buying and using medicines while you are away in the appendix at the back of this book.

Customs officials can sometimes be suspicious of medications you may be carrying (there have been a few horror stories along the lines of 'Innocent Traveller Arrested for Carrying Painkillers') so it's best to keep medicines in their original packaging or container where possible, ideally with a prescription or doctor's letter showing what it is and why you need to take it. If you keep all your medications in an official-looking medical kit, you're less likely to have problems.

Lotions, Potions & Pills

Consider including these for travel to most destinations:

- any prescription medicines, including malaria prevention drugs
- paracetamol (acetaminophen) or aspirin for pain and fever; consider also taking a stronger painkiller like co-codamol or an anti-inflammatory like ibuprofen
- antidiarrhoeals – loperamide (probably the most useful and effective) or bismuth subsalicylate (Pepto-Bismol)

- 'indigestion' remedies such as antacid tablets or liquids
- oral rehydration sachets and measuring spoon for making up your own solution
- antihistamine tablets for hay fever and other allergies, and for itching
- sting relief spray or hydrocortisone cream for insect bites
- emergency bee sting kit containing adrenaline (epinephrine) if you are allergic to stings
- sunscreen and lip salve with sunblock
- insect repellent (DEET or plant-based) and permethrin (for treating mosquito nets and clothes)
- anti-motion sickness remedies (such as promethazine or natural remedies – see p59)
- water-purifying tablets or water filter/purifier
- over-the-counter cystitis treatment
- antifungal cream for athlete's foot, crotch rot and thrush
- calamine cream or aloe vera for sunburn and other skin rashes

In addition, you could consider taking:

- sugar-free chewing gum to keep your mouth moist in dry climates
- cough and cold remedies, and sore throat lozenges
- eye drops for tired or dusty eyes
- multivitamins

First Aid Equipment

You'll want to have at least some of these items with you for most destinations, and probably all of them for more remote destinations:

- thermometer
- scissors
- tweezers – to remove splinters and ticks
- sticking plasters (such as Band-Aids) of various sizes
- gauze swabs and adhesive tape
- bandages and safety pins to fasten them
- nonadhesive dressings
- antiseptic powder or solution (eg povidone-iodine), antiseptic wipes
- wound closure strips or butterfly closures (can sometimes be used instead of stitches)
- needles, syringes, suture kit; cannula for giving a drip (possibly)

Sterile kits containing needles and syringes shouldn't cause you problems at customs if they are sealed and clearly labelled, but carrying loose syringes and needles is not a good idea. If you need to for a medical condition such as diabetes, get a letter from your doctor to say why you need them.

Prescription Medicines

Discuss with your doctor if you need to take the following with you:

- emergency treatment for malaria plus malaria diagnosis kit (see earlier in this chapter)
- antibiotics for treating diarrhoea
- a course of antibiotics for chest, ear, skin etc infections, if you're going to be travelling in remote locations
- antibiotics to treat cystitis
- treatment for vaginal thrush (may be available without prescription in many countries)

For any prescription medicines, ask your doctor for a copy of your prescription to take with you, and a letter of authorisation to keep customs officials happy.

Wilderness Activities & Remote Areas

Items you should consider putting in your medical kit if you are planning on trekking or travelling in remote areas include:

- antibiotic eye and ear drops
- antibiotic cream or powder
- emergency inflatable splints
- blister kit
- elasticated support bandage
- triangular bandage for making an arm sling
- dental first aid kit (either a commercial kit, or make up your own – ask your dentist to advise you)

And Finally ...

If you have any medicines left over at the end of your trip, dispose of them carefully. You could perhaps consider giving them to a hospital or clinic, but don't be tempted to just leave them in your hotel room for the cleaner because medicines are only effective if used appropriately and can actually be harmful otherwise.

ALTERNATIVE TRAVEL KITS

You can make up your own travel kit with your favourite natural remedies, or you can buy a ready-made kit. Unless you're planning to take just a few familiar remedies, it's a good idea to get advice on what to take from your practitioner or local homoeopathic or naturopathic pharmacy. Alternatively, we give some guidance on homoeopathic and naturopathic remedies in the boxed text 'Alternative First Aid for Travellers' on the following page. Some of the texts listed under Books have suggestions for alternative travel kits.

In the UK, Neal's Yard Remedies (catalogue from ☎ 0161-831 7875, or write to: Unit 1, St James's Square, John Dalton St, Manchester M2 6DS) is a long-established supplier of natural remedies. It has a variety of deliciously tempting mini-kits, as well as a 'Travel Roll', which you can either fill with your own remedies or get pre-packed with a selection of first aid remedies.

Also in the UK, Helios Homoeopathic Pharmacy (☎ 01892-537254, fax 01892-546850, email pharmacy@helios.co.uk) has a compact and incredibly comprehensive homoeopathic travel kit containing 36 remedies for travel-related problems (everything from drowning to fear of flying), with a helpful leaflet giving guidance on what to use when. It's probably suitable for someone with prior experience of homoeopathy.

You can order plant-based remedies like echinacea and Sweet Anne (good for digestive upsets) from Joanne Alexander at Snow Mountain Botanicals (☎ 888-743-2642, fax 707-743-2642); check out the web site at www.pacific.net/~smb.

A search on the web brings up more possibilities, including herbal kits from Mountaintop Herbs (www.crisiskit.com), Adventure Medical Kits (www.adventuremedicalkits.com) and Dr Christopher (www.drchristopher.com/special/outdoor.html).

Alternative First Aid for Travellers

Bernadette Saulenier is a naturopath and reiki practitioner who travels regularly between Australia and Europe. She has the following tips for travellers. You should be able to get most remedies in Australia and New Zealand, but if you're going to the Pacific islands, you will need to take what you need with you. As a general rule, these remedies are best used for nonserious conditions and are not intended to replace medical diagnosis and treatment in serious cases.

Diarrhoea can ruin the best planned holiday and, as with anything else, prevention is better than cure. Treat water with tea tree oil, a natural antiseptic: use two drops of tea tree oil in 1L of water and let it stand overnight. Another preventive is to take slippery elm capsules orally before each meal – the powder coats and protects the delicate lining of the bowels against inflammation. If you get diarrhoea, homoeopathic remedies include arsenicum album, carbo vegetalis, podophyllum, ipecac or nux vomica – what to take depends on the characteristics of your illness. Ask your practitioner for guidance on this before you leave.

Constipation is also common when you're travelling: try pear or prune juice, or a tablespoon of linseeds/psyllium husks sprinkled on your food. Remember to drink plenty of water. If you are really desperate, you could try taking a mixture of cascara, senna and chelidonium herbs.

If you're hopping in and out of buses carrying heavy luggage, you're quite likely to get a few bruises. Arnica cream is a great remedy when applied on the bruise immediately (but avoid using it on open wounds and cuts). For bleeding wounds, take arnica 30c under your tongue.

Cocculus drops or ginger tablets are good remedies for preventing motion sickness, and homoeopathic melatonin drops are excellent for jet lag. Gelsemium drops or tablets will alleviate the aches and pains of sore muscles, and taking any form of antioxidant such as grapeseed extract or vitamin A, C or E will help your body to cope with fatigue, stress and lack of fresh air – all common on a long journey.

Mosquitoes hate the smell of geranium, so avoid getting bitten by putting a few drops of geranium oil on your skin. If you get bitten in spite of all your precautions, a drop of lavender oil will soothe the itch. For other bites and stings (spiders, bees, wasps or fleas) a few drops of ledum 30c under your tongue is beneficial.

For sunburn, try a few drops of soothing hypericum oil, which also promotes healing, or comfrey cream. If you're feeling the heat, take the tissue salt of calcium sulphate (Calc Sulph 6x) every 15 minutes until you feel refreshed, or try Dr Bach's Rescue Remedy.

For irritant skin rashes and minor burns, try soothing calendula or comfrey cream. Lycopodium in a homoeopathic form taken orally will help fungal infections of the skin at the constitutional level, but topically you may find tea tree oil, thuja and comfrey creams helpful.

Colds and flu seem to be common wherever you go. Echinacea tablets or vitamin C will boost your immune system and help you avoid illness. If you are stricken, combination 'Q' of tissue salts will help with sinus and throat infections, and herbal tea of thyme or sage will alleviate sore throat and feverish symptoms. Gelsemium will get rid of muscular aches and pains, and allium cepa will help with a runny nose and watery eyes.

For stress or panic attacks, Dr Bach's Rescue Remedy is invaluable. A few drops under the tongue every 15 minutes works wonders. If sleep eludes you, a tincture or tablet of combined valerian, scullcap and passionflower (or any of these herbs alone) is the best cure. Hops is another herb with soothing effect. If you cannot find herbs, a good alternative is to take tissue salts of magnesium phosphate (Mag Phos 6x) before bed.

BOOKS

If you're looking for more information, here's a small selection of some of the many books available on travel health and related issues. Books are published in different editions by different publishers in different countries, but a bookshop or library should be able to track down the following recommendations from the author or title.

A selection of books on wilderness health and safety is listed in the Wilderness Health & Safety chapter later in this guide.

GENERAL REFERENCE

There are several good, general references. Here's a selection of recommended titles.

Travellers' Health by Dr Richard Dawood – authoritative, comprehensive and earnest reference source.

Where There is No Doctor by David Werner – excellent 'how-to-do-it' manual for the medically naive, aimed at people going to live in remote areas of developing countries. There's a companion text (only for sadists, surely), *Where There is No Dentist*.

Bugs, Bites & Bowels by Dr Jane Wilson-Howarth – wonderfully titled, chatty, entertaining and comprehensive.

Your Child's Health Abroad by Dr Wilson-Howarth and Dr Matthew Ellis – detailed guide for travelling parents.

International Travel Health Guide by Stuart R Rose – updated annually and a good source of general information.

If you're looking for a first aid manual, get hold of the authorised manual of your national first aid organisation such as the Red Cross or St John Ambulance Society.

ALTERNATIVE THERAPIES

For something a bit different, try any of the following:

The Traveller's Guide to Homoeopathy by Phyllis Speight – a useful guide, if you can get hold of it.

The World Travellers' Manual of Homoeopathy by Dr Colin Lessel – incredibly comprehensive and full of fascinating detail.

A Handbook of Homoeopathic Alternatives to Immunisation by
Susan Curtis – available by mail order from Neal's Yard
Remedies (for contact details, see the Alternative Travel Kits sec-
tion earlier in this chapter).

BITES & STINGS

If you want more information on potentially dangerous creatures you may come across in the region, check out some of
these titles.

Venomous Creatures of Australia by Struan K Sutherland and John
Sutherland – an excellent first aid handbook.
Bites & Stings, The World of Venomous Animals by John Nichol – a
fascinating read, though not specific to the Pacific region.
Dangerous Marine Creatures by Dr Carl Edmonds – find out all
about the dangers of the deep … and shallows.
Pisces Guide to Venomous and Toxic Marine Life of the World,
Lonely Planet – a comprehensive, fully illustrated guide to
potentially dangerous marine life worldwide.

ON THE MOVE

Getting there is half the fun they say ... If you don't enjoy the moving experience (and many travellers don't), you'll want to read this chapter before you leave terra firma.

FIT TO FLY?

If you're normally fit and healthy, flying shouldn't be any particular problem for you beyond the stresses involved in any form of travelling. However, if you fall into any of the following categories, you should check with your doctor before flying:

▶ if you have heart or lung problems (although as a general rule you shouldn't need extra oxygen during the flight if you can climb a flight of stairs)
▶ if you've had an operation within 10 days of flying, check with the airline if you are able to fly
▶ if you've had blood clots in your blood vessels in the past, as sitting immobile for long periods of time during the flight may make further clots likely
▶ if you're more than 36 weeks pregnant
▶ if you have a bad cold, sinus infection or a middle ear infection, it's best to avoid flying until you're better, as you're at risk of severe ear pain and possibly a burst eardrum – see the following section for more details
▶ if you've been scuba diving, you shouldn't fly for 12 hours after any dive and for 24 hours after a dive requiring decompression stops; note that if you required recompression treatment, you will need medical clearance before you fly – see the Scuba Diving section of the Water chapter for more details

EARACHE & FLYING

Cabin pressure is normally kept at levels equivalent to those at altitudes of 1800m to 2400m (6000ft to 8000ft). At these pressures, gas expands by about 30%. This can cause problems if it is in an enclosed space, such as in the ear. Normally, you cope with this by swallowing, yawning or sucking on a sweet, which has the effect of equalising the pressure between the cabin and your ears. If, however, your ears are blocked for any reason (if you've got a cold or hay fever), you can get a painful pressure build-up, and sometimes your eardrum can burst. It's best not to fly if you've got a cold or severe hay fever, and you should definitely avoid flying if you have a middle ear infection. If you have to fly with a cold, the following measures should help:

▶ take a nasal decongestant, such as pseudoephedrine 60mg four times daily (not suitable if you have high blood pressure), starting the day before you fly
▶ take an antihistamine (p382) before and during the flight (follow the dose instructions on the packet)
▶ try a nasal decongestant spray – use it an hour before the expected time of arrival, and every 20 minutes after this
▶ during the descent, pinch your nose firmly and blow hard down it – this should force the pressure to equalise, and you should feel your ears pop; do this as often as necessary

Burst Eardrum

If these measures don't work, your eardrum may burst. You'll get a gradual build-up of severe pain, followed by sudden relief. You may notice a bit of bleeding from the ear. If this happens, ideally see a doctor to get it checked out. If your eardrum has burst, it'll take about six weeks to heal up.

! *While you wait for your eardrum to heal, avoid getting water in your ear – use earplugs or a cottonwool ball covered in petroleum jelly when you shower or wash your hair. Don't swim underwater (or avoid swimming altogether) until it has healed. If you do swim, take care to protect your ear with earplugs.*

If possible, you should get your ear looked at again in about six weeks. If you have any persistent symptoms, such as discharge from the ear, see a doctor before this.

TRAVELLING WELL

If you're flying, the low cabin air humidity is great for minimising the odoriferous effects of squashing 300 or so stressed people into a closed space for eight or more hours, but it does dry you out. You'll feel better if you drink lots of nonalcoholic fluids – avoid tea, coffee and alcohol, as they can all increase fluid loss. Mineral-water aerosol sprays and skin moisturisers can also be helpful. At cruising altitude, the volume of enclosed gases expands by about a third so you may find your abdomen swells up, and it might be more comfortable to avoid bubbly drinks.

Aromatherapy is great for when you're on the move – try a few drops of rosemary or lavender in a tissue or handkerchief, and waft it under your nose every so often.

Sitting inactive for long periods of time on any form of transport, especially in hot climates, can give you swollen feet and ankles, and may make blood clotting in your leg veins more likely, especially if you are prone to these, or are pregnant. Wriggle your toes while you're sitting and flex your calves or, if you can, get up and walk around. If you are prone to blood clotting, you may want to discuss this with your doctor before you leave, as you may need to take low-dose aspirin or an injection of a blood thinner.

Obviously, you'll need to keep any as-needed medications (such as for asthma or angina) readily at hand during any journey, especially a long one.

JET LAG

If you're flying across three or more time zones, you may experience jet lag. This term describes a syndrome long haul travellers will be all too familiar with: tiredness, difficulty sleeping, headache, irritability, difficulty concentrating, loss of appetite and sometimes diarrhoea or constipation. Some of these effects are due to the physical stresses of the flight, mainly dehydration and immobility, but others are the result of having to reset your body clock to the new time.

Over a 24 hour period, your body experiences rhythmical changes in various functions (like body temperature, levels of hormones and blood pressure), which are designed to prime you to be active during the daylight hours and to sleep during night-time. The trouble is that your internal clock takes time to adjust to a new routine, and when you fly directly to a new time, there's a temporary mismatch between the time your internal clock thinks it is and the actual time at your destination. This results in the set of symptoms we recognise as jet lag.

Most travellers will have crossed a few time zones on their flight to Australia, New Zealand or any of the Pacific islands. If so, jet lag can make you feel below par for up to a week after you arrive. It tends to be more of a problem if you're flying west to east. If you have to cross several time zones, consider having a stopover, as this can help your body adjust.

Unfortunately, there's no wonder pill for jet lag and, considering how many different factors are involved in setting and maintaining body rhythms, there's unlikely to be one in the future. However, you can speed up the adjustment process by helping out the *zeitgebers* or timegivers. These are external influences that impact on your internal rhythms, the most important ones being meal times, sleep times and exposure to bright light. Try the following strategies for reducing the impact of jet lag:

▶ recognise that jet lag may be a problem in the first few days and adjust your itinerary accordingly

- on the plane, set your watch to the new destination time and adjust your schedule to this time
- if it's daytime on arrival, get active and don't give yourself the chance to doze off
- eating is a potent time-setter, so try to take all your meals at the appropriate new time
- it can be torture, but try to stay awake until at least a reasonable bed time
- if you just can't keep your eyelids open, take a short nap, but beware – set your alarm or get someone to wake you
- the first night's sleep may be a bit fragile, but after that things should improve

Drug remedies you could consider to help your body clock to adjust include sleeping tablets or melatonin. Sleeping tablets can help by enabling you to sleep at the appropriate time, but they can make you feel 'hungover' the next day and are not suitable for everyone.

Other less practical options include mind-bogglingly complicated fasting/food regimens (check out the ones in Overcoming Jetlag by Dr Charles F Ehret & Lynne Waller Scanlon – said to be used by the US Army Rapid Deployment Forces) and bright light exposure via special light bulbs (but try carrying those in your pack).

Melatonin

There's been much excitement about this naturally occurring hormone which influences body rhythms. Although melatonin is widely available from naturopathic suppliers, you should be aware that it's not as yet officially sanctioned. This means that it hasn't been fully studied for safety and possible side effects, and the optimum dose hasn't been determined, so it's not available on a medical prescription. If you decide to try it, follow the dosing instructions on the packaging – many different formulations are avialable. Melatonin needs to be taken at an appropriate time before sleep (usually about 8 pm, new time).

MOTION SICKNESS

This most unpleasant of afflictions can strike anyone, and there are plenty of sea journeys on small boats between islands in the Pacific to get you heaving. In case you're fortunate enough not to know, early signs of an impending puke include headaches, dizziness and clammy skin. This is the time to take action. Put this book down ...

Fix your eyes firmly on the horizon and keep your head still (for example, brace it against a headrest). If you're below deck on a ship, lie down and close your eyes. Try eating something bland, like a dry biscuits; tasting or just smelling a lemon is also said to help. Cigarette smoke is guaranteed to make you feel worse, so avoid it as far as possible. Place yourself in the most stable part of the vehicle if you can: between the wings on a plane, in the middle of a boat or in the front seat of a car.

Remedies

You'll find a variety of anti-sickness remedies on the market. Preparations containing ginger or mint (including mint sweets) are helpful, and don't need to be taken in advance. Other remedies need to be taken before you travel. Eating lightly before the journey may also help.

Hyoscine (as tablets or skin patches) is effective for short journeys, but has side effects like dry mouth and blurred vision, and is not suitable for everyone. It's best avoided by children, older people and pregnant women. Hyoscine skin patches are known as Scopoderm in the UK and Transderm-Scop in the US.

Antihistamines (various brand names) are longer-lasting and have fewer side effects. They're generally available without prescription. Some antihistamines may make you drowsy, which can be an advantage on a long journey, but avoid driving and alcohol if you take antihistamines.

Alternatively, you could try something a bit different: special elasticated wristbands are available that work by applying pressure to acupuncture points, or there's a considerably more expensive battery-operated version.

STAYING HEALTHY

Avoiding illness and injury is the key to getting the most out of your trip, wherever you're going. Staying healthy becomes even more important if you're planning to spend some time in a remote location, where medical help is a couple of days away. It's also vital if you're doing outdoor activities such as trekking that rely on your physical – and mental – fitness. If you're aware of potential health hazards and take some basic precautions to avoid them, you shouldn't find it hard to stay safe and healthy. There are some special considerations to take on board if you're planning on doing outdoor activities; these are discussed in greater detail in the Wilderness Health & Safety chapter later in this guide.

ADJUSTMENT

Don't plan on hitting the ground running, especially at the start of a long trip. Allow yourself time to adjust physically and mentally to your new environment and lifestyle. You'll probably need time to recover from jet lag, catch up on sleep and perhaps missed meals, and generally ease yourself into travel mode.

COPING WITH A HOT CLIMATE

If you've gone from a cool, temperate climate back home to a hot tropical one, make sure you give yourself a chance to get used to the heat. Your body has an amazing capacity to adjust to temperature changes, but it doesn't happen overnight. You're probably going to feel uncomfortably hot and easily exhausted for the first week in a hot climate. It takes about this long for your body to make initial adjustments to deal with the temperature change. After this, you'll probably find you can cope with the heat much better, and your capacity for activity gets back to normal.

Most people sweat heavily in the heat, and if you want to avoid serious problems such as heat exhaustion and heat

Health Boosters

Travel can involve many stresses healthwise, leaving you vulnerable to illness at a time you could really do without it. One way to help avoid problems is by making sure you are as fit and healthy as possible before you go. Many travellers, however, take the additional precaution of using remedies to boost their body's powers to fight off infection. You'll probably find it helpful to consult a practitioner to get individually tailored advice, but here's a rundown of some of the options available. Follow the dosing instructions on the packaging or your practitioner's advice, and take basic health precautions as well.

- Acidophilus – one of a number of 'probiotics', this bacteria is present in live natural yoghurt and is claimed to have a beneficial effect on the balance of bacteria in the intestine; it's popularly used by travellers to prevent diarrhoea, although some experts question whether the bacteria would survive the acid conditions in the stomach.
- Aloe vera – an immune enhancer when taken by mouth, this widely available plant also has antiseptic properties when applied topically.
- Cat's claw – originally from the Latin American rainforest, this herb is said to have antiinflammatory and antioxidant properties.
- Echinacea – the top-selling herb in the US, this is a good, readily available (back home at least) general immune-booster.
- Garlic – popular immune booster; often comes in combination with horseradish.
- Glutamine – this amino acid is needed for the immune system to function properly.
- Grapefruit seed extract – said to have antibacterial, antifungal and antiviral activity, this is recommended for intestinal and other infections.
- L-arginine – an amino acid involved in immune function, and promotes wound healing.
- Vitamin C – cheap and readily available in many different forms.

stroke (which is a medical emergency; p282), it's vital to drink plenty of fluids to replace the amount you're sweating out. Cool, plain water is best, although the juice from green coconuts, which is widely available in tropical destinations, makes a refreshing alternative.

- Don't wait until you feel thirsty before drinking; thirst is a very bad indicator of your fluid needs, and if you're thirsty, you're already dehydrated – see p281 for a full discussion of preventing and treating dehydration.
- Always have a supply of water with you and make a point of sipping water regularly while you're out.
- Tea, coffee and alcohol all have a diuretic effect (ie they make you lose fluid), so it's best to go easy on these.

Physical activity generates heat, which means that your body has to work even harder to stay cool if you're exercising. If you're going on an activity-packed holiday in a tropical climate, plan to take it easy during the first week, building up to maximal activity as you acclimatise to the heat.

! Avoid overexerting yourself (and this includes eating a big meal) during the hottest part of the day; it's the perfect time for a siesta or for reading that airport novel – or your guidebook.

As far as clothing is concerned, you need to choose clothes that will protect your skin from the ravages of the sun (and insects) but that will not prevent heat loss. Sunburn makes your body less able to cope with the heat. So body-hugging lycra outfits are probably out, at least off the beach; loose, light-coloured clothing made of natural fibres like cotton are in. (Dark colours will absorb the heat more.) Obviously, you'll need to take any local cultural considerations into consideration when deciding on the best clothing to wear – see your travel guidebook for more details.

Some people are more vulnerable to the heat than others. Children are more prone to heat illness than adults – see the Babies & Children chapter for more information. Older travellers who are less fit may be at greater risk of heat illness, although if you're physically fit, you'll cope just as well as younger adults. Anybody who is overweight may find the heat more of a stress, as the extra padding makes it more difficult for your body to lose heat. People with heart or lung problems are vulnerable to heat stress because the heart has to work harder under hot conditions. If you have an ongoing medical condition, it's worth discussing with your doctor how the heat may affect you.

Prickly heat and fungal skin infections (see the Coughs, Rashes & Other Common Problems chapter for more details) are very common in hot, humid conditions, and can be a nuisance. You can help prevent them by washing regularly with water and carefully drying all those nooks and crannies, especially between your toes.

FOOTCARE

If your feet aren't happy, the chances are you won't be either. It's astonishing what an ordeal walking becomes when you feel every step. The heat can make your feet and ankles swell when you first arrive in a hot climate, and hot swollen feet easily get chafed and uncomfortable. Consider finding room in your pack for a soothing foot spray, moisturiser or balm.

Footwear

If you're not going too far off the beaten track, your best bet is likely to be light-weight walking shoes (the next step up from running shoes). These are supportive where they need to be (around the heel), cushioned where they should be (under the base of the heel and under the ball of the foot), and allow the foot to bend where it's happiest to. Most importantly, you've got a wide range of brands to choose from, so you can find one that suits the shape of your foot best. Unless you're planning on trekking, it's probably best to avoid serious hiking boots because they're heavy and stiff.

Open footwear such as sandals or thongs are tempting in a hot climate but they leave your feet vulnerable to injury (and subsequent infection), and over a long period of time your skin dries out, giving you cracked and painful heels.

Foot Hygiene

If possible, wash your feet at least once a day, and dry them carefully, especially between the toes. Athlete's foot, a fungal infection, is extremely common, especially in hot climates, and can be a real nuisance. If you're a sweaty foot person, consider wiping between the toes with methylated spirits (in the form of pre-injection swabs, available from pharmacists, and won't take up much space in your medical kit).

If you wear open footwear, you can help prevent cracked heels by using a skin-softening agent (such as Sorbelene cream) and a pumice stone to remove dry skin.

SUN

The sun is probably the greatest hazard you'll face anywhere you go in the Pacific region, including temperate New Zealand. Make sure skin cancer is one souvenir you don't come home with.

The Bad News

Sunlight or solar energy is made up of radiation of many different wavelengths, including ultraviolet (UV) rays, the bad guys. UVA rays used to be thought to be less harmful than UVB, but there's plenty of evidence that they are just as bad, so you need to look for sunscreen products that protect against both types. In the short term, UV radiation causes redness, blisters and soreness – sunburn. If you've ever frazzled yourself in the sun, you'll know how painful this can be, but the long-term effects are even scarier. Many of the skin changes that were thought just to be part of the ageing process, including wrinkling, broken veins and pigmented patches ('liver spots'), are now known to be due to sun damage. Worst of all, UV rays can damage the metabolism of skin cells, leading to skin cancer.

Skin damage doesn't just start with sunburn; any time you spend in the sun contributes in the long term. Sun overexposure is thought to result in suppression of the immune system, and may make you more vulnerable to infectious diseases – something to bear in mind when you're travelling.

A suntan is a layer of skin pigment (melanin), which forms in response to sunlight falling on your skin. It can protect against sunburn, but not against the ageing or cancer-inducing effects of UV radiation. In any case, it takes two to three weeks before a suntan can provide good protection against sunburn.

Prevention

If you're somewhere where the sun is almost always shining and you're spending a lot of your time outdoors, it can be hard to be on your guard all the time. It does take a bit of effort, but protection against the sun will hopefully just become part of your daily routine. Sun intensity is greatly increased at altitude and by reflection off water and snow, so you need to take particular care in these situations. The state of the protective ozone layer is another good reason to take care, especially in Australia and New Zealand. The sun is generally at its fiercest during the middle of the day, so it makes sense to stay out of the sun at this time.

The basic message is to do the slip, slop, slap thing:

▶ slip on a shirt – covering up with clothing of a reasonable thickness provides by far the best protection from harmful rays; special protective sunsuits are available for wearing on the beach, and are ideal for kiddies and if you're doing water sports
▶ slop on sunscreen – use liberal amounts of high protection factor (SPF 30+ is currently the highest available), broad spectrum sunscreen on any exposed bits of skin
▶ slap on a hat – a wide-brimmed hat or a legionnaire-style cap with a neck protector will help to keep damaging rays off your face, ears and back of the neck

Sun does just as much damage to your eyes, so you'll need to protect your eyes with sunglasses, ideally wraparound ones.

Note the following traps for the unwary:

- sunscreens need to be applied 20 to 30 minutes before going into the sun and reapplied frequently after that, especially after swimming
- you can get sunburnt through water (snorkelling is notorious for this), so take care to cover up with a T-shirt and use plenty of water-resistant sunscreen
- the ambient temperature doesn't make any difference to the burning power of the sun – you can still get burnt on a cold day if the sun is shining
- you can burn on a cloudy day (because clouds let through some UV radiation) and in shade (from reflected light, often off water)

That Ozone Hole

A layer of ozone, a molecule that consists of three oxygen atoms bound together, exists about 19km to 30km above the earth's surface. This ozone layer plays a vital role as a sort of global sunscreen, by helping to prevent potentially damaging ultraviolet radiation from penetrating the earth's atmosphere. Without the ozone layer, humankind, not to mention other forms of life, would have long ago been killed off from the damaging effects of UV radiation.

In recent years, ozone depletion by manufactured chemicals, mainly chlorofluorocarbons (CFCs), has resulted in the formation of the ozone 'hole'. This is an area of ozone-depleted atmosphere that, for complex reasons to do with winter temperatures, exists over Antarctica, even though most ozone depleters are emitted by countries in the northern hemisphere. The hole isn't static, and waxes and wanes with the seasons, expanding northwards in the southern spring (October and November) before contracting back towards Antarctica in December.

Alarmist reports about the effects of the ozone hole tend to appear every so often, including stories of sheep with singed wool in New Zealand! While these are undoubtedly exaggerations, the damage to the ozone layer is a serious issue, and it is sensible to be extra careful to avoid overexposure to the sun wherever you are in the Pacific region.

Safer Suntanning

If you've come to the Pacific to escape the seasonal gloom of a temperate climate, it can be hard to resist the temptation to stretch out in the sun and make that crawled-out-from-under-a-stone pallor just a distant memory. If staying pale and inter-esting is just not an option for you, then at least take some damage-control measures. Make sure you allow your skin to tan slowly without burning, starting with 15 or 20 minutes exposure a day, increasing this gradually. As soon as your skin starts to feel sore or look red, and preferably long before this, head for the shade. Remember that freckles may be cute but they're also a sign you've already had too much sun.

BEACH & SWIMMING SAFETY

Unless you are seriously hydrophobic, you're going to find it hard to resist the temptation to go for a swim at some stage on your travels in the Pacific region. Swimming is a surprisingly risky activity, and international tourists have something of a reputation when it comes to drownings.

!Rips and strong currents are the most common cause of beach drownings – read the section on Surf & Currents in the Water Safety chapter later for guidelines on what to do if you find yourself caught in a strong current.

Although there will often be lifeguards and safety notices at popular beaches, many beaches in more remote areas will be unpatrolled. If you get into difficulties in the water at these beaches, you're on your own.

▸ Check locally for advice on currents and other swimming hazards – just because there are no warning signs doesn't necessarily mean it's safe.
▸ Play safe and avoid going in if you're unused to surf or you're unsure of your swimming capabilities.
▸ Never run and dive in the water, even if you've checked the depth before, in case it's unexpectedly shallow.
▸ Always be even more vigilant than usual when your children are around water.

▶ Don't swim straight after a meal, as you are more likely to get cramps.
▶ Don't swim if you've had alcohol or you've been doing drugs.

Some marine life in the Pacific ocean and in the waters around Australia can be a danger to you. Get local advice on seasonal hazards, and see the Hazardous Marine Life section of the Water Safety chapter later for the full rundown on potentially dangerous creatures. For example, in Australia, swimming in the ocean off the northern coast is dangerous (and not advised) during October to April because of the presence of deadly box jellyfish.

Maximise your enjoyment of the beach or poolside by bearing some of the following health tips in mind:

▶ sun and heat are major risks – see these sections earlier in this chapter for guidelines on coping with these
▶ swimming at night or after you've had an alcoholic drink or two tends to be especially risky and is best avoided
▶ eye and ear infections are common in swimmers, especially if the water is none too clean – these are covered in the Coughs, Rashes & Other Common Problems chapter later in this guide; wear goggles and ear plugs if you are in any doubt about the cleanliness of the water
▶ fungal skin infections are common in hot humid climates – drying yourself off between swims can help prevent these
▶ wounds suffered at the beach often get infected, usually because they are ignored – clean any cuts and scratches promptly and keep them clean.
▶ if you have any concerns about the cleanliness of the water in the sea or swimin pools, try not to swallow any when you're swimming or doing water sports, as it can be a source of intestinal infections.

Tempting though it is, walking barefoot in or out of the water is probably best avoided, especially as you never know what may be just below the surface of the sand, and coral is sharp stuff. In rural areas of the tropical Pacific islands, you may be at risk of picking up parasites in this way, including hookworm and creeping eruption.

Accidents Can Happen ...

Although travellers tend to worry about picking up a tropical illness in an exotic place, you're actually at far greater risk from accident and injury than from any tropical infection. In fact accidents are the most common cause of death in young travellers. Accidents, especially road traffic accidents, are the main reason for travellers to need emergency medical treatment, including the possibility of a blood transfusion – risky in less developed countries.

When you're on holiday, you tend to take all sorts of risks you probably wouldn't dream of taking at home. It's part of what makes travelling so good, but you do need to use a bit of common sense, especially if you are holidaying in a remote location. You're not immune just because you are on holiday. If you're riding a bicycle, moped or motorbike, a helmet and protective clothing are sensible even if they aren't the local norm.

While we don't want to rain on your beach party, just be aware that alcohol and other mind-altering substances are major factors in accidents of all types in travellers, from dignity-challenging falls to life-threatening road traffic accidents.

Obviously, the risk of having an accident increases if you're doing potentially risky outdoor activities, such as white-water rafting or mountaineering. This is something to take into account when you're planning your trip.

Accidents are preventable to a great extent. Awareness of potential risks, together with good planning for outdoor activities and a few sensible precautions, especially if you are driving or swimming, should see you relatively safe. And don't sit under a coconut tree ...

INSECT BITE PREVENTION

Insects can be a major annoyance as well as a health hazard in the Pacific islands and tropical north of Australia. Subtropical Australia and temperate New Zealand aren't exactly insect-free either, but in these areas insects are more likely to be annoying than a health hazard as such. Here's a summary of the main insects in the Pacific region and the diseases they are responsible for transmitting.

mosquitoes	risk area
malaria	PNG, Solomon Islands, Vanuatu (see map)
dengue fever	all Pacific islands, far north of Australia
filariasis	Pacific islands
Ross River fever	widespread in Australia, especially in the tropical north
Japanese encephalitis	PNG, Torres Strait and Cape York (Australia)
Murray Valley encephalitis	PNG, Australia (mainly tropical north)

ticks	risk area
typhus,	PNG, eastern Australia
spotted fever, tick paralysis	eastern Australia

Currently the only way to minimise your risk of most of these diseases is to avoid getting bitten. Even if you're taking anti-malarials the rise in resistance of the malarial parasite makes bite avoidance a vital prevention measure.

Basic Measures

Like protecting yourself against the sun, insect bite prevention will probably become part of your daily routine. Biting insects are attracted by many variables, not many of which you can directly affect: body heat, body odour, chemicals in your sweat, perfumes, soap and types of clothing. Most mosquitoes are night-biters, but the dengue mosquito bites mainly during the day.

▸ Cover up with long-sleeved tops and long trousers; light-coloured clothing is thought to be less attractive to mosquitoes than dark colours.
▸ Use insect repellents on any exposed skin.

‣ Sleep in a screened room or under a mosquito net and always cover children's beds or cots with mosquito nets; air-conditioned rooms are usually insect-free zones.

‣ Remember day-biting mosquitoes, and avoid shady conditions in the late afternoon or taking an afternoon siesta without the protection of a mosquito net.

‣ Spray your room, tent or campervan with a knock-down insect spray before you retire for the night.

‣ Consider using electric insecticide vaporisers (you'll need a power socket for this) or mosquito coils – both are less effective if you have a fan going.

Insect Repellents

There are many insect repellent products on the market, but the most effective are those containing the compound DEET (diethyltoluamide) – check the label or ask your pharmacist to tell you which brands contain DEET. Some major brands include Autan, Doom, Jungle Formula, Off!, Repel and Rid.

DEET is very effective against mosquitoes, midges, ticks, bedbugs and leeches, and slightly less effective against flies. One application should last up to four hours, although if it's very humid or you're very sweaty, it may not last as long. Different formulations have different concentrations of DEET. The higher the concentration, the longer it will last, with around 50% being the optimal concentration, although there are some longer-acting formulations with lower strengths of DEET. It's a good idea to try a test dose before you leave to check for allergy or skin irritation.

If you're worried about the safety of DEET, be reassured: it's generally agreed that safety concerns over DEET are largely unfounded. However, for children, it's probably best to err on the side of caution – choose a lower strength long-acting cream, and always follow the manufacturer's instructions.

You may prefer to use one of the new lemon eucalyptus-based natural products, which have been shown to be an effective alternative to DEET, with similar action times (although DEET is probably still your best bet in high-risk areas). Other natural repellents include citronella and pyrethrum, but these tend to be less effective and to have a short action (up to an hour), making them less practical to use.

Cotton bands soaked in insect repellent can be useful to wear on your wrists and ankles (especially ankles, as these are a prime target for mosquitoes), and the repellent won't rub off as easily.

! If you're using sunscreen or other lotions, apply insect repellent last, and reapply after swimming if necessary; insect repellent may reduce the protection of a sunscreen.

Insecticides

Permethrin is a pyrethrum-like compound that can be applied to clothes and mosquito nets (but not on your skin). It repels and kills mosquitoes, fleas, ticks, mites, bedbugs, cockroaches and flies. If you're planning on trekking through potentially tick-infested areas, it's probably worth treating your clothes, particularly your trousers and socks, with permethrin before you go.

! You get the best protection against insect bites if you apply a DEET-based product on your skin and use permethrin-treated clothes and nets.

Mosquito Nets

If you're spending some time in the Pacific islands or tropical Australia, consider taking a mosquito net with you. They don't weigh much and don't take up much room. You can just tuck it away in your pack until you need it. Make sure you get one that has been soaked in permethrin, or you can treat your own net if necessary. A free-standing mosquito net (with an integral floor) might also make a handy fly-free zone for outdoor meals and relaxation if you're planning on travelling round Australia in the fly season.

Travel health clinics and travel-equipment or specialist outdoor equipment suppliers generally have a wide variety of mosquito nets to suit your individual needs. Free-standing nets are a great option and widely available; IAMAT (see Useful Organisations in the Before You Go chapter for more details), for example, has a version you could check out.

Other Possibilities

Taking vitamin B1 (thiamine), garlic or brewer's yeast have all been advocated as making you less attractive to insects. They may be worth a try, in conjunction with insect repellent – but bear in mind that they haven't been shown to work in trials. Electronic buzzing devices were a fad for a while but there is no evidence that they work.

SAFE FOOD

In this section we give some basic advice on avoiding problems associated with contaminated food. If you're travelling in Australia or New Zealand, you can probably skip this section, as you're at no greater risk from contaminated food in these countries than in any other developed nation.

○ Staying healthy is also about eating properly, especially when you're on a long trip – for the complete lowdown on eating well, see the Diet & Nutrition chapter later in this guide.

It's generally agreed that food, not water, is the most common source of gastro problems in travellers. Food can be contaminated with disease-causing microorganisms at many stages of the production chain, including during harvesting, transportation, handling, washing and preparation. Many forms of diarrhoea and dysentery (bloody diarrhoea) are transmitted in this way, as well as other diseases such as hepatitis A (common in travellers) and typhoid (uncommon).

You can get sick from contaminated food anywhere but it's more likely when you're travelling, for a variety of reasons. Sewage disposal systems may be inadequate in less developed nations which, together with higher levels of disease in some parts of the population, means there's more chance that food will be contaminated with disease-causing microorganisms. If, for example, a fly lands on your food back home, it probably hasn't had a chance to wipe its feet on a pile of faeces beforehand, but this is not always true elsewhere.

Another key factor for travellers is that travelling usually entails 'eating out' for all your meals for perhaps weeks on end, and you have to rely on other people to prepare your food safely. This is always a risk, and even in countries with supposedly high food safety standards, such as Australia, outbreaks of food poisoning still occur with alarming regularity.

Eating safely is about taking simple precautions to minimise your risk of getting something nasty, it's not about achieving a laboratory ideal. It's down to common sense, plus a little background knowledge. It may mean that sometimes when you're travelling you don't eat exactly what you want to but, hey, what's new!

Safe to Eat

Here are some guidelines on the kinds of things that are likely to be safe to eat in most circumstances. Microorganisms love hot, humid climates, and will multiply gleefully in food left sitting around in these conditions, especially if refrigeration is unreliable or unavailable.

- Heating kills germs, so food that's served piping hot is likely to be safer than lukewarm or cold food, especially if it's been sitting around in the open.
- Fruit and vegetables can be difficult to clean (and may be contaminated where they are grown), but they should be safe if they're peeled or cooked.
- Well cooked meat and seafood is generally OK; raw or lightly cooked meat and seafood can be a source of disease.
- Tinned food is usually safe (check 'best before' dates if necessary).
- Dry food, such as bread, biscuits and plain cakes are usually safe, although it's best to avoid cream-filled goodies, as microorganisms such as salmonella (a cause of food poisoning) love cream.

Finally, your stomach's natural defences (mainly acid) can cope with small amounts of contaminated foods – if you're not sure about something, don't pig out on it!

What to Avoid

Here are some guidelines to help you decide what is likely to be less safe to eat or drink.

- The more food has been handled (for example, through peeling, slicing and arranging), the more chance it has of being contaminated by unwashed hands.
- Food can be contaminated by dirty dishes, cutlery or utensils; blenders or pulpers used for fruit juices are often suspect.
- You can't necessarily tell if food is contaminated by looking at it; food that is seething with disease-causing microorganisms may still look and smell delicious.
- Hot spices don't make food safe, just more palatable.
- Salads, like other vegetables, are hard to clean and may be contaminated where they are grown – if you're in any doubt about hygiene standards, it's best to avoid salads altogether.
- Fruit juices and other drinks may be diluted with unsafe water.
- Freezing doesn't kill disease-causing microorganisms; be wary of frozen food (including ice cream) if refrigeration is questionable (because of power cuts or lack of availability).
- Unpasteurised milk may be offered to you in rural areas but is best avoided, as it can be a source of illnesses such as TB in less developed nations. Boiling milk will make it safe if you're unsure.

Where to Eat

There are no hard and fast rules we can give you, but again, use your common sense. Star rating is certainly no guarantee of food safety, as food poisoning outbreaks on cruise liners and at resort hotels regularly remind us, but in theory, standards are easier to enforce in major hotels than in a food stall in a market, say. However, it's easy enough to stay healthy even if you eat at small, cheap eating places – try to pick busy, popular places that look clean, and choose freshly prepared dishes rather than ones that have been sitting out on display for hours on end.

Street Food

Whether or not to eat 'street food' is one of those classic travellers' conundrums. Common sense tells you that most street vendors probably can't afford to buy high-quality ingredients, and many won't have access to adequate (if any) washing facilities or toilets. And you can't really expect your average street vendor to be up with the latest food hygiene practices. On the other hand ... street food is a way of life in many tropical countries, and arguably very much part of the travel experience. It's definitely your call, but you can minimise the undoubted risks by careful selection, following the guidelines given in this section. Basically, choose hot, freshly cooked items, preferably that have not been touched by the vendor's hand since cooking – this is where carrying your own utensils or a paper plate comes in handy.

Self-catering is a good safe option, but make sure your own food hygiene practices are beyond reproach! Poor food hygiene practices are a common cause of illness in trekkers.

SAFE DRINKING WATER

Water, water everywhere, but not a drop to drink ... You need to drink lots of water to stay healthy, especially in hot climates, but can you drink the water safely? Although contaminated food is probably the most common source of gut infections when you're travelling, water can also be a source of illness, including diarrhoea, dysentery, hepatitis and typhoid.

In countries with good infrastructure and resources, communal water supplies are generally safe from contamination, but you can't rely on this in nations with fewer resources. Contamination of the water supply can occur at some point, usually by human or animal sewage. Your travel guidebook or a reliable local source will be able to give you specific information on water safety at your destination.

In Australia and New Zealand, there's generally no problem with tap water, but contamination of rivers and streams with *Giardia*, a microorganism that causes diarrhoea (see the Diarrhoea chapter for more details), can be a problem if you are trekking in rural areas. Even if the water is cold, this does not mean it is safe.

Unless you are sure the water is safe from contamination, it's best to err on the side of caution.

! If you're not sure, don't drink untreated water and don't brush your teeth in it.

Ice is only as safe as the water it's made from, so it's best to avoid this too. (If you're desperate for a cool drink, seal the ice in a plastic bag before putting it in your drink – but make sure the bag is clean first!) Alcohol has some disinfectant properties, but at drinking strength it won't make water safe to drink. A squeeze of lemon or lime juice can help but, again, you shouldn't rely on it to make your drink safe.

Drinking bottled water is an obvious answer to the water question. As a general rule, it's best to stick to major brands of bottled water, preferably those with serrated tops (this means the bottle can't have been refilled with any old water and sold to you as pure spring water). If you're in any doubt, choose carbonated water (for example plain soda water), as the acidity from carbonation kills off any microorganisms.

The cost of bottled water can add up over a long trip, especially if you're travelling in hot climates, and there's a very real concern over the environmental effect of millions of discarded and unrecycled plastic bottles. If you're trekking or travelling off the beaten track, bottled water is just not practical and may not be available in remote areas. In these situations, you'll have to have some means with you of making water safe to drink. Options are boiling, using chemical disinfectants or using a water purification device. Which method to use depends on where you are and what you're planning to do.

!Make sure you have more than one means of purifying water in case one method fails (for example, take some iodine as well as a pump-action purifier).

Boiling

The simplest and most effective way of making water safe to drink is to boil it, which kills all disease-causing bugs. You just need to bring it to a rolling boil for a minute or two and then let it cool – prolonged boiling is not necessary.

Chemical Disinfectants

If boiling doesn't sound like a practical option, it's relatively easy to disinfect clear water with chemicals. Chlorine and iodine are the chemicals most widely used, and at optimal concentrations both kill bacteria, viruses and most parasites (one exception is cryptosporidium). Iodine and chlorine are both available as tablets or liquids ('tincture' of iodine), and iodine is also available as crystals. You can usually buy them from good pharmacies, travel health clinics or outdoor equipment suppliers.

Factors that affect the ability of these chemicals to disinfect water include concentration, how long you leave the water to stand after adding the chemical, water temperature (the colder the water, the longer it needs to be left to stand before use) and any particulate matter in the water.

Make sure you follow the manufacturer's dosage and contact time if you're using tablets, but as a rule, you'll need to leave the water for at least 20 minutes before drinking it. If the water is really cold, you will need to leave it for longer, sometimes an hour or two; alternatively, you could add the chemicals the night before and leave it to stand overnight. With 2% tincture of iodine you need to add five drops to every litre of water to be purified.

Chlorine is considered less reliable in general than iodine, as it is more likely to be affected by factors such as water alkalinity. Silver tablets are also available but they are not effective against parasite cysts, so they shouldn't be used without filtering the water first.

! *Iodine should not be used continuously to purify water over a long period of time (more than six weeks) as it can cause thyroid problems; iodine should also be avoided if you're pregnant or have thyroid problems, and it's not suitable for children under 12 years of age.*

The taste of chemically treated water can be a major turn-off, but there are ways of neutralising this. Charcoal resins or a carbon filter can remove the taste and smell of chemicals, or you can add ascorbic acid (vitamin C) or flavouring. These need to be added after the treated water has been allowed to stand for the required length of time.

! *If the water is cloudy, chemicals won't be effective because organic matter tends to neutralise the chemical – you'll need to filter the water first, or add alum to precipitate it out.*

Water Filters & Purifiers

No, you don't need to be a rocket scientist to understand what these devices do – it's actually pretty straightforward.

Not sure about the terminology? Simple filters are just sieves or strainers, and their effectiveness depends on how fine they are. Generally, they don't make water safe to drink without further treatment (boiling or chemicals), as they don't remove the smallest disease-causing organisms (viruses and some bacteria), although fine-pore ceramic filters are exceptions. Purifiers are dual action: they filter water and disinfect it (for example with an iodine resin) to remove viruses; often they include a final step to remove the taste of the chemical disinfectant and any other chemicals such as pesticides.

Filters and purifiers can be gravity or pump action. Pump action is probably the more realistic option unless you have plenty of time on your hands, but can be hard work. Water purifiers often contain a carbon filter to remove traces of chemicals used to disinfect the water, but note that using a carbon filter on its own does not make water safe to drink.

It's worth having an idea beforehand of what you're looking for; here's a suggested pre-purchase checklist for purifiers.

- What does it claim to remove? Does it make water totally safe to drink?
- What do you want to use it for? Some devices are suitable for occasional or emergency use, whereas others are good for continuous use over a long period of time.
- What's the flow rate like? You don't want to pump for two hours for a sip of water.
- How portable/breakable is it? Ceramic filters are very effective but need a bit of care, as they can crack.
- How often does the filter need to be replaced? Filters can get clogged and there's a risk of bacterial growth occurring in them, so they usually need to be cleaned or replaced after a while.
- How easy is it to take apart and clean if it becomes clogged?
- Is it endorsed by an independent organisation?

There are some interesting variations available, such as a filter that fits onto a tap and a straw (for reaching those inaccessible puddles ...), so it's worth shopping around to find what you want. Water filters and purifiers are available from most major travel health clinics and from outdoor equipment suppliers, often by mail order. Alternatively, a search on the internet brings up a heap of possibilities.

!Even if you're using a water purifier, choose the cleanest water source possible, and never drink water from rivers, lakes or wells without purifying it first.

PERSONAL HYGIENE

No, we're not talking about tackling BO, but about the importance of washing your hands before you eat! It's obvious perhaps, but if you're used to having efficient waste disposal systems and safe, plentiful water supplies on hand 24 hours a day, you may be a bit rusty on this most basic disease prevention strategy.

Diseases such as diarrhoea, dysentery, typhoid and hepatitis are essentially diseases of poor hygiene. So it's worth reminding yourself to wash your hands before you eat and always after going to the toilet. If you're camping, consider taking a disinfectant gel for this purpose, as you can use this without water, and you won't be endangering the environment. Obviously, this is particularly important if you're preparing and eating food with your hands. Short fingernails are easier to keep clean than long ones. Keep any cooking or eating utensils clean, even if it seems like a chore when you're camping.

! *If you are ill with a gastro upset, avoid preparing food for others, and take particular care over your personal hygiene and bury all waste well away from water courses.*

SEX & TRAVEL

It seems that not even the runs, rickety beds, paper thin walls, sunburn and sand can dampen the ardour of many travellers. Maybe it's the aphrodisiac properties of the heat, or the feeling of freedom travelling can give. Or is it just the beer? Maybe sex is the reason you're going travelling. Whatever the reason, it makes sense to arm yourself with the facts about your risks of getting a sexually transmitted infection (STI), as well as a pack of condoms. STIs are a worldwide problem.

A sexual encounter with a new partner anywhere carries a risk of HIV or one of the other STIs, but it can be even riskier when you're travelling. This is partly because the countries you're travelling in may have higher infection rates for HIV and STIs than your own, but also because when you're travelling you're more likely to be in contact with people who are at greater risk of being infected. More worrying still, surveys have shown that, in spite of the risks, many travellers don't take precautions to protect themselves.

It's easy to think 'it could never happen to me', but it can and does (sex *and* STIs). Anyone who's having sex can get an STI, 'nice' girls and college boys included. You may think you're safe, for example because you're not going to have sex with someone in a high-risk group or you're only going to have sex with fellow travellers. Think again. Who has your fellow traveller had sex with before you? Can you trust them to have been as careful or as aware of the risks as you?

Traditionally high-risk groups are men who have sex with men, people who inject drugs, sex workers, anybody who's had multiple partners and anybody who's had sex with people in these groups. You'll know if you're in the first group, and perhaps you'll recognise and be able to avoid the second and third groups, but are you sure you'd know if someone was in one of the last two groups? It's difficult to be sure of your new partner's sexual history and you may just be getting the edited highlights. 'Sex worker' is a pretty vague category anyway, and starts to look even vaguer when you've included the guy or gal who has sex in return for free meals, drinks or status. You can be fairly sure that you're not going to be the first traveller they've had sex with.

In theory at least, STIs are simple to prevent – don't have sex. But ... for many people, risk reduction is a more realistic option. We're not suggesting you become a celibate saint, but keep your head out of the clouds:

▶ avoid obviously risky situations (use your common sense and don't believe everything your new partner may tell you)
▶ always use condoms if you have sex with a new partner or consider safer ways of having casual sex that don't involve intercourse
▶ you never know when you might need a condom, so be prepared – it doesn't mean you have to have sex

If you do slip up while you're away, don't just pretend it never happened and perhaps put yourself and other partners at risk – arrange for a checkup when you get home.

INJECTIONS & BLOOD TRANSFUSIONS

Injections and other medical or dental treatment procedures can involve infection risks if the needle or equipment is not adequately sterilised. If there are traces of blood or other body fluids on the equipment, there is a risk of infection with diseases such as hepatitis B, HIV and malaria. As a general rule, it's a good idea to avoid injections and any other procedures that involve breaking the skin unless you are confident of the hygiene standards.

If you're travelling to remote areas in less developed nations in the Pacific, consider taking a few sterile needles and syringes in your medical kit for use in an emergency. Obviously, this is only any good if you always carry them on you and are prepared to insist on them being used. Pre-packed 'AIDS packs' are available from most travel health clinics and travel equipment suppliers. A note from your doctor saying why you are carrying them is often a good idea in case customs officials are suspicious.

If you do need an injection, and you're concerned that medical hygiene standards may not be all they should, make sure you see the sterile wrapping opened in front of you. Boiling needles for 20 minutes will inactivate HIV. It goes without saying that it's never a good idea to share needles.

The chance that you will need a blood transfusion while you are away are pretty small. However, it's worth bearing in mind that in less developed countries blood transfusions carry a greater risk of infection than in countries with greater resources. Infections that can be transmitted in this way include HIV, malaria, hepatitis and syphilis. Apart from taking precautions to stay healthy and avoid accidents, the most important point to remember is to have adequate medical insurance that covers emergency evacuation if necessary.

If you are particularly concerned, you could consider joining the Blood Care Foundation (☎ 01732 742 427, fax 451 199, 16 Lonsdale Gardens, Tunbridge Wells, Kent TN1 1NU, UK), a charitable organisation that claims to be able to supply travellers with safe blood and sterile transfusion equipment within 12 hours anywhere in the world, for a membership fee.

DIET & NUTRITION

Eating well is about getting enough of the right nutrients to enable you to function at your best, mentally and physically, making you less vulnerable to illness. When you're travelling, nutritional considerations can be important because your diet may be very different from normal, especially if local foods are unfamiliar to you, or you're constantly on the move – or you're budgeting hard. At the same time, a different lifestyle and new activities (such as sightseeing, which is surprisingly energy-consuming) mean you have different nutritional requirements. Obviously if you fall ill or are injured, you need a good diet to give your body the best chance to recover.

EATING THE RIGHT STUFF

Everybody needs six basics for life: water, carbohydrates, protein, fat, vitamins and minerals. Foods aren't a pure source of just of one type of nutrient – they contain various elements in different quantities, so the best way to make sure you get enough of the right things is to eat a varied diet. You need to eat a variety of foods from each of five core groups:

- bread, rice, pasta and other cereals, potatoes, sweet potatoes and other tubers, such as taro, yams etc – eat lots of these, as they provide carbohydrate, fibre, some calcium and iron, and B vitamins
- fruit and vegetables – eat lots of these, they give you vitamin C, carotenes (vitamin A), folates, fibre and some carbohydrate
- milk & dairy products – eat moderate amounts for calcium, zinc, protein, vitamin B12, vitamin B2, vitamin A and vitamin D
- meat, fish, nuts and pulses (beans, lentils, peas) – these provide iron, protein, B vitamins (including B12, from meat only), zinc and magnesium; eat from this group in moderation
- fat and sugar-containing foods (butter, oil, margarine, cakes, biscuits, sweets, soft drinks etc) – eat sparingly from this group, which mainly provides fat, some vitamins and salt

These recommendations are based on the needs of a healthy person. If you are ill, your nutritional requirements change,

Fast Food, Flaps & Fat

Protein malnutrition has long been a problem in the Pacific islands, because the traditional diet of many islanders especially in rural inland areas includes few sources of protein. However, malnutrition in the form of obesity has recently become a major problem, especially among urban Pacific islanders.

The traditional Pacific island diet is low in fat and sugar, consisting mainly of fresh seafood or meat (occasionally), starch staples, fresh vegetables and fruit. However, the availability of cheap imports has resulted in a diet high in sugar (from processed foods, soft drinks and alcohol) and animal fats (from mutton flaps, turkey tails, tinned beef and fish, and fast food). If you're thinking you haven't seen mutton flaps for sale down at your local supermarket, you'd be right. These are a by-product of the meat industry, and are not considered fit for human consumption in developed nations, although this doesn't stop them from being exported to low-income Pacific nations. Mutton flaps contain an incredible 28% fat, which compares with corned beef at 12% and chicken at 5%.

As a result of diet and lifestyle changes, the Pacific island nations have some of the highest levels of obesity and related 'lifestyle' diseases (including diabetes, gout, heart disease, high blood pressure, intestinal cancer and dental problems) in the world. In Tonga half the women and a tenth of the men are obese. The South Pacific Consumer Protection Programme has reported that 15% of the population of West Samoa has diabetes (five times the rate in Australia or New Zealand), and the incidence of gout and diabetes in Nauru, for example, is the highest in the world.

The Pacific island nations are trying to tackle the problem through public education programs highlighting the risks of obesity, and giving guidelines for healthier food choices, but as many developed nations have found, it's likely to be an uphill battle. The opening of yet more international fast food chains in some of the islands can hardly contribute to the effort.

for example you will need to eat more foods containing protein, vitamins and minerals.

Vitamins & Minerals

These nutrients are needed in small amounts for many of the processes carried out in your body and are essential for health. Although most nutritionists agree that it's best to get what you need through an adequate and varied diet, when you're travelling there are times when it may be a good idea to take multivitamin and mineral supplements.

! Many vitamins and minerals come from fresh fruit and vegetables, so you could consider taking supplements if you think you'll be missing out on these for any reason (for example if you're on a long trek or fresh produce is difficult to find, such as in outback Australia).

Tinned foods are generally a poor nutritional substitute for fresh items, while cooking vegetables tends to decrease their vitamin content. In developed countries, including Australia and New Zealand, basic foods like bread and breakfast cereals are usually fortified with vitamins.

If you have heavy menstrual periods, especially if you have cut out animal products from your diet, you may need to take multivitamin supplements containing iron to prevent anaemia. If you don't eat any foods of animal origin, you will need to take a vitamin B12 supplement. If you're recovering from illness or injury, taking multivitamin supplements may give your body a helping hand.

Energy & Protein

All the starchy staples (known as complex carbohydrates) that make up such a big part of the Pacific island diet are good sources of food energy (although poor sources of protein). Sugary foods are good for supplying an instant energy boost, but complex carbohydrates are broken down more slowly in the body and provide sustained energy over a longer period of time. If you don't have enough carbs in your diet, more protein (from your muscles, if necessary) is used, making less available for growth and repair.

As well as obvious things like sweets and chocolate, good sources of sugar include fruit (drying fruit concentrates the sugar), jam, honey and milk. Sugar cane, a member of the grass family, originated in the South Pacific and has a sugary sap if you chew it. If your blood sugar gets low, you may start to feel weak, wobbly and headachy, signalling that it's time for that chocolate fix.

Protein is an important component of your diet, but healthy adults only need a small amount of protein daily. Protein is important for growth and repair, so it's vital for growing children to get sufficient quantities in their diet. Protein can also help with wound healing, so it can be helpful to increase the amount you are eating if you are recovering from injury.

! Good sources of animal protein include meat, fish, poultry, eggs and dairy foods (milk, cheese etc). Non-animal sources include cereals (bread, rice, oats etc), nuts, seeds and pulses.

Fat is the most concentrated source of energy, providing, weight for weight, just over twice as much as carbohydrate or protein. Foods rich in fat include all the obvious things like oil, butter, and any foods cooked in them; meat; egg yolks and many processed and fast foods. Less obvious foods rich in fat include avocado and nuts. Palm oil and coconut milk are rare plant sources of saturated fats.

Dare we tell you that alcohol provides nearly as much energy as fat?

FADING AWAY?

You may find you lose weight while you're travelling, although you may have to try quite hard in many parts of the Pacific! Fast food is widely available, with its usual saturated-fat overload. However, it is possible you could find you lose weight, especially if you are on a long trip – it's difficult to

A Guava a Day ...

If you are not familiar with some of the fruits and vegetables that are part of the traditional diet in the Pacific islands, it can make it hard to make good food choices.

Coconuts – a source of oil and fibre (copra), as well as coconut flesh (fresh or dried) and juice (from the centre of the fresh nut). Nutritionally, coconut contains fats (coconut flesh is approximately 40% fat, over 90% of which is the saturated type), dietary fibre and small amounts of protein, minerals and vitamins. Fresh coconut flesh has an energy value of 1465kJ (350Cal) per 100g. The juice from the centre of the coconut is a refreshing, low-fat and safe source of fluid but little else. Coconut cream (energy value 860kJ, or 205Cal, per 100g, made from pressing the flesh of coconuts, is high in fats, on average containing about 20g of fat.

Banana – another classic tropical fruit, and a good source of dietary fibre, vitamin C and potassium; bananas are one of very few fruits containing complex carbohydrates. An average-sized banana gives 375kJ (90Cal).

Breadfruit – an important food source in the Pacific, this is a good source of vitamin C, complex carbohydrates and some dietary fibre; energy value is 420kJ (100Cal) per 100g.

Papaya – also called paw paw, this fruit is a good source of vitamin C, carotene (which is converted to vitamin A), dietary fibre and small amounts of other minerals and vitamins. Like pineapples, papaya fruit and leaves contain a protein-destroying enzyme, papain, which is why meat is traditionally wrapped in

feel motivated to eat when it's hot, and a change of diet, falling ill or perhaps just being more active can mean you slim down a bit.

You may have a bit of padding to spare, but keep an eye on how much weight you're losing. Don't allow yourself to lose

papaya leaves before it is cooked in many Pacific islands. Energy value is 185kJ (44Cal) per 150g.

Cassava – also known as manioc or tapioca, this large tuber is a traditional staple in South America and Africa, as well as the Pacific islands. Cassava is a good source of vitamin C, potassium and dietary fibre but it's a poor source of protein. Energy value is 800kJ (188Cal) per 145g.

Koa – also known as mangrove bean, this vegetable is a good source of dietary fibre, with a relatively high salt content compared with most vegetables; energy value is 425kJ (100Cal) per 100g.

Kumera – a type of sweet potato, kumera is high in complex carbohydrates, dietary fibre and carotene (orange-fleshed varieties); energy value is 395kJ (95Cal) per 100g.

Taro – this tuber is cultivated as a staple food all over the Pacific islands; young leaves are also eaten. Taro is a good source of dietary fibre, vitamin C and potassium; energy value is 455kJ (108Cal) per 100g.

Yam – this tuber provides dietary fibre, potassium and some vitamin C, but not much protein. Some varieties have to be peeled and cooked in order to remove bitter alkaloids.

Most fruit and vegetables are good sources of vitamin C, but if you're looking for a mega-dose, you may be interested to know that guavas are one of the richest sources of vitamin C. One guava has the equivalent amount of vitamin C as about five oranges. Kiwi fruit and mangoes are also rich in vitamin C.

too much; this may put you at risk of illness as well as draining you of energy.

! If you find you're losing weight and you're eating a vegetarian diet, remember that you generally have to eat larger quantities of plant foods to get the same amount of energy.

Increase your quota of energy-giving foods, including fats, and consider taking multivitamin supplements. If you're ill, get medical advice; if you have ongoing diarrhoea, for example, you may not be absorbing nutrients properly.

On the other hand, you may find you're one of probably an equal number of travellers who find they put on the pounds when travelling. If this concerns you, remember that maintaining your weight is basically a balance between input and output: if you take in more energy than you're using up, your body will store the extra as fat. However much certain sections of the media may try to convince you otherwise, you can't eat to lose weight.

VEGGING OUT

In the Pacific islands, there are plenty of starch staples to fill you up, but finding a vegetarian or vegan source of protein can be a challenge. If you're headed for traditionally meat-and-two-veg-eating Australia and New Zealand, you'll be pleasantly surprised at the variety of vegetarian and, to a lesser extent, vegan food on offer in the main centres, but don't let this lull you into a false sense of security! Once you leave the main centres, it can be hard to find nutritious non-animal-based food. Although you'll probably be able to get a salad sandwich, vegetable lasagne (possibly) or pizza (but the cheese is unlikely to be vegetarian), there are slim-pickings for vegetarians if you're eating out, and choices are even more limited for vegans. Your best bet is to stock up in the main centres before you set off into the rural hinterland, and be prepared to self-cater.

Although there's a good range of multiculturally-inspired vegetarian and vegan food available in large urban centres in Australia and New Zealand, if you're shopping for food you'll find that it's generally back to the bad old days of reading the small print on food labels to look for animal-based ingredients. And you will need to be a bit wary of foods that

Happy Little Vegemites

Vegemite is an Australian icon, and most Australians were brought up on it. Vegemite's attraction can be something of a mystery to the uninitiated, but once you try it you may well find you're hooked. This dark brown spread in its distinctive yellow-top jar (similar but oh-so-different from the British version, Marmite), is best eaten spread thinly on buttered toast or as a vegemite sandwich (white bread, please!).

Vegemite was originally made by blending yeasts from different breweries, and adding celery, onion and salt. Not the most inspiring of ingredients, you might think, but wait till you try it. Yeast extract is an incredibly rich source of B vitamins, which led to Vegemite being used as a nutritional supplement by the army and hospitals during WWII.

The salt content of Vegemite has raised some concern, and there's currently a move to reduce the amount of salt it contains – gradually, so that consumers' tastebuds don't get a fright. However, for most people the amount of salt they get in their diet from Vegemite is likely to pale into insignificance compared with the amount you get from eating most processed foods. In any case, nutritional analyses suggest that a typical spread of Vegemite on bread contains less salt (112mg sodium), than the bread on which it is spread (132mg sodium)!

are labelled as 'vegetarian', especially in sandwich bars and takeaway joints as they often contain ingredients like cheese (non-veg varieties) and eggs (unlikely to be free-range). For more information you could try contacting the national vegetarian society in the relevant country:

Australian Vegetarian Society (www.moreinfo.com.au/avs) – check out their web site for contact details of the state branches
New Zealand Vegetarian Society (☎ 09-828 9301), National Office, PO Box 77 034, Auckland 1030; or check out the Wellington Branch's web site (http://vegsoc.wellington.net.nz)

You may already be vegetarian or you may decide there are only so many meat pies and sausage sizzles that a person can take, and turn veg on your travels.

! If you've just turned vegetarian, be aware that your body takes a bit of time to adjust to getting some nutrients from plant sources, so take a bit of care with your diet.

Getting enough protein isn't generally a problem, especially if you eat cheese and eggs. Beans are ubiquitous. Nuts are also easy to find and a good source of protein (and vitamin E).

Proteins from plant sources are often deficient in one or more amino acids (the building blocks of protein). Most traditionally vegetarian diets have dealt with this by basing meals around a combination of protein sources so that deficiencies are complemented. Examples of combinations include pulses and rice and nuts and cereal (nut butter on bread).

Because iron from plant sources is less well absorbed than iron from meat, iron deficiency anaemia is a risk if you aren't careful, especially in menstrual-age women. You can improve absorption of iron from food by having a source of vitamin C (for example fruit, fruit juice or vegetables) at the same time as you eat; on the other hand, tea, coffee, and substances called phytates and oxalates in plants reduce the absorption of iron. Vitamin B12 is another micronutrient you need to be careful about, as it is only derived from animal sources. If you cut out all animal foods from your diet, you'll need to take a B12 supplement to make up for this.

Good plant sources of nutrients include:

protein	beans, lentils, bread, grains, seeds, potatoes, nuts
calcium	seeds, green leafy vegetables, nuts, bread, dried fruit
iron	pulses, green vegetables, dried fruits, nuts, plain chocolate

FOOD FOR ACTION

Food is fuel, and if you're active you need lots of it. For example, you can use up to 4000Cal (16,400kJ) a day if you're active in a temperate climate. You need more energy to keep warm in a cold climate, when you might need up to 5000Cal (20,500kJ) a day. You'll feel better and perform better if you maintain an adequate food intake. As a general rule, if you're going to be exercising for more than two hours, you will need to take a snack with you. The best source of energy for action is complex carbohydrates (see the section on Energy & Protein earlier in this chapter), and it's best to eat small amounts often.

If you are planning on camping out in remote areas, you'll need to take with you all you think you will need in the way of food and drink, although you may be able to top up on perishables along the way.

! If you are going trekking in a remote area, never assume you will be able to get supplies along the way (in any case, it wouldn't be fair on local people to expect this).

If you have to carry everything, you'll have to balance up the weight, bulk and energy-giving properties of food items available locally. Bearing in mind the limited culinary possibilities of a portable cooker, as well as the fact that you will have to carry all the fuel you need (don't rely on having a wood fire), you'll want to take lightweight food that can be quickly prepared. If you're going on a long-ish hike, you'll also want to have some variety and decent nutritional value in your diet.

Most trekkers plan on taking enough for three main meals a day: a hot breakfast and evening meal plus a pre-prepared (or at least easily prepared) cold midday meal. In addition, take plenty of between-meal snack food.

! Always take more supplies with you than you think you will need, in case you have misjudged the hunger a trek induces or you have to be out for longer than expected.

Bush Food

If you know what to look for, the bush is full of potential foodstuffs – before Europeans came on the scene, the bush was the only source of food for the population. It's nice to think you could supplement your diet with bush food when you are on a long trek, but you shouldn't rely on it. Berries and fruits will be available in some areas, but you need to know what you are doing. Some bush foods are inedible unless they are ripe, and some need special processing to remove toxins. Many poisonous plants warn you by tasting bitter, but others are more subtle. For example, cycad seeds, a traditional staple of Australian Aboriginal people, taste palatable but are poisonous, and Aboriginal people leach out the toxins first. Many of the early explorers were poisoned by cycads.

What you take depends on what's available locally, but here are some suggestions for good camp and trekking food.

Breakfast

A hot breakfast is good if the weather's cold, but otherwise, you're probably not going to want to do much more than boil the billy.

- instant porridge or other instant cereals – nutritious, light to carry and easy to prepare
- muesli – light, nutritious and doesn't need cooking
- bread or ready made waffles, with golden syrup, honey or condensed milk

Main Meal

Depending on what's available locally, there are endless possibilities. This is probably going to be the focus of your day from mid-afternoon onwards, so it's worth making this meal a good one!

- packet soups and sauces
- instant pasta, noodles, couscous, bulghar, rice, potato

- dehydrated meals – a camping stalwart but leave a lot to be desired taste and digestion-wise; perhaps consider as a fallback
- dried vegetables, for example peas, corn, mushrooms, tomatoes, olives – tasty additions to a meal, and light to carry; need a bit of forethought to prepare (put them to soak while you are setting up camp)
- nuts and seeds
- parmesan cheese – great flavour enhancer, and it doesn't disintegrate in the heat like most other cheeses
- dried herbs, salt and pepper – keep them in old film canisters or buy special screw-top containers
- ready-to-eat vacuum-packed beans and lentils
- antipasti, including roast vegetables, mushrooms, olives – can be decanted into screw-top containers and eaten with rice or pasta, a nice surpise for jaded tastebuds
- stock cubes, dried tomato paste – great for lifting the dullest meal
- instant puddings, instant custard

Lunch, Snacks & Supplementary Items

Again, depends on what is available, but keep it light.

- bread or crackers with nut butter (decant it into a plastic container, if necessary) or honey
- bananas and fresh fruit – good to include if you can
- dried fruits, banana chips, fruit cake
- chocolate, nuts, flapjacks, biscuits, health food bars
- tea, coffee, hot chocolate drink, sugar, powdered milk, condensed milk

○ It's always best to seek help as soon as possible if a child is ill – for more advice, see the Babies & Children chapter.
○ First aid is covered in the appendix starting on p396.

Being ill away from home is always miserable, and it's worse if the medical system is unfamiliar and you can't make yourself understood because of language difficulties. Scarier still is the thought you may have one of those awful tropical diseases you have heard or perhaps read about. Take heart – your body has an enormous potential to fight off infection, and although tropical diseases like malaria and dengue are risks in some areas, you're generally unlikely to get anything very exotic. You're much more likely to get diarrhoea, an infected insect bite or the flu.

IF YOU'RE ILL

In this section we have outlined a basic plan of action to follow if you fall ill on your travels. Most minor illnesses respond to simple, nondrug treatments, so it's always worth trying these first However, in some situations, you will need to get medical help. Use your common sense, but medical help is indicated in the following situations:

▶ if you are seriously ill – you will probably know, but for more guidance, see Signs of Serious Illness later in this chapter
▶ if you've tried all the simple measures without any effect
▶ if there's no improvement in your condition after a day or two

If you are in a country where medications are easily available without prescription, it can be tempting to take matters in your own hand and dose yourself up. However, medicines are powerful drugs and, unless you know what you are doing, you can do more harm than good. Although we give treatment guidelines in this book, these are to help you make a decision about what to do in a given situation; they are not intended to be a substitute for getting medical advice.

As a general rule, only self-medicate if there is no alternative (for example you're in a remote area far from medical help) and you are confident you know what you are doing

Similarly, it's always best to avoid treating fellow travellers unless you know what you're doing.

GETTING MEDICAL HELP

Generally, you shouldn't have any trouble finding a doctor if you are travelling around Australia or New Zealand, or in urban centres in the Pacific islands. Ask at your hotel or try the telephone directory or your guidebook. Alternatively, your embassy (or IAMAT – see Useful Organisations in the Before You Go chapter) can provide you with a list of local doctors. Other possibilities you could try, depending on the circumstances, include the following.

▶ Ring your travel insurance hotline (it's a good idea to carry the number on you at all times).
▶ Most hotels will be able to recommend a doctor, and upmarket hotels may have a doctor attached to the staff.
▶ In an emergency, US citizens could try contacting the State Department's Citizen's Emergency Center (see p24) for advice.
▶ You could try asking other travellers, members of the expat community or members of international aid organisations for the names of reliable doctors.
▶ You could always try contacting your doctor back home for advice, especially for exacerbations or complications arising from preexisting conditions.

In touristed areas, doctors will be used to treating common travellers ailments, and doctors who work in tropical countries have substantial experience in diagnosing and treating tropical diseases (such as malaria) – probably much more than your doctor back home is likely to have!

WORKING OUT WHAT'S WRONG

Try to decide what your main problem is: do you feel feverish? Have you got a headache, diarrhoea, a skin rash or a cough? If you think you know what is wrong, turn to the appropriate chapter later in this book, or you could look up your symptom in the index; otherwise, read on. Here are some simple questions to ask yourself.

- What diseases could I be at risk for? See the summary at the beginning of this book but remember that common things are common, and rare diseases are unlikely.
- Am I in a malaria or dengue fever risk zone? (See the map on p20 and check locally.) If the answer is yes, turn to the section on Fever in the Fever & Hepatitis chapter.
- Have I been in any obvious risk situations recently? Have I been bitten by mosquitoes (malaria, dengue etc) or ticks (typhus, spotted fever), or drunk unpurified water from streams and rivers *(Giardia)*?
- Have any of my travelling companions been ill? If yes, you may be suffering from the same illness.
- Is a sexually transmitted infection a possibility? If so, turn to the HIV/AIDS & Sexual Health chapter.

LOOKING AFTER YOURSELF

If you are ill, whatever the cause, there are some simple things you can do to give your body the best chance of getting better quickly.

▶ Stop travelling and rest up for a while.
▶ Make sure you are as comfortable as the circumstances allow. It's probably worth spending a bit more on a decent room, as you'll be surprised at the difference cheerful surroundings can make.
▶ Drink plenty of fluids (water, weak tea or herbal teas), especially if it's hot or you have a temperature.
▶ If necessary, give yourself a break from alcohol, tobacco and strong tea or coffee.

If you're ill, it's always a good idea to take your temperature (see the following section for guidance on how to do this) and you could perhaps get someone to take your pulse.

Seek medical help if you don't improve after 48 hours (or before then if you get a lot worse).

MEASURING YOUR TEMPERATURE

Take your temperature at regular intervals (four times a day) while you're ill, as this gives you an idea of how ill you are and how quickly you are recovering.

There are three main types of thermometer: mercury, digital and liquid crystal ('fever strip'). Mercury ones are the most accurate, but they're also the most delicate and you can't take them with you in the cabin on a plane. Liquid crystal thermometers are the least accurate, but are convenient – follow the instructions on the packaging. The following instructions are for mercury and digital thermometers:

▸ wipe the thermometer with a small amount of antiseptic solution (or a pre-injection swab) to make sure it's clean
▸ shake the thermometer so that the mercury is down in the bulb
▸ place the thermometer under the tongue; if there is a chance it may be bitten (for example in a young child or if the person is very sick) place it in the armpit or, for young babies, grease it lightly and slip it in the rectum

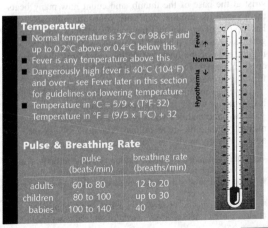

Temperature
- Normal temperature is 37°C or 98.6°F and up to 0.2°C above or 0.4°C below this.
- Fever is any temperature above this.
- Dangerously high fever is 40°C (104°F) and over – see Fever later in this section for guidelines on lowering temperature.
- Temperature in °C = 5/9 × (T°F-32)
  Temperature in °F = (9/5 × T°C) + 32

Pulse & Breathing Rate

	pulse (beats/min)	breathing rate (breaths/min)
adults	60 to 80	12 to 20
children	80 to 100	up to 30
babies	100 to 140	40

▶ leave the thermometer in place for two to three minutes (or follow the instructions on the packet), then remove it
▶ read and make a note of the temperature; temperatures are usually read in degrees Celsius, but may also be read in degrees Fahrenheit

PULSE & BREATHING RATE

Feeling the pulse and measuring the breathing rate are important in a formal medical assessment. Both can provide a great deal of useful information, but only if you know what to look for and how these clues fit in with the rest of the picture. They're probably not going to be that useful to you in most common situations when you feel ill, although they are important to note in an emergency situation – for guidance on how to deal with an emergency, see the inside back cover.

Pulse Rate

To take your pulse, put two fingers on the inside of your wrist at the base of the thumb, and count how many beats there are to the minute; don't use your thumb because this has a pulse of its own that may confuse things. In an emergency situation, if you can't feel a pulse in the wrist, try feeling the side of the neck beside the voice box (the Adam's apple in men) – see the illustrations on the inside back cover for more guidance.

As well as counting the pulse, think about what it feels like: is it strong or weak? Is it regular or irregular?

Some abnormalities you may notice, and what they may mean if you are ill, are as follows. You need to seek medical advice urgently in all these situations:

■ regular fast pulse (eg up to 120 or 140 beats/min) – associated with high fever and serious illness (also severe exertion!)
■ weak, rapid pulse – shock (severe illness, major trauma etc); see inside back cover
■ irregular, very slow or very rapid pulse – heart problems
■ slow pulse in spite of fever – could be typhoid (see p132)

Breathing Rate

Count the number of breaths per minute (get someone else to do this, as it's impossible to get an accurate count on yourself). The breathing rate can be increased in many different situations, including lung problems (such as chest infection or pneumonia) and fever.

OTHER SIGNS

Other things you should check for and note include:

- any rashes, wounds, lumps or bumps
- yellow colour of the skin and whites of the eyes – jaundice
- pale lips and nails, pale inside of eye – anaemia
- blueness of the lips – may indicate a serious lung or heart problem
- unequal or otherwise abnormal pupils of the eyes
- abnormal drowsiness and/or confusion – this always indicates serious illness

SIGNS OF SERIOUS ILLNESS

It'll probably be obvious, but you must seek medical attention urgently if you experience any of the following problems:

- any severe blood loss
- any severe continuous pain
- more than a day without passing any urine

Blood anywhere it shouldn't be:

- blood in urine
- blood in vomit – this may look like 'coffee grounds'; it won't always look bright red
- blood in faeces – may be bright red, more likely to be browny red and mixed in, or faeces may be black like tar (but remember that taking iron tablets can turn your faeces black)
- blood coughed up in spit
- any vaginal bleeding during pregnancy

Fever:

- high fever (more than 40°C or 104°F) that can't be brought down by the measures outlined on p103

- any fever without obvious cause lasting more than two to three days

Problems with your digestive system:

- severe diarrhoea and vomiting lasting more than a day (see p99 for more guidance)
- abdominal pain and vomiting without being able to defecate
- severe vomiting that means you can't take any fluids for more than a day
- severe weight loss (usually more than a tenth of your normal body weight)

'Head' problems:

- convulsions (fits)
- severe headache with neck stiffness and sensitivity to light
- dizziness or extreme weakness, especially on standing

Lumps, bumps etc:

- any sores that won't go away
- any lumps that appear and grow
- any mole that bleeds or changes shape

COMMON SIGNS & SYMPTOMS

In this section, we've summarised some of the main causes of various common symptoms.

FEVER

The term 'fever' means having a temperature higher than normal (see p99), significant fever being 38°C (100.4°F) and higher. It always means that there is a disease process going on, and in travellers it is most likely to be a sign of infection. Producing a fever is thought to help the body's natural defences to fight infection.

Having a fever usually makes you feel pretty rough. You may feel hot and cold on and off, with 'goose bumps' or shivering, and you usually feel completely drained of energy. The fever process itself causes aches and pains (often backache) in your muscles and joints, and headache.

You can feel hot to the touch without having a temperature above normal and sometimes you can feel cold even though your temperature is raised, so it's always worth taking your temperature with a thermometer to be sure. (Trying to decide if you have a temperature by touching your forehead with the back of your hand is notoriously unreliable.) If your temperature is raised, take repeat measurements at regular intervals so you can keep track of any improvement or changes.

Although the pattern of the fever can sometimes be helpful in determining the cause, in practice many diseases don't show the textbook fever patterns, especially in travellers, so it's best not to rely on this.

If you have a really high temperature, you may experience rigors – unpleasant episodes of violent shivering and drenching sweating. They are always a sign of very serious illness, and you should seek medical advice as soon as possible, and immediately try simple measures to lower your temperature.

Note that children can get very high temperatures very quickly and this can be dangerous if it causes convulsions (fits). See the section on p238 for more details.

If you have a fever:

▶ take paracetamol (acetaminophen) – this will help to lower your temperature and relieve any aches and pains
▶ dehydration is a risk with any fever, especially in hot climates, so drink plenty of fluids
▶ help your body to cool down – take cool showers or cover yourself with wet cloths or sponges and turn the fan on
▶ make sure you don't get cold (but don't deliberately pile on the blankets to 'sweat it out' as this is not thought to be helpful)

Having a fever increases your metabolic rate and makes you lose weight. This is just the fever part of the illness; if you have diarrhoea and vomiting as well, you are even more likely to

Illnesses with Fever as a Major Symptom

disease	page	associated symptoms/other clues
flu	p138	may cause generalised aches and pains without any other symptoms
diarrhoea	p107	high temperature indicates a more serious cause of diarrhoea
heatstroke	p282	headache, weakness, muscle cramps
malaria	p125	fever often intermittent, joint aches, chills, headache; also possibly cough, abdominal pain, diarrhoea and jaundice
dengue fever	p122	fever may seem to go, but comes back after a few days; headache, severe aches and pains, rash (possibly)
glandular fever	p143	sore throat, swollen neck glands, no energy
hepatitis	p133	nausea, vomiting, jaundice, dark urine, light faeces
amoebic liver abscess	p121	pain in right upper part of abdomen; may or may not follow episode of diarrhoea
typhoid	p132	often causes a persistent fever, diarrhoea may be a late symptom only
Ross River fever	p319	pain and swelling of the joints, rash
encephal-itis	p320	headache, nausea and vomiting; rarely drowsiness, confusion, fits and coma
tubercu-losis	p193	recurrent evening or night fever, usually with cough
typhus	p327	red rash, distinctive sore at site of tick bite, more likely if you've been trekking in rural areas

lose weight. Try to maintain a basic intake of food while you are ill, and increase it as you start feeling better and your appetite improves. See the Diet & Nutrition chapter for more details. These measures treat the symptoms of fever but not the underlying cause, which is usually an infection.

Causes

Many fevers, as at home, are caused by viral illnesses, such as colds and flu which can start suddenly and rarely last more than about three to five days. With any fever, always consider common causes first:

- runny nose – cold (p138)
- cough – bronchitis, pneumonia (p140)
- sore throat (p142) – tonsillitis, glandular fever
- earache – ear infection (p167)
- facial or sinus pain – acute sinusitis (p140)
- abdominal pain – see following section
- bladder symptoms (p211)
- pelvic infection (p214)
- skin infection (p157)
- toothache – dental abscess (p175)

If you've ruled out all these, then you can start thinking about some other causes of fever, see the table on the previous page.

ABDOMINAL PAIN

It can be notoriously difficult to work out what's causing this – if the pain is severe, it's safer to seek medical advice as soon as possible. To give you some guidance, we've listed a few of the more common scenarios:

- often occurs with diarrhoea, when it's usually crampy; comes in waves and may be relieved by passing wind or faeces; you may have a fever
- constipation is often associated with spasms of pain in the lower abdomen
- central lower abdomen – bladder infection, period pains, pelvic infection
- upper abdomen, just under rib cage, burning, worse after meals – heart burn, indigestion
- upper right abdomen, just under ribs – hepatitis (sometimes), liver abscess, gall stones
- appendicitis – see p151
- severe, colicky (comes and goes) pain that may go down into your pelvis (or testicles in men); could be a kidney stone (p151)

NAUSEA & VOMITING

When you're travelling you often get short episodes of nausea, sometimes with vomiting. They usually settle within a day without any specific treatment. They're usually due to viral infections, but there are many other causes:

- medicines, eg malaria pills, antibiotics
- motion sickness (p59)
- food poisoning (p111)
- diarrhoeal illnesses (p107)
- dehydration or heatstroke (p281)
- meningitis (p192)
- migraine (p173)
- pregnancy (p220)

HEADACHE

Most fevers cause headache. Other possibilities are:

- dehydration, heatstroke (p281)
- migraine (p173)
- stress headache
- trapped nerve (sharp stabbing pains, intermittent)
- neck problems (eg arthritis)
- malaria (p125)
- dengue fever (p122)
- typhoid fever (p132)
- meningococcal meningitis (p192)
- altitude sickness (p289)

SKIN RASH

There are many causes of rashes. See the Skin chapter for a detailed discussion of skin problems, but causes of rashes include:

- glandular fever and other viral illnesses (p143)
- measles and other childhood illnesses (p195)
- fungal infections (p156)
- allergic reactions, dermatitis (p159)
- dengue fever (p122)
- typhus, spotted fevers (p327)

DIARRHOEA

You may as well be prepared: diarrhoea is the most common travel-related illness, and affects about a half to a third of travellers to tropical destinations. Just in case anybody out there is not sure what we're talking about, by diarrhoea we mean passing loose, frequent faeces, often associated with vomiting.

Although there are many causes of travellers diarrhoea (see the boxed text), your risk of getting ill mainly depends on how likely it is that the food and drink you are consuming is contaminated with disease-causing microorganisms. In Australia and New Zealand, this is generally unlikely unless you are drinking unpurified water from streams and rivers in popular trekking areas. In the Pacific islands, standards of hygiene are generally fairly high, and the chance of food being contaminated is low compared with some travel destinations.

You'll probably find that as soon as you go overseas, every traveller you meet has a story to tell about diarrhoea, and it can be hard to separate fact from fiction at times. It's worth keeping in mind some reassuring facts:

■ travellers diarrhoea is generally a short, mild illness lasting on average about three to five days

Causes of Travellers Diarrhoea
So what gives travellers the runs? Various studies indicate that about one-third of cases, usually mild, are due to nonspecific causes, including the following:

■ stress
■ jet lag
■ new foods and a change in eating habits

The rest are divided up as follows:

■ bacteria, the commonest cause
■ viruses ('gastric flu')
■ parasites (including *Giardia* and amoeba)
■ food poisoning

- because of this, you don't usually need to get medical advice or have a laboratory test
- replacing lost fluids and salts is the most important part of treating any watery diarrhoea, whatever the cause
- you don't usually need antibiotic treatment for mild to moderate diarrhoea

○ Travellers diarrhoea is probably the most talked about digestive affliction, but constipation and indigestion are pretty common in travellers too – see the Coughs, Rashes & Other Common Problems chapter for guidelines on dealing with these.

AVOIDING DIARRHOEA

Although we don't want to deprive you of a fascinating talking point during your travels, it's obviously best to avoid getting diarrhoea in the first place. Unhygienic food preparation and storage practices, as well as contaminated water are common causes of travellers diarrhoea. By 'contaminated' we mean containing disease-causing microorganisms, usually from faeces. Hands used to prepare food may not have been washed thoroughly after toilet duty. Flies carry dirt and microorganisms on their feet. In dusty, urban areas, dry faecal matter floats around in the atmosphere, and this can land on food left sitting around.

○ For detailed guidelines on choosing safe food and water, see the sections on Safe Food and Safe Drinking Water in the Staying Healthy chapter.

You can also get diarrhoea from direct contact with an infected person (if you touch hands etc that haven't been washed adequately) or from swimming in contaminated water (by swallowing small amounts). Some infective agents such as *Giardia* can survive even in chlorinated water, and rivers and oceans may be contaminated with sewage.

TYPES OF DIARRHOEA

Different microorganisms cause different types of diarrhoeal illnesses, which may need to be treated in different ways. In this section we've described the three most common types,

Diarrhoea at a Glance

Some characteristics of various diarrhoeal illnesses are summarised here. Just bear in mind that diarrhoeal illnesses are notoriously difficult to diagnose on the basis of symptoms alone and the only way to be sure of the diagnosis is through a laboratory test.

illness	timing	characteristics
food poisoning (p111)	usually comes on soon after eating	symptoms come on rapidly after eating the bad food; tends to cause vomiting predominantly; over in 24 to 48 hours
travellers diarrhoea (p110)	usually strikes about the third day after you arrive	usually caused by bacteria; less bloating and flatulence than with *Giardia*
shigella (dysentery; p110)	two to three days between infection and symptoms appearing	high temperature, blood in faeces, abdominal cramps can be severe
giardiasis (p120)	two to six weeks between infection and symptoms appearing	symptoms are variable but usually sudden onset explosive diarrhoea, associated typically with bloating, cramps and flatulence
amoebic dysentery (p121)	minimum one week, maybe as long as several weeks between infection and symptoms	bloody diarrhoea (not profuse like bacterial causes), cramps, tends to be prolonged
cyclospora	two days to two weeks before symptoms appear	prolonged diarrhoea with weight loss
irritable bowel syndrome (p120)	may start for the first time after an acute attack of travellers diarrhoea	may have alternating diarrhoea and constipation, abdominal pains, but no weight loss
ciguatera (p146)	comes on soon after eating affected reef fish	numbness, tingling sensations, nausea and vomiting; symptoms can persist in a minority of people

although in practice it's often not as clearcut as this makes it seem. The most important things to look out for are: high temperature, blood in your faeces and how severe the diarrhoea is (how much, how often). Full treatment details, including advice on what to eat and drink while you are ill, are given in the subsection, Dealing with Diarrhoea, following.

Watery Diarrhoea

This is the type of diarrhoea you're most likely to get when you are away. The cause varies with your destination, but it's usually bacterial, often a strain of a bacteria called *Escherichia coli*. Relatives of this microbe are normal residents of your gut, but this is a strain that has turned nasty.

The usual scenario is diarrhoea that starts a few days after you arrive, and involves up to six episodes of loose faeces a day. You may feel sorry for yourself, but it doesn't usually make you feel particularly unwell. You may get a low fever (less than 38°C or 100.4°F). Nausea and vomiting are common, especially at the start, but are not a major feature of the illness (compare this with food poisoning – see Vomiting & Diarrhoea later in this section). Stomach cramps, bloating and frequent gas are also common. If you notice blood in your faeces, you've got dysentery – see the following section.

The illness generally resolves itself in a few days (on average three to five). It rarely causes severe dehydration, although the potential is always there and is more of a risk in children and older travellers. Don't panic and start stuffing yourself with medications – you don't usually need antibiotics for this type of diarrhoea, and 'stoppers' are usually best avoided too. The most important treatment measure is to avoid dehydration by replacing lost fluids and salts, which you should start doing straight away.

Bloody Diarrhoea (Dysentery)

Dysentery is any diarrhoea with blood in it. It can be more severe and protracted than the more common watery diarrhoea described earlier, and usually needs antibiotic treatment. Out of every 10 travellers who get diarrhoea, only about one will have dysentery. The most common cause is one of a number of bacteria, including various shigella and salmonella species, but amoebiasis (p121) is a less common cause.

Dysentery usually begins with nonspecific flu-like symptoms, and you often feel really rough, with headache, high fever (38°C and higher), and aches and pains all over. To start with, the diarrhoea is often watery and in large quantities; later it appears to ease and you start to notice blood and mucus (slime) mixed in your faeces. Painful stomach cramps are often a feature of the illness, usually heralding a dash to the little room.

Get medical advice if you have dysentery, as you'll need a laboratory test and a course of antibiotics (see p118). In the meantime, rest and make sure you drink plenty of fluids.

!*If you have dysentery, avoid antidiarrhoeal medications that 'stop you up' because there is a risk of serious complications occurring, including dilation and bursting of the colon.*

Vomiting & Diarrhoea

○ See p106 for a full summary of the many causes of vomiting.

If you suddenly get an attack of nausea and profuse vomiting soon after eating, it's probably due to food poisoning. This is a worldwide problem, but is more likely when you're eating food not prepared by yourself, especially where food preparation and storage procedures may be suspect.

Vomiting is the main symptom, often with stomach cramps and some watery diarrhoea later. You may have a suspicion that you've eaten something that wasn't fresh (such as seafood); another clue is if everyone who ate the same thing comes down with the same illness. Ciguatera poisoning (p146) from toxic fish is another possiblity.

No specific treatment is needed as a rule. You should rest, sip fluids if possible, and wait for it to settle down, which it should start doing in about 12 to 24 hours. Generally, it's best to avoid anti-vomiting medication, as vomiting is your body's way of getting rid of the bad stuff.

DEALING WITH DIARRHOEA

If diarrhoea strikes, don't immediately reach for your medical kit, try some simple treatment measures first:

▶ rest – this gives your body the best chance to fight whatever is making you ill; in any case, being on the move with diarrhoea presents a few logistical problems
▶ drink plenty of fluids – see What to Drink later in this section for more guidance on what and how much
▶ if you feel really rough, take your temperature and note what it is; repeat this to see how the illness is progressing
▶ examine what's coming out of your guts to check for blood or mucus (slime)
▶ be aware of how often you're passing urine and what colour it is, so you can check you're not getting dehydrated – see the section, What to Drink over the page for more details
▶ note any other symptoms you may have – diarrhoea can occur in many other illnesses, including malaria and hepatitis
▶ remember that diarrhoea is contagious so be scrupulous about washing your hands after you use the toilet

When to See a Doctor

Avoid using antidiarrhoeal remedies (apart from oral rehydration salts) and get medical help urgently in the following situations:

▶ if the illness doesn't settle down within 24 hours
▶ if it gets much worse, for example if the diarrhoea is coming out of you in a watery torrent
▶ if there's any blood in your vomit or diarrhoea
▶ if you have a high fever (38°C/100.4°F or higher)
▶ if you have very severe stomach pains or a severe headache
▶ if you can't keep any fluids down because of vomiting for more than 24 hours (less for a child; for example, a couple of hours if they really can't take any fluids)
▶ the diarrhoea doesn't clear up after four or five days, or more than a day in a child with moderate to severe diarrhoea

IF YOU GET DIARRHOEA

got the runs?

↓

basic measures: rest, drink plenty of fluids (ORS essential for children & older travellers) & avoid antidiarrhoeals; check the following:

↓

passing faeces more than six times in 24 hours? ••▶ **YES** •••••▶

NO

↓

can't keep any fluids down because of vomiting? ••▶ **YES** ▶•••••▶ **SEE a doctor OR if no doctor, take antibiotic – see p118**

NO

↓

temperature 38°C or more? •• **YES**

NO

↓

any blood in your faeces? •• **YES**

NO

↓

continue basic measures: rest & fluids

•••••▶ persistent or prolonged diarrhoea (more than seven days)

improvement after finishing antibiotic course?

NO

↓

SEE a doctor OR if no doctor, take a different antibiotic – see p118

113

▶ if you're jaundiced (your skin and the whites of your eyes are yellow; see p133)

!Remember that children very quickly become dehydrated with diarrhoea or vomiting, so you need to seek help more readily for them. See the section on diarrhoea (p239) in the Babies & Children chapter for more details.

What to Drink

You need to replace what's being lost through the diarrhoea and any vomiting: mainly salts (sodium, potassium and chloride) and water. Sachets of oral rehydration salts (ORS) are readily available from pharmacies in most tropical countries. These contain optimum amounts of glucose and salts. Glucose (sugar) is necessary because it encourages the absorption of sodium and water, and it makes you feel better by boosting your energy levels. Follow the instructions and

How Much to Drink

If you're vomiting or feeling sick, try taking small sips of fluid regularly rather than forcing yourself to down a whole glass in one go. You need to drink the equivalent of two average-sized glasses of fluid every time you have diarrhoea. Aim to drink at least 3L of fluid over 24 hours, or more if you're not eating anything at all. (An average-sized glass holds about 250mL of fluid.) Use how much urine you're passing as a rough guide to whether you are drinking enough:

- small amounts of dark urine suggest you need to increase your fluid intake
- if you're passing reasonable quantities of light yellow urine you've got the balance about right

As a rough guide, aim to pass a fullish bladder of light-coloured urine every three to four hours while you're awake.

make up the ORS in the specified quantity of purified or bottled water. There's no magic ingredient in ORS, but the relative quantities of salt and sugar are important.

!You can make up your own solution if necessary by adding six teaspoons of sugar (or honey) and half a teaspoon of table salt to 1L of boiled water. Make it more palatable by adding any flavour you like, for example lemon, ginger or orange juice.

Although ORS is essential in children and elderly travellers, if you're a normally fit and healthy adult and the diarrhoea is mild (up to six bursts a day), you can make do without ORS. Instead, make sure you drink plenty of fluids, including soup (contains salt) and fruit juices (contain glucose and potassium), and eat starchy foods (see the following section).

Other liquids you could drink include purified water, weak black tea with a small amount of sugar added, herbal tea, green coconut juice or, if nothing else is available, soft drinks allowed to go flat and diluted with purified water (but avoid colas if possible).

!Alcohol, strong tea, coffee and other caffeine-containing drinks (such as colas) are all best avoided because they can irritate the gut and promote fluid loss.

It's best to steer clear of dairy products while you have diarrhoea – you can get an intolerance to the sugar in milk when you have diarrhoea, which then exacerbates the problem.

What to Eat

It's easy to get hung up about what, if anything, to eat when you have diarrhoea. But relax, use your common sense and try to tune in to what your body is telling you – if you feel like eating, go ahead. Starchy foods like bread, tubers, sweet potato, rice or salty crackers (and any other local variations on these) are recommended because they encourage absorption of fluids, sodium and glucose in your gut.

Although eating may increase the bulk of your faeces, it shouldn't worsen the illness, so there's no need to starve yourself deliberately. But if you don't feel like eating, don't force yourself to. Unless you've been travelling hard for some time, you're going to be basically well nourished and able to withstand a couple of days with little or no food. It may make you feel a bit wobbly, so add a bit of sugar or honey to your drinks.

Your overworked guts will appreciate small amounts of food at regular intervals rather than great big meals, and this may help make you feel less nauseated, too. You may find that eating brings on stomach cramps and you have to dash to the toilet. This is because of a natural reflex whereby eating increases the activity of the gut, which can get exaggerated in a diarrhoeal illness. It doesn't make you a great dinner companion, but you'll probably find that once you've answered the call of nature you can return to finish your meal! (But remember to wash your hands very thoroughly.)

It goes without saying that it's best to stick to a bland diet while you have diarrhoea and as you recover, and to go easy on fibre providers like fruit, vegetables and nuts. Ripe bananas are good, as they tend to stop you up and are a source of potassium and glucose. (Unripe bananas can be indigestible, making matters worse.) As the diarrhoea clears up and you start to get your appetite back, add in more foods gradually until you're back to normal – this can take some time, up to a week, but if you feel otherwise well, there's no need to worry.

Antidiarrhoeal Remedies

You've probably got a stash of these in your medical kit, but most of the time you're better off just letting the illness run its course.

Antimotility drugs (ie 'stoppers') like loperamide, diphenoxylate (with atropine) and codeine phosphate slow down intestinal activity. These drugs are sold under a wide variety of brand names and are usually available without prescription. Stoppers can be useful if you have to travel on a toilet-less mode of transport or attend an important meeting, but you should treat them with a bit of respect. If you do need to take them, stick to the recommended dose.

It's usually best not to take stoppers for more than 24 hours because of the risk of side effects (swelling and bursting of the intestine, and constipation). Another reason not to take them for longer is that diarrhoea is nature's way of flushing out microbes and their poisons, and stopping this may prevent the illness from settling.

! Note that these drugs should be avoided in children because of the risk of side effects, and you shouldn't take them if you have a high fever or are passing blood or mucus (slime) in your faeces.

Bismuth subsalicylate (Pepto-Bismol) can be useful in treating diarrhoea, although it is less effective than the antimotility drugs. Bismuth shouldn't be taken if you have asthma or if you are taking aspirin, are sensitive to aspirin or have been told to

---

A Word of Warning

You'll probably find many antidiarrhoeal remedies on sale in pharmacies in the Pacific islands. It's best to avoid all but oral rehydration salts, as they are unlikely to be helpful and may actually be harmful. In particular, avoid any containing the following substances:

- tincture of opium or morphine
- clioquinol, which may be marketed as Enterovioform and other names – this is associated with severe side effects
- combinations of remedies (for example an antimotility medication with an antibiotic) are always best avoided

You may see a remedy called kaopectate on sale, but it is not thought to be helpful in treating diarrhoea.

avoid aspirin for any reason. It can cause ringing in your ears and blackening of your tongue. It's not recommended to take large amounts over a prolonged period of time (maximum three weeks).

Alternatively, peppermint oil is an antispasmodic that may be helpful if you're experiencing abdominal cramps. It has no serious side effects. Probiotics such as acidophilus (or lactobacillus), which are found naturally in live yoghurt are popularly taken as protection against diarrhoea, but they haven't shown to be helpful in treating diarrhoea. Homoeopathic remedies for treating diarrhoea include carbo vegetalis and nux vomic, although these are unlikely to be available locally in the Pacific island countries.

Antibiotics

There are some situations when antibiotics are needed – in these situations, it's best to get medical advice rather than to try to treat yourself. If you are seriously ill or the diarrhoea just won't go away, you should seek medical advice on the most appropriate treatment and you'll probably need a laboratory test.

Remember that most cases of travellers diarrhoea do not need treatment with antibiotics, and will clear up on their own in a few days.

If you're travelling in remote areas without access to medical care, you may need to self-treat your diarrhoea with antibiotics. It is notoriously difficult to make an accurate diagnosis on the basis of symptoms alone, but in this situation, you could consider the following treatment:

- severe watery diarrhoea or bacterial dysentery – take a course of ciprofloxacin (500mg twice daily for five days) or norfloxacin (400mg twice daily for three days); children can be given a suitable dose (based on weight) of co-trimoxazole

The Antibiotic Question

There's plenty of evidence to show that taking a dose of an antibiotic (such as ciprofloxacin 500mg, single dose) with loperamide (an antimotility drug) can reduce the length of a diarrhoeal illness quite dramatically. Because of this, some doctors advise travellers to take a treatment dose of an antibiotic as soon as you develop any diarrhoea. Others, however, argue that the benefits are not offset by the risks (including possible side effects of the antibiotic and the emergence of bacterial resistance) and that in any case diarrhoea in travellers is usually a mild illness that will clear up quickly enough on its own. It may be worth taking a treatment dose with you to use for severe diarrhoea if you are travelling in remote areas without access to medical care. Discuss this with your doctor, as it's best to get individual advice on this.

- amoebiasis or giardiasis – take metronidazole (250mg three times daily for five to 10 days) or tinidazole (2g single dose)

Don't take any antibiotic you are allergic to; for more guidance on using antibiotics, see the Medicines appendix.

PERSISTENT DIARRHOEA

You may find that, often after an acute attack, the diarrhoea comes and goes and doesn't clear up. You'll need to get this checked out by a doctor. You'll need a laboratory test to clarify what's causing it so that the appropriate treatment can be prescribed. Use your common sense, but as a rough guide 'persistent' diarrhoea is anything lasting longer than about a week. Infections that can cause persistent diarrhoea include:

- giardiasis
- amoebiasis
- bacteria (eg salmonella or campylobacter)
- cyclospora (a recently identified parasite)

Much less likely causes in travellers include:

Irritable Bowel Syndrome (IBS)

A change in diet, increased stress and possibly food poisoning or travellers diarrhoea can all make symptoms of this common bowel dysfunction more likely. Symptoms include:

- abdominal pain and spasm (often in the left lower abdomen), relieved by passing wind or faeces
- abdominal bloating (due to trapped wind)
- diarrhoea or constipation
- passing ribbon-like or pellet-like faeces

Symptoms may last only a few days or can persist for weeks; they often recur. If constipation is the major factor, an increase in dietary fibre will help. If bowel spasm and pain is the main problem, an antispasmodic such as mebeverine 135mg three times daily or peppermint oil capsules may help. Avoid any foods that make the symptoms worse.

If you are not sure of the diagnosis, the symptoms don't fit the pattern described, you have pain that is new or severe or you are unwell in any other way, you should seek medical advice.

Corinne Else

- intestinal worms
- tropical sprue

Noninfectious causes include:

- post-infectious irritable bowel
- inflammatory bowel disease
- temporary intolerance to lactose, the sugar in milk

Giardiasis

This illness is caused by a single-celled parasite, *Giardia lamblia*, acquired when you ingest food or water contaminated by the hardy cysts of the parasite. The illness usually appears about a week after you have been exposed to the parasite.

Giardiasis can start quite suddenly, with explosive, watery diarrhoea (without blood). More often you get loose, bulky, foul-smelling faeces that are hard to flush away (assuming you have the luxury of flushing, of course), with lots of gas, bloating, stomach gurgling and cramps. You can sometimes get a mild fever and often feel nauseated, with little or no appetite, 'indigestion' and rotten egg burps. Although all these symptoms commonly occur in giardiasis, they are nonspecific symptoms and can occur in other types of diarrhoea.

! You often get noticeable weight loss with giardiasis, as this infection prevents food from being absorbed properly in the upper part of your gut.

It's best to seek medical advice if possible, but if you are in a remote area away from medical help, you could start a course of antibiotics. Options include either metronidazole 250mg three times daily for five to 10 days or tinidazole 2g single dose (tinidazole is not currently available in the USA). You should be able to find one or other of these drugs locally if necessary.

Amoebic Dysentery

This is an uncommon cause of diarrhoea in travellers in Australia, New Zealand and the Pacific. It's caused by a single-celled parasite called *Entamoeba histolytica*, which you get by eating food and water contaminated by the parasite cysts (sounds familiar?). It causes dysentery, ie you get blood and mucus in your faeces. The diarrhoea is often relatively mild and tends to come on gradually. Associated symptoms like fever, vomiting and stomach cramps are much less likely than with giardiasis or bacterial causes of dysentery, although they can occur. Complications can occur if the amoeba migrate to your liver or brain, where they can form abscesses, sometimes without a warning episode of diarrhoea beforehand.

! Suspect an amoebic liver abscess if you have a fever and pain in the right upper abdomen (which may feel tender to pressure), especially if you have been having diarrhoea for a while.

Get medical advice; treatment is with specific antibiotics, as for giardiasis (see earlier).

FEVER & HEPATITIS

In this chapter we cover some important infections causing fever (malaria, dengue, typhoid), as well as hepatitis, the most common vaccine-preventable infection in travellers.

FEVER

In this section, we've grouped some important infections that have fever as their main symptom. Although these are important diseases to be aware of, remember that common things are common – see p104 for a summary of the many possible causes of fever.

○ For guidance on how to take a temperature see p99.

DENGUE FEVER

This viral disease is spread via mosquito bites, and occurs throughout the Pacific islands. Outbreaks have occurred in the tropical north of Australia, mainly in northern Queensland and the Torres Strait Islands.

There is no vaccine against dengue, with none likely in the near future.

!You can avoid dengue by taking steps to prevent mosquito bites – the dengue mosquito bites during the day, so this means putting insect repellent on over sunscreen, if necessary.

Dengue is seasonal to a certain extent, but outbreaks can occur at any time.

Symptoms

The illness usually starts quite suddenly with fever, nausea and vomiting, headache, and joint and muscle pains. The aches and pains can be severe, hence the old name 'breakbone fever'. The fever sometimes appears to settle after a few days, only to reappear a few days later (known as 'saddleback fever'). Typically, you get a fine red rash, often around the

The Rise & Rise of Dengue

Dengue has spread rapidly in the last decade and is now one of the top public health problems in the tropical world. Increasingly, travellers to areas where it occurs are being infected, and the number of cases is expected to continue to rise in the future. At the latest count, there were 50 million new cases annually worldwide – and this is probably a conservative figure.

One of the reasons for the rise of dengue is that the mosquitoes responsible for transmitting the disease thrive in crowded urban areas, where they breed in any container that holds water, including discarded plastic wrapping and old tyres. Dengue mosquitoes are much less common in rural areas and are rarely found at altitudes above about 2000m. Increasing resistance of dengue mosquitoes to insecticides has made control of the disease more difficult. At the same time, air travel has encouraged the spread of the disease throughout the tropics.

On a global scale, prevention of dengue depends on eradication of mosquito breeding grounds, improving urban living conditions and widespread use of insecticides – so don't hold your breath.

third to fifth day, which signals the second phase of the disease, and recovery usually follows soon after.

The illness can last anything from three to about 10 days, settling spontaneously without any specific treatment. However, many travellers report experiencing extreme tiredness with muscle wasting and lack of energy for several weeks or months after, which can be debilitating and may be a good reason to cut your trip short. On the other hand, the symptoms can be mild and you may not realise that you've had it.

Dengue Haemorrhagic Fever

Rarely, you can get a more severe, potentially fatal form of dengue called dengue haemorrhagic fever (DHF), which is associated with uncontrolled bleeding and shock from loss of blood. Although DHF receives a lot of publicity and is frightening, it is rare in travellers. DHF is thought to be due to infection with a second strain of the dengue virus.

! You can get minor bleeding – nose bleeds, bleeding gums, bruising – with simple dengue, so it doesn't necessarily mean you have DHF.

Diagnosis & Treatment
Blood tests can help diagnose dengue fever. There's no specific treatment, but if you think you have dengue fever:

▶ seek medical advice as soon as possible so that the diagnosis can be confirmed and other diagnoses (such as malaria in risk areas) can be ruled out
▶ rest and drink plenty of fluids
▶ take simple painkillers if necessary but avoid aspirin, as this can increase the likelihood of bleeding problems

Keep a look out for signs of DHF, and get medical help urgently if you have any of the following (if DHF does occur, it's usually around the third day of illness):

▶ any worsening of your condition, especially if associated with any of the following symptoms
▶ spontaneous bruising of the skin, nose bleeds, bleeding from the gums, vomiting blood or abdominal pain
▶ signs of blood loss – thin, rapid pulse, restlessness, pale face and cold fingers and toes

Dengue Again?
There are four different strains of the dengue virus. If you get dengue, you develop immunity against the infecting strain, but you are vulnerable to the three remaining strains, so you could get it again. You're more likely to get a severe form of the disease second time around so if you've had dengue in the past, you should discuss the risks with your doctor before you go, and be extremely careful to avoid mosquito bites at all times.

MALARIA

This serious disease is currently a risk all year round in Papua New Guinea, the Solomon Islands and Vanuatu. Malaria is caused by a parasite called *Plasmodium* which is carried by a type of night-biting mosquito present in most tropical and subtropical areas below about 2000m.

When an infected female mosquito bites you, malarial parasites are injected into your bloodstream and get carried to your liver, where they multiply. During this phase you don't get any symptoms.

Symptoms appear when the malarial parasites enter your bloodstream again, which occurs after a variable length of time depending on the type of malaria (usually about one to three weeks, but sometimes up to a year). The malarial parasites enter and multiply in red blood cells, eventually destroying them. This can have effects on many organs in your body, including your guts (causing vomiting and diarrhoea), kidneys (causing kidney failure) and brain (cerebral malaria).

There are four types of *Plasmodium* parasites, but the one of most concern is *P. falciparum*, which causes the most severe disease and is responsible for most malaria deaths worldwide. In the Pacific risk areas, falciparum is the most common type of malaria.

The other types – *P. vivax* (common worldwide), *P. ovale* (uncommon, found mainly in West Africa) and *P. malariae* (uncommon) – are less likely to cause severe complications so rapidly, but infection with any of them still needs to be treated promptly. *P. vivax* and *P. ovale* can remain inactive in the liver for some time and can cause disease several weeks or months after you've left a risk area.

! You can't tell the different forms of malaria apart on the basis of the early symptoms, so you have to assume that any malaria is due to P. falciparum unless proved otherwise (by a blood test).

Malaria can be effectively treated with drugs; the symptoms quickly disappear as the parasites are cleared from the blood. If malaria is treated appropriately, it won't recur. The picture you may have of recurring attacks of malaria is only true when the disease is not treated.

! The most important point to remember about malaria is that it can progress rapidly to severe complications (sometimes within 24 hours), so it is extremely important to seek medical help urgently if you get a fever in a malarial area.

Symptoms

Unfortunately, the symptoms of malaria are very variable and rather nonspecific, making it notoriously difficult to diagnose.

! If you are in a risk area, the most important sign of malaria is a fever of 38°C (100.4°F) or higher.

Textbooks describe three stages: a cold stage when you shiver and your temperature rockets up; followed by a hot stage when you feel hot, flushed and have a high temperature (this lasts for several hours); finally you get a wet stage when you become drenched in sweat, and your temperature falls. We should stress that this is the textbook scenario – in reality the picture is likely to be much more vague, especially if you were taking malaria pills.

Suspect malaria if you have a fever (it may just feel like an attack of flu) with or without any of the following symptoms:

- headache and aching muscles and joints
- nausea and vomiting, or diarrhoea (especially in children)
- cough
- abdominal discomfort and jaundice (yellowing of the skin and whites of the eyes)
- confusion, leading to coma (cerebral malaria)

Remember that you can still get malaria even if you are taking malaria prevention pills.

Diagnosis & Treatment

! Note that it takes at least a week for the disease to appear after an infective bite, so a fever within the first week of your arrival in a malarial area is very unlikely to be malaria (unless you've come from a malarial area).

Malaria can be quickly and simply diagnosed from a sample of your blood, usually taken by pricking your finger. The test may need to be repeated if it's initially negative and you know malaria is likely. Most doctors and clinics in malarial areas will have facilities for doing a malaria blood test, or you can do a test yourself if you have a kit with you. You may be able to buy kits locally in some countries.

If you think you may have malaria:

▶ rest and take steps to bring down the fever – see p103 for guidelines on general measures
▶ drink plenty of fluids
▶ seek medical help as soon as possible for a blood test to confirm the diagnosis
▶ once the diagnosis is confirmed, take the doctor's advice on treatment, as they are likely to be experienced in treating malaria and will know what the most appropriate treatment is for the area you are in

If your symptoms recur or continue despite treatment, seek medical advice as you will need further treatment, and it may turn out not to be malaria.

Don't forget that you will still need to take malaria pills after you recover – get medical advice on what would be most appropriate in your individual situation.

! Malaria can appear after you've left the malaria risk zone – if you get a fever in the weeks or months after you were in a malarial risk area, seek medical help urgently and be sure to tell your doctor where you've been and which malaria pills (if any) you were taking.

Emergency Self-treatment

Self-treatment of any serious disease, including malaria, is not something to be undertaken lightly, but it may be appropriate in certain situations.

- You should only consider self-treatment of malaria in an emergency, ie if you do not have access to medical care within 24 hours of the start of symptoms.
- Emergency self-treatment is a first aid measure only – you still need to get yourself to medical help as soon as possible.

As discussed under Symptoms earlier, it can be difficult to know when to self-treat, but use the following rule of thumb.

! *If you are in a risk area, suspect malaria if you have an otherwise unexplained fever (over 38°C or 100.4°F) that lasts more than eight hours without responding to simple fever-reducing measures.*

Fortunately, the new malaria diagnosis kits (discussed in the Before You Go chapter) mean that diagnosing malaria in yourself is less of the hit-and-miss affair it used to be.

Malaria Treatment Drugs

Although we give currently accepted guidelines here, recommendations change as resistance patterns vary and new facts come to light, so it's best to get the most up-to-date advice from your doctor or travel health clinic before you go, or to seek reliable local advice if necessary. As a general rule:

- you need to take an antimalarial that is different from the one that you were taking as prevention
- because of drug resistance, you need to be sure you are taking the appropriate treatment for the area you are in; inadequately treated malaria can recur later

The reason you need to take a different antimalarial for treatment is because the strain of malaria may be resistant to the antimalarial you were taking. In addition, you are more likely to experience side effects if you take the same antimalarial for treatment as you were taking for prevention.

In Papua New Guinea, Vanuatu and, to a lesser extent, the Solomon Islands, the malarial parasite is highly resistant to chloroquine and sulfadoxine/pyrimethamine (Fansidar). Check with your doctor before you go or get medical advice locally on appropriate treatment, but options for treating malaria in these areas currently include the following:

- atovaquone-proguanil (Malarone) – this is good if you were taking mefloquine or doxycycline for prevention
- mefloquine – can be used if you were taking doxycycline as prevention against malaria
- quinine sulphate – although it's an effective treatment, this drug is tricky to use safely and is not usually recommended for emergency standby treatment in travellers

Emergency treatment with chloroquine or sulfadoxine/pyrimethamine (Fansidar) is not generally appropriate in these areas because of widespread resistance.

Other treatments may come on the market in the near future as malaria experts struggle to cope with the spread of drug resistance worldwide. In particular, you may hear talk of artesunate or artemether in connection with the treatment of malaria. These compounds are related to artemisinin, or qinghaosu, which has been used for over two millennia in traditional medical practice in China. They appear to be safe and effective in the treatment (but not prevention) of severe malaria, but because of fears of the emergence of resistance, use is restricted to some highly drug resistant areas. Another drug on the horizon is Tafenoquine, developed by the US Army.

!Note that the antimalarial halofantrine is now known to cause heart rhythm problems in susceptible people, and these effects are more likely if you have been taking chloroquine, mefloquine or quinine. It is therefore no longer recommended for standby treatment. However, it may still be available in some areas and is better than nothing in an emergency.

Malaria Standby Treatment

Although we have done our best to ensure that these doses are correct at the time of going to print, there are many individual variables to take into account, so you should check with your doctor that these are suitable for you before you leave.

Note that although we give doses for children here, we do not recommend you take children to high risk malarial areas – for more details, see the Babies & Children chapter.

treatment	adult	child
atovaquone/ proguanil (Malarone)	four tablets once daily for three days	11kg to 20kg one tablet once daily; 21kg to 30kg two tablets once daily; 31kg to 40kg three tablets once daily; over 40kg, as for adult
pyrimethamine/ sulfadoxine (Fansidar)	single dose of three tablets	5kg to 10kg half tablet; 11kg to 20kg one tablet; 21kg to 30kg 1.5 tablets; 31kg to 45kg two tablets; over 45kg three tablets
quinine sulphate PLUS:	two 300mg tablets three times daily for seven days	10mg/kg three times daily for seven days
pyrimethamine/ sulfadoxine (Fansidar) OR:	dose as above	dose as above
doxycycline OR:	100mg once daily	over eight years: 2mg/kg twice daily for seven days
tetracycline	250mg four times daily for seven days	over eight years: 5mg/kg four times daily for seven days
mefloquine	two 250mg tablets and a further two six hours later	child 15kg or over: 15mg/kg single dose
chloroquine	four tablets (150mg base) each on days one and two, and two on day three (ie total of 10 tablets)	25mg base/kg over three days

Side Effects & Cautions

These notes are for guidance in an emergency; if possible, get individual advice from your doctor before you go.

Atovaquone plus proguanil (Malarone) This combination drug is highly effective against multidrug resistant strains of malaria. It's also safe and unlikely to cause you any adverse effects.

Mefloquine (Lariam) For more details about mefloquine, see the section on Malaria Prevention Drugs in the Before You Go chapter. Side effects are common at the doses used for treatment, and include lightheadedness, nausea, dizziness and vertigo; more serious side effects occur in about one in 100 people at this dose.

Quinine This is the most effective drug against chloroquine-resistant malaria, but it's quite toxic, so it is not usually recommended for use as emergency standby treatment. It needs to be given with another agent, usually sulfadoxine/pyrimethamine (Fansidar), doxycycline or tetracycline.

Side effects of quinine are common, and include ringing in the ears, muffled hearing and sometimes dizziness, usually on the second or third day of treatment. These side effects usually go away once you stop taking it.

Quinine can cause heart problems, so you need medical supervision if you are on any heart medications, and these problems are more likely if you have been taking mefloquine for prevention. It can also cause your blood sugar to drop.

! *Be aware that quinine is very toxic if taken at more than the recommended dose, and you should always keep it well out of reach of children.*

Sulfadoxine/pyrimethamine (Fansidar) Widely used to treat malaria, although resistance has now emerged in some parts of the world, including Papua New Guinea and Vanuatu. It's generally safe and effective at the doses used for treatment, although it is no longer recommended for use as a preventive agent (because serious skin reactions have been reported when used as a weekly dose).

! You should avoid Fansidar if you are allergic to sulphonamide drugs.

TYPHOID FEVER

Also known as enteric fever, typhoid occurs in most developing countries, including the Pacific island nations. Occasional large outbreaks occur, especially after natural or human disasters, when waste disposal and water supply systems break down. It's rare in travellers, but it's worth taking general precautions to avoid even this low risk.

Typhoid is transmitted via food and water. Symptomless carriers, especially people who are working as foodhandlers, are an important source of infection.

Typhoid is caused by a type of salmonella bacteria, *Salmonella typhi*. Paratyphoid is a similar but milder disease.

Symptoms

These are variable, but you almost always get a fever and headache to start with, initially very similar to flu, with aches and pains, loss of appetite and generally feeling unwell. Typhoid may be confused with malaria.

The fever gradually rises during a week. Characteristically your pulse is relatively slow compared with the fever (eg 80 beats/min for an adult instead of perhaps 100) – but this is something a medic will pick up better than you, so don't agonise over it too much. Other symptoms you may have are constipation or diarrhoea and stomach pains.

You may feel worse in the second week, with a constant fever and sometimes a red skin rash. Serious complications occur in about one in 10 cases, including, most commonly, damage to the gut wall with subsequent leakage of the gut contents into the abdominal cavity. Sometimes this is the first indication of an infection. Other symptoms you may have are severe headache, sore throat and jaundice.

Diagnosis & Treatment

Diagnosis is by blood test, and the earlier it is diagnosed the better. Seek medical help for any fever (38°C and higher) that does not improve after 48 hours. Typhoid is a serious disease and is not something you should consider self-treating.

Rehydration therapy is important if diarrhoea has been a feature of the illness, but antibiotics (chloramphenicol or ciprofloxacin) are the mainstay of treatment, although resistance to chloramphenicol is a growing problem.

VIRAL HEPATITIS

This infection of the liver can be caused by at least five different viruses: hepatitis A, B, C, D and E. Hepatitis A is extremely common worldwide, especially in developing countries, and is a real risk to all travellers. Hepatitis E is becoming more common worldwide, and is a particular threat to pregnant women.

Unlike hepatitis A and E, infection with hepatitis B can persist in about 5% to 10% of people, and these carriers are important sources of infection. Hepatitis B occurs throughout Australia, New Zealand and the Pacific islands, and rates of infection in some populations are high. Hepatitis C is a major cause of blood transfusion-related hepatitis in the west and appears to be a growing problem worldwide, but is not going to be a major worry for you as a traveller. Hepatitis D only occurs in conjunction with hepatitis B infection.

All five viruses cause a similar short-term disease but infection with types B, C or D can cause serious long-term liver problems in a proportion of sufferers. The different viruses are transmitted in different ways:

■ types A and E are spread via contaminated food and water

- types B, C and D are spread via blood or sexual contact; in children, hepatitis B can be transmitted by prolonged contact with a carrier

A blood test can diagnose which type you have, but you'll probably have a good idea anyway.

SYMPTOMS

Hepatitis starts with vague flu-like symptoms, including fever, chills, headache, and joint aches and pains. You usually feel drained of energy; you have no appetite, and smokers often report being turned off cigarettes. These nonspecific symptoms can go on for two to three days, when you get nausea, vomiting, diarrhoea (possibly) and pain in the upper right-hand side of your abdomen. A day or so later you may notice that you're passing dark urine and your faeces are a lighter colour than normal. The whites of your eyes turn yellow, and later your skin starts to look yellow. This yellowing is called jaundice, and occurs because your liver can't clear bile chemicals properly.

!Hepatitis is a much more serious disease in pregnancy, so you must seek medical help urgently in this situation.

Although these are the classic symptoms, hepatitis can be a mild illness without jaundice in many people, especially children, although older people are often more severely affected.

Causes of Jaundice

- viral hepatitis
- glandular fever (p143)
- typhoid (p132)
- malaria (p125)
- amoebic liver abscess (p121)
- medications
- gall bladder disease (may be associated with sudden, severe pain that comes and goes in waves)

You usually find that you start to feel better as the jaundice appears. Hepatitis can leave you feeling very washed out and weak for some time after – about six weeks on average but sometimes up to three months, so be prepared. It might be one reason to come home early if you're on a long trip.

Rarely, you can get serious complications, as a result of overwhelming liver failure. Seek medical help urgently if you get suddenly worse or if you have any of the following:

- severe vomiting and dehydration
- bruising for no reason
- bleeding from your gums or nose bleeds
- blood in your urine or faeces
- confusion and drowsiness

TREATMENT

There's no specific treatment apart from rest and tender loving care. However, you should seek medical advice as soon as possible to have the diagnosis confirmed. You probably won't feel like doing much for a while, so make sure you've got somewhere comfortable to stay. There's no particular need to stay in bed; just do as much or as little as you feel up to.

▷ Drink plenty of fluids, especially if you don't feel like eating because of the nausea.

▷ If you feel like eating, try to stick to a low-fat (the liver has to work harder to deal with fatty foods) and high carbohydrate diet.

▷ Avoid anything that could damage your liver further, such as alcohol and medications like aspirin or paracetamol (acetaminophen).

In fact, it's a good idea to avoid any medications if possible while you have hepatitis, because drugs won't be disposed of as efficiently as normal and can have unpredictable effects.

! If you take the oral contraceptive pill, you'll need to stop taking it (and use an alternative method of contraception) until the illness settles.

Infection with hepatitis B causes a similar illness to type A, but the symptoms can be more severe and there's a higher risk

Hepatitis – Keeping it to Yourself

If you've got hepatitis, you need to take care not to spread it around. With hepatitis A and E, you're most infectious for about two weeks or so before symptoms appear until a few days after the jaundice develops. Pay particular attention to your personal hygiene, don't prepare food for other people, don't share cutlery and avoid sharing drinks or cigarettes. Once you've had hepatitis A or E, you're immune for life.

Anybody you have been in close contact with needs to receive the hepatitis A vaccine (or immunoglobulin) if they haven't been vaccinated, unless they have already developed symptoms.

With hepatitis B, you're infectious for the course of the illness, usually about three to six months, and for about a month before symptoms appear. Take care not to spread the disease (use condoms), let doctors and dentists know of your infection before they carry out any treatment, and you should not donate blood or share needles.

of liver failure. Note that the illness can take up to six months to appear after infection. Persistent infection carries the risk of long-term liver damage and liver cancer in a minority of cases.

! If you think you may have been exposed to hepatitis B, a shot of antibody can help protect against it; alternatively you could start a course of the usual hepatitis B vaccination – discuss this with your doctor.

PREVENTION

Effective vaccines are available against hepatitis A and B; there are no vaccines against the other types of hepatitis. In many countries (including Australia and the USA), hepatitis B vaccination is becoming routine and you may have been immunised at school. For more details, see the Immunisations section of the Before You Go chapter.

In addition, it's advisable to take basic food and water precautions to protect yourself against hepatitis A and E. Shellfish are particularly risky, so are worth avoiding for this reason. Avoid swimming in polluted water.

Protect yourself against hepatitis B infection by avoiding risk situations:

▶ always use a condom if you have sex with a new partner
▶ avoid blood transfusions and other medical (or dental) procedures where possible
▶ never share needles
▶ avoid risk situations like getting your ears or other body parts pierced, having a tattoo or being shaved with a re-used cut-throat razor

COUGHS, RASHES & OTHER COMMON PROBLEMS

When you're travelling, you're just as likely (or unlikely) to get common health problems as you are at home. The difference is that it may not be as easy to get advice on what to do (no family members or familiar doctor to fall back on). If you are on a remote island or trekking deep in the bush, you need to know how to deal with common problems, what to look out for and when to get help.

In this chapter, we've grouped some common respiratory, digestive, urinary and dermatological (skin) problems. Diarrhoea is dealt with in an earlier chapter.

RESPIRATORY SYSTEM

COLDS & FLU

It's not just the culture that's different and exciting, the viruses are too, and even in tropical climates you can get colds and flu. Although flu tends to be a seasonal illness in temperate climates, it's a risk all year round in the tropics. These infections are spread by droplets (for example sneezing) and close personal contact, and you're more likely to get them in crowded urban environments.

Colds and flu have very different symptoms.

! *Flu tends to start quite suddenly, often with a high temperature, and it can make you feel pretty dreadful, with headache and generalised aches and pains.*

You may have a runny nose and sore throat with flu, and often a dry cough that can last for several weeks. Although the illness usually lasts a few days, it can leave you feeling tired and out of energy for some time.

! *With a cold, you don't usually get a high temperature, but you do get the runny nose, sore throat and cough.*

Colds usually go away in a few days without any special treatment; flu tends to take a bit longer. Apart from these illnesses being miserable wherever you are, complications like sinusitis, chest infection and ear infection are more likely when you're travelling.

Recognise the symptoms of a cold or flu as a sign to take it easy for a couple of days.

! *Unless you get complications, antibiotics are no use because colds and flu are caused by viruses, not bacteria.*

Drink plenty of fluids, especially if it's hot and you have a fever, and take simple painkillers if necessary for any aches or pains and to lower a fever, if you have one. (Aspirin is best avoided in tropical areas, in case your fever turns out to be dengue.) Once your appetite returns, make sure you eat well (especially vitamin-containing fresh fruit and vegetables).

You can make your own cold remedy by adding honey or sugar to lemon or lime juice and top up with boiled water. Echinacea with or without zinc is a popular plant-based cold remedy, although it may not be available in the Pacific islands.

When to See a Doctor
The trouble with flu is that the symptoms are so nonspecific that lots of diseases can mimic it. This can be a problem in tropical areas, when it can be hard to tell if you have flu or dengue (or malaria). To give you some guidelines, you need to see a doctor if:

▶ your temperature is over 39°C (102°F) and it can't be lowered by general measures (see p103)
▶ you don't feel better after two days – it may not be flu after all
▶ you feel breathless, start to cough up green spit or have chest pain – this may indicate a chest infection
▶ you think it could be malaria or dengue fever – the symptoms can be identical
▶ you have a severe headache, neck stiffness and hypersensitivity to light – you may have meningitis

SINUSITIS

This usually follows a cold, and can be a pain – literally. The sinuses are air-filled cavities in the skull above the eyes and on either side of the nose, designed to make our heads lighter so that they don't drag on the ground. If the lining of the cavities becomes infected and the normally empty spaces fill with mucus or pus, it causes you pain.

Symptoms are headache (usually over your forehead) or face pain, which is worse when you strain or bend over. Your forehead or cheeks may feel tender when you press them, and you feel something dripping down the back of your throat. Typically the pain isn't there when you get up, but comes on during the morning, reaching a crescendo about lunch time before gradually receding. It's possible to be quite ill with it, with a fever and aches and pains.

Try inhalations of steam, menthol, eucalyptus, Tiger balm or tea tree oil as a first measure, together with simple painkillers. If this doesn't help, you could try taking a nasal decongestant like pseudoephedrine hydrochloride 60mg four times daily (though not if you have high blood pressure). Antihistamines may also help.

If you're really ill with it and have a fever, you'll probably need a course of antibiotics – see a doctor if possible. If not, suitable antibiotics are co-amoxiclav 250mg three times daily or cefaclor 250mg three times daily.

> *!Flying can make the pain worse, so start taking a nasal decongestant the day before you fly or use a nasal decongestant spray. Underwater diving also makes it worse, so avoid diving until you feel better.*

CHEST INFECTION

This can follow an illness like flu or a cold, or it can just come on, when it's often due to a viral infection. It usually starts with an irritating, dry cough and a feeling of tightness in the chest. You may have a mild fever. After a day or so, you start coughing up yellow or greenish gunk. It usually clears up on its own in about a week. Antibiotics aren't usually needed (they don't work against viral infections).

When to See a Doctor

There are some situations when you will need to see a doctor:

▶ you're pretty sick, with a high fever – it may be malaria (in risk areas) or a more serious chest infection
▶ you're still coughing, with no improvement, after a week
▶ you're feeling increasingly short of breath
▶ you have pain in your chest on coughing or taking a deep breath
▶ you cough up blood

If you do need antibiotics, appropriate treatment would be a broad-spectrum antibiotic such as amoxycillin 250mg three times a day (not if you're allergic to penicillin); if you're allergic to penicillin, another option is erythromycin 250mg four times a day (see the Medicines appendix for more details on suitable antibiotics).

ASTHMA

Symptoms include a cough, wheeze, chest tightness and shortness of breath, which may be worse at night or brought on by exercise. If you're asthmatic, you'll probably know about it before you go travelling, and you should take a plentiful supply of your usual medicines with you.

It is possible that asthma may start for the first time while you are travelling, especially if you are travelling in polluted urban areas. It's very common in children and young adults, and appears to be a disease of 'westernisation'. Some drugs can make it worse and should be avoided, the most common one being aspirin. If you're worried, seek medical advice so that appropriate medication can be prescribed if necessary.

! If you are very short of breath or wheezy, you should seek help urgently.

HAY FEVER

This common condition, known officially as allergic rhinitis, is usually due to an allergy to something in the air you're breathing, such as pollen. If you're trying to decide whether your symptoms are because of a cold or an allergy, if they persist and you otherwise feel reasonably well, it's probably hay fever.

Hay fever involves lots of nose blowing. Other symptoms include sneezing, and itchy eyes, roof of the mouth and sometimes ears, too. Your chest may feel tight, as you can get asthma with it (see the previous section).

If you know you're susceptible to hay fever, it's a good idea to bring all your usual remedies with you. If it's being a real nuisance, try antihistamine tablets to start with (see the Medicines appendix for more details), but if this doesn't control it, you could try a nasal spray containing steroids (the amount used won't cause any general problems), such as beclomethasone dipropionate spray. It needs to be taken regularly to have the best chance of working.

SORE THROAT

You can get an uncomfortable throat if you're travelling in dry and dusty situations, or if you're mouth-breathing because your nose is blocked or you're doing strenuous exercise. Drink plenty of fluids, eat moist foods like fruit and vegetables, and consider chewing sugar-free gum if you can get hold of it.

A sore throat can also be caused by infection, usually viral, and you often get a viral eye infection (conjunctivitis – see p169) at the same time. You may have a sore throat on its own, or it may be associated with a cold, flu or glandular fever (see the following section). A sore throat usually clears up on its own after a few days without any special treatment.

Simple measures for treating sore throats are to gargle regularly with salty water (buy some table salt and put a few spoonfuls into a glass of purified water) or a solution of soluble aspirin or paracetamol (acetaminophen). Having lots of

Causes of Sore Throat

- heat and dust
- viral infections, colds and flu
- bacterial infections ('strep' sore throat)
- glandular fever (infectious mononucleosis)
- toxoplasmosis, acquired from infected cat or dog faeces
- sexually transmitted infections (eg gonorrhoea; p186)
- diphtheria (p194)

warm drinks will also help: add some grated ginger, lime juice and sugar (or honey) to a cup of hot water.

When to See a Doctor

About a third of sore throats are caused by a bacterial infection. The reason this matters is that some bacterial throat infections can occasionally lead to serious complications, especially in children. Unfortunately, the only sure way to tell bacterial and viral sore throats apart is by a laboratory test, but as a rule of thumb, you need to seek medical advice for a sore throat in the following situations:

▶ if it's severe – for example you can't swallow solids
▶ if it's persistent (more than five days without any improvement)

In this situation, you'll need a course of antibiotics, such as co-amoxiclav 250mg three times a day or cefaclor 250mg three times a day (see the Medicines appendix for more details).

GLANDULAR FEVER

Suspect this viral disease if you have a severe sore throat that doesn't settle with antibiotics. Apart from sore throat, look out for swollen glands (lumps in your neck, armpits and groins) and fever. You may also notice that you're jaundiced (yellow skin and whites of the eyes). Very occasionally, glandular fever can lead to a serious complication – bursting of the spleen (one of your internal abdominal organs).

!If you have glandular fever and you develop abdominal pain, particularly in the left upper part of the abdomen, you need to seek medical advice urgently.

Glandular fever can only be confirmed by a blood test, and there's no specific treatment. It can leave you feeling weak and washed out weeks, sometimes months, afterwards. Other viral infections can cause similar symptoms.

COLD SORES

Cold sores are caused by a herpes virus infection which recurs periodically. If you've had these before, sunlight, and the stresses of travel or illness may make them recur. You usually know when one is coming on because you'll feel a burning sensation on the edge of your lip followed by the appearance of a blister, usually the next day. They take about a week to clear up. Acyclovir cream (5%) can be effective if you apply it as soon as you feel the burning starting – take a tube with you. Using a lip salve with sunblock can help prevent recurrence.

Secondary bacterial infection is a risk, so try to avoid touching the sore with your fingers. This is good practice anyway, as you can introduce infection in your eye if you then rub your eyes.

MOUTH ULCERS

These are more likely to occur if you're stressed or if you're taking proguanil as an antimalarial, but otherwise they're a bit of a mystery. Regularly swishing your mouth out with salty water or an antiseptic mouthwash (such as chlorhexidine), or even just applying a small amount of toothpaste to the ulcer can help, although all these measures will sting at first.

DIGESTIVE SYSTEM ────────────

If you find travelling to be a bowel-loosening experience, as many do, diarrhoea is dealt with in its own chapter earlier in this guide.

INTESTINAL WORMS

Worldwide, infection with intestinal worms affects about one-third of the population, mainly in developing countries, particularly tropical countries. In general, travellers are unlikely to be affected, but if you are on a long trip, especially if you've been roughing it or spending time in rural, tropical areas, it's possible you could pick up a light infestation along the way.

Worm infestations generally cause few symptoms, unless the infestation is very heavy (unlikely in travellers). The first you may know of it is when you glance in the toilet and find there's something looking back at you.

Roundworms and threadworms are acquired through eating contaminated food or water (unwashed vegetables are common culprits), or can be passed directly from person to person. A light infection with roundworms rarely causes any symptoms, but should be treated because the worms can sometimes get caught in narrow openings internally and cause blockages.

!*Threadworms cause intense anal itching, especially at night – you may have had an infection in childhood.*

Threadworms are small, white and thread-like, and you may notice them wriggling in your faeces or on toilet paper.

Other worms, such as hookworms and strongyloides, develop in the soil and can penetrate the skin of bare feet. Both types of worm find their way to the gut, sometimes causing a cough as they pass through the lungs. Untreated, they can live in your gut for years. Hookworms suck blood, so if the infestation is heavy, it can cause anaemia.

Treatment of worm infestation is with special anti-worm medicines, such as mebendazole, albendazole or piperazine (for threadworm), which may be available without prescription. Note that mebendazole is not suitable in pregnancy or in children under two years of age.

The Revenge of the Fished ...

Certain species of marine reef fish can poison you if you eat them. This is due to the accumulation in the fish of naturally occurring **ciguatera toxins** from species of algae that live in seaweed growing on dead coral. It's common in certain localities, and especially around the Pacific islands. Many species of warm-water fish can be affected, but most commonly involved are groupers, barracudas, snappers, jacks, mackerel and triggerfish.

There are no hard and fast rules as to which fish to avoid, as toxic fish occur sporadically, and even when they do, not all fish of a certain species will be toxic. It's unlikely that you will be served toxic fish in a restaurant, but if you're buying fish or eating fish you have caught, always ask around locally for advice on ciguatera. The toxin is not affected by cooking, freezing or drying, and the fish tastes no different to normal.

Symptoms usually come on within six hours of eating the toxic fish. Initial symptoms include numbness and tingling around the mouth, which may then spread to your arms and legs. Typically you get nausea, vomiting and diarrhoea with it. Other symptoms include sensory alterations involving hot/cold sensations, dizziness and muscle weakness. The cardiovascular system can be affected, resulting in low blood pressure and irregular pulse.

Ciguatera poisoning usually resolves within a few days, but in severe cases, sensory symptoms can persist for weeks and even months. Very rarely death can occur because of the effects on the heart and breathing mechanism. There is no

Tapeworms

These can be acquired by eating raw or lightly cooked infected meat, especially pork and beef, or through contact with dogs or by eating salads and vegetables contaminated with dog faeces (hydatid disease). You don't need to worry unduly about these, as they are rare in the Pacific region, and

specific first aid treatment, but you should get medical help urgently if you think you may be affected.

If fish such as tuna, mahi mahi, bluefish, sardines, mackerel, amberjack and abalone are not kept properly refrigerated, they can cause **scombroid (or histamine) poisoning**. Often the fish will taste peppery or sharp, then within half an hour of eating it, you get headache, flushing, nausea, vomiting, diarrhoea, dry mouth and sometimes an allergic rash and wheezing. The syndrome doesn't last long (eight to 12 hours) and it's rarely dangerous. However, if your symptoms are severe, especially if you experience difficulty breathing, you must seek medical advice urgently as you may need adrenalin (epinephrine) treatment.

Shellfish also do their bit to encourage us to leave them alone. In the presence of **red tides** (caused by a type of plankton at certain times of the year) clams, mussels and oysters can cause numbness and paralysis within half an hour of eating them. Other types of shellfish poisoning include a short-lived illness caused by eating contaminated mussels, giving you nausea, vomiting, diarrhoea and abdominal cramps.

Take a bit of care when eating seafood:

- ask locally for advice on what species are best avoided
- avoid raw seafood, and remember that steaming doesn't necessarily make it safe
- you can't tell if seafood is toxic by looking or smelling
- get medical help urgently if you experience pins and needles, numbness or paralysis after eating seafood

extremely rare in travellers. Tapeworms generally cause few symptoms, but some types cause cysts to develop in your body tissues, which can have serious effects.

Effective treatment of tapeworm infection is available with specific drugs (niclosamide or praziquantel), although surgery is required to treat cysts.

Prevention

With all intestinal worms, prevention is the main aim:

▶ don't walk barefoot in rural areas
▶ take basic food and water precautions and wash your hands before eating
▶ avoid undercooked meat and fish
▶ steer clear of dogs

If you have been on a long trip, spending time in rural, tropical areas, it's probably a good idea to get a laboratory test done on your faeces when you return to check for worms.

CONSTIPATION

Far less has been written about travellers constipation, but it is a least as common as travellers diarrhoea. Plenty of factors conspire to stop you up while you're travelling, including immobility if you're stuck on a bus, plane or train for hours on end, not drinking enough fluids, disruption to your normal routine, jet lag and a change of diet. A lack of privacy and time to relax can be enough to bring on constipation if you have a shy bowel, or you may find it difficult to get used to squatting (although this is supposed to be a more 'natural' way of defecating). Drugs you have been taking, such as antidiarrhoeals, can cause relatively intractable constipation.

The end result is being unable to defecate as often as normal, which can make you feel bloated and uncomfortable, with no appetite and no energy. If you have piles, being constipated can worsen them.

If you know you are prone to constipation, consider bringing your own supply of bran with you or a reliable remedy you know. Otherwise, try a few simple measures before diving into the nearest pharmacy or your medical kit.

▶ Make sure you're drinking plenty of fluids, especially if you are in a hot climate.
▶ Try to increase the fibre in your diet by eating more fruit (peeled) and vegetables (cooked and peeled) but avoid bananas, which

can stop you up. Porridge, pulses, nuts and dried fruit are also good fibre providers. Prune juice is another old favourite.

▶ A cup of hot, strong coffee can get things moving, especially first thing in the morning, while a large meal can have the same effect (remember that if you're not eating much for any reason, there's not going to be much coming out, either).

▶ Alcohol has a laxative effect, if you need an excuse.

▶ Finding a decent toilet may help – perhaps consider changing hotels.

▶ Exercise has many benefits, including stimulating your guts.

Finally, if you feel like going, don't be tempted to hang on or the moment will pass, and you will forever regret it.

If simple measures fail, you could consider taking something fairly gentle like lactulose syrup (15mL twice daily, takes about 48 hours to work) or senna, a gut stimulant (two to four tablets at night, works in eight to 12 hours).

PILES & OTHER ANAL PROBLEMS

Piles are swollen veins around the anus, either on the outside (external) or inside (internal), occasionally popping out when you strain. Constipation (because of straining), diarrhoea, or carrying heavy packs, especially up mountains, can exacerbate the problem.

External piles can be excruciatingly painful. The pain can be relieved by cutting them open (still with us?) but this needs to be done by a medic, ideally under sterile conditions. Otherwise, you may need to take painkillers and hotfoot it down the mountain.

Internal piles can be uncomfortable, with a feeling of something popping out when you strain and may cause itchiness around the anus. Local anaesthetic creams, such as those containing lignocaine, can help.

If you get excruciating pain when you pass faeces, especially if you've been constipated, often with bright red blood on the toilet paper, you probably have an anal fissure, a small split in the anus. It can be very painful, but there's no specific treatment apart from taking care to keep the area clean and dealing with any constipation you may have.

Anal itching may be caused by threadworms, chafing and poor hygiene. Check your faeces for little, white wriggling worms or, if you just have to know, you can put a piece of tape across your anus at night and examine it for worms in the morning. Treatment is with an anti-worm medicine.

INDIGESTION

A change in diet, stress, anxiety and spicy foods can all make 'indigestion' (burning pains in your upper stomach) and heartburn (burning in your gullet, often with an acid taste in your mouth) more likely when you're travelling. The discomfort is often worse when you're hungry and just after meals. Smoking and alcohol exacerbate it.

!If you have a gastric or duodenal ulcer, or are taking treatment for one, this may make you more susceptible to gut infections, so it's best to discuss this with your doctor before you go, as you may be able to change to a different anti-ulcer medicine that makes this less likely.

Simple measures to ease the symptoms of indigestion include eating small, regular meals (for example don't eat a huge meal just before you go to bed). Consider stopping smoking and cutting back on alcohol or at least giving yourself a break for a few days. It can be difficult in some places, but try to avoid spicy, hot foods. Milk and yoghurt can be soothing, as can eating plain, starchy foods like bread, potato or rice.

You could consider trying antacids (there are many products available without prescription; take them between meals and at night), although stomach acid has a protective effect against infective agents, so this may make you more vulnerable to gut infections.

!You need to seek medical help urgently in the following situations: if the pain is severe and not relieved by any of the

measures suggested, if it wakes you at night, if it seems to go through to your back, if you have had a stomach or duodenal ulcer in the past or if you vomit blood.

APPENDICITIS

If you have still got your appendix, acute appendicitis is a possible cause of severe abdominal pain. It's reasonably common in both adults and children, and you should consider it if you experience abdominal pain that's colicky or constant, and increases in severity over a short period of time (12 to 24 hours). Symptoms can vary, but typically they are as follows:

▶ central abdominal pain that may be colicky (comes and goes) or constant, and which moves to the right lower abdomen after a few hours, becoming constant
▶ nausea, loss of appetite and sometimes vomiting
▶ mild fever but not usually very high
▶ diarrhoea in some cases, but it's not usually very severe
▶ the right lower abdomen is tender when you press on it

Seek medical help urgently if you think appendicitis may be a possibility, as you'll need surgery if the diagnosis is confirmed. It's potentially extremely dangerous if it's not treated quickly.

URINARY PROBLEMS

Because bladder infections (cystitis) are much more common in women, this is covered in the Women Travellers chapter.

!Men travellers who experience urinary symptoms (including burning on passing urine, passing small amounts frequently) should always get medical attention as soon as possible.

KIDNEY STONE

Dehydration (and other conditions) can cause chemicals in the urine to harden and form small stones in the kidney. If a stone becomes stuck in the tube leading from the kidney to the bladder, it causes excruciating pain. The pain usually starts suddenly on one side, in the back just below the ribcage, spreading round to the groin in the front. Characteristically, the pain is gripey (ie it comes and goes in waves) and you can't stay still with it. It can be so severe that it makes you vomit.

Most (95%) kidney stones eventually work their way down to the bladder and get passed out within about a day or so. However, you should seek medical help if possible, as you will probably need a strong painkilling injection.

! If you have a fever, this indicates that the kidney is infected, which is a medical emergency.

If the pain subsides and has not returned after 12 hours or so, this means you have probably passed the stone, but it's a good idea to get this checked out as soon as possible, or when you get back if you're on a short trip.

! Make sure you drink plenty of fluids, especially if you are active in a hot climate, to prevent further problems.

PROSTATE PROBLEMS

While there's no reason why you shouldn't travel if you have symptoms of prostate enlargement, it's probably a good idea to discuss this with your doctor in advance, especially if you are going to be travelling in remote areas. That way, you can work out strategies for dealing with any problems that might arise while you're away. The main concern is if you become unable to pass urine at all; in this scenario you will need to have a tube (catheter) inserted up the penis into the bladder to drain it manually. It's not something that you can accurately predict, so in certain situations it might be appropriate to take a sterile catheter set with you.

! If you are unable to pass any urine at all for more than 24 hours (you'll probably feel very uncomfortable before this) seek medical advice urgently.

Painful Testicle

You should seek medical advice urgently if you develop a sore testicle. If the pain started suddenly, and the testicle is swollen and red, it may be due to torsion. This is when the testicle gets twisted, which cuts off its blood supply – with the risk of irreversible damage. This is an emergency situation, as you may need surgery to fix the problem.

If the pain has come on more gradually, it may be due to a hernia or an infection, often a sexually transmitted one such as chlamydia (common) or gonorrhoea (less common). You may have noticed other symptoms, such as a discharge from the penis, and the testicle will feel hot and tender. You may have a fever. You will probably need a course of antibiotics to treat the infection, so it's best to seek medical advice.

Pain in the testicle can be due to a problem elsewhere such as stones in the urinary tract, when the testicle will look and feel normal to the touch.

SKIN PROBLEMS

○ For first aid of cuts, burns and scalds, see the First Aid appendix.

Although there's a great line-up of weird and wonderful 'tropical' skin diseases, the most common skin problems you are likely to suffer are much more prosaic: insect bites (and secondary bacterial infection), sunburn, fungal infections and prickly heat.

INSECT BITES

Mosquitoes and other insects inject a small amount of saliva when they bite, which sets up a reaction in the skin, causing itching and swelling. People vary in their response to bites – some people, often women, are particularly sensitive to them, and bites can swell up alarmingly, often forming a blister.

Bites are usually most troublesome when you first arrive – mosquitoes seem to be able to smell a fresh tourist skin as soon as you step off the plane. In theory at least, you become desensitised to bites (ie they cause less itching and swelling) with time. Why some people get bitten more than others is something of a mystery, and to do with factors such as body odour, different habits and activities and different immune response to bites.

Insect bites commonly get infected (called secondary bacterial infection because it is secondary to the bite), especially if you scratch them – it's best to try hard not to. Signs of infection are yellow or yellow-brown crusts on the bites, and redness spreading around the bite. Infected bites can be painful but they are usually just even itchier than uninfected bites. Bathe infected bites regularly in clean water and protect them from dirt; you may need a course of antibiotics if they don't clear up (see also the boxed text 'An Itch to Scratch' in the Bites & Stings chapter).

SUNBURN

We'd like to think, of course, that after following all the advice about preventing sun damage on p65, you won't need to read this section, but just in case ...

The trouble with sunburn is that it comes on gradually, unlike burns from other causes, and you often don't notice it until it's too late. Sunburn can vary from just a mild redness with some soreness to more severe swelling with blistering.

With mild sunburn, you can take the heat out of the burn by covering it with a damp cloth and turning the fan on; simple painkillers may also help. There are lots of skin treatments you could try – the best known are perhaps calamine cream (messy but effective) or aloe vera gel, but there's also a huge selection of commercial 'after sun' products. It's best to avoid greasy creams, as these trap the heat and make further damage likely.

Natural remedies you might like to try include lavender essential oil applied undiluted to the area, comfrey cream or hypericum oil.

Sun Hypersensitivity

Taking certain medicines can make you hypersensitive to the effects of the sun – you may find you burn more readily and badly than is normal for you. It's something that your doctor or pharmacist will probably warn you about. If you are taking medicines for a preexisting condition, this is something you should check with your doctor before you leave. Medicines that can cause problems like this include:

- tetracycline antibiotics, including doxycycline (may be prescribed as a malaria preventive)
- ciprofloxacin (antibiotic that may be prescribed for diarrhoea)
- anti-inflammatory painkillers like ibuprofen and diclofenac
- the contraceptive pill (rarely)
- thiazides (diuretics for blood pressure control and heart problems)
- nalidixic acid (antibiotic often prescribed for bladder infections)
- sulphonamide antibiotics eg co-trimoxazole (unlikely to be prescribed under normal circumstances)

The sun tends to make atopic dermatitis (eczema) worse, although it can improve psoriasis. Sunlight can trigger cold sores, if you get these.

If the burn is more severe and has blistered, there's a risk of secondary infection. Take steps to avoid this by keeping the area clean and covered. For a smallish area of blistering sunburn, an antibacterial cream like silver sulphadiazine 1% (Flammazine) is useful – spread it on liberally and cover the whole area with a dry sterile dressing. You'll need to reapply the cream and change the dressing daily until it has healed up. For larger blisters, it's best to get medical attention.

Take care not to get burnt again, especially if peeling has left areas of unprotected new skin. Cover up and use plenty of water-resistant sunscreen on exposed areas.

Skin Cancer

Australia has one of the highest rates of skin cancer in the world, and you'll find it's a high-profile issue in the region. Worldwide, changes in attitudes towards sun exposure and tanning in recent decades have led to rising rates of skin cancer. Risk factors include fair skin, living in tropical or subtropical areas of the world, short intense bursts of sun exposure, sunburn in childhood, and prolonged sun exposure. The more moles (raised freckles) you have the greater your risk.

If you're in a high-risk group, it's a good idea to keep a lookout for early signs of skin cancer. There are different types of skin cancer but melanoma is the most dangerous form, and tends to affect people in their 30s and 40s. Tumours vary in appearance, but they often look like irregularly shaped and coloured moles. If you notice any of the following signs in a mole or freckle, see a doctor as soon as possible:

- rapid increase in size
- any change in shape or colour
- itching, oozing or bleeding
- any increase in thickness or change in the surface

! Note that widespread severe sunburn is a serious condition that needs to be treated like any other extensive burn (p402) – you will need to get medical help urgently. In the meantime, rest, drink plenty of fluids and try any of the cooling measures suggested for mild sunburn.

FUNGAL INFECTIONS

These infections flourish in hot and humid conditions, and are extremely common. If you already have a fungal infection before you leave, you'll probably find it gets worse when you're travelling.

Fungal infections can affect different parts of your body, and are given different names accordingly: scalp (tinea capitis), body (ringworm), crotch (jock itch, tinea cruris) and feet (athlete's foot, tinea pedis). They all produce a reddened, flaky area of skin, which is sometimes itchy. Ringworm lesions tend to be round, spreading outwards with a clear area in the centre. If your scalp is affected, you may get bald patches in your hair. Athlete's foot usually affects the skin between your toes, and can be a real nuisance, especially if you're trekking. If the skin splits, it can be painful.

Another fungal infection common in the tropics is tinea versicolor (also called pityriasis). You may first notice it on your shoulders, chest and back, when patches of your skin don't tan.

Prevention

Fungal skin infections aren't exactly going to kill you, but they can be uncomfortable, and it's worth taking steps to prevent them:

▶ wear loose-fitting, cotton clothing
▶ wash regularly and dry yourself carefully, especially between the toes, the groin area and under the breasts

Treatment

Fungal skin infections are generally treated with antifungal creams, usually available without prescription. These include clotrimazole, ketoconazole, miconazole and nystatin, and need to be applied twice daily for at least a couple of weeks. Widespread infections may need to be treated with antifungal tablets. Calendula tincture may be helpful, applied directly to the affected area.

It's best to get medical advice on treatment options for tinea versicolor, but these usually include treatment with selenium sulphide shampoo or an antifungal cream, although sometimes antifungal tablets may be recommended.

BACTERIAL INFECTIONS

○ For more guidelines on preventing and treating bacterial skin infections, see the First Aid appendix.

Cuts and scratches are much more likely to get infected in the warm, humid climate of the tropics, and it's often hard to keep them clean when you're on the road. Because of this, you need to take a bit more care of any wounds than you would normally at home, however insignificant they may initially seem. Severe skin infections can make you seriously ill with blood poisoning.

!Scratching insect bites is probably the most common cause of skin infections in travellers – prevent insect bites in the first place, and if you get bitten, try hard not to scratch.

Hot, humid conditions make boils and abscesses more common, too. Swimming in less than clean water can give you folliculitis, a rash of pimples caused by infection of the hair follicles.

Impetigo is a common bacterial skin infection that typically affects children but may also occur in adult travellers. It usually starts on the face, often around the mouth or from a mosquito bite. Blisters appear on the face, and may look like a cold sore at first. These then burst, forming golden, crusty sores, which can spread quickly to different areas of the skin. Impetigo is very contagious, and can easily be spread by fingers and towels or face cloths. Treat impetigo as follows:

▶ wash the crusty sores regularly (twice a day) with soap and water or an antiseptic solution like povidone-iodine
▶ apply an antibiotic cream (such as fusidic acid three times daily for five to seven days) on the sores after washing the crusts off
▶ if it's very severe or doesn't respond quickly to treatment, you'll need a course of antibiotics (eg flucloxacillin or erythromycin if penicillin-allergic)

PRICKLY HEAT

This uncomfortable rash is very common in tropical environments and is particularly common in travellers arriving from temperate climates, although it can strike any time. It's caused by blockage of the sweat ducts. As sweating tries to occur in the blocked glands, you get an uncomfortable prickling sensation, hence the name.

! Prickly heat is very common in babies and children; nappy rash is also more likely to be a problem in hot climates – see the Babies & Children chapter for more details.

At its mildest, prickly heat consists of a rash of painless clear blisters without any redness. These usually burst quickly and don't cause any other problems.

The next step up is prickly heat proper. You get itchy areas of redness, with spots and small blisters, usually in covered, sweaty areas like around your waist, chest or back, under the breasts or in the groin. You may get it on the backs of your knees or in the elbow creases. Babies and young children commonly get it on their heads.

Because the problem is the build-up of sweat in the blocked ducts, treatment is aimed at preventing sweating.

- Stay cool: reduce exertion, use fans, cool showers, damp cloths or an air-con hotel.
- Wear loose cotton clothing.
- Wash with water: overuse of soap, which destroys the skin's natural oils and defences, is thought to be one causative factor.
- Calamine, calendula or comfrey cream applied directly to the rash can be soothing.
- Try taking antihistamine tablets to help stop the itching.
- Watch for signs of secondary infection – see p399.

Prickly heat usually clears up in a few days. Rarely, it can refuse to go and ends up as a widespread rash. Because your sweat ducts are blocked all over, this affects your heat-controlling mechanisms and you can get a rare form of heatstroke because of it. This form is more likely after you've been several months in a hot climate. See p282 for more on heatstroke.

DERMATITIS

Dermatitis is a general term for an itchy skin rash. It's very common worldwide and can be caused by a whole range of

Causes of Itchy Skin Rash		
condition	page	characteristics
dermatitis (allergic or irritant reactions)	p159	often on hands or other exposed areas
prickly heat	p158	armpits, waist, groin, head (in babies and children)
fungal infections	p156	sweaty areas: armpits, groin, under breasts, between toes
insect bites	p153	any exposed area
scabies	p163	intense itchiness, especially at night
reaction to medicines	p375	rash all over
creeping eruption	p165	moving red tracks, usually on feet and legs

factors, from simple chemical irritation to reactions to plants and insects. It may be an in-built tendency in some people, when it can occur without any obvious cause. In this situation it's known as atopic dermatitis or eczema, and may be associated with asthma or hay fever. Most people with eczema will have had it for some time, often since childhood, and it is unlikely to develop for the first time on your travels.

Itching is the main feature of any dermatitis, with thickened, red and often cracked skin. There may be some blistering, particularly if it has been caused by contact with a plant. Where you get it depends on what's causing it: eczema usually affects your hands, inside of the wrists and backs of the knees; contact dermatitis, caused by something you've touched, will appear wherever contact was made.

If you haven't had dermatitis before and it suddenly appears when you're travelling, it's most likely to be due to contact with something ... the question is what. It may be a chemical irritant, for example soaps or detergents, or something that you are allergic to, for example an ingredient in a new skin lotion or a plant you've touched or brushed past.

Some unlucky people can get a dermatitis, often with blistering, as a result of mild to moderate sun exposure – consider this possibility if it only occurs on parts of your body that have been exposed to the sun. Or, it could be a reaction to the suncream you're using. Or it could just be sunburn.

It's not always easy to work these things out but a bit of common sense and a certain amount of trial and error can help. For example, in this case you could see if covering up or changing suncream helps. Don't forget that you can develop a sensitivity or allergy to something you have used without problems in the past.

Treatment

Most contact dermatitis will gradually settle once the irritant or allergy-causing substance is removed. If you can work out what the culprit is, avoid it! Otherwise, finding the cause only really matters if it doesn't go away.

If the rash is mild, try liberally covering it with a moisturiser like aqueous cream or white soft paraffin. (The trouble with 'cosmetic' moisturisers is that they can contain ingredients that may exacerbate the rash, but if you've got nothing else, it may be worth giving them a try.) Calendula or comfrey cream may also help.

If this doesn't work, a weak steroid cream can help, such as hydrocortisone 1% cream or ointment, and is quite safe to use for a short period of time. You may find that if the skin is thick, for example on the palm of your hand, a stronger steroid cream is needed, such as betamethasone 0.025% or 0.1% cream. If the skin is cracked and weeping, it's likely to be infected, and an antibiotic cream will be helpful.

! If a steroid cream makes a rash worse, stop using it – you've probably got the diagnosis wrong! Steroid cream on its own will make fungal and bacterial infections much worse.

All steroid creams should be used as sparingly as possible, twice a day. Don't use anything stronger than hydrocortisone

Contact Irritation

Many tropical plants cause blistering or itching on contact. Members of the poison ivy family, includes mango trees and cashew trees, are notorious for producing skin irritation and inflammation. In some of the Pacific islands, beware of painful stinging nettles If you're walking through heavily vegetated areas, you may brush against one of these plants or their fruit, although if a rash appears, it can be hard to identify the cause.

Contact with some little critters can produce skin irritation. Blister beetles are found worldwide, especially in warm, dry climates. They're about an inch long, with slender bodies encased in shiny green or blue wing cases. If you touch one or one gets crushed on your skin (or blown into your eye), it causes a burning sensation like a nettle sting and later a blister. Calamine cream can help soothe the irritation, which usually clears up in a matter of hours. Cantharidin, the irritant substance produced by the beetles, was used as a medicine for over 2000 years to treat various ailments, including bladder troubles, warts and impotence. It's extremely poisonous if taken internally.

Fuzzy caterpillars are best avoided as they can cause an irritant rash with swelling and blistering. If you do get stung, try to remove all hairs by using a piece of sticky tape. Ice may help to soothe the irritation. If the hairs get in your eyes, they can cause conjunctivitis.

1% on the face or genital area. If you're using these creams for the first time, discuss it with a doctor or pharmacist beforehand, if possible.

SKIN INFESTATIONS

As a general rule, the standard of accommodation is pretty high in most countries in the region, and you're unlikely to be at risk of any of skin infestations unless perhaps you stay over in a village leaf hut when you're in a rural area.

Scabies

Scabies is common worldwide, and is associated with poor living standards. It's caused by a tiny mite which is passed by intimate contact with an affected person. Scabies infestation causes intense itching that can persist even when the mites themselves have gone. Secondary infection following scratching is very common. Scabies mites are not known to transmit any diseases.

Lice

Lice can infest various areas of the body, including scalp, body and pubic areas (crab louse). They cause itching due to bites. You may not see the lice themselves, as they're transparent, but they lay eggs that look like white grains attached to hairs. Lice are passed by close contact between people (sexual intercourse for pubic lice) and via infected bedding or clothing.

Bedbugs

Bedbugs are 3mm by 4mm oval insects that live in mattresses, cracks in the walls etc, but not on you. They merely visit you when it's dark for a meal. Bites, which can be itchy, are usually in a line of two or three on your face, arms, buttocks or ankles, anything accessible. Use an insecticide in your room or, better still, find another place to stay. There's been much debate about whether bedbugs can transmit HIV, as in theory at least it's a possibility, but there is no evidence to suggest they do.

Fleas

Neither human nor animal fleas can live on you but they do like to visit for a meal. You may notice itchy bites, usually in groups around the ankles or at the margin of clothing, and secondary infection is common. Kill the fleas with an insecticide and wash yourself and your clothes. Find another hotel if you can. Although fleas are widespread, they very rarely cause disease.

Treatment

You can soothe itching from bites with calamine cream applied to your skin, or take an antihistamine tablet. Scabies and head lice infestations can be treated with an insecticide lotion, such as malathion or permethrin lotion (preferably), usually available without prescription. For scabies, you need to cover your whole body apart from your head (except in young children) and leave it ideally for 24 hours, but overnight treatment (10 to 12 hours) is probably adequate.

With scabies, you need to wash all your clothes and anything you've been sleeping in (such as your sleeping bag and liner) to prevent reinfection. Anybody who has shared a bed with you will also need to be treated.

To treat head lice, apply the lotion to your head and leave for it for 12 hours before washing off. Alternatively, use any hair conditioner and get a (good) friend to comb through your hair – the lice just slip off. You'll need to repeat this every three days or so for two weeks after the last louse spotted. Treat anyone you share a bed with as well. The empty egg cases can stick around after the lice themselves have gone.

Treat body lice by getting rid of them: wash all bedding and clothing in hot water (kills the lice). Treatment of pubic lice is covered in the HIV/AIDS & Sexual Health chapter later in this guide.

DISEASES CAUSING RASHES

Skin rashes can occur as part of a more generalised disease. It's usually obvious, because you have a fever and other symptoms such as sore throat or nausea and vomiting in addition to the skin rash. Some diseases that are associated with a skin rash include:

- the 'childhood' illnesses (which can occur at any age if you haven't had them before): measles, rubella and chicken pox
- glandular fever and other viral infections (p143)
- food poisoning (p111) or allergies
- dengue fever (p122)
- tick-transmitted fevers (p327)
- meningococcal meningitis (p192)
- worm infestations of the gut (p145)

CREEPING ERUPTION

Also called cutaneous larva migrans or the geography worm, this rash is caused by the larvae of various worms, usually the dog or cat hookworm, which are passed in their faeces. It occurs worldwide, but it's much more common in hot, humid environments, which encourage development of the larvae. You're at risk anywhere contaminated with dog and cat faeces, usually by walking barefoot or sitting on sandy beaches.

You can get mild itching and a rash when the larvae first enter your skin, but the real fun begins when they start to migrate a few days later. They produce intensely itchy red tracks that advance slowly day by day. They're desperately hoping you're a cat or dog, as they can't live in humans and will die after a few weeks.

You could just wait for them to die naturally, but you're probably not going to want to leave it that long. Treatment is by freezing the head of the track with ethyl chloride spray or with anti-worm medicine (such as thiabendazole directly on the track or albendazole tablets by mouth). As for any skin condition in the tropics, look out for secondary infection.

A similar rash can be caused by intestinal worms, but they tend to be much speedier.

EARS, EYES & TEETH

Problems in these areas are relatively common when you're travelling, and can make life uncomfortable.

EARS

Apart from sunburnt ears, the most common ear problems in travellers are earache when flying (see the On the Move chapter for more details), swimmer's ear and ear infection after a cold.

EARACHE

The most common cause of earache is fluid build-up behind the eardrum during or just after a cold. This will respond to simple painkillers and doesn't need antibiotic treatment.

Sometimes earache is due to infection, either in the outer ear (the bit you can stick your finger into) or in the middle ear (the bit behind the eardrum). Try pulling on your ear lobe – if the pain increases, it's a problem in the outer ear (see Swimmer's Ear); if not, it's a middle ear problem (see Ear Infection).

Earache in both ears is unlikely to be due to infection. It's more likely to be due to blockage by mucus, and it may respond to decongestants (such as pseudoephedrine) or antihistamines.

Earache sometimes isn't to do with your ears. Problems outside the ear – such as in the jaw, throat or teeth – can sometimes cause earache and may be the reason why treatments for ear problems don't help your symptoms.

SWIMMER'S EAR

This outer ear infection is very common in swimmers, and in hot, humid conditions generally, and is sometimes called 'tropical ear'. Swimmer's ear is very itchy, and you may notice a discharge, as well as earache. If it's very painful, it may indicate that you have a boil in the ear canal.

Simple painkillers will help relieve the discomfort. Warmth also helps – you could try putting a water bottle filled with warm water and wrapped in a towel against your ear. You could also try aluminium acetate eardrops (which help toughen the skin of the ear canal) or antibiotic eardrops. These usually contain an antibiotic as well as a steroid and, often, an antifungal too (such as neomycin with hydrocortisone and polymyxin B sulphate). Note that antibiotic eardrops should not be used for longer than a week because long term use can lead to secondary fungal infection.

To give the infection a chance to get better, make sure you don't get water in your ear for at least two weeks; use earplugs if you're washing your hair, taking a shower or swimming, and avoid swimming underwater.

Allergic reactions, for example to eardrops or swimming pool water, can also cause itching. If so, try to keep your ears dry and think about stopping the eardrops.

If your symptoms haven't settled in a week, see a doctor, as you may need a change of antibiotic or treatment to clean out your ear canal.

It's tempting, but avoid cleaning your ears out with the corner of a towel, a cotton bud or anything else, as this makes infection much more likely.

EAR INFECTION

Typically, you get this middle ear infection during or just after a cold. It starts as a blocked feeling in the ear and progresses to pain, often with a fever. Later, you may notice a discharge from the ear (for example on your pillow) if your eardrum bursts, followed by relief from the pain.

If it doesn't start to get better in 48 hours, see a doctor, as you'll probably need a course of antibiotics (usually amoxycillin). In the meantime, simple painkillers will help the discomfort and to bring any fever down. Warmth against your ear may help. You should avoid putting eardrops or getting water in your ear in case your eardrum has burst (see the On the Move chapter for more details).

DEAFNESS WITHOUT PAIN

This is usually due to wax. Don't attempt to poke anything in your ear, as this can make infection more likely. Try wax-dissolving eardrops (such as Cerumol) or warm almond or olive oil. If this doesn't work, your ears may need to be syringed out.

EYES

This section was compiled by Graeme Johnson, an ophthalmic surgeon based in Sydney, Australia.

CONTACT LENS WEARERS

Maintaining your usual hygiene standards can be difficult, especially if you're roughing it. If necessary, you can use boiled and cooled water in place of your usual cleansers. Take extra care to wash your hands with soap and water before handling the lenses.

If your eye becomes red or irritated, remove the lens, clean and sterilise it and leave it out until your eye is better. Bathing your eye in clean salty water may help. If your eye hasn't improved after 48 hours, you should seek medical advice, as you may have an infection.

DRY, ITCHY EYES

Air conditioning, especially in aircraft, can exacerbate dry eyes and allergic eye conditions. Take lubricant drops with you (available without prescription from pharmacies) and use them frequently. Note that anti-allergy drops containing a decongestant ingredient shouldn't be used more than every few days – these are eyedrops that usually claim on the packet to make red, tired eyes look white.

Eye Wash

If you've got an eye bath, this is obviously designed for the purpose, but good substitutes include any small container or glass, or an egg cup. If you have a ready-made saline (salt) solution, you can use that; or you can make up your own by dissolving a level teaspoon of salt in about 600ml (a pint) of boiled and cooled water or by adding a pinch of salt to a cup of water.

Fill the eye bath or container, bend your head over it with your eye open and blink rapidly in the water. You could get someone to pour the water into your eye if you prefer, but you'll get pretty wet. Alternatively, get someone to soak a tissue or a clean cloth in the water and squeeze it into your eye from a height of a few inches while you are lying down.

SOMETHING IN THE EYE

Dust, particles of sand and insects can get blown into your eyes. Try washing it out, or, if the particle can be seen on the white of your eye or under the upper eyelid (turn the eyelid over a match or a small key), it can be gently removed with the corner of a tissue or (even more gently) a cotton bud. The clear central part of the eye is too sensitive for you to be able to do this. If you can't wash the particle away, see a doctor, who may be able to remove it after anaesthetising the eye.

RED, STICKY EYE

If your eye is red and sticky, and you've got gunk in the corner of it, you've probably got an infection (conjunctivitis). Conjunctivitis is quite common, especially in children, and can be caused by touching your eyes with dirty hands or swimming without goggles in unclean or polluted water.

You know you've got conjunctivitis if your eye feels irritated, as though there is something stuck in it, and it looks red and bloodshot. You get sticky yellow pus in the corner of your eye, which may be gummed shut when you wake up in the morning. You may find bright light difficult to tolerate.

Conjunctivitis can be due to a bacterial or viral infection. Bacterial conjunctivitis usually quickly affects both eyes, whereas viral conjunctivitis is more likely to affect one eye only, and you don't get such a copious discharge. Viral conjunctivitis often comes with flu or a cold.

Treatment

Bathe your eye frequently in clean (boiled and cooled) plain or salty water. Try not to touch or rub your eye, as this makes the infection more likely to spread to your other eye.

! *If the redness doesn't clear up in a couple of days or you've got ready access to medical care, see a doctor, as you will probably need a course of antibiotic eyedrops or ointment.*

A common and effective antibiotic for eye infections is chloramphenicol (used as eyedrops or ointment); alternatively, sulphonamides tend to be more generally available. Start by putting one drop in every two hours, reducing this as the redness and irritation improve. If you've got an ointment as well, apply the ointment at night before you go to sleep. If you've got ointment alone, apply it three to four times daily.

Ointment should be put directly into the eye, as follows: hold out the lower eyelid and squeeze about 1cm of cream into the pouch made behind the lid, then close the eye on it.

Bacterial conjunctivitis usually improves (ie the redness clears up) in two to three days, but you need to continue using the drops or ointment for three more days to make sure. If you don't notice any improvement within 48 hours of using the antibiotic, it may be that the cause is not bacterial. Viral conjunctivitis won't respond to antibiotics – it will clear up on its own, although it may take a week or two.

! *As a rule, you should avoid using eyedrops containing a combination of an antibiotic and steroids (the names of these usually end in '-sone' like betamethasone), as this can sometimes cause a serious problem if the infection is not bacterial.*

Trachoma

This type of conjunctivitis, spread by flies, is most common in dry, rural areas of Australia and many of the Pacific islands. Untreated and repeated infection results in serious damage to the eyes, and it's a major cause of blindness worldwide. Before you get too alarmed, it's not a big risk for you as a traveller in the region. Effective treatment is available, with antibiotic eyedrops (chlortetracycline) or tablets.

HAEMORRHAGE

Another cause of red eye is a haemorrhage on the surface of the eye, on the white of the eye. It can look fairly spectacular, but if your sight is unaffected and you don't have any pain, there's nothing to worry about. You don't need any specific treatment and it will clear up in a week or so.

STYE

If you develop a painful red lump on the edge of your eyelid, it's probably a stye. This is a bit like a pimple anywhere else. It usually clears up in a couple of days without any special treatment. Try putting a clean cloth soaked in clean hot water (not scalding) on your closed eyelid, and do this several times a day.

If it doesn't go away, it might be something called a chalazion. This is a blocked and infected gland in the eyelid, and you'll need to see a doctor about it.

BLACK EYE

If you receive a blow to the eye, you may get a black eye. This is due to bruising around and behind the eye, usually with swelling of the eyelids, but your sight is not usually affected (unless your eyelids are so swollen, you can't open them, of course). If your sight is not normal, then you need to get medical advice as soon as possible. Minimise the bruising by putting an ice pack (or anything cold, including snow) on your closed eye.

OTHER EYE INJURIES

You can get a scratch on the eye if the branch of a bush or tree whips back in your face. You'll know because it's painful immediately, which may become worse after an hour or two. If you put a pad on the eye, this makes it more comfortable, although if you're trying to walk on rough ground, this is not easy with one eye! Keep the pad on for a few hours or even a couple of days if the pain persists, although you might find it's more trouble than it's worth.

If you've got a tube of antibiotic eye ointment (such as chloramphenicol), you could use that. If the abrasion is not too deep, it should heal in one or two days.

A blow to the eye can cause bleeding inside the eye, which your travel companion may see as a fluid level of blood in the iris (the coloured part of the eye). This is a potentially dangerous situation – seek medical help urgently; in the meantime, rest in bed with the eye covered.

LOSS OF VISION

!*If you lose your sight, partially or totally in one or both eyes, you need to seek medical help urgently.*

If you suddenly lose your sight (from blurring to total loss) without any pain, it could be due to a haemorrhage inside the

Signs of Serious Eye Problems

If you experience any of the following symptoms, you should seek medical advice urgently:

- any blurred vision or loss of vision that can't be improved by blinking or washing your eye
- sudden loss of vision
- painful eye, especially if it is also unusually sensitive to light
- double vision
- eye injury followed by loss of vision or blood in the eye

Migraine

Bear in mind that migraine headaches can be associated with flashing lights or other eye symptoms such as tunnel vision. The visual symptoms usually last about 20 minutes, and may or may not be followed by a headache. If you have had it before, you will know what it is, but it can be frightening the first time you experience it.

All sorts of factors can trigger migraines when you're travelling: tiredness, movement, stress and sunlight. Try taking simple painkillers as early as possible to prevent the attack worsening. Natural remedies like feverfew can be helpful (although you will need to have a supply with you).

eye or detachment of the retina (the back of the eye). You may notice a curtain obstructing part of the vision in one eye, which may be preceded by seeing lightning flashes on one side of the vision. Retinal detachment can also follow injury.

If you have blurring or loss of vision associated with intolerance of light and severe aching pain in the eye, it could be due to inflammation inside the eye (iritis) or glaucoma (where the pressure inside the eye is abnormally high). Glaucoma is more likely to occur in older people. Both these conditions need urgent medical attention.

Partial loss of vision associated with giddiness (especially if you experience weakness in an arm or leg) is likely to be a stroke – a blockage of the blood vessels in the brain. This is more likely to occur in older people.

TEETH

UK-based dentist Iain Corran gives you the complete low-down on staying out of the dentist's chair while you're away.

Dental problems are common when you're travelling. Your diet often consists of lots of sugary drinks (soft drinks, fruit juices etc), and practical difficulties can mean that you take a break from your usual dental hygiene routine just when it's needed most.

PREVENTION

The two main preventable causes of dental problems are tooth decay and gum disease, which can lead to cavities, sensitive teeth and bleeding from your gums. Keep your teeth healthy while you are on the road with a few basic precautions:

▶ avoid sugary foods and drinks, especially carbonated soft drinks; try to get into the habit of rinsing your mouth out with clean water after you eat

▶ keep your mouth moist in dry climates (eg by chewing sugar-free gum), as saliva neutralises the tooth-decaying acid formed by bacteria in the mouth

▶ brush your teeth, ideally with a fluoride toothpaste, at least once a day; if you run out, try using a small amount of salt instead on a moist brush

▶ use dental floss or tape (toothpicks are a widely available substitute if you run out); floss can come in handy for a multitude of minor repairs, so is well worth tucking into your pack

If you're on a long trip, remember to pack a spare toothbrush! However, if you can't get a replacement, you can use your finger as a toothbrush, possibly with a small piece of cloth around it.

! *Where drinking water is suspect, remember to use bottled, boiled or purified water for brushing or flossing your teeth.*

TOOTHACHE

There are lots of causes of this most unpleasant of symptoms: an injury to a tooth, a filling breaking or falling out, or tooth decay, leading to a tooth abscess.

Unless your toothache settles quickly, you're going to need to find a dentist or doctor. In the meantime, take painkillers (such as co-codamol) regularly. Don't put aspirin directly on a painful tooth, as this can cause a sore patch on the gum. If you have oil of cloves with you, this can help relieve the pain when applied to the offending tooth on a clean cotton bud, although applying it may be uncomfortable. Wash your mouth out regularly (after meals) with warm salty water. Try to avoid sugary foods, hard foods and hot and cold foods. It goes without saying that you should avoid biting on the tooth.

If the pain is severe and unrelieved, perhaps with a bad taste in your mouth, you've probably got a tooth abscess, and you may need to have the tooth extracted eventually, although root treatment may save the tooth (but you'll need a good dentist). Seek medical or dental help urgently, but if you're in a remote area away from help, start taking a course of antibiotics, for example amoxycillin, erythromycin or metronidazole, or whatever you have with you (so long as you're not allergic to it – see the Medicines appendix for more guidance).

! If your face becomes swollen or you develop a fever, you must seek medical help as soon as possible, as it means that the infection is spreading. In the meantime, drink plenty of fluids and start a course of antibiotics.

Another cause of pain in the mouth is a gum abscess, which can occur around a partially erupted wisdom tooth or when the gum has receded around a tooth, but hopefully both of these will have been picked up by your dentist before you left. Treatment is the same as for a tooth abscess.

BROKEN OR LOST FILLINGS

If you bite on something hard, you may break a filling: you may feel a sudden pain, a gap where the filling was, and pieces of the filling in your mouth. As an immediate measure, rinse your mouth out with some warm salty water (add a couple of teaspoons of salt to a glass of boiled and cooled water) to clear any debris from your mouth.

If you have some temporary filling material (from your dentist or a commercial kit), you can use it to plug the hole up, or you can use a piece of sugar-free chewing gum. It's important to plug it up so that the hole doesn't get filled with food, which can cause more problems. You'll need to get dental treatment for a permanent filling as soon as possible. If you're on a short trip, and it's just a small surface filling, it could wait for a week or so until you get back.

If the filling has cracked rather than fallen out, you may notice that it's sensitive to hot/cold/sugary foods and drinks. A cracked filling can lead to toothache, so try to get a permanent filling placed in the tooth as soon as is convenient.

As a general rule, avoid sugary, hot and cold foods in all these situations.

CHIPPED TEETH

This can be caused by a fall, or a direct blow to the tooth. It can cause toothache immediately or after a delay, and an abscess can develop. You need to seek treatment as soon as possible as you may need root canal treatment or, possibly, extraction of the tooth. In the meantime, take painkillers if necessary.

CROWNS & VENEERS

If a crown comes out, stick it back in and then find a dentist to glue it back on. If a crown breaks (usually front porcelain ones), it's unlikely that you'll be able to get a new one made, but you should be able to find a dentist to put a temporary crown on, which should last you till you get home.

If a veneer cracks, chips or breaks off, you probably don't need to get dental treatment until you get home, as it's not likely to cause any damage to the tooth if it is not replaced in the short term. A rough edge may initially cause some irritation.

TOOTH KNOCKED OUT

If you can find the tooth, wash it in milk (better) or clean water and, if practical, place it back in the socket to reimplant it. Get dental help as soon as possible. If it's in a child, remember that milk teeth won't need to be replaced.

If it is not practical to attempt to reimplant the tooth (for example if it's chipped or broken or you've got other injuries in your mouth), keep the tooth in milk, and try to get a doctor/dentist to attempt to reimplant it. Reimplantation may not be successful, but it is worth trying.

! *If more than two hours have passed between the tooth being knocked out and reimplantation, the chance of success is slim.*

If you are left with an open socket, rinse your mouth out with warm salty water. Don't rinse too vigorously, as this may dislodge the clot forming in the socket. Avoid strenuous exercise for a few hours.

If there is persistent bleeding from the socket, place a clean piece of cloth across the top of the socket and bite onto it for 20 to 30 minutes. If bleeding persists, seek expert advice as soon as possible, as you may need stitches.

If the socket becomes painful and infected, get medical advice as soon as possible for specialist treatment and a course of antibiotics.

HIV/AIDS & SEXUAL HEALTH ──

For a general discussion about sex and travel, including how to avoid sexually transmitted infections (STIs), see the section on Sex & Travel in the Staying Healthy chapter earlier in this book.

HIV/AIDS ──────────────────────

Acquired immunodeficiency syndrome (AIDS, or SIDA in French) describes the collection of diseases that result from suppression of the body's immune system by infection with the human immunodeficiency virus (HIV). HIV targets cells in the blood that are an important part of your immune system, which protects you from infections. At present, although there are effective (but toxic) treatments that can keep AIDS at bay for a period of time, there is no known cure.

! AIDS is a worldwide problem, and travellers are generally more at risk of acquiring HIV than people who don't travel.

HIV INFECTION & AIDS
There aren't any immediate signs of infection, although you may get a glandular-fever-like illness a few weeks after infection, with fever, aches and pains, a skin rash and swollen glands. After this you may have no more symptoms for 10 years or more, although this time of being HIV-positive is very variable. This is the danger period in terms of passing the infection to others, because you're healthy and you may not realise that you've got HIV. Eventually, your immune system starts to show signs of strain, and the syndrome of AIDS starts.

! A blood test can indicate if you're infected or not, but it won't show positive for about three months after you may have been exposed to HIV.

HIV & YOU

Wherever you are, you can put yourself at risk of HIV infection if you:

▸ have sexual intercourse with an infected person (men with women or men with men)
▸ share needles with HIV-infected injecting drug users
▸ receive an infected blood transfusion or injection, or have a medical or dental procedure with inadequately sterilised equipment

Other potential risk situations to be aware of include tattooing, ear and body piercing, and using cut-throat razors.

MINIMISING YOUR RISKS

Wherever you go, it's sensible to take some basic common-sense precautions.

Safer Sex

Using a latex condom (*preservatif* in French) is extremely effective at preventing transmission of HIV (and other STIs). Condoms are widely available from pharmacies, vending machines and other retail outlets in Australia and New Zealand. In the Pacific islands, condoms are generally available from pharmacies in the main centres, but are unlikely to

What are the Risks?

The risk of acquiring HIV per exposure varies enormously, from one in 20 to one in 1000 for different types of sexual intercourse, one in 20 for needle sharing, to near certainty for a contaminated blood transfusion. In general, it's twice as easy to transmit HIV from men to women than the other way round, and receptive anal intercourse is especially risky. Many other factors can affect the risk, including the stage of infection (early and late are the most risky), the strain of HIV and whether you have another STI. Having another STI increases your risk of getting HIV, and if you are already infected, it increases the chance of you passing it on.

be available in more remote islands. You may have trouble tracking them down in some places (the Solomon islands, for example) as there's often considerable church opposition to their use and they tend only to be given to married couples.

Take a supply of condoms with you if you're going to the Pacific islands. Extra-strong condoms are unlikely to be available, so if you think you'll need these, take some with you. The heat can cause rubber to perish, so check your condom carefully before use, especially if you've been carrying it around in your pack for a while. If you're buying condoms locally in the Pacific islands, check expiry dates and choose ones that haven't been left lying around in the sun. Use only water-based lubricants, as petroleum or oil-based lubricants can damage rubber.

! You may feel awkward about discussing condoms because of cultural differences or a worry that you might be seen as 'forward' or as having planned it, but it's a small price to pay for peace of mind and your good health.

Your local health centre, any travel health clinic and any sexual health clinic will be able to provide you with more information on safer sex or, if you have access to the web, you could check out the UCSF safer sex site (www.safersex.org) for more info.

Other Precautions

HIV/AIDS is not only transmitted through intimate contact. It's obviously a good idea to take care to avoid accidents and injury that might mean you would need surgery or a blood transfusion. Admittedly, infection risks from blood are very low in most Pacific nations, and in Australia and New Zealand the risk is no higher than in any other developed country.

! Never share needles with other injecting drug users, as injecting drug users are a traditionally high risk group for HIV/AIDS and other infections.

Fact or Fiction?

It can be confusing trying to separate fact from fiction with HIV, but here's the current wisdom on it:

- a vaccine against HIV is looking promising, but there's a long way to go, so don't throw away those condoms just yet
- worldwide, most HIV infections are acquired through heterosexual sex
- the more sexual partners you have, the more at risk you are for HIV/AIDS
- you can be perfectly healthy for 10 years or more after infection before any signs of the disease show up
- you can't tell by looking at a person if they are infected or not
- HIV can be transmitted through infected blood transfusions
- HIV is not thought to be transmitted by saliva
- acupuncture, tattooing, ear and body piercing, injections and other medical and dental procedures with unsterilised equipment can all transmit HIV infection
- HIV is a sensitive little virus and needs pretty intimate contact to be transmitted – it's not transmitted by hugging, social kissing, using the same toilet seat or sharing a cup
- it's not passed in swimming pools
- insects like bedbugs and mosquitoes do not transmit HIV

IF YOU'RE WORRIED

Nobody's a saint, especially on holiday. If you are worried you may have put yourself at risk of HIV infection:

▶ don't sit and brood on it – phone an AIDS helpline as soon as possible to talk about your concerns; either wait till you get home or, if you're on a long trip, phone a local number
▶ protect any subsequent sexual partners by always using a condom
▶ make an appointment with your doctor or a sexual health clinic when you get back to discuss what to do next

In Australia, you could try some of the following telephone helplines, depending on which state you are in, or check out the Australian Federation of AIDS Organisations web site (www.afao.org.au), which has heaps of useful information, including listings of sexual health clinics nationwide:

- AIDS Country Line SA ☎ 1800 888 559
- AIDS Line Tasmania ☎ 1800 005 900
- AIDS, Hepatitis & Sexual Health Line (Victoria) ☎ 03-9347 6099 or 1800 133 392 (toll free within Australia)
- NSW Infoline ☎ 02-9332 4000 or 1800 415 600 (toll free)
- WA Helpline ☎ 08-9429 9933 or 1800 199 287 (toll free)

In New Zealand, try contacting:

- AIDS Hotline ☎ 0800-802-437 (toll free within New Zealand)

In the Pacific islands, AIDS helplines are few and far between, but there's one in Guam:

- AIDS Hotline (Guam) ☎ 734-2437

Remember that an HIV test won't be able to tell you either way for about three months after the risk situation.

You may have heard about a 'morning after' treatment for HIV, called post-exposure prophylaxis. It's a cocktail of anti-viral drugs that, in theory, stops HIV infection getting a hold after you've been exposed to it. Although it may be of value for health workers who accidentally get jabbed by contaminated needles, its use after sexual exposure is very controversial. It's not guaranteed to work, and there are enormous practical problems associated with its use – it's extremely expensive, several different drugs have to be taken every day for at least six weeks and it can cause unpleasant side effects. For most travellers this isn't an option, and you shouldn't rely on it.

HIV/AIDS IN AUSTRALIA, NEW ZEALAND & THE PACIFIC

No country in the world is unaffected by the HIV/AIDS epidemic, but Australia, New Zealand and the Pacific island nations have generally been less severely affected than some other parts of the world.

Pacific Islands

HIV/AIDS occurs in the Pacific islands but, with the exception of Papua New Guinea, spread has so far been minimal. However, it's likely to increase in future as social and cultural changes evolve (for example, in some cultures there is less sanction against pre-marital sex than there used to be). A concomitant rise in tourism and international travel is likely to contribute to the problem.

HIV & STIs in Papua New Guinea

PNG is said to have some of the highest ratest of STIs in the world. Gonorrhoea, chlamydia, syphilis and herpes are common and donovanosis and trichomoniasis are also prevalent in some areas. Be aware that there is a large sex worker industry in PNG, which may not be obvious to you as a traveller. For example, many women attend bars and discos to meet expats and travellers and exchange sex for money and drinks. Recent studies have shown an HIV prevalence of approximately 15% in sex workers in Port Moresby.

Although data are very limited it seems likely that unless fairly drastic action is taken soon Papua New Guinea is on the brink of an HIV/AIDS epidemic of significant proportions. As in Africa, HIV infection is mainly passed by men having sex with women, as well as from mother to child in pregnancy. There is a complex interaction of risk factors, which include changing social and economic factors, increasing migration of the population (presenting greater opportunities for casual sexual encounters) and deterioration of the limited health services available.

The prevention and treatment of STIs and HIV/AIDS in PNG is a complex and problematic issue, attracting much pessimism. However, significant progress in prevention and care of HIV and STIs is being made. A National AIDS Council was recently set up to help tackle the problem and a recently completed AusAID NGO project has provided training for many health workers in the area of STIs and HIV.

Australia & New Zealand

In Australia and New Zealand, HIV infection has mainly been through sex between men. Because of effective public education campaigns, targeting of at-risk groups and the adoption of safer sexual practices, the incidence of HIV infection has declined considerably since the 1980s. However, the proximity of countries with relatively high levels of infection to the north and the popularity of travel among Australians and New Zealanders makes these countries vulnerable to renewed spread of HIV infection. Because of this, there are federal and state campaigns aimed at informing travellers about HIV/AIDS and encouraging condom use.

SEXUALLY TRANSMITTED INFECTIONS

There's a long history of an association between travel and STIs. Most famously, Christopher Columbus and his crew have been accused of initiating an epidemic of syphilis that spread through Europe in the 16th century. The two world wars were both associated with epidemics of STIs and, more recently, the spread of HIV through Africa can be directly related to long-distance truck routes. When Europeans came onto the scene in the south Pacific, they didn't just bring a different cultural viewpoint with them, they brought STIs too.

Although some of the traditional STIs like syphilis and gonorrhoea have faded from the picture somewhat in developed countries like Australia and New Zealand (at least among non-indigenous people), they are generally on the increase in many Pacific island nations as migration, urbanisation, poverty, travel and changing cultural values result in greater opportunities for risky sexual behaviour.

DIAGNOSIS & TREATMENT

Some STIs cause no symptoms or only mild symptoms that may go unnoticed; sometimes fertility problems are the first sign you have an infection. If STIs do cause symptoms, these are usually an abnormal vaginal or penile discharge, pain or irritation during intercourse or when you urinate, and any blisters, lumps, itches, rashes or other irritation on or around your genitals or anus.

! *Because STIs can go unnoticed, it's best to get a checkup when you get home if you had unprotected intercourse while you were away.*

If you notice any symptoms, it's best to get expert help as soon as possible. You can't tell accurately from your symptoms what infection you're likely to have, and you can often have more than one STI at the same time. Taking the wrong treatment or inadequate treatment leaves you at risk of future complications like infertility, or you may think you're cured when you're not. Try to find a reputable doctor or STI clinic for a thorough examination and laboratory tests, and see your doctor when you get back so they can confirm that the infection is gone and there are no other problems. If you think you may have an STI:

- ▶ seek medical advice for investigation and treatment
- ▶ self-medication is best avoided, as it can be disastrous
- ▶ your partner will need treatment too
- ▶ avoid intercourse (assuming you still feel like having sex) until you have finished a course of treatment
- ▶ play fair and don't spread it around

Many STIs (including gonorrhoea and syphilis) can be simply and effectively treated with antibiotics if they're caught early. However, others (including chlamydia and gonorrhoea) can make you seriously ill and may have long-term effects, especially if they are not treated early. These include infertility, liver disease (hepatitis) and an increased risk of cervical cancer (genital warts).

! *Note that hepatitis B is the only sexually transmitted infection for which there is an effective vaccine (see p30) – discuss with your doctor.*

Getting Medical Advice on STIs

STI clinics are available in most hospitals in large towns in Australia and New Zealand or you can go to a family planning clinic or any general practitioner. There are STI clinics in some major centres in the Pacific islands, but they are generally called by the bad old names like VD clinic or venereodermatology clinic, and, for local people, there is still significant stigma attached to being seen visiting one. The service you get is unlikely to be quite as caring and understanding as you might expect back home, so be prepared. Other options are to visit a private practitioner or a family planning clinic. Local people tend to try traditional medicines first or to self-medicate with remedies bought from pharmacies, sometimes with disastrous results. Only if this doesn't work are they likely to visit a doctor or clinic. As they are quite likely to receive a strict admonishment not to come back in addition to their course of antibiotics, it's hard to blame them.

In the following sections we've summarised a few details about some of the STIs you may be at risk of acquiring. We haven't included specific antibiotic treatments because the sensitivity of infections to antibiotics varies from region to region and with time, and it's near impossible to diagnose STIs without a laboratory test. In any event, you always have time to find medical help.

Trichomoniasis is another STI that women may be at risk for – see p215.

! *Remember that some less obvious infections can be transmitted through sexual intercourse, including viral hepatitis (p133), pubic lice (p163), scabies (p163) and diarrhoea (p107).*

GONORRHOEA

Caused by a bacteria, this STI occurs worldwide, affecting hundreds of millions of people. It usually causes a penile or vaginal discharge and burning on urination (or a sore throat if you've been having oral sex). It can lead to serious complications like pelvic inflammatory disease and infertility if it's not treated promptly. Gonorrhoea used to be effectively treated with high-dose penicillin, but multiple antibiotic resistance is a major problem worldwide, and treatment is now usually with one of the newer antibiotics. You'll need a couple of checkups to make sure it has gone completely.

SYPHILIS

This historic disease occurs in three stages, and can cause serious complications in a proportion of sufferers if it's not treated early. Initially, it causes a painless ulcer (on your genitals, rectum or throat) and a rash. Later you may get a feverish illness with painful ulcers and rashes, and later still (up to 50 years) you can get problems involving major blood vessels or the brain. Diagnosis is by a blood test. Treatment needs to be administered and monitored by an expert, and usually involves multiple injections of penicillin.

CHLAMYDIA

Known as the silent STI because it often causes mild or no symptoms, this infection is extremely common worldwide. It

---

Condoms

What condoms will NOT protect you against:

- genital herpes
- genital warts
- pubic lice

Condoms WILL help protect against STIs transmitted through the exchange of body fluids, including:

- HIV
- hepatitis B and C
- gonorrhoea
- chlamydia
- syphilis

is also known as NSU, and if symptoms are present they're similar to gonorrhoea but milder. It's a major cause of pelvic inflammatory disease and infertility in women. Antibiotic treatment is effective at treating this condition.

GENITAL HERPES

This is a very common cause of genital ulceration. Herpes ulcers occur in clusters and are often very painful; they can recur. Genital herpes is caused by a similar virus to the one responsible for causing cold sores on your lips. Cold sores can be transmitted to the genitals by oral sex. Any genital ulcers make transmission of HIV more likely.

With genital herpes, the initial infection is usually the worst, and can last about three weeks. You can feel quite miserable with it, with a fever, aches and pains, and swollen glands. Once you have herpes, you are liable to have recurrences, but subsequent attacks are usually less severe, and you may recognise and be able to avoid triggers like stress or being run-down.

Treatment is with simple painkillers; bathe the ulcers in salty water or a mild antiseptic solution, or try applying a local anaesthetic jelly to the ulcers. Antiviral drugs (such as acyclovir 200mg five times daily for seven days) can help shorten the length of an attack and reduce the severity, but they are expensive and only moderately effective.

! It's best to avoid any sexual contact while you have an attack of herpes or if you notice a sore or ulcer on your genitals.

GENITAL WARTS

These are usually painless, and can appear on the vulva, vagina, penis or anus. Warts can be painted with an acid solution that makes them dry up and fall off, or you sometimes need to have them removed in hospital, where they can be frozen or burnt off. Occasionally, they may need to be surgically removed. They can recur; often there's no obvious trigger, although smoking and stress may be contributory factors.

Fortunately, genital warts usually disappear completely, but in women they are associated with cancerous changes in the cervix, so it's important to have regular cervical smear tests if you have been infected.

CHANCROID

This highly infectious STI occurs in tropical and subtropical areas, where it is the most common cause of genital ulcers. Worldwide, it's more common than syphilis. The ulcers are painful (and can get secondarily infected) and you often get swelling of the glands in the groin. It is much more common in men than in women, and it often occurs with syphilis. Antibiotics are effective against chancroid.

LYMPHOGRANULOMA VENERUM

This is caused by types of *Chlamydia* (see earlier in this section) and occurs worldwide, though it's uncommon in Australia, New Zealand and the Pacific. Symptoms are variable, but you may notice a blister or small painless ulcer or, more commonly, tender swelling of the lymph glands with fever and general aches and pains. Late problems, if it's not treated, include bladder and rectal problems and swelling of the genitals (genital elephantiasis). Antibiotic treatment is effective in the early stages.

DONOVANOSIS (GRANULOMA INGUINALE)

This STI is rare in most developed countries but high rates of infection exist in some developing countries, including Papua New Guinea. In the decades following the arrival of Europeans in New Guinea, serious outbreaks of donovanosis and gonorrhoea occurred. Donovanosis is a problem in aboriginal communities in Australia, and it is thought to have been introduced to PNG by labourers from northern Australia. Donovanosis is a chronic disease, causing genital ulcers that can spread to other areas of the body. Antibiotic treatment is effective, but may need to be prolonged over several weeks.

RARITIES

In this chapter we've listed (in alphabetical order) some infections you're generally going to be at very low risk of getting, except under special circumstances. If you think you might have one of these diseases, see a doctor.

BRUCELLOSIS

This infection, also known as undulant fever, occurs worldwide. It is transmitted by ingesting unpasteurised milk and dairy products or through contact with meat from infected animals, mainly cows, pigs and goats. Symptoms include headache, fever, chills, sweating and abdominal pain. The fever comes and goes, with night sweats and morning chills. Sometimes the illness comes on more gradually, with weakness and exhaustion being the main symptoms. Untreated, the infection can last months or even years. It's rarely fatal, and can be effectively treated with antibiotics. It's one more reason for avoiding unpasteurised milk on your travels.

CHOLERA

This bacterial disease is a rare cause of diarrhoea in travellers. It is transmitted via contaminated water and food, especially seafood, including crustaceans and shellfish (which get infected via sewage). Cholera is occasionally reported in some of the Pacific islands.

!The risk of most travellers acquiring cholera is extremely low, especially if you take some basic food and water precautions. There is a vaccine available but it is not usually recommended because it has very limited effectiveness.

Although in many cases cholera just causes a mild diarrhoea, about one in 10 sufferers get a severe form of the disease. In this form, the diarrhoea starts suddenly, and pours out of you. It's described as 'ricewater diarrhoea' because what comes out is watery and flecked with white mucus. Vomiting and muscle cramps are usual, but fever is rare. In the worst-case scenario, cholera causes a massive outpouring of fluid (up to 20L a day). Mild cholera is a self-limiting illness, meaning that it will end in about a week without any specific treatment.

Cholera can usually be treated effectively by fluid replacement, although some more severe cases may require antibiotic treatment (usually tetracyclines, although drug resistance is a growing problem.

If you think you may have cholera or you develop diarrhoea within five days of returning from an area where cholera occurs, seek medical help immediately; in the meantime, start fluid replacement therapy immediately.

FILARIASIS

Worldwide, this disease affects about 120 million people. It occurs in all the Pacific islands, and is caused by infection with parasitic worms that are transmitted via mosquito bites.

The long thread-like worms (filaria) cause damage to the lymph drainage system. Elephantiasis, painful swelling of the limbs and genitals, is a severe late consequence of the disease. (You may have seen or heard of male sufferers having to carry their enormously enlarged genitals in wheelbarrows – an image that is bound to stick in your mind.) Elephantiasis can affect the arms, legs, breasts or scrotum, and there is usually an associated thickening and wrinkling of the skin, which is supposed to resemble elephant skin, hence the name 'elephantiasis'.

However, not all infections lead to elephantiasis. There may be no symptoms at all with light infections, or you may get fever, painful swellings of the lymph glands (such as in your armpits, groin or elbows) and, for male travellers, swelling of the testes, with scrotal pain and tenderness. Symptoms usually develop about six months after infection.

Filariasis is extremely rare in travellers, as it takes prolonged (three to six months at least) and intense exposure to the parasite for infection to become established.

Infection can be diagnosed with a blood test, and effective drug treatments are available. There is no vaccine against lymphatic filariasis; the only prevention is to avoid mosquito bites.

HANSEN'S DISEASE (LEPROSY)

This ancient disease occurs in most parts of the world, but especially in the tropics, and you may see sufferers while on your travels. Because of the social stigma attached to the name 'leprosy', it's now officially known as Hansen's disease, after the person who first identified the causative organism in 1873. It's caused by a bacterium which attacks nerves. In the most severe form of the disease, feeling is deadened in the sufferer's fingers and toes, making them vulnerable to injury and infection. It's very hard to catch, and you won't get it from touching sufferers.

MENINGITIS

This is a general term for any infection of the lining of the brain and spinal cord. Many different infectious agents can cause meningitis, including bacteria and viruses. Viral meningitis usually settles without any treatment, whereas bacterial meningitis caused by meningococcal infection can rapidly cause death.

Meningococcal meningitis is spread by breathing droplets coughed or sneezed into the air by an infected person (often healthy carriers of the bacteria). Epidemics occur occasionally in different parts of the world, and are most common in poor, overcrowded areas. It can occur at any age, although young children are at particular risk.

Symptoms of meningitis include:

- fever and chills
- severe headache
- neck stiffness – bending your head forward is difficult and causes pain
- nausea and vomiting
- sensitivity to light – you prefer lying in a darkened room
- blotchy purple rash (may appear in meningococcal meningitis)

Meningococcal meningitis is an extremely serious disease that can cause death within a few hours of you first feeling unwell, so you should get medical help urgently if you have any of the symptoms listed. Treatment is with large doses of antibiotics (usually penicillin, cefotaxime or chloramphenicol) given intravenously.

If you've been in close contact with a sufferer, seek medical advice, as you can protect yourself from infection by taking antibiotics, usually rifampicin or ciprofloxacin (not suitable for children).

TUBERCULOSIS (TB)

Called consumption in the old days because people just wasted away with it, TB is making a comeback globally, for a variety of reasons, including the rise in HIV/AIDS, drug resistance and air travel. Papua New Guinea has the highest rate of infection in the Pacific islands.

TB is a bacterial disease. Only a proportion (15%) of people who become infected go on to develop the disease, as the TB bacteria can lie dormant for years. If your immunity is lowered for some reason, for example due to poor nutrition or another disease like HIV/AIDS, the disease can appear.

TB is transmitted by breathing in droplets expelled through coughing, talking or sneezing. Only people ill with pulmonary (lung) TB are infectious. Your risk of being infected increases the closer you are to the person and the longer you are exposed to them. You can also get a form of TB through drinking unpasteurised milk from an infected cow.

TB is rarely seen in short-term travellers, as you need close contact with a sufferer with active disease to catch it. It is a risk if you are planning to live or work closely with members of the local population or you are planning to stay for more than a few months in one of the Pacific islands.

There have been concerns about the risk of catching TB on a long-haul flight, as a result of some well publicised cases of passengers being infected during a flight. However, this is not thought to be related to the practice of recycling cabin air, but it is related to how close you are sitting next to a TB sufferer. There's not a great deal you can do about this (we can see it now: would you like a window seat? an aisle seat? a seat next to a TB sufferer?).

TB classically affects the lungs but it can affect almost any other part of the body, including your joints, bones, brain and gut. Pulmonary (lung) TB is the most common way in which TB shows itself in adults. Symptoms develop slowly, often over the course of several months, and include weight loss, fever, night sweats and cough with blood-stained spit. Diagnosis is by a laboratory test of your spit.

TB is not something you're going to be self-treating, so seek specialist advice if you think you may be infected. Treatment is with a combination of antibiotics over a prolonged period of time (six to eight months, but sometimes up to a year). Multidrug-resistant TB is common worldwide and is a major headache to treat.

VACCINE-PREVENTABLE INFECTIONS

Immunisation programs and higher living standards have made many previously common infections rare in developed countries, but you may be at more risk of them when you're travelling in less-developed countries where immunisation programs may be less comprehensive and levels of disease higher.

○ For details about immunisations, see the Immunisations section of the Before You Go chapter.

DIPHTHERIA

Vaccination against this serious bacterial disease is very effective, so you don't need to worry about it if you are up to date with your shots. Diphtheria occurs worldwide, but has been controlled by vaccination in most developed countries. It mainly affects children and causes a cold-like illness, which is associated with a severe sore throat. A thick white membrane forms at the back of the throat, which can suffocate you, but what makes this a really nasty disease is that the diphtheria bug produces a very powerful poison that can cause paralysis and affect the heart. Otherwise healthy people can carry the disease-causing microorganism in their throats, and it's transmitted by sneezing and coughing. It can also cause a skin ulcer known as a veldt sore, and vaccination protects against this form too. Treatment is with penicillin and a diphtheria antitoxin, if necessary.

MEASLES

Measles starts a bit like a cold, then appears to get worse, and a fever develops. At about the third or fourth day, a rash appears on the skin, starting on the face and moving down. The rash is red and raised. It starts to fade after about five days. You can get ear and chest infections with measles, and also diarrhoea. Occasionally, severe complications (affecting the brain) can occur, which is why you should seek medical advice if you think you may have measles. Although it's often thought of as a childhood illness, measles can occur in adults and tends to be much more severe when it does.

MUMPS

Mumps is a viral infection of the salivary glands. You feel generally unwell and you may notice swelling around the jaw, extending towards the ear and associated with pain (especially when eating). It usually resolves after about a week without any special treatment. There is a risk of infection affecting the testicles in adult men who get mumps, although not in children.

RUBELLA

Rubella (German measles) is generally a very mild illness, a bit like a mild cold, associated with a pink, non-raised rash that starts on the face and spreads downwards. However, it

Polio

As a result of successful immunisation programs, no new cases of this viral disease have been reported in the Pacific region for the last few years. You still need to be up to date with your polio immunisation to make sure that this serious disease doesn't make a come-back in the future. Polio is spread from person to person by coughing and sneezing, and through contaminated food and water. Although it mainly causes a flu-like illness and sometimes diarrhoea, paralysis of a limb or the respiratory muscles due to damage to nerves can develop in a proportion of sufferers, and can sometimes causing breathing difficulties and death.

can cause severe problems in unborn children, so it is extremely important to be immunised if you are a woman of child-bearing age.

TETANUS

You probably know that you have to be up to date with this vaccination, but do you know what you're being protected against? Spores of the tetanus bacterium are widespread in soil and some animal faeces, and occur worldwide. They can be introduced into your body through injury, for example through a puncture wound (even a very trivial one), a burn or an animal bite. The tetanus bacteria produce a toxin in your body that causes severe, painful muscular contractions and spasm leading to death through spasm of the respiratory muscles. It used to be known as 'lockjaw' because of the spasms of the jaw muscles. Tetanus needs specialist treatment in hospital.

Clean any wound immediately and thoroughly with soap and water or antiseptic and, if you haven't been vaccinated against tetanus within the last 10 years or the wound is particularly dirty, get medical advice on having a booster dose of the tetanus vaccination as soon as possible (you may need a booster even if your vaccination is up to date).

MENTAL WELLBEING

If you're jetting off to an exotic destination, you probably don't expect stress or other mind problems to be high on the travel health agenda. Then again, heat, unfamiliar surroundings and lifestyle, and perhaps a lack of home comforts can mean that your holiday falls short of the stress-free nirvana you anticipated.

TRAVELLERS STRESS

Everything that makes travelling good can also make it stressful. You have to cope with a different physical environment as well as a new lifestyle; your normal points of reference are absent, and you are cut off from your usual support network of family and friends. Unfamiliar social and cultural cues can make communication more difficult, even if you appear to speak the same language, making you feel alienated and alone.

Often the lead-up to the trip has been less than relaxing as you rush around trying to get things done before you leave, and you often have jet lag to contend with on top of this. And then you're expected to enjoy yourself ...

Unless you're on a short trip, you may find it helpful to factor in some time (and emotional space) for adjusting to your new situation. Remember:

- ▶ stress can make you less able to cope, with even minor difficulties and setbacks seeming like insurmountable hurdles
- ▶ you may feel frustrated and angry, taking your frustrations out on your travelling companions and other people you have to deal with
- ▶ stress can make you feel anxious or depressed, irritable, tired, unable to relax, and unable to sleep (although this is often due to external causes)
- ▶ because you don't feel 100%, you may think you are physically ill, especially as the physical manifestations of anxiety can easily be mistaken for illness – see Anxiety later in this chapter
- ▶ stress affects your immune system, making you more vulnerable to infections; being physically ill affects you emotionally, often making you feel low and less able to cope

▶ if you know you are sensitive to stress or you've had emotional problems before, you may find, at least in the short term, that travelling exacerbates your problems

Half the battle is recognising that the way you're feeling is because of stress rather than some worrisome tropical disease you've caught. An acute stress reaction is to be expected to some degree at the start of your travels and will probably ease by itself over the course of a few days, but you might want to activate some damage-control measures:

▶ take some time off to unwind: quit the tourist trail for a few days and do something completely different
▶ rest and try to catch up on any missed sleep (as a result of jet lag, overnight journeys, noisy hotel rooms etc)
▶ on the other hand, exercise is a great de-stresser, and worth a try if you've been stuck on trains or buses
▶ catch up on missed meals – stress is very energy-consuming
▶ try a de-stressing routine such as aromatherapy, massage, yoga, meditation, tai chi or just lying on a beach
▶ talk with fellow travellers: they may be going through the same experience
▶ herbal teas such as chamomile or the ubiquitous kava can have a calming effect on stretched nerves

Stress Effects

Stress is thought to play a significant part in some conditions; don't be surprised if you get the most severe headache you've ever had or the worst PMS of your life while you're away. Be prepared, and take plentiful supplies of your favourite remedies. Conditions thought to be affected by stress include:

■ tension headaches (by definition!)
■ migraine (p173)
■ asthma (p141)
■ eczema (p159)
■ irritable bowel syndrome (p120)
■ premenstrual syndrome (p206)

CULTURE SHOCK & TRAVEL FATIGUE

People experience a well recognised set of emotional reactions following any major life event; when this occurs as a result of living (or travelling) for an extended period of time in a culture very different from your own, it's called culture shock. The culture shock syndrome is a well known hazard of living overseas for any length of time. It's unlikely to strike hard on a short trip, but you may notice it if you're on a long trip, especially if it is compounded by travel fatigue.

Culture shock can be thought of as a sort of psychological disorientation resulting from a conflict between your deeply ingrained cultural values and the different cultural cues and behaviours of the society you have relocated into. However broad-minded you may hope you are, deep down we all have a fundamental assumption that our own culture is right.

Culture shock doesn't happen all of a sudden – it progresses slowly, and affects some personalities more than others. Sometimes it doesn't progress, and you may get stuck at one stage. If you've been travelling a while, you'll probably recognise some of the stages and symptoms as identified by Myron Loss in *Culture Shock – Dealing with Stress in Cross-Cultural Living*:

- euphoria, when everything is new and exciting
- hostility as the novelty wears off and the differences start to irritate – you may feel critical of your host country, stereotyping local people; you may feel weepy, irritable, defensive, homesick, lonely and isolated, perhaps worried about your physical health
- adjustment is when you start to feel more comfortable in your new lifestyle and with the new culture
- adaptation occurs when you lose that 'us and them' feeling

Here are some strategies you could try for minimising the impact of culture shock on yourself as well as on people you may come into contact with:

▶ accept that everyone experiences some degree of culture shock, and be prepared to recognise the symptoms as such

▶ find out about the country, people and culture before you go and when you're away – surprisingly, it doesn't have a huge effect but there are other good reasons for doing it

▶ look after your physical health – it's easier to feel positive if you feel well

▶ friendships and keeping in touch with home can help you feel less isolated

▶ you don't achieve anything by succumbing to the temptation of disparaging everything local

▶ having a sense of humour can help you keep your head above water – just think what good stories you'll be able to tell later

Travel fatigue is bound to affect you after you've been on the road for many months. It's a combination of culture shock, homesickness and generally feeling fed up with the hassles and inconveniences of life on the road. Definitely time for a rethink.

ANXIETY

A certain degree of anxiety is a natural reaction to a change in lifestyle and environment, and you'll probably accept it as

Anxious Feelings

Anxiety is the body's way of preparing for an emergency: the so-called fight or flight reaction. Certain physiological changes occur, which can have all or some of the following effects:

■ palpitations, missed heartbeat or discomfort in chest
■ overbreathing, shortness of breath
■ dry mouth and difficulty swallowing
■ stomachache, bloating and wind, diarrhoea
■ having to pass urine frequently
■ periods stop
■ premenstrual syndrome
■ tremor and aching muscles
■ 'pins and needles'
■ headache
■ dizziness and ringing in the ears

such. But there are situations when anxiety is a worry, either because it's over the top or because you misread the symptoms as something else.

Anxiety can take a number of forms, any of which can strike you for the first time when you're away, especially if you're a worrier by nature. If you have any preexisting anxiety-related problems, travel may exacerbate them.

If you recognise that anxiety is a problem, try some of the suggested short-term strategies for coping; you'll probably want to discuss longer-term methods of anxiety reduction with your doctor when you get home, especially if the problem is new or persistent. This is important because some physical diseases like thyroid and diabetic problems can cause anxiety symptoms, and your doctor may want to test for these.

Generalised anxiety often affects worriers; you feel restless, irritable and tired, stretched to the limit, with tension headaches and sleep problems. Any of the strategies for stress reduction listed at the beginning of the chapter may help; you could also try cutting out coffee and strong tea, both of which make tension symptoms worse. Drug treatment is usually only indicated if your symptoms are very severe and disabling.

! Remember that alcohol withdrawal, perhaps after a binge or if you're a habitually heavy drinker, can be a cause of acute anxiety; it's best to avoid binges in the first place, and if you are a heavy drinker, it's best to cut down gradually.

Panic attacks can occur without warning and can be terrifying. They're marked by frightening physical symptoms as well as thoughts, and there's rarely a recognisable trigger. You feel like you're suffocating, you can't get enough air, and have palpitations, light-headedness, faintness and pins and needles. Often you have a feeling of being outside yourself, and everything seems unreal.

You'll probably recognise the symptoms if you've had an attack before, but if it's the first time, you may think you're dying. Sounds silly, but breathing in a controlled way in and out of a paper bag for a short time can help the symptoms of a panic attack. This is because when you panic, you start to overbreathe, and this causes you to feel light-headed and gives you pins and needles.

The main thing is to recognise what's happening, and to be reassured that you're not having a heart attack, and that it will pass eventually. Some general stress reduction is probably a good idea in the short term.

DEPRESSION

The blues can strike any time, even when you're on holiday. Stress, anxiety, disappointment, isolation and poor physical health can all make an attack of the blues likely. You know you've got it bad when you feel teary, listless and tired; you can't be bothered to do anything and nothing is enjoyable any more. You lose interest in sex and food (although sometimes you over-eat instead), you may have trouble sleeping and you just want to withdraw from the world.

Any physical illness can make you feel low, but some diseases are known for causing depression and fatigue, often for prolonged periods of time. Some notable culprits are viral diseases like flu, glandular fever, hepatitis and dengue fever; malaria is another. Other causes are anaemia and low thyroid function.

If it's just a simple case of the blues, you'll probably find that you bounce back in a few days, especially if you can identify and deal with the cause.

▶ Try any or all of the de-stress strategies suggested earlier and re-assure yourself that it will pass.

▶ If you know you suffer from depression, try anything that has worked in the past.

▶ Exercise is known to stimulate the production of endorphins, which are natural feel-good factors.

▶ Maybe it's time to stop and re-think what you're doing, and perhaps to head home.

If your depression is a follow-on from a physical illness, it may be reassuring to recognise that this is the reason you are feeling low. It's also worth seeking medical advice, as anti-depressant drug treatments may be helpful in this situation.

!If you think you may be depressed and things haven't improved over a couple of weeks, you should think about getting medical help. Depression is an illness, and it can be successfully treated with medication ('conventional' antidepressants or herbal remedies such as St John's wort) or counselling. Severe depression can be very frightening and if it's not treated, you're at risk of suicide.

DELIRIUM & ALCOHOL WITHDRAWAL

Any serious physical illness, but especially infections, can cause delirium. This shows itself as confusion, restlessness, disorientation, sometimes hallucinations, and it can be difficult to persuade someone who is delirious to stay in bed or to take treatment. Treatment of the underlying illness will settle it. If you or someone you are with is this ill, seek medical attention urgently; in the meantime, take steps to bring down the fever and make sure the person doesn't hurt themselves.

Alcohol withdrawal is a specific form of delirium, and strikes people who are habitually heavy drinkers who suddenly stop (as can happen if they're ill and miss their usual alcohol intake). It's a serious, life-threatening condition, which needs medical advice urgently.

MEFLOQUINE

The antimalarial mefloquine (see p36) can cause a variety of symptoms, from abnormal dreams to panic attacks, depression and hallucinations. They're all more likely if you've had emotional problems in the past, and your doctor will usually have recommended an alternative drug in this case. If you're taking mefloquine, it will probably have been prescribed well before you leave, and you'll have had a chance to deal with any potential problems before you go. However, if you do experience problems while you're away, stop taking it and

Strange Experiences

Some serious illnesses like schizophrenia could theoretically be kick-started by the stress of travelling. If someone you are with starts experiencing unusual things like visual or auditory hallucinations and delusions, they may need urgent medical help. They may not recognise that they are ill, which can make it frightening and confusing.

seek medical advice about alternative protection. Since mefloquine is only taken once weekly, you should be able to organise an alternative antimalarial without any break in protection.

DOING DRUGS

If you do decide to take drugs, be aware of the legal and health consequences first. By definition, these substances affect your mental state – this is after all the reason for taking them – but they can have unwanted or unexpected effects, especially if you're taking them for the first time. Kava, the 'Pacific drug', in its many local incarnations is unlikely to cause you any harm in the quantities normally consumed, although it can make you feel nauseated.

- Acute anxiety or panic attacks are common with marijuana (and LSD or mescaline), and are more likely if you're taking it in a stressful situation or for the first time.
- Acute paranoia ('persecution complex') can occur after taking marijuana, cocaine, crack, amphetamines or ecstasy, and can be extremely frightening.
- Overdose can be fatal anywhere, but especially where you can't rely on the emergency services.
- If you're injecting drugs, never share needles with other users – because of infection risks.

Anxiety attacks or acute paranoia are likely to resolve without any specific treatment, although they may be pretty unpleasant at the time.

One Too Many ...

If you wake up regretting that last stubby or Hawaiian cocktail, remember that dehydration, especially in hot climates, causes many of the symptoms of a hangover. Drink plenty of water before you go to sleep and if you wake up in the night (quite likely after all that fluid), make yourself drink another glass or two of water. There are plenty of commercial hangover remedies on the market, but you're probably better off drinking plenty of water to counter dehydration, eating (if you can) because alcohol can make your blood sugar drop (another reason why you feel unwell after a binge), and taking antacids if your stomach is giving you hell.

Enjoy yourself by all means, but use a bit of comon sense. You're much more likely to have an accident and injure yourself if you've been drinking, and you'd be crazy to risk driving if you're over the limit – not only is your own judgement impaired but you'll probably have to contend with other drivers in even worse states. Before you begin a session, assess the potential risks – how are you going to get back to your hotel, for example.

Just be aware that there's no quality control on the drugs you buy, and locally available substances can be unexpectedly strong or may be mixed with other harmful substances. You're at the mercy of sellers when it comes to quality of ingredients, and their main concern is unlikely to be your good health.

!*Because unexpected reactions – including accidental overdose – can occur any time, never take drugs when you are alone.*

WOMEN TRAVELLERS

Travelling can present some particular problems for women, and some women's health issues are a bit more tricky to cope with on the road.

MENSTRUAL PROBLEMS

These are common when you're travelling. Although they are not usually serious, menstrual problems can affect your enjoyment of the trip.

MENSTRUAL-FREE TRAVEL

If you need to, it is possible to take measures to temporarily prevent menstruation – this might be something to consider if you're going on a trek in a remote area, for example. Discuss this with your doctor before you go, but options include the following.

▶ If you're taking the combined oral contraceptive pill, you could carry on taking the pill without the usual break (or skip the seven days of inactive pills), although it's not advisable for more than three cycles at a time and, if you're unlucky, you may have some breakthrough bleeding.

▶ For a short trip, norethisterone (a progesterone) can be used to postpone a period. You need to start taking it three days or so before menstruation is due to begin and continue until the end of the holiday (for up to two to three weeks); menstruation occurs again two to three days after stopping. The dose is 5mg three times daily and side effects are rare, but it's not suitable for long term use, and it's not a contraceptive.

▶ An injected progesterone contraceptive produces light, infrequent periods or none at all in most women – great for when you're travelling. However, you need to have injections every eight to 12 weeks and the effect on menstruation is initially unpredictable.

PREMENSTRUAL SYNDROME

If you normally get period pains and premenstrual bloating, you may find these are worse while you are travelling, for a variety of reasons – physical and psychological stresses,

Mentioning the Unmentionable

Disposal of used tampons and sanitary pads can be a major concern (and not just when you are travelling), especially in remote or environmentally sensitive areas. So what do you do?

- Despite the inconvenience, the most environmentally responsible action is to carry everything out with you (take plenty of rubbish bags) and dispose of them somewhere more convenient later.
- You could burn them; this is another environmentally responsible option but it's hardly practical.
- If you are in the wilderness, you could bury them, but you will need to dig a decent-sized hole and cover it well, and it's not generally recommended because they decompose poorly and animals dig them up.
- Reusable items are available from specialist shops selling environmentally friendly products, but they do rely on you having access to adequate water and washing facilities.
- Some women travellers recommend using a rubber cap device, worn in the vagina and similar to an upside-down diaphragm. It has to be removed every six to 12 hours to be rinsed and emptied, then replaced. Between periods you carry it in a cotton bag in your luggage. The Keeper is one brand, and (wouldn't you know it) there's a web site (www.keeper.com) where you can find out more.

unaccustomed heat and prolonged immobility on long journeys). If you think this could be a problem, take a good supply of a painkiller or any other remedies that you know work for you. Alternatively, you could consider starting the oral contraceptive pill before you leave, but it's best to sort this out in plenty of time before you go.

Remedies that may be helpful include evening primrose oil, which can be taken in capsule form or as the oil, and vitamin B6, magnesium or calcium supplements. Or you could try the delightfully named Chaste tree (Vitex agnus castus) or dong quai, a herbal treatment widely used in Asia for menstrual problems.

LIGHT OR ABSENT PERIODS

You often find that your periods disappear or become irregular when you're on the road, probably because of the mental and physical stresses of travel and the change to your usual routine. Other causes are pregnancy, drastic weight loss and hormonal contraceptive problems. Obviously the most important cause to exclude is pregnancy (see later in this chapter).

There's usually nothing to worry about, although if you don't have a period at all for more than about three or four months, it's a good idea to get a checkup. Periods usually get back to normal once you have finished your travels.

! New, severe period pains can be a result of a vaginal infection or a tubal pregnancy (if there's a chance you may be pregnant), so seek urgent medical advice in this case.

HEAVY PERIODS

Light or absent periods are great, but you can find that your periods become heavier or more frequent while travelling, so be prepared for either possibility!

! If your periods are heavier than usual, you may develop a mild anaemia; boost your diet with fresh fruit and green vegetables, or consider taking a multivitamin and iron supplement.

Heavy bleeding is often due to hormonal problems. If you suffer heavy persistent bleeding for more than seven days, which shows no sign of lessening, you need to get medical advice. Treatment is usually with norethisterone (a progesterone tablet) 5mg three times daily for 10 days. Bleeding should stop by the end of the course and you can expect to have a period about seven days after finishing the course. If the bleeding does not stop, you will need further treatment. Norethisterone is not suitable if there is any chance you may be pregnant, or if you have a history of gynaecological problems or are otherwise unwell – you must seek medical advice urgently in all these cases.

MENOPAUSAL & POSTMENOPAUSAL TRAVELLERS

If you get hot flushes, hot weather and stress can make these worse. It's probably worth discussing this with your doctor before you go so you can work out ways of dealing with it. If you're not taking hormonal replacement therapy, this could be an option to consider. Try simple measures to keep cool such as wearing loose cotton clothing, not overexerting yourself, resting during the heat of the day and, if evening flushes are a problem, make sure you have a room with a fan or air-conditioning. Cool drinks and eating small, frequent meals may also help.

Many natural remedies can be helpful for menopausal symptoms, including the herb dong quai (for flushes), St John's wort (Hypericum perforatum, for depression), ginseng (to reduce sweating) and Bach flower remedies, so check these out with your practitioner before you go, and take a good supply with you.

Dry, itchy skin can be a problem at and after the menopause. The physical hazards of travelling can exacerbate this, so take care to protect your skin from the sun and wind by using sunscreen and moisturisers.

Cystitis (see Bladder Infection later in this chapter) can occur at any age but is very common after menopause, and travelling can make an attack more likely.

If you're postmenopausal, and you're not on HRT, you need to seek medical advice for any vaginal spotting or bleeding that occurs, although if you're on a short trip, this can probably wait until you get back.

HRT & TRAVEL

As for any medication, it's best to take a plentiful supply with you. If you have an implant, will it be due for renewal while

Breast Lumps

If you notice an irregularity or lump in your breast while you're on the road, see if it disappears after your period. If it's still there, and you're going to be away for some time, seek medical advice so that it can be checked out. If you're post-menopausal, it's a good idea to have it checked out as soon as possible.

you are away? If you are going to be travelling in the heat, sweating and swimming may mean patches stick less well, so you might want to consider changing to a tablet or gel preparation before you go.

If you're taking a preparation that induces bleeding, it may be possible to change to a different one that induces periods every three months instead of every month if a period is going to be inconvenient while you're travelling. Periods can be postponed by manipulating your progestogen dose, but because this can sometimes lead to heavy bleeding, it's best to discuss this with your doctor before leaving.

HRT makes you slightly more prone to thrombosis (blood clots) in your leg veins, especially if you're immobile for long periods of time, for example on a long flight or bus journey:

▶ take regular walks
▶ when you're sitting during a journey, wriggle your toes and flex your calf muscles
▶ support stockings or tights are an option but not a very attractive one in a hot climate
▶ drink plenty, as dehydration makes clotting more likely

If you have been on HRT for some time and you develop heavy or irregular bleeding while you are away, it could indicate a problem with the lining of your womb (such as thickenings called polyps or even early cancer), and you should seek medical advice as soon as possible.

BLADDER INFECTION

Also called cystitis, the main symptom is having to empty your bladder frequently – great when you're travelling! Although you have to go more frequently, you only pass small quantities of urine, often with pain or a burning feeling and sometimes an ache in your lower abdomen.

Cystitis is often due to infection by bacteria that normally live in the bowel. It's very common in women. The reason for this is that, compared with men (who relatively rarely get cystitis), the tube leading to the bladder in women is short, making it easy for bacteria to enter the bladder. This is also why bladder infections often occur after sexual intercourse, and are more likely if you use the diaphragm for contraception.

If you think you've got cystitis:

▸ drink plenty of fluids to help flush the infection out; citrus fruit juice or cranberry juice can help relieve symptoms
▸ take a non-prescription cystitis remedy (these usually contain an alkalinising agent like potassium citrate, sodium bicarbonate or sodium citrate) to help relieve the discomfort; alternatively, add a teaspoon of bicarbonate of soda to a glass of water
▸ if there's no improvement after 24 hours despite these measures, you may need a course of antibiotics

Get medical advice; most antibiotics will treat simple cystitis, treatment is usually a single dose or a three-day course. Suitable antibiotics include trimethoprim (600mg single dose; not suitable in pregnancy), amoxycillin (take two 3g doses 12 hours apart) or nalidixic acid (1g four times daily for seven days). Avoid any antibiotic you are allergic to – see the Medicines appendix for more details.

!If you have the symptoms described earlier, you almost certainly have cystitis, and it will almost certainly respond to a course of recommended antibiotics. If it doesn't, or if the symptoms recur quickly, you should seek medical advice so a urine test can be done to clarify what's causing your symptoms.

If cystitis is left untreated, there's a risk of the infection spreading to the kidneys, which causes a much more serious illness.

! *Symptoms of a kidney infection include a high temperature (38°C/100.4°F and higher), vomiting (sometimes) and pain in the lower back – you should seek medical attention in this case.*

Just to confuse the issue, about a third of women with symptoms of cystitis don't have an infection at all (it may be a sort of 'irritable bladder' syndrome), so it's definitely worth trying some simple non-antibiotic measures first. It's worth bearing in mind that 'cystitis' can be caused by a sexually transmitted infection, so you should get this checked out if you are concerned, especially if you have any other symptoms such as an abnormal vaginal discharge.

! *Help prevent cystitis by drinking plenty of fluids and making sure you don't hang on too long – empty your bladder at regular intervals.*

VAGINAL INFECTIONS

If you've got a vaginal discharge that is not normal for you (more copious, abnormal colour, smelly) with or without any other symptoms, you've probably got an infection.

- ▶ If you've had thrush before and you think you may have it again, it's worth self-treating for this (see the following section).
- ▶ If not, get medical advice, as you will need a laboratory test and an appropriate course of treatment.
- ▶ It's best not to self-medicate with antibiotics because there are many causes of vaginal discharge, which can only be differentiated with a laboratory test.

Although candidiasis ('yeast' infection) is probably the best known cause of vaginal problems, and the one women are most likely to self-diagnose, it's worth remembering that it probably accounts for only 20 to 30% of all vaginal infections, which is a relatively small proportion. Sexually transmitted infections are an important cause of vaginal discharge.

THRUSH (VAGINAL CANDIDIASIS)

If you don't already know, symptoms of this common yeast infection are itching and discomfort in the genital area, often in asssociation with a thick white vaginal discharge (said to resemble cottage cheese). It's due to an overgrowth of the vaginal yeasts, usually the species called *Candida albicans,* which are present normally in the vagina and on the skin.

Many factors, including diet, pregnancy and medications, can trigger this infection, which is normally kept at bay by the acid conditions in the vagina and the normal balance of organisms. Heat, the oral contraceptive pill and antibiotics can all make an attack more likely, so it's no surprise that it's even more common when you're travelling.

! Although candidiasis is not a sexually transmitted infection as such, it makes sense to treat your regular partner with an antifungal cream on the genital area for five days.

You can help prevent thrush by wearing cotton underwear and loose-fitting trousers or a skirt; it's a good idea to wash regularly but some soap and bath salts can make vaginal irritation and candidiasis more likely, so are best avoided.

If you have thrush, a single dose of an antifungal pessary (vaginal tablet), such as clotrimazole 500mg is an effective and convenient treatment. Short courses of three to 14 days are also available but are less convenient. Alternatively, you can use an antifungal cream (for example clotrimazole 1% or econazole nitrate 1%) inserted high in the vagina (on a tampon) instead of a pessary. The treatment can be used even if you're on a period. Antifungal cream can be used in addition to a pessary to relieve vulval itching. A vaginal acidifying gel may help prevent recurrences.

!If you know you are prone to thrush, take a supply of pessaries or cream with you in your medical kit.

If you're stuck in a remote area without medication, you could use natural yoghurt (applied directly to the vulva or on a tampon and inserted in the vagina) to soothe and help restore the normal balance of organisms in the vagina. Sitting in or washing with a weak solution of vinegar or sodium bicarbonate may also help. If thrush is really being a nuisance, some nonspecific strategies you could try are cutting down on sugar and alcohol, and eating more plain live yoghurt.

BACTERIAL VAGINOSIS

Also known as nonspecific vaginitis or *Gardnerella* vaginitis, bacterial vaginosis is the most common cause of abnormal vaginal discharge. It can cause a range of symptoms, but the most common are odour (fishy) and discharge (white-grey).

Although it is more likely if you are sexually active, there's no evidence that it is transmitted by intercourse. It's not caused by any one organism – instead there's a general change in the whole vaginal environment, with the good guys, the lactobacilli that normally keep the vagina healthy, being replaced by a variety of bad guys. Treatment is with an antibiotic, usually metronidazole 500mg twice a day for seven days.

SEXUALLY TRANSMITTED INFECTIONS

○ For a more detailed discussion of STIs, see the HIV/AIDS & Sexual Health chapter earlier in this book.

Prevention is definitely the aim with sexually transmitted infections (STIs). Symptoms include sores in the genital area, an abnormal vaginal discharge and sometimes cystitis symptoms.

- Having an STI can make you more vulnerable to HIV infection.
- STIs need to be diagnosed and treated properly, as they can cause chronic pelvic inflammatory disease or infertility later, so it's worth finding a doctor or clinic to get it checked out.

- It's important that your partner is treated for the STI as well.
- You may have an STI even if you have no symptoms – if you think you may have put yourself at risk, get a full checkup when you get home.

Trichomoniasis

This sexually transmitted infection often occurs at the same time as other STIs. Symptoms include vaginal discharge (thick yellow), itchiness and sometimes discomfort on passing urine. About 50% of women with the infection don't have any symptoms. Men rarely have any symptoms, but partners must be treated to prevent re-infection. Treatment is with an antibiotic, usually metronidazole either in a single dose of 2g or 250mg three times daily for seven days.

CONTRACEPTION

It makes sense to discuss your contraceptive needs with your doctor or a specialist family planning clinic well in advance of travelling. Even if you're planning on celibacy, it's always worth being prepared for the unexpected.

There's a whole range of options available to you, so if one method doesn't suit, there's plenty more to choose from. Seek professional advice, but the following table summarises the major players, with some of the pros and cons for travellers.

!New sexual partner? Go 'double Dutch' – use a barrier method in addition to a non-barrier method to protect yourself against HIV and STIs (and babies).

If you need to, you shouldn't have any trouble re-stocking in Australia and New Zealand or the main centres in the Pacific islands (although you may not be able to get your usual brand).

ORAL CONTRACEPTIVE PILL

If you are crossing time zones or travelling at night:

▶ combined oral contraceptive (COCP) – make sure that you do not leave more than 24 hours between pills

Missed a pill?

If you miss a pill (either the combined oral contraceptive or progestogen-only pill), take the missed pill straight away and take the next pill on time, even if it is the same day.

You'll need to use a different form of contraception for the next seven days in the following situations:

■ progestogen-only pill: if you took it more than three hours late
■ combined pill: if you took it 12 or more hours late

For the combined pill, if the seven days extend into the pill-free gap (or into the inactive pill interval), you should start the next course straight away without the usual break.

▶ progesterone-only pill (POP) – the timing needs to be much more precise with this; if you're more than three hours late, you'll need to take additional contraceptive precautions for the next seven days

If you have vomiting or diarrhoea, it can mean that the hormones are not absorbed properly and therefore that you are not protected. For either the COCP or POP:

▶ if you vomit or have severe diarrhoea less than three hours after taking the pill, take another pill
▶ if more than three hours, or if vomiting and diarrhoea persists, take the pill as normal, but take additional contraceptive precautions for the rest of the cycle

You should stop taking either the COCP or POP and use an alternative method of contraception if you get hepatitis (jaundice), as the jaundice can interfere with the usual way in which the body deals with the pill.

Some common broad-spectrum antibiotics (such as ampicillin) can reduce the effectiveness of the COCP (but not POP); the UK Family Planning Association advises that you should use additional contraceptive methods during a short course of these antibiotics and for seven days afterwards (the leaflet

method	advantages on the road	disadvantages on the road	protects against STIs?
combined oral contraceptive pill	effective and reliable; periods may be lighter and PMS less	only effective as long as you remember to take it! diarrhoea and vomiting, and some antibiotics, can reduce effectiveness; fluid retention may be worse in hot climates	No
progestogen-only pill	useful for a selected group of women (eg older women, heavy smokers, migraine sufferers); not affected by antibiotics	effectiveness reduced by diarrhoea and vomiting; small margin for error if you forget to take it	No
hormonal implants	effective and reliable; nothing to remember or lose; not affected by diarrhoea and vomiting or antibiotics; periods usually lighter and may disappear; injection lasts eight or 12 weeks	irregular bleeding can be a problem, especially at first; if you're going to be away on a long trip you will need to arrange when and where to have the next injection	No
intrauterine copper devices ('the coil')	convenient – nothing to remember or lose; reliable	STIs more likely to cause long-term problems, so this method is not advisable if casual sex is likely; tubal pregnancy may be more likely	No
intrauterine progestogen	convenient and reliable; period pains are improved and periods are usually lighter and may disappear; STIs less likely to cause problems than with the coil and less risk of tubal pregnancy	periods may be unpredictable at first	No
diaphragm or cap	no hormonal side effects	hygiene may be a problem when travelling; difficult to replace if lost; you need a refit (diaphragm) if you lose a lot of weight (4kg or more)	some STIs but not HIV
female condom	available over the counter; less likely to rupture than male condoms	useability could be improved, but sense of humour may help	Yes
male condom	readily available; no mess – important if washing facilities are in limited supply; can be carried just in case	can split or leak – needs to be used correctly to be effective	Yes

accompanying the pill packet will give you more guidance on which drugs to be careful with, but if in doubt, take extra precautions anyway). If you get to the end of the pill packet during the week after finishing the antibiotics, start the next packet straight away and take additional precautions.

INTRAUTERINE DEVICES (IUD)

If you can't feel the strings, you should assume you are not protected and use an alternative contraceptive method until you can get it checked out by a doctor.

! You should seek medical advice urgently if you develop low abdominal pain, especially with a fever and vaginal discharge; if you miss a period; or if you develop unusually heavy or painful bleeding.

BARRIER METHODS

For details on condoms, see the HIV/AIDS & Sexual Health chapter. A couple of points to bear in mind:

▶ heat can cause rubber to perish, so check your diaphragm for holes periodically, and try to keep it in a cool place
▶ consider taking a second diaphragm with you, especially if you are going to be away for a prolonged period of time

EMERGENCY CONTRACEPTION

In an emergency, you can try to prevent pregnancy following unprotected intercourse by taking the 'morning after' pill. This contains high doses of oestrogen, which helps prevent the fertilised egg from settling in the lining of the womb. Another method of preventing pregnancy is to have an intrauterine contraceptive device inserted within five days.

If possible, see a doctor who can prescribe the so-called 'morning-after' pill. You need to take two doses 12 hours apart, and you need to take the first dose as soon as possible within 72 hours of unprotected intercourse. The high dose of oestrogen may cause nausea and vomiting. If you vomit within two hours of either dose, the dose should be repeated. You should not take the morning-after pill if you are suffering from a severe migraine at the same time. Your next period may be either early or late. If you are taking the oral contraceptive pill, continue taking it as normal.

! The morning-after pill is not 100% foolproof; it's for emergencies only, not for use as a regular method of contraception.

The morning-after pill usually prescribed contains ethinyloestradiol 50 micrograms and levonorgestrol 250 micrograms. The dose is two tablets followed by another two 12 hours later. The important ingredient is oestrogen (usually in the form of ethinyloestradiol). If it's not practical to seek medical advice, then see if you can buy a pill containing the same dose of oestrogen (check the packet or ask the pharmacist to tell you), and treat yourself as indicated in the previous paragraph. If you can't find a high-strength pill, you could use a 'normal' contraceptive pill, as follows:

▶ if the pill contains 20 micrograms of oestrogen, take five pills and then another five 12 hours later
▶ if the pill contains 30 micrograms of oestrogen, take three pills and another three 12 hours later

AM I PREGNANT?

So what do you do if you think you may be pregnant? If you suspect it may be a possibility, your suspicions may be confirmed if you miss a period or have an unusually light one. Other signs are enlarged, tender breasts and, although this is usually a later sign, nausea ('morning sickness').

Get a pregnancy test as soon as possible so you know for sure – you can buy a kit from most pharmacists in major cities; otherwise, go to a doctor, clinic or hospital and ask for a pregnancy test to be done. A pregnancy test won't show positive before the first missed period. If you do a test and it is negative but you still think pregnancy is a possibility, wait two weeks and then repeat it.

In the meantime, it's probably best to continue (or start) using a reliable contraceptive method (there is no evidence that the contraceptive pill harms the fetus, for example, so it's probably best to continue taking it until you know for certain that you are pregnant, especially if you are still sexually active).

If you're happy to be pregnant, see a doctor as soon as possible for blood tests and advice, and see the following section.

If you decide you want to terminate the pregnancy, you'll want to sort this out as soon as possible (and definitely before the 12th week of pregnancy, counting day one of pregnancy as the first day of your last menstrual period). If you're travelling in the Pacific islands, you'll probably want to consider going to Hawai'i, Australia or New Zealand or back home for the procedure. In less competent hands, abortion carries significant risks of infection, blood loss and infertility, so it's worth getting the best possible care.

PREGNANT TRAVELLERS

The days of seeing pregnancy as an 'indisposition' are long gone, and many women either choose or end up having to travel while they are pregnant, without any adverse effects on mother or fetus. However, there are some important considerations to bear in mind if you are planning to travel while you're pregnant. The information included in this section is to give you an idea of the issues that are involved – you should get medical advice well before you plan to go on any trip.

If you have had complicated pregnancies before or you're expecting twins, it would be best to postpone your trip.

WHEN?

Most doctors would suggest that the best time to travel in pregnancy is during the middle 12 weeks, when the risk of complications is less, the pregnancy is relatively well established and your energy levels are getting back to normal.

Before the 12th week, there is a relatively high risk of miscarriage (which could require surgical treatment like a scrape of the womb lining or even a blood transfusion) or a tubal pregnancy, which occurs in about one in 200 pregnancies. Tubal pregnancy nearly always requires surgical treatment and is an emergency situation. In addition, many women experience morning sickness in the first three months (sometimes for longer), which could make travelling less than enjoyable. Occasionally, it can be severe enough to require treatment in hospital. More mundane, but just as incapacitating for travelling, is needing to empty your bladder more frequently as the enlarging womb takes up more room in the pelvis and presses on the bladder.

!Note that most airlines prohibit flying after the 36th week of pregnancy (sometimes this can be waived if you have a doctor's certificate to say that there are no complications) – this is because they don't want to risk a woman going into premature labour on a flight, not because there's thought to be any intrinsic danger to the pregnancy.

In the last three months, major complications such as premature labour, blood pressure problems and problems with the placenta can all occur, so you would probably not want to risk a trip of any length during this time.

WHERE?

You need to go somewhere with a reasonable standard of medical facilities, in case complications occur while you are away. For the same reason, it's probably not a good idea to plan a trip to remote areas when you are pregnant, in case you need urgent medical treatment. Scuba diving (assuming you would want to do it in mid-pregnancy) is not advisable.

IMMUNISATIONS

You don't need many immunisations for travel in the Pacific islands, and you don't need any special ones for Australia and

Malaria Prevention in Pregnancy

Travel to malarial areas is not recommended but if necessary, preventive medication is considered safer than risking the disease in pregnancy. Chloroquine and proguanil are considered safe in pregnancy, although you may need a folic acid supplement with proguanil. Mefloquine can be used in the last 24 weeks of pregnancy, although it shouldn't be used for emergency treatment. If prevention fails, quinine is known to be safe in pregnancy for emergency treatment (for more details, see Malaria in the Fever & Hepatitis chapter.

New Zealand. Generally, it's best to avoid all vaccinations in the first 12 weeks of pregnancy, as there's a theoretical risk of harm to the fetus and miscarriage. In addition, 'live' vaccines ideally should be avoided at any time during pregnancy. Live vaccines include oral typhoid and hepatitis A vaccine (but not hepatitis A immunoglobulin). Hepatitis A is a much more serious illness in pregnancy, so it's important to have the immunoglobulin injection, as well as to take food and water precautions. An inactivated polio vaccine can be used instead of the usual oral live vaccine in pregnant women if necessary. A tetanus booster can be given safely in pregnancy, and tetanus protection is conferred to the newborn.

SPECIAL CONSIDERATIONS

All the predeparture preparations discussed in the Before You Go chapter apply if you're pregnant, but there are some special considerations for pregnant travellers. If this is your first pregnancy, it's probably a good idea to read up on it before you go so you have an idea of what to expect (such as tiredness, heartburn etc) and are familiar with any minor problems that may arise. Discuss these with your doctor, and work out strategies for coping in advance.

!*Make sure you are clear on what your travel health insurance covers you for during pregnancy.*

It's a good idea to take a well stocked medical kit with you, with suitable medications for common problems, so that you are clear on what you should and shouldn't take while you are away. You should avoid non-essential medications when you are pregnant. Don't take any medications while you are away unless you know they are safe in pregnancy (read the information leaflet or packaging, or ask a reliable doctor or pharmacist).

Long flights or bus rides increase the risk of blood clots in the legs, so if possible try to get up and walk around, drink plenty of water and consider wearing support stockings to reduce this risk on a long flight.

Every traveller should take steps to avoid illness, but it's even more important in pregnancy, when illnesses can have more severe effects on both your health and your baby's: prevent insect bites, take food and water precautions, and avoid risk situations for accidents.

During pregnancy your immunity is lower; infections, such as cystitis and chest infections, can be more severe and should be treated with antibiotics early – get medical advice. In the tropics you may be less tolerant of the heat. Rest, drink plenty of fluids and give yourself lots of time to adjust.

It's a good idea to make sure you eat a well balanced, nutritionally sound diet during the trip, avoiding potential problem foods like raw or partially cooked eggs, peanuts and peanut products, and soft cheeses. And all the general advice about not smoking and being careful with alcohol obviously holds true wherever you are.

BABIES & CHILDREN

Australia, New Zealand and most of the Pacific islands are great destinations if you're travelling with children as, depending on your destination, the health risks are relatively few. The main health challenges children are likely to face in the region are are basically:

- sunshine – a hazard wherever you go in the region
- heat – can be a problem in tropical Australia and the Pacific islands, especially if your children are not used to it
- water safety – beaches, surf, swimming pools and waterholes are a significant hazard for children
- insects and the diseases they carry – these are mainly a problem in tropical Australia and the Pacific islands; malaria is a serious risk at any age but it's more dangerous in children
- limited medical facilities – bear this in mind if you are going to some of the Pacific islands (especially if you are going off the beaten track), and in remote areas of Australia or New Zealand where medical help, although available, is likely to be at least a few hours away
- nappies (diapers), formula feed – likely to be in short supply outside main tourist centres in the Pacific islands

As well as the potential health risks of your destination, you need to take into account the age and temperament of your children, and what sort of trip you're planning. Babies are easy to feed (especially if they are exclusively breastfed), they're relatively easy to carry around in a sling and you don't need to worry about them getting bored by sightseeing. On the other hand, they are a concern if they get sick, they can quickly become dehydrated and are very sensitive to heat and sun. Toddlers are more complicated to feed, transport around and to keep amused and safe, particularly around water.

BEFORE YOU GO

Good preparation is the key to a successful trip with babies or children, so it's worth putting a bit of effort into this before you go. Lonely Planet's *Travel With Children* provides useful insight and practical guidance on travelling with children.

SOURCES OF INFORMATION

See the Before You Go chapter earlier in this book for contact details of travel health clinics and other information sources. Some travel health providers and other commercial health-related organisations have good leaflets and information sheets for travelling parents, including Nomad Travellers Store & Medical Centre (listed under Sources of Information & Advice in the Before You Go chapter) and the UK-based chain of pharmacies, Boots the Chemist.

Many of the travel health web sites listed in the Before You Go chapter have special items on travelling with children, although some are more informative than others. Try the TMVC web site for a good, helpful summary written from personal experience.

DOCTOR & DENTIST

It's a good idea to make sure your child is as healthy as possible before you go. Discuss basic illness prevention strategies and work out a plan of action for common problems that you may face while you are away, such as diarrhoea and fever.

If your child has an ongoing condition like eczema, diabetes or asthma, it's best to be clear about what to do if the condition worsens while you are away, and to make sure you have a plentiful supply of any medications they normally take.

It's worth making sure your children have a dental check-up before going away, and remember to leave enough time for any treatment to be carried out if necessary.

IMMUNISATIONS

It's just as important for your children to be protected against diseases through immunisation as it is for you. They should be up to date for all routine childhood immunisations and, in addition, they'll need the same travel-related vaccines as you

– see the Immunisations section in the Before You Go chapter for more guidance on this.

Most fully immunised school-age children won't need further doses of routine immunisations, but babies and younger children who haven't completed their normal childhood immunisations may need to complete the schedules earlier than normal. Discuss this with your doctor when you start planning your trip.

Note that some vaccines have age limits or are best avoided in childhood – discuss this with your doctor. For example:

- diphtheria and tetanus (usually with pertussis, as DTP) – the first dose can be given at six weeks of age if necessary
- polio can be given at six weeks if necessary
- measles can be given at six months of age if necessary (it's normally given as part of the MMR vaccine at 15 months of age)

Travel-related vaccines your child may need if you are going to one of the Pacific islands for any length of time include the following:

- hepatitis A vaccine can be given from the age of one year (two years in the US); younger children should have immunoglobulin
- typhoid vaccination isn't normally given under two years of age
- hepatitis B and tuberculosis (not used in the US and some European countries) have no lower age limit

If your child is going to have a reaction to an immunisation, this will usually occur about 48 hours after the injection and generally settles with a dose or two of paracetamol (acetaminophen) syrup or suppositories. Note that children can go on to have further reactions and sometimes develop rashes 10 days after the immunisation, so the earlier you get this organised before you go, the better.

MALARIA PREVENTION

Malaria exists in Papua New Guinea, the Solomon Islands and Vanuatu, as well as the Torres Strait Islands in Australia.

! Malaria is very dangerous in children, and you should think very carefully before taking children to malaria risk zones – discuss this fully with your doctor.

For more general information on malaria risk and prevention, see the Malaria Prevention section of the Before You Go chapter earlier in this book.

If you do take children into a malarial area, it's absolutely vital to protect them by taking steps to avoid mosquito bites and by giving them antimalarial drugs. It may be necessary to carry a dose of malaria treatment for your child if you are going to a remote area without access to medical help – discuss this with your doctor before you go.

Chloroquine, proguanil and quinine are known to be safe in children of all ages, and mefloquine can be given to babies over three months. Mefloquine should be avoided if your child has any history of seizures. Doxycycline should not be given to children under 12 years because of potential side effects (may stain teeth and retard growth). Note that if you are taking antimalarials yourself and you are breast feeding your child, you will still need to give your child antimalarials.

! Be careful to keep antimalarials out of reach of children – even a few tablets overdose of chloroquine can be fatal in small children.

Getting your children to take their malaria pills can be a real challenge, as only chloroquine is available in suspension form (in some countries). You may have to resort to crushing the tablets into a powder and disguising them in a small amount of food or drink.

! If it's a battle to persuade your child to take the medication, it can be tempting to stop as soon as possible; however, it's very important your child carries on taking antimalarials for four weeks after leaving a malarial area – otherwise, they are at risk of getting malaria.

NAPPIES, FORMULA FEED & BABY FOOD

Be prepared for these items to be much less readily available if you are going outside the main tourist centres in any of the Pacific island nations, so take a supply with you. You shouldn't have trouble finding them in most places in Australia and New Zealand. Washable nappies and liners tend to take up less luggage space than disposable nappies and are more eco-friendly.

MEDICAL KIT & MEDICATIONS

It's a good idea to take a child-specific medical kit in addition to your own basic medical kit (see the What to Take section in the Before You Go chapter). If your child takes any medications regularly (for asthma, eczema or diabetes, for example), remember to take a good supply of these with you. Otherwise, a basic medical kit for children should include most of the following.

- Remedies for pain and fever, for example paracetamol (acetaminophen) syrup or suppositories for little ones, Junior paracetamol (acetaminophen) for older children or ibuprofen paediatric syrup.
- Antibiotics for common ailments like ear infections or coughs – discuss this with your doctor, but you could consider these if you are planning on going to remote areas where you may not have ready access to medical care or supplies. Suitable antibiotics include co-amoxiclav, cephalexin or clarithromycin (if your child is allergic to penicillin). See the section on Antibiotics in the Medicines appendix for more details.
- A plentiful supply of oral rehydration salt sachets, barrier cream for nappy rash, calamine cream or aloe vera gel for heat rash and sunburn, motion sickness remedies, sunscreen, antiseptic wipes and antiseptic liquid or spray.
- Sterilising tablets are a good idea for cleaning feeding utensils, or you might want to consider taking a sterilising unit with you.
- Plastic spoons (5mL and 2.5mL) are useful for measuring out doses of liquid medications. A plastic syringe (5mL or 10mL) can be handy for giving medicine (and fluids) to a reluctant patient.

Medications to Avoid

Some medicines may be fine for adults but not for children, because of the risk of side effects. Some common drugs to avoid in children include:

- for pain and fever: aspirin
- antibiotics: ciprofloxacin and doxycycline
- antidiarrhoeals: loperamide, diphenoxylate, bismuth (Pepto-Bismol)
- antimalarials and malaria treatment: mefloquine before the age of three months; doxycycline

If you are at all uncertain about the dose or if the medicine is suitable for children, check with a doctor before giving it.

If you do need to give your child medication when you are away, remember children need a child-sized dose, and not all medications are suitable for children. Follow the dosing instructions given by your doctor or on the packet. Doses are generally worked out from how much your child weighs.

ON THE MOVE

Long journeys aren't always a bundle of fun with children, so be prepared! Consider arranging your itinerary to minimise the number of long journeys you have to do, or consider alternative means of getting around (such as flying instead of taking a two day bus journey). For toddlers or older children, travelling at night may be one solution, although it might be exhausting for you. Take a selection of travel games, puzzle books, reading books, colouring books and electronic games. A new toy might just provide enough interest to last a journey.

Children (and adults) can get thirsty and hungry on journeys very quickly, which is one preventable reason for bad temper. Consider making up some milk beforehand if you're bottle feeding (although it won't keep long in a hot climate) or you can get bottles with powder and water that you can mix up when you need. It's always a good idea to take a few snacks and cartons of drink for giving out to little ones on the journey. A change of clothing and plenty of wipes and tissues are always a good idea to have on hand for the inevitable spills.

EAR PAIN & FLYING

On flights, air pressure changes can cause ear pain in babies and young children. Older children can be encouraged to blow their noses, which should help their ears to pop. Younger children and babies can be given decongestant nose drops if necessary (get these from your doctor or pharmacist before you go) as well as paracetamol (acetaminophen) syrup to ease the pain. Give the syrup approximately one and a half hours before landing. If you are bottle feeding during the flight, try to sit your baby or toddler upright as far as possible, as feeding can sometimes increase the ear discomfort.

Coping with Jet Lag

Travelling eastwards is potentially the most difficult for your child to cope with. Allow your child to get plenty of sleep. You could consider using a mild sedative, for example an antihistamine like promethazine. When you arrive, slot your child into their new routine immediately. Serve their meals at the correct time and put them to bed at the local time. Also, spend plenty of time outside because light (particularly sunlight) and physical activity in the first half of the day will help the body clock to adjust faster.

Be aware that our body temperature falls during the night and initially this will occur in the middle of your new day. Even though you may have travelled to a warmer climate, your child may require warmer clothes for a few days before their body clock adjusts.

John Mason

!If your child has an ear infection or a bad cold, you should postpone flying until it is better.

TRAVEL SICKNESS

This is extremely common in children, and can turn even a short journey into a trauma. Consider using an anti-sickness remedy like promethazine (follow the dosing guidelines, and note that it's not recommended for children under two years) or ginger. Promethazine has the added advantage that it often makes your child sleepy – possibly sanity-saving on a long journey – although the effects are very variable. A naturopathic soothing alternative is chamomile.

STAYING HEALTHY

Children can be very adaptable to climate and time changes but they are more susceptible to infections and accidents.

FOOD, WATER & CLEANLINESS

If you are going to the Pacific islands, you need to be a little more careful about food, water and general cleanliness than you would be normally. If possible, breastfeed babies and young toddlers, as this reduces their risks of getting diarrhoea through ingesting contaminated food and water. It's probably best to stick to boiled, cooled water or bottled water. Iodone is best avoided in children under 12 years, although chlorine tablets are an alternative. You'll probably want to avoid giving children carbonated and other soft drinks, but packet fruit juices, green coconut juice and UHT milk are usually available and make safe substitutes. If you can, try to prepare any food for babies yourself, making sure that the utensils you use are sterile (take sterilising tablets with you).

Children who are crawling or just walking are particularly at risk of diseases spread via dirt, so take care to wash hands and faces frequently throughout the day, especially if you're travelling on public transport, and discourage wandering hands in the mouth, eyes and nose as far as possible. A supply of wet wipes can be invaluable, especially on long journeys.

If you get sick with diarrhoea yourself, be extremely careful to wash your hands after using the toilet to avoid passing diarrhoea to your child. be careful with nappies etc if your child has diarrhoea to prevent it passing to you.

DIET & NUTRITION

New foods can induce surprise and a reflex refusal, stress and new surroundings can distract children from eating and the heat often reduces even the healthiest of appetites. Try to introduce new foods gradually, perhaps starting before you leave, and consider taking a supply of familiar dry foods with you to provide an element of continuity. If you are in the Pacific islands, and the local cuisine is not proving a hit, western-style dishes are usually available, especially in touristed areas.

! Even if your child isn't inclined to eat, fluids are a must, especially if it's hot.

INSECT BITES

Biting insects carry a number of serious diseases, including dengue in all the Pacific islands and the tropical north of Australia, and malaria in a few areas, so it's extremely important to protect your child from bites. For more details, see the section on Insect Bite Prevention in the Staying Healthy chapter, but the main messages are to make sure your child is covered up with clothes, socks and shoes, and to use insect repellents on exposed areas – either DEET-containing repellents or the new natural repellents containing lemon eucalyptus. Permethrin-soaked mosquito nets are very effective at preventing bites at night and during daytime naps (the mosquito that spreads dengue bites during the daytime).

Try to discourage scratching of bites if they do occur, as this often leads to infection. Keep fingernails cut short and use calamine cream or a sting relief spray to ease irritation.

ACCIDENTS & OTHER HAZARDS

Children tend to be accident-prone at the best of times, but the hazards are even greater when you're travelling, so you need to be even more vigilant than normal. Many hotel rooms and restaurants are not built with children in mind and may have a nightmare-inducing lack of safety features, particularly where windows and balconies are concerned. Some precautions to think about taking:

▶ be on the look-out for potential risk situations and unsafe features
▶ try to be aware of what your child is doing at all times, especially if they're playing outside
▶ consider using a harness for toddlers when you're travelling or walking in crowded places
▶ make sure your child has some form of identification on them at all times, including details of where you are staying
▶ if you're planning to travel by car, consider taking a child safety seat with you (although you should be able to pick one up without difficulty in Australia and New Zealand, if necessary)
▶ drowning is surprisingly common – be particularly vigilant around swimming pools or at the beach, and remember that drowning can occur in shallow water as well as deeper water
▶ check new beaches for debris, discarded hypodermics, glass and tins, as well as various offerings left by people and animals

Children's natural curiosity and fascination with all creatures great and small make them more vulnerable to insect and spider stings, snake bites and animal bites. For more details on these hazards, see the Bites & Stings chapter later in this book.

CUTS & SCRATCHES

In hot, humid climates these can easily become infected, and it can be difficult to keep children clean, especially if they are running or crawling around. You'll need to take a bit more care of these than perhaps you would normally. Wash any break in the skin carefully with soap and water or antiseptic solution (or an antiseptic wipe if you haven't got access to water) and keep it covered with a sterile, non-adherent, non-fluffy dressing (a sticking plaster is fine if the wound is

Poisonous Plants

Small children are attracted like magnets to plants, particularly if the plants are colourful and look appetising. Toddlers will eat almost anything, regardless of taste. Children need to be supervised, especially if they are somewhere outdoors with access to plants and bushes. Contact with some plants and grasses may go unnoticed until a reaction occurs.

Some plants and grasses can cause toxic or allergic reactions when they come into contact with bare skin, so it's best to make sure your child is covered up if they are playing in grassland. This will help protect them from insect bites, too.

If you catch your child eating a plant, keep a sample for identification. Watch for any symptoms, and encourage your child to drink plenty of fluids to help dilute any potential toxic effects. If possible, seek expert advice. If this is not available, you can induce vomiting by giving your child ipecacunha syrup (if you can find it) – but be aware that some experts believe children should never be given ipecacuanha. This is usually only effective within four hours of eating a suspect plant, but it may be worth trying while you find medical help.

John Mason

small). It's probably worth checking your child carefully at the end of each day for cuts, scratches and potentially problematic bites. Itchy insect bites are a common source of infection, which is a good reason for making a strenuous effort to avoid them in the first place.

SUN

Anyone can get sunburnt but little ones are especially vulnerable. Keep children and babies covered up (for example with a long-sleeved T shirt and long trousers or skirt and hat, or an all-over sunsuit). Apply liberal amounts of the highest factor sunscreen you can find on any exposed skin and reapply it frequently. Keep your child out of the sun during the middle of the day when the sun is at its fiercest. Not only is sunburn miserably painful for your child, it's thought to be a major risk factor for skin cancer in later life.

HEAT

If your child is not used to a hot climate, they will need time to acclimatise. Children tend to acclimatise relatively easily, but young children (with their greater surface area relative to their body mass) can lose fluid through sweating very rapidly and become dehydrated and vulnerable to heatstroke (see p282). Babies and young children may not be able to tell you how hot they're feeling, so if you're feeling the heat, check to see how your child is coping, and in particular whether they are dressed appropriately. Try to discourage mobile youngsters from rushing around in the heat of the day.

Because babies and children can become dehydrated relatively easily, they require a significant increase in their fluid intake. As a general rule you can double their fluid intake. Consider sprinkling a little extra salt on their food, as salt can be lost through sweating, especially to start with. You could also encourage them to eat lots of juicy fruit and vegetables. Keep an eye on how much urine they are passing – small amounts of dark urine or dark urine-stained nappies in babies mean you need to increase their fluid intake.

! *Baby or toddler-carrier backpacks are a handy way to carry children, but it can be easy to forget how exposed they are to the elements.*

COLD

Children are very susceptible to the cold, as they lose heat very rapidly, especially if they are immobile in a carrier, so wrap them up well and check them regularly for signs of cold. Appropriate layers of clothes are vital, including mittens and warm hats. Give children plenty to eat and drink, as they can use up their energy reserves quickly and this makes them more vulnerable to the cold.

STINGS

Children seem to attract bees and wasps like the proverbial honey pot, so take plenty of insect repellent (although this is less effective against stinging insects like bees and wasps) and be prepared to apply sting relief spray and lots of sympathy. If you know your child is allergic to bee stings, discuss this with your doctor before you leave, as you will need to take an emergency kit containing adrenaline (epinephrine) with you (see the Bites & Stings chapter for more details).

IF YOUR CHILD FALLS ILL

Children are at risk of the same diseases as you are when you are away, so unless otherwise indicated, you can follow the guidelines given in the main text (but remember that children need different doses and possibly different drugs – see the Medical Kit & Medications section earlier in this chapter for more details).

! Because children can't always tell you what's wrong and in many cases don't show typical symptoms of diseases, it's even more important to seek medical help at the earliest opportunity, and always seek medical help urgently if you have any concerns about their condition.

Even in Pacific island countries where medical services may be more limited than you are used to, local doctors and health-workers will be experienced in dealing with all common childhood problems.

IS MY BABY/CHILD UNWELL?

Children can quickly change from being well and active to becoming ill, sometimes seriously ill. In young children especially, the signs can be quite subtle and difficult to interpret, which can be a worry.

As the parent, you will know your child best of all and any change in their behaviour should be taken seriously – listen to your sixth sense. This is particularly true of young children. Babies up to six months may become quieter than usual, miserable and crying. They may not want to feed or drink or they may develop more specific signs, such as diarrhoea, a cough, vomiting or a rash.

Older babies and toddlers may just not 'perform' as well as you are used to. They may stop walking, stop sitting up, stop feeding themselves or being as generally developed as you are used to. Children of this age are unable to tell you what's wrong and this may be the only sign before a rash or a cough appears.

! Don't rely on a child's skin temperature as an indication of whether they have a raised temperature or not. Always carry and use a thermomete (preferably a digital one or a fever strip – less accurate but easy to use).

It is important to have an actual reading of the temperature. A cold child to touch may have a raging temperature and the other way round.

! If you have any cause for concern, check the temperature and make sure your child is taking at least enough fluids to pass urine twice a day, even if they have gone off their food.

FEVER

This is very common in children wherever they are, and is always a cause for concern. In addition, a high temperature can sometimes cause a convulsion in babies and young children. Skin temperature is a confusing and unreliable sign – see the previous entry. If you think your child has a fever, for example if she's flushed and irritable and obviously unwell:

▶ take her temperature (see p99 for how to do this) and take it again 30 minutes later as a check
▶ put your child to bed, remove most of her clothing (perhaps covering her up with a cotton sheet) and make her comfortable (under a mosquito net if necessary)

▶ wipe her face and body with a sponge or cloth soaked in tepid (not cold) water or place her in a tepid bath to help lower the temperature
▶ giving paracetamol (acetaminophen) syrup or tablets every four to six hours will also help to lower the temperature
▶ prevent dehydration by giving small amounts of fluid often – make up oral rehydration salts with bottled or boiled water, or packet or fresh fruit juice diluted half and half with safe water; give 5mL every 15 minutes for the first hour

Conditions like viral infections, colds, ear infections, urine infections and diarrhoea are common causes of fever. If you've been travelling in malarial risk areas, you must always consider the possibility that it could be malaria.

Take steps to lower the temperature and seek medical help urgently in the following situations:

■ if the temperature is over 37.7°C (100°F) in a baby of less than six months
■ if the temperature is over 39°C (104°F) in any infant or child
■ if your child has had fits in the past
■ if it could be malaria; malaria should be suspected with ANY high fever if you are in a malarial area

Febrile Convulsion

If your child's temperature quickly rises high, she may have a fit, whatever the cause of the fever. This generally occurs in young children up to five years of age. If this occurs:

■ try not to panic
■ don't try to restrain your child's movements, but do remove any sharp objects from the area to prevent her injuring herself
■ don't put anything in her mouth
■ when the movements subside, roll her onto her side so that she can breathe freely
■ comfort her when it has stopped, then take measures to cool her – fans, tepid spongeing, tepid baths, paracetamol
■ seek medical help

- if the fever shows no sign of improving after 24 hours (take your child's temperature regularly to show you if it's going up or down)

MALARIA

○ For more details on malaria, including emergency treatment, see the section on Malaria in the Fever & Hepatitis chapter earlier.

Children can rapidly become very ill with malaria – which is why it is not advisable to travel with children to malarial areas – and it's easy to miss the diagnosis because the symptoms can be very vague.

! You need to suspect malaria if your child develops a fever with or without flu-like symptoms that persists for more than eight hours if you are in or have visited a malarial area within the last few months. Seek medical help urgently for a blood test and treatment.

If you are in a remote area without access to medical help, you'll need to give your child emergency standby treatment while you seek medical help – make sure you discuss this with your doctor before you go.

DIARRHOEA

Children, especially young children and babies, are more like-ly than adults to get diarrhoea when they are away. They also tend to get more severe symptoms, and for longer. It's partly because children tend to be less discrminating about what they put in their mouths and it's hard to keep little hands clean, but it may also be because they have less immunity to disease-causing bugs.

Babies and children can become rapidly dehydrated through diarrhoea and vomiting, and it can be difficult to make sure they drink enough. The best fluids to give children are oral rehydration salts (ORS). You need to start giving them ORS as soon diarrhoea or vomiting appears – you can make ORS more palatable by adding flavours (such as the juice of an orange), or look for ready flavoured sachets of ORS. Avoid food if they are actively vomiting.

You don't need to give your child ORS if you're breast-feeding, but make sure you're taking in enough fluid yourself. If your child is being fed a milk-based formula, you need to replace this with ORS until the diarrhoea is better. As the diarrhoea improves, introduce diluted milk feeds, then solids. For older children, follow the same dietary guidelines as for adults, avoiding milk and milk-based products until your child is on the mend.

The World Health Organization gives the following guidelines for the quantity of fluid replacement:

under two years	one half to one quarter cup per loose stool
two to 10 years	one half to one cup per loose stool
over 10 years	as for adults (see p114 for more details)

If children are vomiting, allow the stomach to rest (for example for an hour) before trying to give fluids, then reintroduce fluids very slowly – 5ml every 15 minutes for the first hour, and building up from there. If your child is refusing to drink, try giving small amounts by teaspoon or syringe every few minutes.

Seek medical help earlier rather than later, especially if you notice any of the following symptoms developing:

■ prolonged vomiting and diarrhoea
■ refusal to take fluids
■ listlessness
■ fever
■ blood or mucus in the diarrhoea

In children, faeces may take 10 to 14 days to return to normal, sometimes longer, following an episode of diarrhoea. As long as the faeces are not too frequent, you shouldn't worry about slightly loose faeces in an otherwise fit and recovered child.

Note that symptomatic antidiarrhoeal medications ('stoppers') are not generally recommended in children and should be avoided. If your child is ill enough to need antibiotics, you should seek medical advice; if you are in a remote area away from medical assistance, co-trimoxazole is a suitable antibiotic option (see the Medicines appendix for more details).

As a general rule, avoid giving your child any antidiarrhoeal remedies (apart from ORS and recommended antibiotics).

TUMMY ACHE

This is a very common complaint, as it is in adults. The causes are many and varied, some serious – see p105 for more details. If your child is prone to tummy aches, the stress of travelling may make them more likely while you are away. Otherwise, situations when you should seek medical help include:

- any tummy ache with a fever – could be malaria, typhoid, bladder infection etc
- severe tummy ache that is continuous for more than three hours – could be appendicitis
- tummy ache with profuse vomiting and diarrhoea – the danger is dehydration
- tummy ache that's not normal for your child, especially if he's generally unwell

COLDS, COUGHS & EARACHE

Children are particularly likely to succumb to new germs in new places, so be prepared! Asthma (cough, wheezing) may occur for the first time while you are away, and can be frightening especially if you or your child have not experienced it before. You should seek medical advice if your child is having difficulty breathing, especially if you notice that their ribs are being drawn in with each breath.

Swimming can make ear infections more likely – see p166 for more details. If your child has grommets in their ears, your doctor will generally advise that they shouldn't swim.

PRICKLY HEAT & NAPPY RASH

Prickly heat tends to be more of a problem in children than in adults. Calamine cream can soothe the irritation, and you can help prevent the rash by dressing children in loose cotton clothing, bathing them often and drying them carefully, especially any skin folds and under their arms.

Nappy rash can be a lot worse in the heat. Take a good supply of barrier creams (such as petroleum jelly or zinc and castor oil cream or Sudocrem). Wash the affected area with water after your child has a poo, dry it well, apply barrier cream and try to keep the nappy off as much as possible.

If the affected area is red and painful and the rash doesn't clear up with simple treatment, it may be due to a fungal infection. In this case, try applying an antifungal cream (options include clotrimazole, or Canesten; or an antifungal with hydrocortisone if it is very red and painful) applied twice daily. Check their mouth, as they may have a fungal infection (thrush) there as well, indicated by white patches that are difficult to remove. Treatment is with antifungal drops (such as nystatin). Remember to change rubber teats and feeding utensils as soon as treatment is started and halfway through.

AFTER YOU GET BACK

Consider getting a checkup for yourself and your children if you've been on a long trip or have been travelling rough. Children are more likely to pick up intestinal parasites such as worms if you have been in rural, tropical areas of the Pacific islands, so a test for this is a good idea when you get back. This is a simple test done on a faeces sample, and can be arranged easily by your family doctor. Remember the possibility of malaria if your child gets an unexplained fever after you get back, particularly within the first month or so but up to a year after. Make sure your doctor is aware that you have been travelling and where.

TRAVELLERS WITH SPECIAL NEEDS

You don't have to be able bodied or in perfect health to travel, but make sure you know what to expect and are prepared for it. A short trip to a tourist centre or urban area with well developed medical services may not present any major difficulties, but you may want to think more carefully about longer trips, especially to remote areas.

- Medical advice – get advice from your doctor or specialist on health problems you could encounter when you're travelling and what to do about them.
- Documentation – take with you a written summary from your doctor of your medical problems and any treatment you are currently on or have received in the past.
- Travel insurance – important for all travellers, but particularly if you have special needs (check that it covers you for preexisting illnesses); a policy that provides a 24-hour hotline is handy.
- Medical facilities – good services are available in Australia and New Zealand, but services are more limited in the Pacific islands, and emergency services may be nonexistent in remote islands.
- Practical difficulties – travellers with disabilities will probably find that facilities in the Pacific islands generally lag well behind those in most western countries.
- Medicines – although you should be able to replace most medicines while you are away (especially if you are going to Australia or New Zealand), it's best to take a plentiful supply with you, as well as any equipment you need, like syringes, needles, blood or urine tests, and any arthritis aids or inhalant devices.
- Bracelets or tags engraved with your medical conditions, medications and any drug allergies – see Useful Organisations in the Before You Go chapter for contact details of one company.
- Flying – make sure you let the airline know well in advance about any special requirements you have. Your doctor or the medical department of the airline you're travelling with will be able to give you advice on potential health hazards of flying. For example, the lower oxygen availability in aircraft cabins may be a problem if you suffer from severe heart or lung problems.

!Travelling can be very physically demanding, so your itinerary needs to be realistic and to have the flexibility to allow for rest days, sick days and any unexpected difficulties.

MEDICAL CONDITIONS & TRAVEL

Some medical conditions may make you less able to cope with the physical and environmental challenges of travelling; for example, if you have a heart or lung condition you may find the heat more difficult to cope with. Some medical conditions can make you more vulnerable to infection, and you may need to take additional preventive measures to counteract this. Common travel-related ailments such as diarrhoea and vomiting can be more of a problem if you have ongoing medical conditions, especially as they can affect the absorption of medicines. It's not all bad news, however – being in a hot climate may improve conditions like arthritis and lung problems.

If you have an ongoing medical condition, it's worth seeing your specialist physician before you go for advice on any special hazards travel may pose for you. It's also worth getting in touch with your local support group or a national disease foundation, as they may be able to provide you with specific advice and contact details of similar organisations where you are going. Some useful organisations are listed in the following section.

Check what medical facilities are available locally in case you need to call on them. Your doctor or travel health clinic or any of the information sources listed in the Before You Go chapter should be able to give you information on this; in addition, a brief run-down is given in the Medical Services appendix of this book. If you are on a cruise or an organised tour, find out what provisions they have for dealing with medical problems.

SUPPORT GROUPS & INFORMATION SOURCES

If you have any special health needs, most major national or state disease foundations or support groups should be able to provide you with information and advice on travel-related health issues. In this section we've listed some recommended resources to get you started; you could also try your doctor, specialist physician or a travel health clinic.

Arthritis – the US-based Arthritis Foundation (☎ 800-542-0295 or 206-547-2707) produces an excellent, extremely comprehensive guide for those with arthritis, *Travel and Arthritis*; you can also access it online (www.orthop.washington.edu).

Dialysis – Creative Age Publications (☎ 800-442-5667), 6728 Densmore Ave, Van Nuys, CA 91406 USA, produces a directory of dialysis centres worldwide, or check it out online (http://eneph.com/html/thelist/listglobalpg.html).

Heart conditions – for general information, US travellers could try the American Heart Foundation (☎ 212-953-1900, fax 687-2339, www.ahf.org), 320 East 43rd St, New York NY 10017; in the UK you could try the British Heart Foundation (☎ 020-7935 0185, fax 7486 5820, www.bhf.org.uk), 14 Fitzharding St, London W1H 4DH; and in Australia, you could ring the Heartline information service on ☎ 1300 362 787.

US-based travellers with disabilities could contact one of the following organisations:

Access Foundation (☎ 516-887-5798), PO Box 356, Malverne, NY 11565

Mobility International USA (☎ 541-343-1284, www.miusa.org), PO Box 10767, Eugene, OR 97440

Society for the Advancement of Travel for the Handicapped (SATH, ☎ 718-858-5483, sath.org/index.html), 26 Court St, Brooklyn, NY 11242

In the UK, the Royal Association for Disability & Rehabilitation (RADAR, ☎ 020-7250 3222, fax 250 0212, www.radar.org.uk), at 12 City Forum, 250 City Rd, London EC1V 8AF, produces three holiday fact packs (UK£2 each), which cover planning, insurance and useful organisations, transport and equipment, and specialised accommodation.

Australians and New Zealanders can contact the National Information Communication Awareness Network (NICAN, ☎ 02-6285 3713, fax 6285 3714, www.nican.com.au), at PO Box 407, Curtin, ACT 2605.

The *Global Access* web site (www.geocities.com
/Paris/1052) has lots of information for travellers with disabilities, as well as links to related sites.

OLDER TRAVELLERS

When you're older you're more likely to have the time and,
possibly, the money to travel. If you're normally fit and
healthy, you shouldn't be at any greater risk of problems than
younger travellers. Statistically, older travellers are less likely
to fall ill than younger ones (possibly because you are less
likely to take risks). However, as you get older, you're more
likely to have ongoing medical conditions, and exacerbations
of ongoing medical conditions are the main cause for hospi-
talisation and evacuation of older travellers.

If you have an ongoing medical condition, good preparation
helps to minimise the chances of problems while you are away.
You can get information and advice on health issues from any of
the information sources listed in the Before You Go chapter. For
more general advice, you could try your local senior citizen's

Physical Fitness

Negotiating your way around large airports and other transport terminals often involves a considerable amount of walking, as well as standing around and perhaps having to carry
heavy luggage. Sightseeing can also be surprisingly exhausting, especially in the heat. If you're out of the habit of doing
much exercise, it's probably a good idea to start a gentle
exercise program before you go. If you're planning a trek or
other strenuous exercise, it is essential to start training in
advance. You can avoid activity-related injuries by warming
up and stretching properly before you start and when you
finish.

Finally, don't be overambitious with your travel itinerary –
it's better to do less comfortably than to push yourself too
hard and perhaps regret it.

advice centre, or a national organisation such as the American Association of Retired Persons (☎ 202-434-2277, 800-424-3410), 601 E St NW, Washington DC 20049, USA.

IMMUNISATIONS & MALARIA PREVENTION

Being older doesn't mean you're immune! Immunisations are just as important as for younger travellers, and perhaps more so, as immunity wanes with age. It's a good idea to get this checked out as early as possible, in case you need the full course of an immunisation, which can take a few weeks. For more details of the travel-related immunisations you may need for your trip, see the Immunisations section of the Before You Go chapter. In addition to these, if you are over 65 it's a good idea to be immunised against flu and possibly pneumococcal disease before you travel. You may be more at risk of the flu and pneumonia when you're travelling, and you don't want to waste your trip being ill.

If you need to take antimalarials, be aware that some antimalarials may interact with your regular medications (for example, mefloquine can interact with beta blockers, a heart medicine), so it's a good idea to check this with your doctor.

MEDICAL CHECKUP

As well as getting travel health advice, it's worth having a medical checkup before you go, especially if you are planning on doing any strenuous activities in climatic extremes. If you have any medical conditions or you've recently had surgical treatment, check with your doctor that you are fit to travel. If you are fit to travel, it's a good opportunity to discuss any potential problems you may encounter while you are away and to clarify what to do about them if they do occur.

If you intend to go scuba diving, you will need to have a medical performed by a specialist diving doctor. This is particularly important, as older divers and those with preexisting medical conditions are more likely to suffer serious problems, and if you are in the Pacific islands, you will probably need to be evacuated to specialist facilities in Hawai'i, New Zealand or Australia. See the section on diving in the Water Safety chapter later in this book for more details.

DENTAL CHECKUP

This is a always a good idea, particularly if you are going away for more than a couple of weeks. If you wear dentures, have them checked before you leave home, and make sure you wear in a new pair of dentures before you go, in case adjustments need to be made to make them comfortable. Consider taking a spare pair with you; if you have an old pair, your dentist may be able to modify them to make them useable in an emergency. Getting a new set of dentures while you're away could be a major problem. However, simple temporary repairs may be carried out by a dentist, or you can make a simple repair yourself like sticking a tooth back on or sticking a broken denture back together using glue. If you use an epoxy glue, be careful not to put them back in your mouth before the glue has set ...

EYES

If you wear glasses, remember to take a spare pair with you, as well as the prescription in case you need to replace them. Take a plentiful supply of any eyedrops you use, although eyedrops that need to be kept refrigerated can be a bit problematic – keep them in the middle of your luggage, and investigate whether there is a fridge you can have access to at your accommodation.

MEDICAL KIT & MEDICATIONS

It's sensible to take a well stocked medical kit, including a plentiful supply of any regular medications plus a bit extra. Always keep a supply on you, as well as a back-up supply in your luggage, in case your luggage goes walkies.

The What to Take section in the Before You Go chapter gives detailed guidance on items you could consider taking

Medicines

If you take any regular medications, bear in mind that these could interact with medicines you may be prescribed for a travel-related problem when you are away.

- Some medications can make you very sensitive to the effects of the sun – see p155 for more details.
- Pseudoephedrine hydrochloride (decongestant) – avoid if you have raised blood pressure.
- Hyoscine (for travel sickness) – best avoided if you have glaucoma or prostate problems.
- Antimalarials can interact with some heart drugs.

with you. In addition, if you suffer from prostate trouble, you could consider taking a sterile catheter set with you if you are going to remote areas away from medical help – discuss this with your doctor if necessary.

ON THE MOVE

Keep any regular or as-needed medications (for angina, for example) in your hand luggage so you can access them readily during the journey if necessary.

Sitting for long periods of time, especially in the heat, can make your feet and ankles swell. Also, when you're older, you're at greater risk of developing blood clots in your leg veins if you sit immobile through a long journey. Some medical conditions can also make this more likely. Discuss this with your doctor but try the following strategies:

▶ wriggle your toes, flex your calves while you are sitting down
▶ get up and move around periodically if you can
▶ drink plenty of fluids (nonalcoholic) to prevent dehydration, which makes your blood more likely to clot
▶ your doctor may advise you to take low dose aspirin (75mg) for three days before, during and after the flight; alternatively, some doctors may suggest an injection of a blood-thinning agent like heparin

If you're crossing lots of time zones, jet lag can be a problem – for guidelines on minimising the impact of jet lag, see the On the Move chapter at the beginning of this book.

STAYING HEALTHY

All the general, common-sense measures suggested in the Staying Healthy chapter earlier in this book are just as relevant to older travellers.

With increasing age, you have fewer sweat glands and they work less efficiently. This means that you are likely to feel the heat more and be more vulnerable to problems like heat exhaustion and heatstroke (see p282). Take time to acclimatise, avoid strenuous exercise in the heat, especially when you first arrive, and drink plenty of fluids. With age, your blood vessels get stiffer and less reactive, making you more likely to faint in the heat. Being in a hot climate makes you sweat more, and it's easy to become dehydrated, especially if you are taking medications to promote fluid loss, such as diuretics for a heart condition. Discuss this with your doctor before you leave, as you may need to adjust your medications while you are away. If you are overweight or have a medical condition such as heart or lung problems or diabetes, you will be more vulnerable to the effects of the heat.

Several studies have shown that older travellers are less likely to suffer from diarrhoea while travelling, perhaps because you are more discerning about where and what to eat than younger travellers. In any case, if you are planning on travelling through Australia and New Zealand, digestive upsets are no more likely than if you were travelling in your home country. If you do get diarrhoea and/or vomiting, follow the guidelines given in the Diarrhoea chapter, and remember that this may mean your usual medications are absorbed less well. You're also at more risk of dehydration, so seek medical help earlier rather than later.

Constipation is a common complaint even (or especially) when you are travelling – see the section on constipation in the Coughs, Rashes & Other Common Problems chapter for more details. Keep up your fluid intake, and eat lots of fresh fruit and vegetables. If you are prone to constipation, take a supply of a remedy you know works for you.

As you get older, wounds are slower to heal. The hot, humid conditions of the tropics exacerbate this and make infection more likely, so it's worth taking particular care to avoid insect bites and injury. If you do get a cut or scratch, take good care of it to save you trouble later.

! If you fall ill, seek medical advice as soon as possible, and remember that the more drugs you are taking, the more likely they are to interact and cause unwanted effects. Always tell any doctor treating you of any conditions you have and any medications you are on. Have good insurance!

DIABETIC TRAVELLERS

This section was written by Michelle Sobel, a Type 1 diabetic who has never let her condition get in the way of her travels.

Preventive self-care is your aim, wherever you travel. Prepared and in good diabetic control, you're in the best position to enjoy your experiences abroad.

The level and type of care offered to diabetics varies from country to country. In Australia and New Zealand, you can expect a similar level of care to that available in any other developed country. In the Pacific islands, general medical facilities are more limited outside of the main centres; however, diabetes is a common and growing problem in the region, so doctors and healthworkers are likely to be familiar with the needs of diabetic travellers. Find out before you go what to expect at your destination. National diabetic associations are usually the best source of information on local diabetic care, and national diabetes organisations at home often have information for travellers. You could try contacting any of the following:

International Diabetes Federation (www.idf.org), 1 rue Defacqz, B-1000 Brussels, Belgium – maintains a list of diabetic associations around the world

American Diabetes Association (www.diabetes.org) National Office, 1660 Duke St, Alexandria, VA 22314, USA

British Diabetes Association (BDA Careline ☎ 020-7636 6112, www.diabetes.org.uk), 10 Queen Anne St, London W1M 0BD, UK – produces a useful leaflet on travel with diabetes, as well as a number of country guides for diabetics

Diabetes Australia (☎ 02-6230 1155, www.diabetes.org.au), National Office, 1st Floor, Churchill House, 218 Northbourne Ave, Braddon, ACT 2161, Australia

Diabetes NZ (☎ 03-434 8110, fax 434 5281, email info@diabetes.org.nz), PO Box 54, Oamaru, New Zealand

Alternatively, check out www.diabeticresource.com (click on 'Travel'). A useful publication you could consider getting is the *Diabetic Traveller's Companion* by Nerida Nichol.

INSULIN & OTHER DIABETIC SUPPLIES

Before you leave, call the relevant manufacturer to get information on the availability abroad of diabetic supplies like test strips, medication (oral and insulin) and glucose meters. Consumer-friendly meter and pump manufacturers will advise you on repair, replacement and delivery policies if your equipment malfunctions or is lost abroad.

Take two to three times the medical supplies you expect to use (in carry-on, waterproof packs) to protect against loss or damage. On day trips, I carry two half bottles (instead of one or two full bottles) of insulin so there's backup in case of breakage. Also, it's a good idea to retain generic-name prescriptions (even if invalid abroad) and medication inserts, as medications may have different brand names in different parts of the world.

To reduce bulk, try insulin pens over syringes. However, note that manufacturers state that at room temperature some insulin pen cartridges (particularly some slow-acting and

Insulin Concentrations & Glucose Readings

Be aware that insulin may be sold in different concentrations from country to country. If you have to replenish abroad, use the appropriate syringe with the appropriate concentration. If you mix and match syringes and concentrations (for example if you use U-40 insulin in a syringe marked 'for U-100 insulin only'), you'll be at greater risk of over or under-injecting insulin.

Note that most nations measure blood glucose in mmol/L; the US, however, primarily uses mg/dL. Different meters report glucose readings using either or both of these standards.

- To convert mmol/L to mg/dL, multiply the glucose reading by 18 (ie 4mmol/L = 72 mg/dL).
- To convert mg/dL, divide the glucose by 18.

pre-mixed insulin) may have shorter lives (as short as seven or 14 days) than vials (which last about a month).

Note that having syringes and meters on your person can sometimes prompt questions from customs and other officials, so make sure you carry on you at all times documentation from your doctor explaining your need for syringes, insulin and meters.

Some diabetic care providers suggest reusing sharps, at your own risk. Consult your physician about reusing, and ask for advice on sterilising syringes and needles if necessary. Always discard needles and lancets appropriately when dull, and never share sharps or meters.

If you find you are running out of supplies in a place with limited resources, be prepared (financially and time-wise) to make a detour to a better-stocked country (such as Australia or New Zealand). For extended travel and for emergencies, consider making preparations before you go for medical supplies to be mailed to you. Packaging is available to insulate insulin from heat and physical damage in the mail.

ON THE MOVE

Crossing time zones can be problematic, especially for insulin-dependent diabetics. Before you leave, take a copy of your itinerary to your diabetic care provider and ask for specific guidance on adjusting your individual protocol en route and as you acclimatise. As a rule, though, keep your watch on home time until the morning after you land.

It's always important to check blood sugars frequently to modify dosages, mealtimes and food choices, and flying presents its own issues. If you make adjustments based on how you feel – a very unreliable indicator whether you're travelling or not – hyper and hypoglycaemic reactions are almost inevitable. Remember that jet lag can further impair your ability to tell highs and lows.

STAYING HEALTHY

Before you go, discuss with your doctor or specialist what to do if you get sick, as well as dosage adjustments, immunisations and other general travel-related health issues. Unaccustomed physical activity, erratic sleep and meal times, unfamiliar foods, climate change, altitude sickness and stress are just some of the many variables that can aggravate control while you are away. All the potential effects of unstable blood glucose (like disorientation, headaches and lethargy) are especially unwelcome when you're away from home.

When you're travelling, insulin-dependent diabetics need to take particular care to prevent hyper and hypoglycaemic reactions. Ideally, monitor at least six times daily; if possible, bring two meters as well as visual blood glucose strips as backup. Carry emergency food, foil-wrapped ketone strips and glucagon. In the event of a reaction, wearing a medical bracelet showing that you are a diabetic (see MedicAlert under Useful Organisations in the Before You Go chapter) can help prevent misdiagnosis (symptoms are often otherwise presumed to be induced by alcohol or illegal substances).

All diabetics should follow basic guidelines to prevent foodborne illness. If you do (or don't) take extra risks and end up ill, know what you need to do to prevent highs and lows related to illness. Touring with supportive companions is a good idea; if you're travelling solo, check in with contacts. Cell phones are handy.

Wounds in hot, humid climates get infected easier and faster – always keep your feet dry, clean, and comfortable. Never walk barefoot, even on the beach. In hot or remote regions, take special care to stay hydrated. Pack extra supplies of medication, food and water. Protect your skin from the sun (severe sunburn can elevate blood sugars).

Keep insulin chilled in thermoses or insulated cool packs. Gels that freeze when shaken can protect insulin for a few hours. Make sure you don't freeze insulin, and don't place it directly against ice. Keep insulin out of direct sunlight. And ask hostels, friends etc to refrigerate your supplies when they have the opportunity.

HIV-POSITIVE TRAVELLERS

If you are HIV-positive, travelling poses some special problems, although this depends to a certain extent on your CD4 count. It's essential you get specialist advice on this before you travel (from your doctor, specialist physician or travel health clinic).

As a rule, live vaccines (which include oral polio, oral typhoid, measles, mumps and rubella) are best avoided if you are HIV-positive.

! You are generally at greater risk of travel-related illnesses, and if you do get ill, illness may have a greater impact on you.

It's even more important to take great care over what you eat and drink, and you may want to consider taking antibiotics to prevent diarrhoea – discuss this before you go. You are at greater risk than non-HIV-positive travellers of some illnesses, such as tuberculosis and hepatitis A, although you are not at any increased risk of malaria.

Bear in mind that attitudes towards HIV infection may be very different in some Pacific islands to what you are used to. Although Australia, New Zealand and some Pacific island nations ask for HIV testing for work permits and long stays, you're unlikely to be asked for this if you're going for a short holiday.

You should be able to get more information on all these issues from your national HIV/AIDS organisation. Some useful organisations include the following:

Terrence Higgins Trust (☎ 020-7831 0330, www.tht.org.uk), 52-54 Grays Inn Rd, London WC1X 8JU, UK

Australian Federation of AIDS Organisations (AFAO; ☎ 02-9281 1999, www.afao.org.au) – an excellent source of information and contacts on all aspects of HIV/AIDS

National Association of People Living With HIV/AIDS (Australia ☎ 02-9281 1999 or 0416 311 833)

New Zealand AIDS Foundation (☎ 303-3124, fax 309-3149), PO Box 6663, Wellesley St, Auckland, New Zealand – there are also regional offices in Auckland, Hamilton, Wellington and Christchurch

On the web, there's good medical information for HIV-positive travellers at www.travelhealth.com/aids.htm and on the CDC site at www.cdc.gov/travel/hivtrav. Another good resource you could check out is aegis.com (with loads of good links for a variety of HIV-related issues).

WILDERNESS HEALTH & SAFETY

Australia, New Zealand and the Pacific islands provide endless opportunities both for water sports and for adventuring on land, from trekking and mountaineering to skiing, rock climbing, cycling and caving. Trekking is known as 'bushwalking' in Australia and Papua New Guinea, and 'tramping' in New Zealand but for simplicity, we've stuck to using the generic term 'trekking' in this guide. For safety issues associated with water sports, see the Water Safety chapter.

Outdoor adventuring anywhere carries risks, and this is especially important to bear in mind if you are in a remote area without immediate access to emergency services. It's important to take the wilderness seriously, even if you are experienced in wilderness activities – adventurers can and do regularly die in wilderness situations in Australia, New Zealand and the Pacific islands, often because they were not properly prepared and failed to take adequate precautions. Don't let this be you! Make sure you find out – and follow – some basic safety rules before you go off adventuring.

For any wilderness activity, you need to be able to answer, or at least to have considered, the following questions.

■ What could go wrong? Have I taken steps to make sure this is as unlikely as possible?
■ How would I get help if something does go wrong?
■ If something goes wrong, do I have the necessary skills or equipment to deal with the situation until help arrives?

With these questions in mind, here are some basic safety rules to follow.

▶ Get as much information about the activity, route, risks and appropriate safety precautions before you go.
▶ Make sure you let someone know of your intentions and expected date of return – no-one is going to come looking for you if they don't know you're out there.
▶ Do a first aid course before you go and take this guide or a dedicated first aid or wilderness survival guide with you.

Safety in Numbers

One of the most important safety issues to take on board when you're planning any sort of wilderness activity is not to go solo. It's best, if possible, to go in a small group – four is usually considered the minimum number. This way, if someone in the group has an accident or is taken ill, one person can stay with the casualty and the others can go for help.

Also, many of the signs and symptoms associated with excess heat or cold (or altitude) are much more likely to be noticed by other people than by you. Because of this, it's vital everyone watches out for each other. Never leave someone on their own if they're showing symptoms. Of course, you'll also want to self-check for aches, pains, cold areas, numbness, dizziness and any other symptoms that aren't normal for you. And most problems, even seemingly insurmountable ones, turn out to be much less daunting when there are second, third and fourth opinions on how to tackle them.

▸ Make sure you are properly equipped before you set off.
▸ Be prepared to delay starting if you are not feeling one hundred percent or the weather looks risky.
▸ Keep within your capabilities – it's good to challenge yourself, but it doesn't have to be an ordeal.
▸ Stretching before you exercise and warming down after helps make muscle strains less likely.

If you are going to remote areas for more than a few days, make sure you know how to recognise and deal with common illnesses, including coughs and flu, intestinal upsets, skin infections, and malaria (in risk areas).

INFORMATION SOURCES

If you're looking to find out about wilderness health, safety and survival issues before you go (recommended if you are planning on doing any serious adventuring), there are lots of good resources you could try.

Publications

There are many of these on the market, providing general and more specific advice on coping with outdoor hazards. Here's a selection to get you started:

Being Outside by Tim Macartney-Snape – comprehensive overview of health, safety and general outdoor survival issues

Hiking & Backpacking: A Complete Guide by Karen Berger – comprehensive, easy to read and practical guide to all aspects of walking in the wilderness, and there's a second guide with more specialist information, *Advanced Backpacking: A Trailside Guide*

The Backpacker's Handbook by Chris Townsend – the how-to guide for all aspects of backpacking and trekking from a veteran outdoor adventurer

Medicine for Mountaineering (edited by J Wilkerson) – the classic reference for travellers likely to be more than 24 hours from medical care

Bushwalking in Australia and *Tramping in New Zealand* (Lonely Planet) – both guides have a comprehensive Health & Safety chapter, as well as detailed information on walks

Bushwalking and Camping by Paddy Pallin – includes sections on bush first aid, as well as outdoor hazards

Safety in the Bush by the Hobart Walking Club – good sections on bush first aid and bush safety issues.

Bushwalking and Mountaincraft Leadership, Handbook of the Victorian Bushwalking & Mountaincraft Training Advisory Board, Sport & Recreation Victoria – authoritative and comprehensive manual.

The New Zealand Mountain Safety Council (☎ 385 7162) PO Box 6027, Te Aro, Wellington, publishes a number of excellent pamphlets, including *Bushcraft*, *Mountaincraft*, *Outdoor First Aid*, *Hypothermia*, often available at information centres and hostels

Safety in the Mountains, Federated Mountain Clubs, PO Box 1604, Wellington

If you're interested in learning how to trap, skin and eat a wild animal or how to construct a mess hall from just a few twigs, you could check out some of the following books: *Australian Bushcraft Handbook* by L Lannoy and Horowitz Grahame; *The Bushman's Handbook* by HA Lindsay; or *The Ten Bushcraft Books* by R Graves.

Internet Resources

If you have access to the web, Princeton University's Outdoor Action Program (www.princeton.edu/~oa/altitude.html) is a great resource, with detailed information on heat, cold, altitude and other wilderness safety issues, as well as heaps of links to related sites on a wide variety of outdoor activities, including mountain biking, hiking, caving and mountaineering.

Other Information Sources

In Australia, national park offices and rangers are the best source of information on track and weather conditions, as well as any safety concerns, including total fire ban days. The national park offices are state and territory run, and there is a central office in each state and territory capital.

In New Zealand, contact the appropriate national park headquarters or the local Department of Conservation office for local information about current track and weather conditions, as well as safety advice. The DOC's head office can be contacted on ☎ 471 0726, PO Box 10 420, Wellington, NZ.

RADIOS & EPIRBS

If you're going off the beaten track in an unpopulated or remote area for any length of time or sea kayaking, it's sensible to have some means of raising the alarm if the need arises. Cell phones can be handy (and light if you're on foot), but they don't work in most wilderness areas. The alternative is to take a radio or possibly an EPIRB (Emergency Position Indication Radio Beacon) with you. You can often hire equipment for the length of your trip, at reasonable rates. You should be able to get information on radios from the national parks organisations or local tourist information services in Australia and New Zealand.

EMERGENCY RESCUE PROCEDURE

If you or one of your group has an accident (even a minor one), or falls ill while you are out in the wilderness, you'll need to

Let Someone Know

If you are planning a trip in the wilderness, whether you are hiking, cross country skiing, sea kayaking or outback driving, the best insurance you can have is to let someone know of your plans. Always inform someone reliable of your route and estimated return date so that if you do run into difficulties, the alarm can be raised.

At the start of many overnight treks in popular hiking areas in Australia and New Zealand there are intention books which you should fill in. In outback Australia, if you are driving to remote, unpopulated areas, you should register your intentions at the last town.

If there isn't a formal 'intention book' system (not likely, for example, in the Pacific islands) you could consider letting the folks back home know via a brief phone call; alternatively, leave the information with your hotel, other travellers or the local park office.

The system only works if you let people know when you get back so that unnecessary and expensive rescues aren't initiated. Otherwise, the system runs a risk of falling victim to the 'cry wolf' syndrome – or you may end up having to pay for previously free services.

decide on your best course of action – not always easy. Obviously, you will need to take into consideration your individual circumstances, including where you are and whether you have a radio or some means of direct communication with you, but some basic guidelines are as follows (see also the section on Getting Lost later in this chapter):

▶ use your first aid knowledge and experience, as well as the information in this guide if necessary, to make a medical assessment of the situation

▶ for groups of several people, the accepted procedure is to leave one person with the casualty, together with as much equipment, food and water as you can sensibly spare, and for the rest of the group to go for help

▶ if there are only two of you, the situation is more tricky, and you will have to make an individual judgement as to the best course of action in this situation

▶ if you leave someone, mark their position carefully on the map (take this with you); you should also make sure they can be easily found by marking the position with something conspicuous, such as bright clothing or a large stone cross on the ground

▶ you can try attracting attention by using a whistle or torch, lighting a smoky fire (use damp wood) or waving bright clothing. Shouting is tiring and not very effective

Be realistic – in many remote areas, especially in the Pacific islands, self-evacuation is going to be your only and best option, especially as rescue may be delayed or difficult due to transport problems and communication difficulties.

! *The internationally recognised distress signal is six whistle blasts or six torch flashes, followed by a minute's rest, then the signal repeated. The answer is three blasts or flashes followed by a minute's rest, then repeated.*

The uncertainties associated with emergency rescue in remote wilderness areas should make it clear to you how important careful planning and safety precautions are, especially if you are going in a small group.

FIRST AID KIT

See What to Take in the Before You Go chapter for suggestions on what to include in a basic travel medical kit. For adventuring in remote areas, you'll need to include a few extras, including:

- radio
- waterproof matches
- paper (waterproof) and pencil
- length of cord (for crossing rivers etc)
- whistle
- torch
- bivvy (survival) bag, supply of plastic bags or survival blanket

WEATHER

You are extremely vulnerable to all the vagaries of the weather when you are doing outdoor activities – ignore them at your peril. Make sure you know what to expect in terms of potentially severe weather conditions and factor this in at the planning stage. Be prepared to modify or even call off your plans if appropriate. Torrential tropical rains, for example, bring a real risk of flooding and make tracks treacherously slippy and river crossings dangerous.

FOOD & WATER

If you don't get this aspect of your trip right, you run the risk of turning the outing into an unwelcome ordeal, as well as jeopardising your health. The section on Food for Action in the Diet & Nutrition chapter earlier in this guide gives guidelines on fuelling up.

Water is a major issue, and you need to give some thought to this before you set off. In temperate climes and tropical rainforests, water is often available in abundance (although you may need to purify it before it is safe to drink), but in arid areas you need to plan how much to carry with you and to have reliable information on where you can refill. National park rangers and returning walkers are often the best source of information. In many areas, you'll have to let water availability dictate your itinerary.

It is said that you can survive only three days without any water – don't test it out!

Through normal body processes, you lose 2L to 3L of water a day. If you are sweating a lot because of the heat or activity, you can lose a lot more. You need to replace this amount through drinking water and moisture taken in through food. Individual requirements vary, but most people need 4L to 6L a day, more in extreme temperatures. A 2L water bottle is probably sufficient for a day's outing in mild weather. Cold

Giardia

Clear water is not necessarily safe water! Water in river and streams in many wilderness areas in Australia, New Zealand and the Pacific islands may be contaminated with the cysts of the *Giardia* parasite. You only need to drink one or two cysts to get giardiasis, a form of diarrhoea (see the Diarrhoea chapter for more details about symptoms and treatment).

Why is *Giardia* present in otherwise pristine wilderness areas? One reason is thought to be poor hygiene practices by trekkers, mainly by not burying faeces adequately, or by burying them close to waterways. Trekkers may have brought the infection with them from previous destinations, especially if they have been travelling internationally. In addition, the parasite is found in some domestic and wild animals, and may reach the water supply from them. So even in unpopulated areas, don't assume the water is safe:

- take some means of purifying water with you – see p79 for more details
- be careful about basic hygiene – wash your hands before preparing or eating food
- bury faeces in an adequately deep hole, well away from waterways

dry air can make you lose moisture, especially if you are active. See the Climate & Altitude chapter for more details on heat and dehydration.

DRIVING OFF THE BEATEN TRACK

Driving in remote, rural areas, especially in the Australian outback, is not to be taken lightly and requires a certain amount of planning. Many routes are through unpopulated areas, and the climate is harsh. If you are going off the main road, always carry a good map of the area, and always let someone know what you are planning. Make sure you have sufficient spare parts and equipment with you.

Some basic rules to bear in mind:

- fuel – you'll need to plan carefully where to get this and consider carrying extra fuel with you on some routes; if you run out, it's likely to be a long way to the next fuel stop
- water – this is scarce in the Australian outback, so you must carry all you need with you; a minimum of 20L in suitable containers is recommended
- radio – essential if you are driving off the main road for any length of time; although hire vehicles don't generally come complete with a radio, there are companies you can hire them from
- fatigue – in Australia, the distances involved are often vast; stop and rest at least every two hours
- wildlife – roads are generally unfenced and animals such as cattle, kangaroos and camels often wander onto the road; avoid driving at dusk or at night, when the wildlife is most active
- flooding – always check the depth indicator first if you have to cross a flooded causeway or bridge; caution is always the best part of valour in this situation
- off-roading – don't do it! You will probably be trespassing, you may do considerable damage to the environment, and you're going to feel pretty stupid if you get bogged

For more detailed information on all aspects of outback driving, check out Lonely Planet's *Outback Australia*.

Lost or Broken Down

If your vehicle breaks down or you get lost, especially if you are not on the main road, don't leave it – a large, sun-reflecting vehicle will be easier for rescuers to spot than you would be. If you have a radio (strongly advised for remote areas), signal for help. Don't waste your precious water, and take stock of your food situation.

Bogged Vehicle

Hopefully, this will never happen to you because you'll avoid getting in the situation in the first place. Driving on soft surfaces requires special skills – if you don't know what you are doing, you shouldn't risk it.

Finding Your Way

If you are out and about in the wilderness, being able to read a map accurately and use a compass are vital skills to have. It's worth doing a bit of homework on this at the planning stage of your trip. Consider going on an orienteering course, or check out one of the many manuals available on the subject. One recommended guide is the Ordnance Survey's *Land Navigation* by Wally Keay.

Something to bear in mind: if you've bought your compass in the northern hemisphere, you'll find that it goes wonky in the southern hemisphere (because of the earth's magnetic variation), so you'll need to buy a southern hemisphere compass when you arrive.

If you do get bogged, don't spin your wheels – you'll only dig yourself in further. Try to get your vehicle out using whatever equipment you have. Otherwise, stay with your vehicle and wait for assistance.

TREKKING

If you decide to go on a trek of any length, here's a quick health and safety checklist.

Preparation

All the general principles discussed at the beginning of the chapter apply, especially letting someone know of your plans and when to expect you back.

- Fitness – trekking can be a strenuous activity, particularly if you're not in peak physical condition, so make sure what you are planning is within your capabilities and that there is some flexibility built into your plans in case you find you need to bail out at any stage.
- Training – some pre-trek fitness training is a good idea, and will reduce the likelihood of sprains, falls and overuse injuries.
- Equipment – make sure you are fully prepared for the environmental conditions you're likely to encounter and take a well

A Sauté in the Woods ...

If you plan to go camping or trekking in remote areas, you can't rely on fire as a means of cooking. In fact, many national parks have banned the use of campfires altogether. You will need to carry a portable cooker. There are several types of on the market, but the most practical are ones that use a variety of liquid fuels, such as kerosene, petroleum or white gasoline. Gas canister stoves are popular with backpackers and slightly safer than liquid fuel stoves, but remember that gas canisters are not permitted on aircraft at all.

If you're new to the joys of using a camp stove, it's probably a good idea to have a few practice runs in the kitchen at home. Burns from portable stoves are common. It's important to use your camp stove safely, especially if you are using it inside your tent:

- if you need to re-fill your stove, do it outside the tent
- light your stove outside the tent and keep the stove close to the door so that you can push it out in an emergency
- make sure the tent flaps are tied back to prevent them from falling in the flames
- if you are cooking inside your tent, make sure it is well ventilated or you run the risk of carbon monoxide poisoning with liquid fuel stoves
- be careful to avoid fuel spills, and keep your hair and clothes out of reach of the flames
- take a pan grip or have a thick cloth handy for handling hot pans, and try not to stir the food once it's on the stove in case of spillages

See the First Aid appendix for guidelines on how to treat burns and scalds.

stocked medical kit (see the Before You Go chapter earlier in this guide).
- Footwear – running shoes and sandals are not much use on a trek in rough terrain, so unless you can get hold of a decent pair of walking boots, consider changing your plans.

- Map and compass – a reasonable map of the area is vital, especially if you are going without a guide (but is a good idea anyway), but it's no good if you can't follow it.
- Insurance – check that your insurance covers you for trekking, and consider joining a local emergency rescue organisation.

Although this is only relevant for a few places, including Mt Wilhelm in Papua New Guinea and Mt Cook in New Zealand, if you are going to be walking at high altitude (over about 2500m), make sure you know how to recognise and deal with altitude sickness (see p288).

On the Trek

Be prepared to hire a guide if necessary – essential for many trails in Papua New Guinea.

- Water – don't assume there will be water along the way unless you are told there is by a reliable source; otherwise, you'll need to carry all your water requirements with you.
- Food – again, you shouldn't rely on food being available along the way; take plenty of food with you, including energy-giving snacks like chocolate and dried fruit.
- Tiredness – this makes accidents and injuries more likely, so eat properly throughout the day, take regular rests and don't push yourself too hard, especially towards the end of the day.
- Protect yourself against insect bites (p69) and leeches (p323); carry a compression bandage to treat snake bite (except New Zealand).

Blisters & Footcare

The scourge of trekkers, blisters (and calluses) occur when there is repeated friction to the skin. Prevention is all-important.

! Make sure your footwear is well worn in before you set off sightseeing or on a hike. At the very least, wear them on a few short walks before you leave – don't plan to wear them in for the first time while you are away.

Your boots should fit comfortably with enough room to move your toes, and be sure your socks fit properly. If you're going to be doing lots of walking, it's worth investing in socks specifically made for walkers. Socks made from a synthetic fibre called orlon have been shown to decrease the size and frequency of blisters. Wet and muddy socks can also cause blisters, so slip a spare pair of socks in your daypack and change your socks when necessary. Keep your toenails clipped but not too short.

If you are planning on trekking and you haven't time to toughen the skin of your feet up by graduated walking, you could consider soaking your feet in a solution of potassium permanganate for 20 minutes daily (add a teaspoon of crystals to 4L of warm water) to toughen the skin. In the army, new recruits were once told to urinate on their feet to toughen the skin, but this won't endear you to your travelling companions.

If you do feel a blister coming on, or you find you have developed one at the end of the day, take immediate action.

▸ Apply a simple sticking plaster or preferably one of the special blister plasters that act as a second skin, and follow the instructions on the packaging for replacement. 'Second skin' products reduce the shearing forces that cause blisters.
▸ It may be worth stretching the offending part of the shoes or wearing a different pair of socks.
▸ If the blister looks as if it is about to burst or is already broken, apply an antiseptic ointment such as chlorhexidine to reduce the risk of infection, and cover it with a thick pad of sterile gauze (preferably over a nonadherent dressing like melolin). If you've got hydrodermic dressings such as duoderm with you, apply it and leave it in place for seven days or so.

If the blister hasn't already burst, it's best to leave it, as it won't get infected as long as it is intact.

CYCLING

Australia and New Zealand, in particular, are great mountain biking destinations, with miles of unsealed tracks crisscrossing the wilderness. If you're considering a short or longer cycle tour, here are some basic health and safety tips to consider.

Health & Fitness

It's a good idea to get fit on a bike if you plan on doing more than a couple of days of cycle touring – practise riding an average daily distance two or three days in a row. Before you set off, be sure to warm up and stretch properly. On the ride:

- take regular breaks during the day
- consider having a massage in the evening
- avoid sore hands from gripping the handlebar on rough roads for long periods by changing hand position (if possible), relaxing your grip on the handlebars and taking frequent rests
- be prepared for climatic extremes
- remember to drink plenty of fluids, especially if it's hot, and avoid cycling during the hottest part of the day
- take snack food with you for any ride that's more than about an hour long

Equipment & Cycling Technique

This can make a big difference to your enjoyment and comfort, as well as safety on the ride.

- If you're hiring a bike, check it over carefully – make sure the brakes work and check the wheels and tyres.
- Wear safety gear – helmet (essential), sunglasses, cycling gloves and two layers of clothing (helps prevent road rash if you come off your bike) – and check your bike on a daily basis.
- Learn the local road rules, ride in single file and ride defensively.
- Make sure your bike is adjusted for you – check the seat and handlebar height, and that the seat is parallel to the ground.
- Take lights with you if you're intending to ride at night.
- Balance the load on your bike and keep the weight low to the ground, preferably with panniers.
- Learn to spin the gears (70 to 90 revs per minute), not push them – this way you'll avoid sore knees from pushing big gears.

Resources

For more information, try the following resources:

The Bicycle Touring Manual by Rob van der Plas – a useful guide for serious tourers

www.cyclery.com and www.ctc.org.uk – both these web sites have good information on health and safety issues for cyclists

Australian Cycling Federation (☎ 02-9764 2555, fax 02-9764 2888), 14 Telopea Ave, Homebush West, NSW, Australia

NZ Mountain Bike Association (☎ 07-378 9552) PO Box 371, Taupo

For the complete low-down on cycle touring in Australia and New Zealand, you could check out Lonely Planet's cycling guides to these destinations.

CAVING

If you're planning on going caving, be aware of the potential risks and don't attempt anything that is beyond your abilities. Even a minor injury underground can entail major difficulties in getting the casualty to the surface, and caves are usually in relatively isolated areas, away from medical help. As for any wilderness activity, never go caving alone, and always let someone know where you are going and when to expect you back. If you're a novice, you'll probably be going with an experienced leader or group, but it's a good idea to be aware of some basic safety rules.

▶ Wear a helmet – falling rocks can be a hazard, and wet surfaces can be slippery, so protect yourself from head injury.
▶ Take a light source – caves are dark, so take a good torch (flashlight) with you, plus back-up lights.
▶ Wrap up – caves are cold and wet and, especially in temperate climates, hypothermia is a real risk; use the layer principle to protect yourself against the cold.

It's easy to get lost in caves, so stick with your leader and take note of junctions and any other significant features. Other hazards include:

■ falling or unstable rocks – watch out above and below
■ flash floods are always a risk, as a result of rain storms or snow melt
■ getting stuck – tight spots can be a bit daunting, especially if you are relatively inexperienced; if you do feel you're stuck, stay calm, breathe out slowly (this will make your chest shrink) and ease yourself out

! Scuba diving in caves is extremely risky – don't even think about it unless you are a very experienced caver and diver.

As far as nasty diseases are concerned, there are a couple to be aware of, but they are not a huge risk:

- leptospirosis (Weil's disease) – bacterial disease transmitted through rat or bat urine; you can get infected if you scrape yourself against the cave walls or by swimming in contaminated water – see p299 for more details
- histoplasmosis – you can get this fungal chest infection by inhaling dried bat droppings in small confined spaces; causes a fever, headache, chest pains and cough about two weeks after you've been exposed – there's no specific treatment, but you should seek medical advice, as it can make some people very ill

Scorpions and snakes can live around caves, so be wary of where you put your hands. Various small biters (including sandflies, mosquitoes, ticks and leeches) live in and around the entrance to caves – cover up and apply insect repellent.

Resources

For more information, you could try contacting:

Australian Speleological Federation (http://rubens.its.unimelb .edu.au/~pgm/asf), PO Box 388, Broadway NSW 2007, Australia
NZ Speleological Society (☎ 07-878 7640) PO Box 18, Waitomo Caves

EMERGENCY SITUATIONS

Hopefully, you will have prepared well, followed all the safety precautions and used your skills to keep out of trouble. However, here are some guidelines if you do find yourself in a sticky situation.

GETTING LOST

This can be surprisingly easy, and every year even experienced walkers get lost and disappear in wilderness areas in

Australia, New Zealand and the Pacific islands. Although it is less likely on major, popular trails, it is always a possibility, even on a half day walk. Prevention, as always, is the best cure: take a guide if necessary (most of the walks in Papua New Guinea should not be attempted without a guide), and always take the best available map and a compass. And make sure you know how to use them.

So if you get that heart-stopping, goosebump-inducing, gonad-shrinking feeling that you are totally lost in the wilderness, what do you do? First off, allow yourself a limited brief panic, then try any or all of the following:

▶ stop, have a drink and a snack, and think about it – resist the urge to keep going just in case the path is over the next rise
▶ try to work out where you are – think about how long you've been walking and which direction from the last known point
▶ have a look round for any prominent landmarks, take a compass reading and use your map
▶ back-track to your last known point – but only if you are sure you can
▶ aim for a landscape feature you can identify on your map, from which you can work out your position
▶ stay put and wait for rescue (but only if someone knows you're out there) or another walker to pass by – this is clearly not a practical option if you're walking somewhere remote such as highland or jungle areas of Papua New Guinea

EMERGENCY NIGHT OUT

If you are lost or you misjudged the time (avoid this with better planning next time!), you may have to spend an unplanned night out in the wilderness. This shouldn't be too much of a drama if you have plenty of equipment and emergency rations with you, but if haven't, it can be somewhat nerve-wracking. You're likely to be tired and, temperatures can plummet at night, especially in highland or desert areas. Your aims are to prevent hypothermia and to maintain your morale.

▶ Find a sheltered spot, out of the wind or rain; make a snow cave or a shelter from ferns if necessary.

▶ Before you get cold, remove wet clothing and put on all the extra clothing you hopefully have with you.

▶ Make sure you are insulated from the cold ground – sit on a sleep mat or blanket.

▶ If you have a bivvy bag with you, get inside it, and invite everyone else in too, to keep warm.

▶ Divide up your rations; eating and drinking regularly will help keep you warm.

▶ In the morning, make your way back – hopefully you'll get back before an unnecessary search is put out.

SEVERE STORMS & LIGHTNING STRIKES

Thunder storms, with lightning, torrential rain and high winds can occur at any time of the year. They can be scary wherever you are, but especially if you are out in the open. Although high winds can be alarming, your greatest risk is from lightning. (In Australia, for example, statistically lightning poses a greater threat than any other natural hazard.) Lightning has a penchant for crests, lone trees, gullies, caves and cabin entrances, as well as wet ground.

▶ Secure caravans and campervans against strong winds.

▶ If you can, shelter in a hard-top vehicle or solid building.

▶ Never shelter under trees!

▶ If there's no shelter, curl up as tight as possible, with your feet together and a layer of insulation between you and the ground.

▶ Make sure you're not sitting next to metal objects like walking poles or metal-frame backpacks, and stay away from fences, fishing rods, umbrellas etc; get off your bike.

▶ Move immediately if you hear buzzing on nearby rocks or fences, or your hair stands on end.

▶ If you're swimming or surfing, get out of the water; if you're boating go ashore.

▶ Don't use the telephone during a storm.

RIVER CROSSINGS

These are a common cause of drowning in trekkers, especially in New Zealand and tropical rainforest areas, so take extreme care. If there's a strong current and the water is higher than your knees, it will be too hard to cross without the help of other people.

! Never try to cross a river in flood – if there is no emergency crossing further upstream, back-track, take another route or wait until the river subsides before crossing.

If you have to cross any fast-flowing rivers, choose a good spot to cross – for example, where the river widens into several channels – and a good exit point. Take one arm out of your pack, and unbuckle it so that if you feel yourself getting swept away, you can slip out of it easily. Use a stick to feel the river bed before putting your feet down, cross at an angle with the current, and walk side-on to the direction of flow so that the water can flow more easily round your body. If there are several of you, link arms and cross the river together.

! If you feel yourself being swept downstream or you fall, immediately slip out of your pack and manoeuvre yourself into a face-up floating position with your feet facing downstream; use your arms to move to the bank or a shallow area.

River water can be very cold, especially if it is snowmelt, so beware of hypothermia and muscle cramps.

BUSHFIRE

In Australia, bushfires regularly cause deaths. You'll see fire risk signs during the danger period, indicating how high the fire risk is. On total fire ban days, no naked flame is allowed anywhere outdoors and you'll be fined if you are caught transgressing. Quite apart from this, you'd be plain daft – there's a good reason for the ban. This means no campfire and no gas stove, so you'll be glad of those emergency biscuits you packed. If you are caught in a bushfire in a car:

▸ stop at a clearing
▸ turn the ignition off, and put your hazard lights and headlights on
▸ keep doors, windows and vents closed

▶ lie under a woollen blanket until the firefront has passed

The petrol tank is unlikely to explode. After this, if you need to, get out of the car, still covered by your blanket, and walk to already burnt ground.

If you're on foot and you are caught in a bushfire, try to find shelter. If there is no shelter:

▶ cover your skin up – wrap yourself in a heavy, pure wool blanket if you have one to hand
▶ move away from the main firefront and towards the rear of the main fire
▶ try to move onto open or already burnt ground
▶ if you can't avoid the fire, lie face down under a bank, in loose earth, in a hollow or get in a dam or stream (but not a water tank)

DUST OR SAND STORM

Don't try to move far in a dust storm, as you're very likely to get lost. Instead, if you are in a vehicle, try to park it in a sheltered spot. If there's no shelter to be found, park it with the engine facing away from the direction of the wind to help prevent the dust or sand getting in. Keep doors and windows closed and wait for it to pass. If you're caught out in the open, try to find shelter, perhaps behind a log or boulder, and cover your mouth and nose with a piece of clothing.

AVALANCHE

This is uncommon in Australia but relatively common in mountainous areas of New Zealand. Snow can drown you, so cover your nose and mouth. Try to swim towards the top of the snow pile before it freezes. If you can't reach the top, make a large hole around you as quickly as possible before the snow freezes, and wait for rescue.

BLIZZARDS

Snow can fall suddenly and unexpectedly, even in summer, in highland areas of Australia, New Zealand and Papua New Guinea. Unless you are close to shelter, don't move far during a whiteout, as it's easy to get lost or to have an accident. Make a makeshift shelter or snowcave and wait until it passes.

NATURAL DISASTERS

Although relatively unlikely, you may find yourself facing a hazard such as an earthquake or a cyclone on your travels. The following advice follows guidelines set out by the Australian Emergency Management Authority (http://home.ema.gov.au) and in the US National Disaster Education Coalition guide (www.redcross.org/disaster/safety/guide.html).

EARTHQUAKE

Earthquakes don't usually give any advance warning, so it's a good idea to have a contingency plan in case you suddenly feel the earth move. Some guidelines on what to do in an earthquake are as follows:

▸ drop, cover and hold; move only a few steps to a nearby safe place
▸ if you are indoors drop under a sturdy desk or table, hold on, and protect your eyes by pressing your face against your arm; if there's no table, choose a safe place against an inside wall where nothing can fall on you
▸ if you are in bed, hold on and stay there, protecting your head with a pillow
▸ if you are outdoors, find a clear spot away from buildings, trees and power lines, and drop to the ground
▸ if you are in a car, slow down, drive to a clear place, and stay in the car until the shaking stops

Remember that aftershocks are common, and if you feel one, drop, cover and hold on, as described above, each time.

HURRICANES AND CYCLONES

Hurricanes and cyclones don't generally arrive without warning. If a hurricane or cyclone is expected, heed any advice given locally, and be prepared to evacuate if necessary.

▸ Make sure all windows, doors and shutters are fastened firmly.

▶ If you are not expected to evacuate, stay indoors, away from windows until it is safe to come out.

▶ If you are driving, stop somewhere that is clear of trees, power lines and streams.

▶ Note that the 'eye' of the storm does not necessarily mean that the storm is over; after the eye passes over, the winds blow from the opposite direction, and can break trees and buildings damaged in the first onslaught.

▶ If floodwaters rise, climb onto higher ground and wait for rescue.

If you decide to move during or just after a cyclone or hurricane, be aware that high winds and flooded roads are hazards.

TSUNAMI

A tsunami is a destructive sea wave caused by events under the sea such as an earthquake, volcanic eruption or landslide. Most tsunamis occur in the Pacific Ocean, with many Pacific islands and New Zealand being most at risk in the Oceanic region. Small tsunamis occur in Australia every so often, with the northern half of Western Australia at highest risk. In July 1998, a tsunami hit Papua New Guinea's West Sepik coast, causing massive devastation and the death of up to 2000 people.

The Pacific Tsunami Warning Centre helps to monitor seismic activity around the region and to issue warnings on potential tsunami-producing earthquakes.

If you hear of a large earthquake in the region, wait for a tsunami warning, and be prepared to be evacuated or at least to move from lowlying areas to high ground. Tsunamis are sometimes preceded by a rapid rise or fall in sea level – if you are in a sea vessel, move immediately to deeper water. If a tsunami warning is given, follow the advice of the local emergency centres. Don't play tourist with a tsunami – you may be too close to escape.

CLIMATE & ALTITUDE

Although altitude is only going to be relevant to the relatively small proportion of travellers who make their way to Aoraki-Mt Cook in New Zealand or some of the higher peaks in the Papua New Guinea highlands, most travellers to Australia, New Zealand or the Pacific islands will need to know about the effects of extremes of heat and cold.

HEAT

Generally, your body is able to adapt to the heat pretty well, although you need to give it time – full acclimatisation can take up to three weeks. The most important change that occurs with acclimatisation is that you sweat more readily and in larger quantities. Sweating helps cool you down, as heat is lost when sweat evaporates off your skin.

Heat and dehydration can affect your physical performance and mental judgement, even if you're not ill as such. This is especially important when you need to rely on these, such as when you are out bushwalking.

FLUID REPLACEMENT

You can lose an astonishing 2L of fluid an hour in sweat, more if you're doing strenuous physical activity, and if you don't balance this by drinking more, you are in danger of dehydration and heatstroke. In hot climates you need to drink a lot more than in a cool climate, and this is true even when you have acclimatised. Don't rely on thirst to prompt you to drink – by the time your thirst mechanism kicks in, you'll probably already be dehydrated. How much urine you're passing is a much better indicator of how dry you are. If you're only passing a small amount of concentrated (dark yellow) urine, you need to drink more. Cool fluids are absorbed more rapidly than warm ones.

Humid Tropics Versus Arid Desert

In the Pacific islands and the tropical north of Australia, the humidity is typically high. This means that, instead of evaporating and hence cooling you down, the sweat tends to pour off you instead. This is why humid heat usually feels worse than dry heat. If you're in coastal areas the sea breeze can help to make the temperature more pleasant but inland, especially if you are walking through the forest, the heat and humidity can be unbearable. Fanning will encourage the sweat to evaporate and so cool you down. Because of the ever-present insects, cover up with loose clothing to help prevent bites, and sleep under a mosquito net (take one with you). You'll need to drink lots, so make sure you have a plentiful supply on you. Leeches are a problem in most damp, shady areas, so tuck your trousers into your boots. Sturdy footwear is vital – it will not only protect your feet from cuts and scratches, but also against hazards such as ants, snakes and spiders.

Much of central Australia is arid desert. In the daytime, temperatures can soar, and there's often a scorching desert wind that dessicates your skin and makes your eyes and throat feel dry and gritty. If you are in rural areas, there's generally very little to shade or shelter under. Wear a wide-brimmed hat and loose clothing to protect against the sun, and drink lots of water. Protect your eyes from the sun and dust with wrap-around sunglasses. Chewing sugar-free gum can help to keep your throat from feeling like the bottom of a cockatoo's cage, and keep a moisturising lip salve handy. Depending on the time of year, you may need to wear a fly net.

As a rough guide, an adult needs to drink about 3L of fluid a day in a hot climate or 5L and more if you're doing a strenuous physical activity such as trekking.

Sweat contains water and salts. As you acclimatise, your body learns to conserve salt better, and less is lost in sweat. You generally lose more water than salt in sweat, and your main

Dehydration

Any condition that leads to an excessive loss of body fluids can cause dehydration, including heat, fever, diarrhoea, vomiting and strenuous physical activity. Signs of dehydration are:

- nausea and dizziness
- headache, and dry eyes and mouth
- weakness and muscle cramps
- passing small quantities of dark urine
- raised temperature

Treatment is to drink lots of fluids. Oral rehydration salts (ORS) are best at replacing lost salts as well as fluid, but any (nonalcoholic) fluid will do.

requirement is to replace water. At first you can lose more salt than normal, but so long as you're not on a salt-reduced diet, you should still be able to make it up from your diet without needing to add extra salt. The current thinking is that you don't need to actively replace salt unless you experience symptoms, usually muscle cramps, or are doing strenuous exercise. As a rule, salt tablets are best avoided – our diets tend to be relatively high in salt anyway, and too much salt can cause kidney and heart problems in the long term.

Physical fitness makes you more able to cope with heat stress and quicker to acclimatise, but you still need to take care to replace lost fluids.

FAINTING

This is quite common when you first arrive in a hot climate, and it's more likely to affect older travellers. It occurs because heat causes the blood to pool in your legs when you're standing, meaning that less blood reaches your brain, causing you to feel dizzy and faint.

If you find you have to deal with a fainting travel companion, lie them down and raise their legs so that their feet are at a higher level than their head. Use fanning and spraying with cool water to help cool them down. When they come to, give them fluids to sip.

HEAT STRESS

Heat can cause a range of symptoms, from relatively mild discomfort to more serious heat exhaustion and potentially fatal heatstroke. Although these conditions are usually described as separate entities, in practice they overlap to a certain extent, so it's best to treat any heat illness as heatstroke. Mild heat illness can progress to a more severe one if you don't take action to prevent it. If you've been in a hot climate before, you'll probably recognise some of the symptoms of mild heat stress:

- heavy sweating; your skin feels moist and cool
- tiredness and irritability
- nausea and loss of appetite
- prickly heat rash
- muscle spasms or twitching
- muscle cramps – painful, occur in your limbs and abdomen

If you experience any of these symptoms, take this as a sign to take a break from the tourist trail. Rest in a cool environment or take a cool shower or bath, and drink lots of water. If you have muscle cramps, drink oral rehydration salts (ORS) as well as plain water (or add a little extra salt to your food), and massage your muscles to ease the spasms. Applying ice packs (if available) or a cold compress to your muscles can help.

Heat Exhaustion & Heatstroke

Both conditions are more likely to occur if you've experienced heavy and prolonged sweating, without adequate fluid replacement or sufficient time for acclimatisation. The two conditions overlap to a degree, so if you're not sure of the diagnosis, always treat for heatstroke. You are unlikely to be capable of recognising or treating severe symptoms of heat exhaustion or heatstroke in yourself – keep a look-out for signs of these disorders in your travel companions.

Symptoms to look out for include:

- heavy sweating, with cold, clammy skin
- headache, dizziness and nausea or vomiting
- tiredness, weakness and restlessness
- muscle cramps

If you take the person's temperature and pulse, you'll find their temperature is normal and the pulse is fast. The aim of treatment is to cool the person down and to encourage them to drink plenty of fluids:

▶ lie the person down in the shade; apply wet cloths to their head and body and fan them
▶ as soon as you can, move them to a cool environment such as an air-conditioned room
▶ encourage them to take sips of water
▶ get medical help if they continue to vomit or show no signs of improvement

If untreated, heat exhaustion can progress to heatstroke. In heatstroke, sweating stops and you get a dangerous rise in body temperature. Heatstroke can be fatal. Signs include:

- confusion, headache
- lack of sweating; skin feels hot and dry and looks flushed
- incoordination, confusion, fits and unconsciousness
- raised body temperature

Heatstroke can be rapidly fatal, so you need to take immediate action to lower the person's temperature while you get medical help:

▶ get medical help or arrange evacuation urgently
▶ move the person into the shade or a cool environment
▶ if they're conscious, give them cool water to sip
▶ apply ice packs (wrap in cloth first), wet cloths and fan them; sponging or spraying with cold water can also help

COLD

New Zealand and south-eastern Australia basically have a temperate climate, so the cold is a major hazard if you are walking or camping out. In addition, the weather can be extremely changeable at any time of the year, so you have to be prepared, mentally and physically, for all kinds of weather. Temperature decreases as altitude increases, and even in the tropics it can get very cold in highland areas. You may start walking in a warm valley but when you reach the summit, you can be sure it's going to be very much colder. In arid inland areas (much of central Australia), daytime temperatures can soar in the hot sun, but as soon as the sun goes down, temperatures plummet.

PREVENTION

You're generally more likely to die of the cold than the heat if you are bushwalking – in New Zealand, for example, the cold is a major hazard for trampers, and a few die every year because of exposure (hypothermia). If you are out and about in the cold, you need to know how to avoid hypothermia and what to do if it does occur.

Hypothermia, or generalised body chilling, occurs when your body loses more heat than it can produce. You don't need incredibly low temperatures to become hypothermic, just the right combination of circumstances.

! *Hypothermia is more likely in wet and windy conditions, especially if you are tired and hungry.*

Bear in mind that you are more at risk of hypothermia if you have little body fat for insulation, although there isn't a great deal you can do about this in the short term! Older travellers are more vulnerable to the cold, as are children, especially if they are being carried (such as in a backpack child carrier). An added problem is that children may not let you know how they're feeling until it's too late.

Avoiding hypothermia means being well prepared and equipped. Whatever the weather is like when you set off, make sure you are prepared for the worst possible conditions.

Bags & Blankets

'Space blankets' are a popular cold weather survival aid, but there are doubts about their effectiveness in the field. You're probably better off using a sleeping bag or other thermal layers, depending what you have with you. Carry lots of plastic bags with you – covering yourself up with these prevents further heat loss through evaporation, and can double as protection from rain.

▶ Wear (or have with you) appropriate clothing, including windproof and waterproof layers – lots of thin layers are warmer than one thick layer, and more versatile. Lightweight synthetic pile fabrics are popular and will dry off quicker than wool, but silk and wool are also good.
▶ Wear a hat – heat is lost through radiation from your head, so covering your head can make a big difference.
▶ Don't let yourself get tooo tired – have frequent rests throughout the day.
▶ Food equals heat, so make sure you eat and drink regularly.

! Always carry plenty of fluids and carbohydrate-packed goodies, and snack regularly throughout the day.

Even though it's cold, you still need to watch out for dehydration and sunburn. You'd be crazy to drink alcohol or do drugs in harsh environmental conditions – alcohol encourages heat loss and also affects your judgement.

! Immersion in cold water, for example if you fall in a mountain stream, can rapidly cause you to become hypothermic.

TREATMENT

Hypothermia can come on gradually and take hold before you realise, so it's important to recognise the signs early. Watch for subtle early signs of hypothermia in your travel companions. These are what Rick Curtis of the Princeton Outdoor Program calls the 'umbles' – stumbles, mumbles, fumbles and grumbles:

- exhaustion, clumsiness
- feeling cold, numb extremities, shivering

More severe hypothermia is indicated by:

- mental and physical lethargy
- disorientation and inability to understand simple questions
- slurring of speech
- lack of judgement and irrational behaviour
- visual problems
- collapse and loss of consciousness

Take immediate action:

▶ find shelter from wet, wind and cold – use a tent, large plastic bag or survival bag
▶ cover the casualty's head and extremities, and insulate them from the ground (put a blanket or piece of clothing underneath them)
▶ remove cold or wet clothes, if possible, and replace with warm, dry ones
▶ rewarm by using blankets, sleeping bags and body-to-body contact (zip two sleeping bags together and get in with the cold person to help warm them up)
▶ you can use hot packs or hot water bottles (or improvise) to help warm a person , but remember to wrap these up first to prevent the risk of burns
▶ if they are conscious, get them to drink warm, sweet fluids; don't give alcohol

! Severe hypothermia is a very serious condition – you need to get medical help or arrange evacuation immediately. Handle the casualty carefully and don't rewarm them too fast, as this can be dangerous.

CHILBLAINS

These are the most common form of cold injury and the least dangerous. Chilblains can occur if your bare skin is repeatedly exposed to low temperatures (above freezing). They usually affect fingers and toes, and appear as red, swollen, itchy and tender areas. Chilblains heal up on their own in one to two weeks.

Prevent chilblains by wearing warm mittens (rather than gloves) and socks, and suitable footwear. There's no specific treatment, except to keep them clean and covered.

Natural remedies that have been recommended include calendula or witch hazel tinctures for unbroken chilblains, or hypericum ointment for broken chilblains. Comfrey ointment is soothing for any skin inflammation.

FROSTBITE

When your tissues get so cold they freeze, this is frostbite. It occurs when you're at temperatures below freezing for prolonged periods of time without adequate gloves or footwear. High winds, high altitude and badly fitting boots can all make frostbite more likely. Fingers, toes, ears, nose and face can all be affected. It's unlikely to be a problem for most travellers.

Prevent frostbite – cover all exposed skin with waterproof and windproof layers in cold conditions and if you notice your hands or feet turning numb, stop immediately and warm them up by body to body contact if necessary.

A frostbitten part looks white and waxy; it's painless while frozen. Get medical advice as soon as possible. Mild frostbite can be reversible. If you can be evacuated promptly or you are near medical facilities, you can thaw the affected part by immersing it in hot (just bearable to touch) water for half an hour or so. As it starts to warm up, the pain can be pretty severe. The thawed part will swell up, so be sure to remove any rings from your fingers first.

Never rub the affected part to warm it up, as this can cause further damage.

Don't attempt to thaw the part unless you are within reach of medical help.

SNOW BLINDNESS

Snow blindness is sunburn of the backs of the eyes and is caused by sunlight reflected off snow. It could be a risk if you are mountaineering in New Zealand. Prevent it by wearing goggles or sunglasses with UV protection. It gives you a gritty feeling in your eyes, extreme sensitivity to light, redness and temporary blindness several hours after exposure.

There's no specific treatment apart from relieving the pain (for example by putting cold cloths onto your closed eyes), and it usually heals completely in a couple of days. Antibiotic eye drops are not necessary. You can make emergency eye protection by cutting slits in cardboard or cloth.

ALTITUDE

You'll have to try quite hard to get high enough for altitude to be an issue in the Pacific region. Unless you are going mountaineering on Aoraki-Mt Cook in New Zealand or doing serious peak bagging in the Papua New Guinea highlands, this is not going to be an issue for you.

You're not usually at risk of altitude illness until you reach about 2500m but it is possible to get symptoms from about 2000m upwards. You're very unlikely to get problems if you stay at altitude for less than about six hours. Going above 3500m, about 50% of trekkers experience symptoms of mild altitude illness and about one in 20 have life-threatening severe altitude illness.

As you gain altitude, the air becomes thinner and less oxygen is available. Humans are able to function – and live – at high altitudes through adaptation. At first, the rate and depth of your breathing increases; later you get an increase in heart rate and in the number of red blood cells and their ability to use oxygen. Although you can acclimatise sufficiently in a couple of days to a particular altitude, full acclimatisation takes about three weeks.

PREVENTION

The most important risk factor for altitude sickness is how rapidly you ascend. For example, if you fly from Lai to Kegsugl in Papua New Guinea and don't give yourself time to acclimatise before tackling Mt Wilhelm, you are almost guaranteed to get symptoms. The best way to prevent acute mountain sickness (AMS) is to allow rest days for acclimatising, and not to ascend too quickly. Don't over-exert yourself in the first few days at altitude.

▶ 'Climb high, sleep low' – as far as possible, sleep at a lower altitude than the greatest height you reached during the day.
▶ If you have any symptoms of AMS, stop ascending until the symptoms have gone.
▶ Descend immediately if your symptoms persist or worsen in 30 to 60 minutes.

! Never trek alone at altitude – you may not recognise the symptoms of AMS in yourself and you may not be able to get to safety if you are ill.

If you plan to trek at altitude, make sure you know where the nearest medical facility is.

Another option for preventing AMS is with drugs, usually one called Diamox (acetazolamide). This is a controversial issue, and in any case it's unlikely to be necessary in New Zealand or Papua New Guinea. Although there are some situations where drug treatment is useful, the bottom line is that if you follow the rules of gradual safe ascent, you shouldn't need drug treatment. For more information about Diamox, discuss this with your doctor before you go.

MILD AMS

Above about 2000m, it's common to get mild symptoms of AMS, which usually come on gradually. These include:

■ headache
■ loss of appetite

- nausea and vomiting
- tiredness and irritability

You may also notice that you're a bit unsteady on your feet, and you may feel a little short of breath. Because symptoms of AMS are so nonspecific, it can be difficult to distinguish them from flu, colds or jet lag, if you've recently arrived – if in doubt, assume it's AMS. Having difficulty sleeping is very common at altitude – you may find it hard to get to sleep, have vivid dreams and wake up frequently. Symptoms of mild AMS are unpleasant, but they usually disappear after two to three days, as long as you don't go any higher. The main concern with mild AMS is that it can progress to more severe forms if you ignore it or go higher.

The best treatment for any form of AMS is descent, but mild symptoms of AMS can be treated with simple measures:

▶ rest up for a couple of days
▶ drink plenty of fluids, as dehydration is common at altitude
▶ take simple painkillers (or an anti-inflammatory such as ibuprofen) for the headache
▶ try a motion sickness remedy (p59) for nausea and vomiting

Some important points to bear in mind:

▶ never ascend with any symptoms of AMS
▶ always descend promptly if your symptoms are moderate to severe or getting worse, or there's no improvement in mild symptoms after two to three days
▶ seek medical advice if necessary, but don't let this delay descent

SEVERE AMS

About one in 20 people will develop more severe forms of altitude illness, usually at 3500m to 4000m and above, but sometimes lower. Severe AMS includes high altitude pulmonary oedema and high altitude cerebral oedema.

In high altitude pulmonary oedema (HAPE), fluid accumulates in your lungs, preventing you from breathing properly. It can follow from mild AMS or it can come on suddenly without any warning. The main symptoms are:

- breathlessness at rest or a persistent cough (common early symptoms)
- coughing up pink, frothy sputum
- tiredness and weakness

If fluid collects within your brain, you get high altitude cerebral oedema (HACE). This condition is rare, but it is life-threatening. Symptoms include:

- severe headache, unrelieved by simple painkillers
- change in behaviour, confusion and disorientation
- double vision
- unsteadiness
- drowsiness and coma (unconsciousness)

Severe AMS, HAPE and HACE are all medical emergencies and you need to act immediately.

▶ Seek medical advice if possible but don't let this delay descent.
▶ Descend immediately (even 500m can help).
▶ Use oxygen by mask, if possible.

WATER SAFETY

In this chapter we discuss potential hazards associated with immersing yourself in water. If you want to know how to make water safe for drinking, see the section on Safe Drinking Water in the Staying Healthy chapter.

○ For guidelines on the emergency resuscitation of a drowning person, see the inside backcover.

SURF & CURRENTS

If you're not a confident swimmer or you're not used to big waves, it's best to err on the side of caution. Strong currents can be a risk on many ocean beaches. Even if you are swimming in the relatively safe confines of a lagoon, watch out for strong currents flowing from the lagoon out into the open sea. Always ask around locally about hazardous currents and tides. Understand the ocean, and learn a bit about waves, wind and tides, and know your limitations. Surf Life Saving Australia is responsible for providing rescue services across Australia's beaches, and publishes a handy information sheet on surf and beach safety (accessible on the web at www.slsa.asn.au).

Waves

These are caused by wind blowing over the ocean surface. There are three main types of waves:

- plunging or dumping waves – these are your classic 'crashing' wave, and break with force, especially where there are sandbanks and at low tide
- spilling waves – these are where the crest 'spills' down the face of the wave; they can form 'tubes' if the sandbank is low, which are the best waves for surfing
- surging waves – no white foam, and because they are deep, they can knock you off your feet and drag you back out

Currents

A rip is a strong current that takes water back out to sea. It often occurs when water has built up between a sandbar and

Between the Flags

As for any outdoor activity, water sports aren't without hazard, but if you use your common sense and don't take unnecessary risks you should stay safe.

In Australia, the higher than usual number of beach drownings over the summer of 1997/98 has provoked the BeachSafe initiative, an awareness-raising and public education campaign to reduce the number of beach drownings. A report by Surf Life Saving Australia (SLSA) identified international tourists as a major at-risk group.

Most of Australia's most popular beaches are patrolled by volunteer lifeguards. To help ensure the safety of swimmers and surfers, red and yellow flags on the shore indicate the safest area to swim. If you're swimming at a patrolled beach, always swim between the flags, and if you get into difficulties, stay calm, raise your hand and wait to be rescued. Never ignore warning signs at a beach – they're there for a good reason.

Obviously it's not possible for SLSA to patrol every one of Australia's 7000 or so beaches, and most drownings occur outside patrolled areas. If you're swimming on an unpatrolled beach in Australia, New Zealand or the Pacific, you'll be on your own if you get into difficulties.

- Never do any water sports alone.
- Make sure you are familiar with survival and self-rescue techniques before you set out.
- Use your common sense and don't take unnecessary risks.

the shore, which then has to go back to sea. Strong currents can also occur as water is funnelled off the reefs when the tide is going out, and between reef passages. A rip tends to take you out to sea, not down under the water. Rips can be very difficult to spot, even if you're looking for them.

Telltale signs of a rip current include colour (it may be darker than the water on either side), a rippled effect on the surface of the water and a trail of surf extending beyond the surf zone.

Side shore currents flow parallel to the shore and can wash you quite a way down the beach, where conditions may be less safe. Don't stray too far from the shore in this situation, and watch the shoreline to make sure you don't drift too far along. Swim in to the shore before you float too far away from your starting point.

Getting out of a Rip Current

If you do get into a rip, you may feel yourself being dragged out to sea, or you may be sucked underwater if it passes through a rocky passage. To avoid getting into serious trouble:

▶ don't panic – this will tire you out quicker
▶ get out of the rip current by swimming parallel to the shore, then catching the waves back in; don't swim against the current, as you'll just exhaust yourself

If you are unsure of your swimming abilities and there are people on the beach, raise an arm above your head to indicate that you are in trouble, and tread water (you can stay afloat for a surprisingly long time) until you are rescued. Alternatively, you could try conserving your energy while you wait for rescue by allowing yourself to float in the water in fetal position, raising your head just when you need to take a breath.

CRAMPS

These muscle spasms can be extremely painful and may occur for a variety of reasons, including swimming in cold water, tiredness, overexertion or dehydration. It starts as a twinge at first, often in your calf, then the pain builds up and is only relieved by resting the muscle. Massaging and stretching the muscle, for example by pulling on your toes while straightening your leg, can help. Cramps are potentially dangerous if you are in rough seas or you're a weak swimmer. Try to rest the muscle, then use it gently.

Help prevent cramps by warming up well and stretching before starting any activity. Warming down after any strenuous activity is important too.

WATER POLLUTION

Quite apart from any aesthetic considerations, swimming in polluted waters is bad for your health. Water pollution is a worldwide problem. Pollution is commonly caused by sewage outflow into the ocean, and this is most likely to be a problem if you're swimming on beaches around populated, urban areas – avoid city beaches if you can. Other sources of pollution in rivers and oceans include mining waste, chemical spills, industrial by-products, fertilisers and pesticides. Pollution tends to be worse after torrential rain, as surface contaminants get washed away and sewage channels overflow.

It's possible to pick up intestinal infections (diarrhoea and hepatitis) from polluted water, by swallowing small amounts when you are swimming. Children are particularly at risk because they often swallow water when they swim. Swimming in polluted water can make infection of cuts and grazes more likely. Direct contact with chemical pollutants in the water can cause irritation to your skin and eyes, as well as uncertain, possibly carcinogenic, long-term effects.

Chlorinated pools that are well maintained should be safe, although some diarrhoea-causing parasites (such as *Giardia* and cyclospora) are able to survive chlorination. You can't get diseases like HIV from swimming in pools.

Some tips for avoiding potential problem areas:

▸ stick to well maintained chlorinated pools or ocean beaches far from urban settlements and the mouths of rivers, streams and storm-water drains
▸ avoid swimming in sluggish rivers in urban areas
▸ do a quick check for floating objects before you get in the water
▸ if in doubt try not to swallow any water

SNORKELLING

If you don't fancy the palaver and expense of scuba diving, snorkelling is a great alternative. Here's a quick safety checklist for would-be snorkellers:

Surfing Safety Tips
Peter Neely, author of Indo Surf & Lingo, *has the following tips for safe surfing.*

The surfing lifestyle is all about fun and freedom, but you need to take a few simple precautions to avoid unwanted injuries.

Sun Protection
Possibly the most dangerous aspect of surfing is sunburn, which can keep you out of the surf for a few days. In the long term, sunburn can cause potentially fatal skin cancer.

- Use waterproof suncream (ideally SPF 30); apply it before you go out, and reapply it regularly.
- Wear a lycra wetshirt in the surf. A cap protects your eyes in the water too.
- Avoid surfing when the sun is at its most intense, between 11am and 3pm.

Check the Conditions
When you arrive at a new surf spot, it pays to watch the line-up for at least 15 minutes before paddling out.

- What is underneath the water? Any rocks or shallow ledges? If you're surfing over a coral reef, always wear protective rubber boots and maybe a wetsuit.
- Where do the local surfers paddle out from? Where do they exit the surf?
- Are there any rips? If caught in a rip, always paddle *across* it, not against it.

▶ it's easy to get sunburnt on your back and the backs of your legs when you're snorkelling – wear a T-shirt and use plenty of water-resistant sunscreen
▶ beware of currents (listen to local advice), use flippers, and don't snorkel alone
▶ before you get into the water, plan how you are going to get out

- How often do the big sets come? Can you handle that size wave?
- Where do the locals end their ride? Is there a dangerous end section they avoid?

Dangerous Creatures

Sharks are universally feared by surfers, but you are unlikely to see one, and attacks are even rarer. Avoid surfing in river mouths and be watchful around sunset. Other hazards include jellyfish, sting rays, blue ringed octopus and stone fish. Be watchful when surfing in on-shore winds which carry these stingers towards shore. For more details, see the section on Dangerous Marine Life later in this chapter.

Be Prepared

- Travel with a simple first aid kit.
- Drink plenty of water before and after surfing to prevent dehydration.
- Practise long swims before your trip to increase stamina.
- Swim between the flags on a patrolled beach where life-savers are on duty.
- Stretch before and after each surf.
- Never surf alone.

Equipment

Make sure your board has no sharp edges – repair dings smoothly, sand sharp edges off your fins, use a rubber nose guard and most importantly attach a new legrope before your trip.

Happy surfing!

– getting into the water from a coral ledge is pretty simple, but getting back out, especially if the sea is rough, can be much more difficult
▶ if you're snorkelling over coral, take care not to get cuts and grazes
▶ beware of potentially hazardous marine creatures

SEA KAYAKING

If you're going out for anything more than just an hour's try-out, bear in mind some basic safety rules:

▶ study the weather and ocean conditions before you set off, and be prepared to delay the expedition if necessary
▶ wear a personal flotation device (PFD; life jacket) and helmet – many drownings occur when a person is knocked unconscious, and a helmet is a simple safety insurance
▶ take appropriate safety equipment with you: lights (for night journeys), flares, a mirror (for signalling during the day), whistle (should be attached to your PFD), and an Emergency Position Indication Radio Beacon (EPIRB) are all items you should consider taking with you
▶ remember that however far you paddle out, you're going to have to paddle back the same distance, and chances are, the wind will be against you

In addition, all the usual guidelines for safe outdoor adventuring apply:

▶ let someone know what your plans are and when to expect you back so they can raise the alarm if necessary
▶ protect yourself against the elements – sunburn and hypothermia are the main risks
▶ it's easy to get dehydrated and dehydration can make you feel tired and the trip an ordeal – take adequate water supplies and remember to drink regularly, without waiting until you feel thirsty
▶ similarly, if you're going out for longer than a couple of hours, you're going to need to take adequate supplies of food with you – ward off tiredness by snacking regularly

Kayaking on the open sea can be very different from a training course in a sheltered bay – recognise and stick within your limitations. Consider doing a refresher course, if necessary, to remind yourself of some basic skills.

Blown Out to Sea

Offshore winds, blowing you out to sea or causing you to capsize, are probably the main risk if you're sea kayaking (assuming you have a basic skill level). Offshore winds can be very deceptive – conditions at your launch point can seem calm even if they are not further out. Look for white-capped waves offshore, especially if the spray is being blown sea-wards, and remember that wind strength increases as you go from land to open sea. A continuous sand dune ridge or line of cliffs provides shelter from offshore winds, but where this shelter is broken by, for example, a narrow bay entrance, a narrow fiord or river valley, offshore winds get funnelled through, increasing in strength and causing turbulence.

!If you find yourself getting gradually blown out to sea, imme- diately turn towards the beach or the nearest shelter, and stick as closely as possible to the shoreline.

RIVERS & WATERWAYS

If you're inland and sweltering in 40°C heat, or the ocean is out of bounds because of the jellyfish season, you probably won't be able to resist taking a dip in a waterhole or river. Great idea, but bear in mind some potential hazards:

▶ strong undercurrents, and eddies in waterfalls, especially after a downpour further upstream, can sweep you off your feet and drag you under – look out for warning signs before you plunge in
▶ watch out for crocodiles – see the following page
▶ biting insects and leeches tend to be plentiful around waterways, so watch out
▶ beware – mountain streams can be very cold, even in summer, and the cold can make your muscles cramp up

For guidelines on how to cross rivers safely, see the Wilderness Health & Safety chapter.

Leptospirosis (Weil's Disease)

Although rare, it is possible to get this bacterial disease from contact with water contaminated by animal urine (usually dogs and rats). You're probably at greatest risk of this if you're an 'adventure traveller', especially if you're swimming or doing

Crocodiles

If you're going to the wetlands of northern Australia or the Pacific islands, you need to know how to avoid becoming croc fodder. Pacific crocodiles come in two varieties: saltwater and freshwater, known locally in Australia as salties and (you've guessed it) freshies. In Australia, legal protection of crocodiles has been in force since the late 1960s and early 1970s, bringing the population back from the brink of extinction. As you dabble your toes in the water (if you dare), ponder on the fact that there are currently more than 100,000 crocs in the wild in northern Australia.

The freshwater crocodile is a small, shy, narrow-snouted relative of the infinitely more dangerous saltwater croc. Every year salties claim a few foolhardy victims. These fearsome creatures are not film extras.

Just to confuse you, salties can be found in both salt and fresh water, and can come a long way inland, especially following flooding. Crocodiles can move very fast when they want to. There are warning signs at many waterholes in the Top End of Australia – don't ignore them, they are for real. Salties are found in mangrove swamps in most of the Pacific islands, and sometimes in mangrove swamps around Darwin in Australia. If you're not sure about the risk, get local advice from park rangers or the police; if there's no-one to ask, assume the worst! Some vital safety rules:

- never swim or paddle in water that could contain a saltie
- never clean fish by the edge of waterways, don't leave food scraps on the bank
- never camp close to the water's edge – salties can attack you in your tent

Although the freshwater crocodile is much less dangerous, it could still give you a nasty nip if provoked.

Treatment for a crocodile bite is basic first aid – see the First Aid appendix.

water sports (canoeing, rafting or caving). It's more common after a period of heavy rainfall or flooding. The bacteria enter your body through breaks in your skin or through your nose or eyes. You can get mild flu-like symptoms, about 10 days after infection, but sometimes a more severe illness results, with high fever, vomiting, diarrhoea and red, irritated eyes. The illness can occasionally progress to jaundice and severe liver failure, and even death in about one in 100 affected people.

You should seek medical help as soon as possible if you think you may have leptospirosis. After the diagnosis is confirmed, treatment is with antibiotics (usually penicillin or doxycycline).

AMOEBIC MENINGITIS

This serious disease is a rare hazard of swimming in warm fresh water, including thermal springs, stagnant ponds or lakes and inadequately maintained public heated swimming pools. It has been reported in Australia, Papua New Guinea and, particularly, New Zealand, as well as elsewhere in the world. It's caused by infection with a microorganism present in the water, and affects the brain. Symptoms appear three to seven days after immersion, and include sore throat, severe headache and neck stiffness. It's a serious disease with a high fatality rate. Seek medical help urgently if you think you may be affected.

You get the disease by diving, jumping into or swimming underwater in warm fresh water, when water is forced up into your nose. Take heed of any warning signs, and don't dive or put your head underwater in affected water.

SCUBA DIVING

Diving is a prime attraction for many visitors to Australia and the Pacific. Diving is a fantastic sport, allowing you to enter another world. However, diving accidents do happen, often involving beginners, and can be fatal or cause permanent injury. To dive safely, you need to have done the proper training and have a good understanding of the risks involved and how to minimise them.

DIVING CERTIFICATE

To dive, you will need a diving certificate issued by a major diving organisation (PADI, NAUI etc) – it's a bit like a driving licence when you're hiring a car. To get a certificate, you need to complete a diving course. You can either do this before you go or at a dive centre at your destination. Once you've got your diver's card, you can dive anywhere you want.

! Diving is not suitable for everyone; if you intend to go diving, it's a good idea (and sometimes mandatory) to have a diving medical checkup to make sure you are physically fit to dive, especially if you are on any medications or you have a medical condition.

Some dive centres may just want you to fill in a questionnaire, but ideally you should get a proper diving medical checkup before you leave. Age is not a barrier to diving in itself, but conditions that may make diving unsuitable for you are heart or lung disease (including asthma), ear or sinus problems and any fits or dizzy spells.

INSURANCE

This is vital! You will need specific diver insurance that covers evacuation to a hospital or recompression chamber and subsequent treatment, something that will otherwise cost you thousands of dollars. Divers Alert Network (DAN – see the boxed text for details) offers this, as do some other organisations (such as PADI). Note that some dive operators won't let you dive unless you have this insurance.

! In an emergency situation, use the services available at the time but make sure you contact your insurance provider as soon as possible.

RECOMPRESSION FACILITIES

You should always make sure you know where the nearest hyperbaric chamber is, especially if you are planning on diving in more remote areas – check with your dive operator before you start. Note that recompression facilities are limited on the Pacific islands, and you are likely to need to be evacuated to facilities in Australia, New Zealand or Hawai'i.

DIVING RESOURCES

As part of the services it provides for divers, DAN has a Medical Information Line (☎ 1-919-684-2948, 9 am to 5 pm

DAN Emergency Hotlines

DAN is an international nonprofit organisation providing expert medical information and advice for the benefit of the diving public. DAN does not directly provide medical care, but it does provide advice on early treatment, evacuation and hyperbaric treatment of diving-related injuries, and maintains emergency hotlines.

In a dive emergency in Australia, New Zealand or the Pacific islands, ring the Dive Emergency Service (DES) hotline:

- ☎ 1800 088 200 (toll free within Australia)
- ☎ +61-8-8212 9242 (outside Australia)
- ☎ +64-9-445 8454 (DES New Zealand)

The DES on-duty doctor will assess the situation and advise on a course of action.

For general queries and information about diving health and safety, contact DAN (www.dan.ycg.org) as follows:

- ☎ 919-684-2948 (or toll free ☎ 800-446-2671 from within North America)
- DAN SEAP Head Office Australia (☎ 03-9886 9166, fax 9886 9155), PO Box 384, Ashburton, Vic 3147, Australia
- DAN SEAP New Zealand (☎ 09-4455036, fax 4455973), PO Box 32340, Devonport, Auckland, New Zealand

Monday to Friday), or you can email your query (see the boxed text on DAN for contact details).

There are plenty of good books on all aspects of diving, including health and safety. To get you started, you could try any of the following:

Encyclopaedia of Recreational Diving by PADI – a useful, basic text

The Diver's Handbook by Alan Mountain, a comprehensive, well thought-out guide covering most aspects of diving

Scuba Diving Explained – Questions and Answers on Physiology and Medical Aspects of Diving by Martin Lawrence

Lonely Planet's new Pisces series has specialised diving guides, including all the best sites of Australia and the Pacific islands.

DIVING & ANTIMALARIALS

If you're taking mefloquine (Lariam) for protection against malaria, you need to be aware that diving isn't recommended while you are taking it. This is because mefloquine can cause dizziness and balance problems, especially in the first few weeks of taking it, and it can make fits more likely in susceptible people. If you are planning on going diving and need to take antimalarials, mention this to your doctor before you leave so you can be prescribed an alternative if necessary.

If you are taking any medications, check with a diving medicine specialist (such as DAN) that it is safe to dive.

DIVING SAFETY TIPS

Although most dive centres are very safety-conscious, fierce competition between dive schools at some popular dive sites can mean that corners are cut and safety standards suffer as a result. Some basic rules for safe diving are as follows.

When you're choosing a dive school, look for:

■ small instruction groups – about four to six learners to one instructor is probably the most you'd want

- experienced diving instructors; there should always be a dive-master on board any dive charter
- good, well maintained equipment
- boats should have a two-way radio, oxygen and medical kit, and there should always be someone on board (with diving equipment) while divers are underwater

Before the dive:

▶ don't dive if you're feeling physically or mentally below par
▶ avoid going in if you are uncertain about the water or weather conditions
▶ check rental equipment carefully before using it
▶ never dive after taking alcohol or doing drugs

On the dive:

▶ always follow your dive leader's instructions – but be aware that there are good and less good divemasters; ask around beforehand
▶ be aware of your limitations and stick within them
▶ never dive in murky water – you won't be able to see and avoid hazards
▶ keep a watch on your diving companions for signs of difficulty – the 'buddy' system
▶ stop diving if you feel cold or tired, even if it's not the end of the dive
▶ try not to panic if you find yourself in difficulties – instead, take some slow deep breaths and think through what you need to do
▶ avoid touching or picking up things underwater – they may be harmful to you and you may be harmful to them; it's usually illegal to take anything from a marine park

Even if you are an experienced diver, if you haven't been on a dive for a while, consider doing a refresher course before you take the plunge, or ask to be taken on a site tour if you're uncertain about conditions or navigation in the area.

DIVING & HEALTH

Described here are some of the main problems that may be associated with diving. Note that these are not the only problems that can occur. A good training course should provide you with more information, or you could consult any of the resources mentioned earlier.

Decompression Sickness

Also known as 'the bends', decompression sickness is one of the most serious hazards of diving – make sure you know what it is and how to avoid it.

Breathing air under pressure (as when you're diving) forces quantities of nitrogen (a major component of air) to dissolve in your blood and body tissues. If the pressure is later released too quickly (for example you ascend too fast), nitrogen can't be eliminated in the usual way and bubbles of gas form in the blood stream and body tissue.

Symptoms depend on where the bubbles are. Bubbles in the bloodstream can block circulation and cause stroke-like symptoms, such as blackouts and weakness of one side of the body. The most common form of decompression sickness is where bubbles form in large joints (joint bends) like the shoulder and elbow, giving you pain that increases to a peak some hours after the dive, then gradually subsides. Skin bends can occur, giving you itches and a rash over your body. In spinal bends, you get back pain that typically circles your abdomen, followed by pins and needles in your legs, unsteadiness and paralysis. Inner ear bends make you dizzy and unable to balance.

Recompression Treatment of the bends is by recompression in a hyperbaric chamber, which causes any bubbles to dissolve again, followed by slow, controlled decompression. This allows all the dissolved nitrogen to be eliminated without forming bubbles.

! *Recompression treatment is usually effective but you need to get to a recompression chamber as soon as possible, because any delay could result in further damage, which may be irreversible.*

Prevention You can never guarantee that you won't get the bends, but you can do a lot to make it very unlikely. Dive tables are available to give you guidance on safe dives but they obviously don't take your individual condition into account.

!Never dive if you are feeling unwell in any way, avoid strenuous activity before you dive and drink plenty of fluids to prevent dehydration.

Be particularly careful to avoid diving if you're dehydrated, as this can slow down the rate at which nitrogen is eliminated from the blood. Sea sickness, alcohol the previous evening and heat can all make you dehydrated.

Nitrogen Build-Up Nitrogen build-up can be a problem if you're on a diving holiday, doing multiple dives a day or diving on consecutive days, and is the most common cause of decompression sickness at diving resorts. Taking a day off can allow any nitrogen that has built up to be eliminated.

Nitrogen Narcosis
Also known as 'rapture of the depths', this occurs below depths of about 30 to 40m, and is due to the build-up of nitrogen in the blood to levels at which it has toxic effects on the brain. Symptoms can be quite frightening, and include a feeling of detachment from reality and apprehension, sometimes leading to panic. In addition, your thought processes slow down and you lose your concentration. Symptoms clear if you ascend 5 to 10m. Nitrogen narcosis is one reason why it is vital for divers to be on the lookout for signs in other members of the team, and to be familiar with an emergency drill for this situation.

Pressure Effects
The increased ambient pressure underwater can cause problems if the pressure is not equalised within various air-filled cavities in the body, including the lungs, ears, sinuses, teeth cavities and gut. Lung barotrauma (damage due to pressure)

is a very serious condition, often caused by not breathing out on ascent from a dive. Symptoms are variable but include chest pain, dizziness and unconsciousness. Treatment is by recompression in a hyperbaric chamber.

Ear and sinus pain can be quite severe, and you should avoid diving if you have a middle ear infection (see p167), sinus trouble, a cold or hay fever. If you get dental pain while diving, it may be due to cavities in your teeth, and you should see a dentist as soon as is convenient.

HAZARDOUS MARINE LIFE

The oceans and reefs around Australia and the Pacific islands (and much less so, New Zealand) are home to a variety of fascinating and often beautiful life forms, some of which can be a danger to you. If you're swimming or diving in the sea, learn to recognise and avoid the villains. The risk of encountering a potentially dangerous sea creature is fairly small, so long as you use a bit of common sense:

▶ seek out and heed advice on local dangers
▶ don't walk along reefs in shallow water
▶ don't go diving or snorkelling when the waters are murky (this may attract predators and you won't be able to see them coming)
▶ unless you're a marine biologist and know what you are doing, don't touch or feed any creature underwater
▶ it's a good rule never to put your hands or feet somewhere you can't see first
▶ most marine creatures are not aggressive – if you don't threaten them, most will leave you alone

In this section we outline some of the more noteworthy hazards to be aware of. All things considered, it's probably best to give that midnight skinny dip on a tropical beach a miss.

SHARKS

! *Treatment of a shark or barracuda bite is basic first aid for a*
• *traumatic injury – see the First Aid appendix.*

For many people, shark attack is their ultimate marine fear, and Australia and the Pacific have something of a reputation for sharks. However, only about a hundred or so shark attacks are reported around the world annually – compare that with the number of people who go swimming and diving every year!

Sharks occur in all oceans of the world but attacks tend to be reported from warmer waters, perhaps because more people swim in warmer waters. Of the many types of sharks that occur, only a few are known to be a danger to humans. Great white, tiger and bull sharks are thought to be the most dangerous, while mako sharks and the weird-looking hammerhead are also known to attack humans occasionally. Although sharks are basically sea creatures, the bull shark is known to swim upriver, and has been reported in rivers in Australia as well as elsewhere.

Ask about sharks (and other marine hazards) locally. Great whites are more common around seal colonies, which swimmers and divers should avoid for this reason. Spearfishing and line fishing may attract sharks. If you decide to swim in an area known to have sharks, here are some tips on avoiding trouble:

▶ don't swim or dive where fishermen are cleaning their catches (not an attractive option anyway)
▶ avoid swimming in murky waters or with an open wound
▶ be careful at dusk, as this is when sharks feed

In Australia, some beaches prone to shark attack (such as those around Sydney) are netted. Although it doesn't keep sharks out altogether, netting is very effective in reducing the likelihood of shark attacks.

In the unlikely event that you spot a shark, don't panic – freezing may make the shark lose interest in you, or try to move away slowly. The less you look like a frantic seal to the shark, the better; sharks have poor eyesight and are attracted by movement and smell. If the shark does take a lunge at you, push it away with something solid (such as a camera, an oxygen tank or a knife, if possible) – don't use your hands, as shark skin is very rough and the abrasion may increase its interest.

CORAL

Coral is sharp stuff and if you brush against it, you're very likely to injure yourself (and the coral). Coral wounds are notoriously troublesome, mainly because they tend to be ignored at first. Coral is covered in a layer of slime that is full of marine microorganisms, and small particles of coral, including its stinging cells, are often left in the wound.

If you ignore a coral wound, there's a good chance it will get infected and take ages to heal up. Treat any coral cut promptly, however small and insignificant it seems, as follows:

▶ rinse the wound with plenty of pure water (eg bottled water), perhaps using a small brush or a syringe (with or without the needle) to flush out any small particles
▶ apply an antiseptic solution such as povidone-iodine
▶ apply an antibiotic cream or powder (eg mupirocin 2%) to the area
▶ cover it with a dressing
▶ watch for signs of infection (p399)

You can cause irreparable damage to the coral when you come into contact with it, so it's mutually beneficial to avoid getting cut by coral in the first place.

▶ Don't walk or swim over reefs.
▶ Maintain correct buoyancy and control when you're diving on reefs.
▶ Always wear shoes in the water – flip flops (thongs) or sports sandals are good.

Fire Coral

These come in many different forms, and are another good reason not to touch any corals. They can deliver a powerful sting – treat by dousing with vinegar.

SEA SNAKES

These beautiful creatures are found throughout the Pacific, around Australia and New Zealand. They're often very inquisitive, although not usually aggressive. However, their venom is extremely toxic, so you should give them a wide berth. Unlike venomous fish bites, sea snake bites are not painful. Bites look like two or more small dots or scratch marks. Although sea snake venom is very poisonous, the quantity of venom injected is rarely enough to cause serious problems. Symptoms of poisoning may not appear for several hours, and include pain and stiffness, weakness, dry mouth, difficulty swallowing or speaking, thirst and respiratory failure.

! You need to get medical treatment urgently for any sea snake bite, as their venom is very toxic.

First aid treatment in the meantime is as for any snake bite:

▶ keep the casualty calm
▶ apply a pressure bandage (see p398)
▶ immobilise the limb by splinting it (this helps prevent the toxin from spreading)
▶ be ready to perform emergency resuscitation if necessary

JELLYFISH

Despite their ethereal appearance, jellyfish are carnivorous animals. They catch their prey by discharging venom into it from special stinging cells called nematocysts. Most jellyfish stings are just uncomfortable, but some species found in the waters aound Australia and the Pacific islands are capable of causing severe, potentially lethal stings. In general, stings on thick skin like the soles of your feet are likely to cause fewer problems. Children are more likely to suffer a severe reaction to stings.

! Get local advice on jellyfish risk areas and times, and don't swim at isolated beaches if there's a risk of dangerous jellyfish being about. Wearing a wetsuit or a lycra bodysuit may protect against stings in the jellyfish season, but would you want to risk it?

Sea Lice

Sea lice, also called sea bather's eruption, are thought to be the tiny larvae of thimble jellyfish. They can be a problem in any tropical waters. They sting and cause an uncomfortable rash, especially if they get caught in your swimming suit. Shower thoroughly after getting out of the sea. Calamine lotion may relieve the pain.

Dangerous Jellyfish

Avoid contact with any jellyfish, especially ones with long, trailing tentacles. Box jellyfish (right; also known as sea wasps) are found in tropical coastal waters, creeks and rivers. They are some of the most deadly jellyfish in the world. These jellyfish have large, box-shaped bells, with long stinging tentacles that trail out behind them. Box jellyfish venom can affect the heart and breathing mechanism, and can cause ulceration and scarring of the skin. Children have died within minutes of being stung. In Australia, antivenom is kept by many life-saving clubs in the north. Stings are excruciatingly painful, and the casualty will often suddenly scream, run out of the water and collapse on the beach. The area of the sting looks like it has been whipped, with swollen purple lines.

Chriropsalmus is another large, deadly jellyfish, occurring throughout tropical waters. It causes similar a similar effect to the box jellyfish.

The Irukandji is found along the northern coastline of Australia. It's quite small, and stings are painful but not severely so. The pain and any swelling tends to disappear in half an hour or so. Typically, casualties experience other symptoms soon after the sting, including nausea, vomiting, sweating, and muscle cramps. No deaths have been known to have been caused, but you need to get medical help to deal with the symptoms of poisoning.

The Portuguese (or Pacific) man-of-war (right; also known as bluebottles) occurs widely throughout the warmer waters of the world. Stings have caused deaths, but are more likely to be just painful. The man-of-war consists of a gas-filled, bluish float on the surface of the water, underneath which there are stinging tentacles. Large numbers of these jellyfish are sometimes blown inshore. Stings are extremely painful, with swelling and blistering at the sting site. Symptoms of poisoning include fever, chills, muscle cramps and paralysis, rarely leading to death.

! Dead man-of-wars are often washed up on shore and they may still be able to sting – don't touch any jellyfish on the beach.

Treatment

! Don't wash jellyfish stings with water or rub them, as this can encourage stinging cells to fire and can make the pain worse.

You will need to get medical help urgently for severe stings, especially if dangerous species are known to be in the area. In the meantime:

- get the casualty out of the water
- remove any bits of tentacle with tweezers or a gloved hand
- pour vinegar on the affected area (this doesn't help the pain, but it prevents stinging cells left in the wound from firing)

▶ be prepared to start emergency resuscitation if necessary – see inside backcover

For painful stings, ice packs or local anaesthetic sprays, creams or ointments may help, but strong painkilling injections may be needed. Antivenom may be available for some stings (for example box jellyfish).

STINGRAYS

These beautiful creatures (right) are widespread in tropical and subtropical waters. Stingrays aren't aggressive but because they like to lie half-submerged in mud or sand in the shallows, you may step on one accidentally. If you do, you'll certainly know, as rays whip up their tails in self-defence and can inflict a nasty ragged wound. They also inject venom through special spines in their tail, which can cause severe poisoning.

While stingray injuries are relatively common, and usually minor, severe poisoning is rare. First aid treatment of a ray injury is as for dangerous marine fish (see the following section). You need to clean any stingray wound very carefully, as otherwise infection is common.

! *Always shuffle your feet when in the shallows to give sting rays, stonefish and other creatures a chance to get out of your way.*

DANGEROUS MARINE FISH

! *Some fish are poisonous if they are eaten – see the section on p146 for more details.*

Relatively few fish are dangerous to humans, but there are a couple of species that produce venom capable of causing severe poisoning and sometimes death. Of these, stonefish (below right) and scorpionfish (below left; including butterfly cod and lionfish) are probably the most dangerous, and occur in most tropical waters. You'll know if you've been stung, as stings from venomous fish are extremely painful.

Stonefish have the dubious distinction of being the deadliest of all venomous fish. Stonefish are as ugly as scorpionfish are beautiful, and they are masters of disguise: they lie half-submerged in sand, mud or coral debris, looking exactly like (you guessed it) a stone. As with sting rays, the danger is stepping on one accidentally.

Stonefish stings are said to be the most devastatingly painful of any marine sting. The pain is immediate, causing the casualty to writhe around in agony. There is usually a puncture mark at the sting site, which develops a characteristic blue discolouration. The whole limb swells up. Severe poisoning may lead to collapse and even death. There is a stonefish antivenom, which should be given as soon as possible after the sting.

Scorpionfish are much easier to avoid, as they are distinctive and easily recognised, and the chances of you being stung by one are pretty remote. No antivenom is available.

Treatment

Hot (nonscalding) water helps to break down the toxins and is surprisingly effective at relieving pain from venomous fish stings. General treatment principles are as follows:

- ▶ if any spines are poking out, try to remove them gently (be sure to protect your own hands)
- ▶ wash any surface venom off with water
- ▶ immerse the wound in hot (nonscalding) water for up to 90 minutes or until the pain has gone, or apply hot packs
- ▶ wash the wound thoroughly once the pain is under control and apply a clean dressing
- ▶ rest with the limb raised
- ▶ seek medical help for antivenom (for a stonefish sting) and pain control if necessary

BLUE-RINGED OCTOPUS

This deadly creature is found in tropical waters, and is often washed up into rockpools at low tide. People sometimes get poisoned when they don't realise what they are, and pick them up. Naturally, the octopus bites in self defence. They are surprisingly small, varying in size from 2cm to 20cm. The ringed marks, normally yellowish brown, turn a bright blue when the octopus is under threat. Symptoms appear within a few minutes and include tingling sensations of the mouth and tongue, followed by increasing paralysis and collapse.

You must get help urgently. While you are waiting:

- ▶ wash out the wound with any water or antiseptic available
- ▶ apply a pressure bandage (see p398) to the affected limb and immobilise it (to prevent spread of the poison)
- ▶ be prepared to start resuscitation if breathing stops

CONE SHELL

Fish-eating cones are found in tropical and subtropical waters. They kill their prey by harpooning them with a poisonous barb, which has been known to cause death in humans. The pain from a sting can be excruciating, and may be followed by generalised symptoms, including paralysis. Treatment is as for blue-ringed octopus bite, with pressure bandaging, immobilisation and resuscitation if necessary.

CROWN OF THORNS

These impressive reef creatures are a hazard if you tread on them by accident or brush against them while diving. They inject venom from the base of their spines, which can break of and remain embedded in you. If the spines are not removed, they can cause pain, swelling and generally make you feel unwell for several weeks or months.

Remove any spines you can see, making sure not to break them. Immerse the affected area in hot (nonscalding) water, which will help ease the pain, then immobilise the limb. Seek medical advice as soon as possible.

SEA URCHINS

Sea urchins should be treated with care. If you step on one with bare feet, their spines can become embedded and are difficult to remove. One species is capable of causing generalised poisoning. If you step on one, remove any spines you can with tweezers, taking care not to break them off. Run hot (nonscalding) water over the wound to relieve the pain, then apply antiseptic to the wound. Applying meat tenderiser, made from the flesh of the paw paw (papaya) fruit, to the area may be helpful. Keep a careful lookout for breathing difficulties – seek medical help immediately if these develop.

OTHER STINGERS

Various other marine creatures can cause problems if you come into contact with them. Some sponges can cause severe itching and anemones can also give you a painful sting, so don't put inquisitive fingers on their tentacles. You've probably got the message now: look but don't touch!

BITES & STINGS

Bites and stings from insects and other small critters are probably going to be the main wildlife hazard you face on your travels in Australia, New Zealand and the Pacific.

MOSQUITOES & FLIES

○ For the complete lowdown on preventing insect bites, see p69.

MOSQUITOES

If there's a downside to a tropical paradise, mosquitoes (below) and other biting insects are probably it. As the sun sets, so the mosquitoes rise (although day-biting mosquitoes are responsible for transmitting dengue in risk areas). Mosquitoes are more of a problem in Australia (particularly the tropical north) and the Pacific islands, and less so in temperate New Zealand.

However, mosquitoes can be a nuisance in summer in New Zealand, especially on the west coast of the South Island.

Worldwide, mosquitoes play an astonishingly important role in the health of people in tropical and subtropical regions of the world through their role as carriers of some major tropical diseases. If there was any justice in this world, mosquitoes would get the diseases they carry. In the Pacific region, mosquitoes transmit malaria, dengue and filariasis. In parts of Australia, mosquitoes are responsible for transmitting Ross River Fever (and related diseases). In New Zealand, mosquitoes don't carry any diseases.

It's not just the diseases mosquitoes carry; it's also the fact that they have honed to perfection the art of maximal irritation, from the high-pitched whine as they approach their target to

An Itch to Scratch

How best you stop the itch from insect bites is one of those hotly debated questions that every traveller has an opinion on. It's important not to scratch those bites because, if you break the skin, you're very likely to get a troublesome infection. You could try one of the many commercial anti-sting relief sprays, although antihistamine creams or sprays are probably best avoided. They are widely available without a prescription but they may cause an allergic skin reaction, which makes the problem worse. Other tried and tested options include calamine cream, tea tree lotion, lavender oil or hydrocortisone cream (applied sparingly, and not if the bite looks infected). If the itching is driving you mad, you could try taking an antihistamine tablet.

Or if you happen to be standing underneath a frangipani tree, try a Pacific island remedy: pick a leaf and rub some of the milky sap that oozes from the broken stem onto the bite.

the maddening itch of bites that waxes and wanes throughout the day. Worse still, if you give in to the urge to scratch the bites open, you run the risk of infection developing, especially in hot, humid climates.

Ross River Fever

In many areas of Australia, mosquitoes are responsible for transmitting infections such as Ross River Fever and Barmah Forest Virus. The risk of acquiring these diseases if you are in urban areas is low, but if you are going to be staying in rural areas, it's worth taking steps to prevent mosquito bites.

These infections cause polyarthritis – pain, stiffness and swelling of the joints. You may also get a rash and flu-like symptoms (fever, headache, chills). The aches and pains can persist for weeks or sometimes months, and some people experience prolonged fatigue and depression. Most people recover fully, and have no long-term effects.

Diagnosis is by a blood test. There is no specific treatment, apart from treatment for aches and pains.

Encephalitis

Some viral diseases spread by mosquitoes can cause inflammation of the brain (encephalitis), outbreaks of which occur sporadically in the Pacific. They are generally a very small risk to you as a traveller. Japanese encephalitis is now known to exist in some of the Pacific islands, including Papua New Guinea and the Torres Strait Islands, and there has even been a case in mainland Australia. Similar viral diseases, Murray Valley Encephalitis and Kunjin virus, occur in northern and occasionally south-eastern Australia. These diseases occur in rural areas. Pigs and sometimes water birds act as reservoirs of infection. An effective vaccine is available against Japanese encephalitis but it is not generally recommended for travellers to the Pacific region because the risks are so low.

Symptoms vary from barely noticeable to severe, and sometimes fatal. They usually include fever, headache, nausea and vomiting. In a small proportion of cases, symptoms of brain involvement occur after a few days, with lethargy, irritability, drowsiness and confusion. Rarely, fits and coma occur. Victims may be left with mental or physical disability.

There's no specific treatment, but you should seek medical help as soon as possible if you think you have encephalitis. In the meantime, rest, drink plenty of fluids and take simple painkillers if necessary.

SANDFLIES & BLACKFLIES

These tiny (2mm to 3mm long) flies are widespread in coastal and inland areas throughout Australia, New Zealand and the Pacific islands. Female sandflies feed on blood, causing extremely itchy bites, usually around your feet and ankles. In some parts of the world, sandflies are responsible for transmitting various diseases, but not this is not a significant risk in Australia, New Zealand or the Pacific.

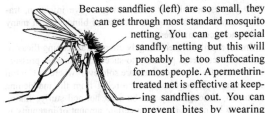

Because sandflies (left) are so small, they can get through most standard mosquito netting. You can get special sandfly netting but this will probably be too suffocating for most people. A permethrin-treated net is effective at keeping sandflies out. You can prevent bites by wearing shoes, socks and long trousers and by using insect repellent containing DEET on any exposed skin.

Blackflies (called *nonos* in French Polynesia) and other tiny flying insects can drive you mad in some areas, especially as they tend to go for your face and, worst of all, your ears. Bites are extremely itchy. The usual strategies of covering up and using insect repellent may work, but you may find they drive you indoors. They are not responsible for transmitting any diseases in Australia, New Zealand and the Pacific.

FLIES

If you've ever been to country Australia in the summer, you'll know why these warrant a mention. Bush flies are the scourge of the great Australian outdoors, and will probably be an enduring memory of any outback trip you take. They are not as much of a problem in urban areas, but as soon as you get into the bush, you'll find swarms of these small flies arrive within minutes. They are attracted to moisture, so you'll find they try to get up your nose and into your mouth and ears. It's a source of some amazement that even in the most remote, least populated and apparently lifeless areas of the outback, such as on the edge of Lake Eyre in Central Australia, within minutes of emerging from your vehicle you'll be inundated with flies.

To put it in perspective, although they can drive you wild and make picnicking outdoors practically impossible, they are unlikely to cause diseases and they are mainly a problem in the summer months (October to April). In Central Australia, flies are responsible for transmitting an eye infection, trachoma, which is an important cause of blindnesss in many indigenous communities.

Insect repellents aren't hugely effective at keeping flies off, and your best bet is probably to succumb to market pressure and wear a fly net. These nets are sold everywhere in Central Australia, and provide welcome relief from the maddening irritation, although they can be a bit hot and stuffy. Taking anything by mouth requires a certain amount of ingenuity to prevent flies from getting trapped inside the net (to be avoided at all costs). A hat with corks dangling from it is a temptingly silly option but not particularly effective and you'll probably get as tired of the corks bumping your face as of the flies crawling up your nose. If the flies aren't too bad you may get by just with the 'Australian salute': waving your hand in front of your face.

HORSEFLIES

Also called March flies, these are much larger than bush flies. They are blood suckers and inflict an uncomfortable bite. These bite through thin or close-fitting clothing and can be a nuisance in summer months if you are bushwalking in Australia or New Zealand. Using insect repellent and wearing loose clothing may help; otherwise, try carrying a twig or fly whisk to keep them off.

BEES, WASPS & ANTS

These insects are found worldwide. Stings are generally not dangerous in themselves, but they can cause a severe allergic reaction in some people who are sensitive to them, which is a medical emergency. Bright clothes and perfume may attract bees. Children often get stung, especially if they're eating outdoors. If you have drinks outdoors, check first before you gulp it down, in case there's a bee or wasp floating in it. Using a straw is a good safety precaution.

Bees leave their stings behind but wasps and ants usually do not. If the sting is still visible, remove it with a pair of tweezers, taking care not to squeeze the venom sac (the bulbous bit at the end furthest from the skin). The pain and swelling of a sting can be relieved with an ice pack or a cloth soaked in cold water. or you could try one of the many commercial sting relief sprays, or calamine lotion, tea tree or lavender oil.

If the sting is in the mouth or throat, you will need get medical help; in the meantime, try to remove the sting, and suck on an ice cube.

Some people can develop an allergy to bee, wasp and ant stings and get a severe reaction if they are stung.

If you know you are allergic to stings, you should carry with you an emergency kit containing antihistamines and adrenaline (epinephrine) to be used if you are stung – discuss this with your doctor before you leave.

You should seek medical help for stings in the following situations:

- if you've been stung in the mouth or throat, especially if the area swells rapidly
- if you get rapid swelling from a sting anywhere
- if it's followed by breathing difficulties or signs of shock – rapid pulse, pale clammy skin, breathlessness, sweating, faintness

In an emergency, ie if a severe allergic reaction occurs and no medical help is available, treatment is as follows:

- get the casualty to lie flat, and raise their feet
- give an injection of adrenaline/epinephrine (1 in 1000) 0.3mL into the top of the casualty's arm or thigh
- get medical help urgently

LEECHES, TICKS, SPIDERS & SCORPIONS — LEECHES

Leeches are common in forested areas throughout most of Australia and many of the Pacific islands. They don't transmit any diseases but their bites can get infected if you don't keep them clean. There is something about leeches, however, that can reduce even the most tranquil nature lover to a state of blind hysteria.

Leeches are usually found in damp, forested areas, often near streams or rivers. They attach themselves to you as you pass by. They're usually a couple of centimetres long, and unfed they look like thin black worms. After they've been attached to you for a while they swell up and look like black blobs.

If you don't want to get grossed out by leeches, take some preventive measures:

▶ check all over for them if you've been walking in infested areas
▶ use insect repellent (preferably containing DEET) on your skin to discourage them
▶ wear long trousers and closed shoes; tuck your trousers into your socks or wear gaiters to prevent leeches dropping down your boots
▶ considering soaking your clothes and boots in an insecticide such as permethrin

Once a leech has attached itself to you, it produces a substance that prevents your blood clotting and then it drinks its fill. Once full, it will drop off spontaneously. A leech can suck up to 10 times its weight in blood within half an hour. You probably won't even notice when the leech attaches itself.

Although leeches will spontaneously drop off if you leave them, unless you have nerves of steel, you'll probably want to remove them before this. Try not to pull them off in a state of panic. If you do this, they may leave their mouthparts behind, which makes infection of the bite more likely.

! Tried and tested methods for getting leeches to drop off include applying alcohol, vinegar or salt to the attached end; alternatively – cruel but possibly the simplest – put a lighted match to the unattached end.

After the leech has dropped off, clean the wound carefully with antiseptic and apply pressure to stop the bleeding. It can take some time – keep applying a steady pressure, raise your limb and try not to keep removing the bandage to see if the bleeding has stopped.

TICKS

Ticks (right) are a hazard if you're bush-walking or picnicking in scrub or grassland in eastern Australia and Papua New Guinea. Although they ticks do attach themselves to humans, they are basically blood-sucking parasites of wild and domestic animals and birds. Domestic dogs often pick them up. There are many different types of ticks, but you shouldn't have trouble recognising them.

It's best to avoid contact with these little critters because some species can transmit fairly nasty diseases, usually through bites, but also by contact with their body fluids.

▶ Get reliable local advice on likely problem areas (usually scrubland or pastures with long grass).
▶ Wear long trousers and boots, and tuck your trousers into your boots.
▶ Use insect repellent (containing DEET) on any exposed areas and consider soaking your clothes in an insecticide (such as permethrin) if you are planning a trek in tick or mite country.
▶ Check your body regularly all over for ticks and mites if you have been walking in infested areas, as they often go unnoticed until you get undressed.
▶ Use an insect net at night and sleep up off the ground if possible.
▶ Animals, wild or domestic, may be a source of ticks, so avoid close contact with these.

If you find a tick attached to you, resist the impulse to pull it off directly, as its body will just separate from the mouthpiece, which makes infection much more likely. Tick body fluids can transmit infection, so avoid handling it with your bare hands as far as possible. If you do, wash your hands thoroughly soon afterwards.

The idea is to induce the tick to let go – various methods have been advocated in the past, including burning the tick off or applying chemicals to it, but these are no longer recommended, as they can be harmful to you and may make the tick's contents more likely to contaminate you.

! The most effective and safest method to remove a tick is to use a pair of tweezers to grasp the head (not the body, or this will squeeze the contents into the wound and make matters worse) and pull gently, as shown in the illustration.

After the tick has dropped off, clean the wound thoroughly and apply an antiseptic solution like povidone-iodine. If tick parts get left behind, try scraping them out (under sterile conditions as far as possible) or get medical help to do this.

There are many different types of ticks and mites, capable causing a variety of diseases in humans, some more serious than others. In general, you are very unlikely to get any of these diseases, but they are a possibility if you've been trekking or camping in tick-infested areas.

! If you fall ill (eg with a fever or rash) after being in tick or mite country, get yourself checked out by a doctor as soon as possible.

Tick Paralysis

A type of tick found in the coastal strip of eastern Australia from Queensland down to eastern Victoria can produce paralysis and, rarely, death. Some people develop an allergic reaction to these ticks. If you're bushwalking or picnicking in this area, you may pick up some of the tiny, pin-head sized ticks without being aware of it. Over the course of a day or two the tick slowly enlarges as it sucks blood. It often hides above the hairline or in skin creases. If paralysis occurs due to a toxin produced by the tick, it usually appears about the fifth day. Deaths due to tick paralysis are extremely rare, and a tick anti-toxin is available.

If you notice any unusual symptoms or paralysis after a tick bite, seek medical help immediately.

Typhus

This disease is transmitted via tick bites and occurs in Papua New Guinea (as well as other parts of the world), but it is extremely rare in travellers. A form of typhus, called Queensland Spotted Typhus occurs in Queensland, Australia. Initially, a swelling appears at the site of the tick bite that enlarges and later forms a black scarred area. A variable time after the bite (four days to two weeks) a fever develops, and you get a headache and swelling of the glands near the bite. You may also notice a skin rash that spreads over your whole body, cough, eye irritation and abdominal pain. In its most severe form it can be fatal, but it is unlikely to reach this stage in you. Get medical advice as soon as possible for appropriate antibiotic treatment (usually a course of tetracycline).

SPIDERS

Although most spiders you may see on your travels are unlikely to be harmful, there are a few species that are best avoided.

Australia

Australia's arguably two most venomous spiders are the red-back and the funnel web. The red-back is found in all parts of Australia, and is a close relative of the black widow spider. They are particularly common in summer. Only the female red-back is potentially dangerous. It has a shiny black abdomen, about 1cm in diameter, with a distinctive red stripe. Most bites occur because the spider is trapped in clothing or under a pile of garden rubbish. The bite is initially painful like a bee sting, then the pain becomes more severe, and spreads to other parts of the body. In severe cases, it can cause paralysis and even death. However, an antivenom is available and is effective at preventing paralysis.

The Sydney funnel-web spider is a much nastier type altogether, and one of the most dangerous spiders in the world. This time it's the male of the species that is dangerous. In spite of their name, funnel-webs live in cylindrical web-lined burrows in rock crevices or house walls, with white trip lines running out to salient surrounding points. The Sydney funnel-web is black and hairy, with distinctive paired spinarets projecting out of the end of its abdomen, like two extra legs.

One of the reasons why funnel-webs have a reputation for being so deadly is that they are aggressive and will rear up when they feel threatened. The other reason they are scary is that their venom is extremely potent. It contains an unusual toxin that attacks the nerves, causing muscles to twitch, and perspiration, tears and saliva to flow copiously. The effects of the venom may wear off in a couple of hours, but you must get to hospital as soon as possible. An antivenom is available, and since it has been in use it has been very effective in reducing the number of deaths from funnel-web poisoning. In fact, no deaths have been recorded since the antivenom was first produced.

The Sydney funnel-web, as its name indicates, is found only in and around Sydney, but there are other types of funnel-webs that live in the rainforests of Queensland and eucalypt

Close Encounters in the Outhouse

You'll probably have your closest encounters with wildlife of the eight-legged variety when you're bushwalking or camping out. Most bites, if they occur, will be no more dangerous than an insect sting but it may give you a bit of a scare. Before you flop down for that well earned rest, just check what you are flopping on.

And wouldn't you know it, spiders just lurve outside toilets (because of the insects they attract). Before outhouses were phased out, two-thirds of red-back spider bites were to the groins of victims! If you don't want to feel an eight-legged tickle on your bare backside, some precautionary measures are in order.

Make sure you give plenty of warning as you approach (stamp firmly on the ground) and have a good look round before entering. If you're planning on sitting down, check under the seat first (a long stick is particularly handy) – it's astonishing how saucer-sized huntsmen spiders fit under toilet seats, but they do, legs and all. Having done a thorough check, you can now shut the door (it's best to keep this open up until now in case you need to beat a hasty retreat), relax (if you can) and get on with it. A final caution – before you reach for that considerately placed toilet roll or paper towel, just check what's nestling within the folds.

If you're squatting in the bush, just bear in mind that it is not unknown for spider bites and, less commonly, snake bites to occur in this situation. Experienced bush squatters tend to do plenty of bush beating first to scare off potential predators.

forests further south. Just don't put your hands in any tree ferns without checking first.

Some other spiders, such as the white-tailed spider, commonly seen in houses, may be responsible for a condition called necrotising arachnidism, in which bites cause extensive ulceration of the skin. All things considered, you're probably best to give a wide berth to any creepy crawlie with more than six legs.

New Zealand

The katipo is New Zealand's only venomous creature, and hence a source of much national pride. This diminutive specimen is related to black widow and red-back spiders, and a bite is potentially dangerous although very few deaths have been recorded. An effective antivenom is available in most hospitals, and can be given even a few days after the bite.

The katipo is found in coastal areas, apart from the far south. It lives in small webs in the undergrowth or in driftwood, and is only likely to bite if you disturb it. It is similar to other black widows in appearance, with a shiny black body about 6mm long, and a bright red patch at the tip. Only the female is dangerous. If you wear closed shoes, you should be able to minimise this (small) risk.

Pacific Islands

The black widow is probably the most notorious venomous spider and is found in most warm areas of the world (it's closely related to the Australian red-back spider and the New Zealand katipo). Only the female bites, and she is black or brown, about 25mm long, with a distinctive red hourglass shape on the underside of her abdomen. The male black widow is usually too small to bite, and he gets eaten by the female after mating. Black widows tend to live outdoors, hanging from webs under and around dwellings and outhouses.

Black widow spider venom affects the nervous system and can be fatal. The bite is painless at first, but in severe poisonings, intense pain develops several hours after the bite, followed by muscle spasms, abdominal pain, nausea and vomiting, and breathing difficulties.

Prevention

There's no need to be paranoid, but it is sensible to take steps to be aware of the risks, and to take steps to avoid close encounters with spiders:

- shake your clothes out and check in your boots before putting them on
- check under the seat in outhouse and pit toilets, as these are favourite spider haunts
- check the ground before you sit down
- sleep off the ground and use an insect net
- take notice of any local advice on particular risks

First Aid for Spider Bites

If you get bitten by a spider:

- don't panic!
- use the pressure immobilisation technique as described for snake bites (see p398) to prevent the venom from spreading EXCEPT for red-back spider bites in Australia, where this is not helpful, as the venom spreads so slowly, and compression will increase the pain
- get medical help as soon as possible for any spider bite; antivenom is usually available in the case of bites by potentially dangerous spiders

If you can trap the offending spider without further harm to yourself, this is useful for identification. Even mangled remains of spiders can be subjected to tests and identified.

SCORPIONS

These shy creatures are found throughout the tropics and subtropics, especially in dry desert areas. Several species are found in Australia and the Pacific islands, but they don't generally cause anything worse than a painful sting. Bites from bigger scorpions are likely to cause greater pain and swelling but don't generally cause generalised poisoning. In Australia, the further north you go, the bigger the scorpions are. As a general rule, the larger the pincers on a scorpion, the less potent the venom.

If you're not sure what a scorpion looks like, think of a tiny land lobster, except that the tail curls upwards. Scorpions grip their prey with their front pincers and use their tails to inject poison. Scorpions are nocturnal creatures, so you're very unlikely to see them. They're not aggressive, and you're only likely to get stung if you step on one by accident. Take precautions against this:

▸ always check your shoes before putting them on in the morning if you are camping out
▸ take care when lifting or moving rocks
▸ if you're camping, clear your camp site of rocks and other debris

An ice pack or a cold compress may help if you do get stung. If you get severe pain and swelling, seek medical help, as you may need painkilling drugs and observation in hospital.

CENTIPEDES

These multilegged creatures are found throughout Australasia and the Pacific. They can inflict a painful bite with their fangs, although they are unlikely to cause generalised poisoning. Centipedes wave a pair of pincer-like appendages from the back of the body when they are annoyed, but their fangs are actually hidden under the head at the front of the body. The larger the centipede, the more severe the bite. Centipedes get bigger the nearer the equator you are. They're easily avoided, but take care if you are clearing a site for your tent or to sit down.

SNAKES

Some of the world's most dangerous snakes occur in Australia and Papua New Guinea. Of the 130 or so species of land snakes in Australia, about 80 species are venomous and, of these, about 15 species are known to be dangerous, which is a high proportion compared with other parts of the world. There are a few venomous species on the other Pacific islands, although the toxicity of their venom is not well studied, and no snakes in New Zealand. You need to be aware of this risk, especially if you are planning on bushwalking or camping in rural areas; you need to know what to do if you get bitten, as help may be a some hours away if you are in a remote area; and you need to be able to recognise the signs and symptoms of snake poisoning.

SNAKE FANGS

The fangs of venomous snakes are hollow, or have narrow grooves down one side, allowing venom from a reservoir behind them to be injected into the prey when the snake bites. The fangs of Australian and Papua New Guinean snakes are usually smaller than most dangerous snakes from other regions of the world. This is thought to be one reason why these snakes produce such potent venom, to make up for their small bite. This means that fang marks from a dangerous snake bite may be so small they are hardly noticeable. Because snakes replace their fangs from time to time, you won't necessarily have two fang marks from a snake bite.

SNAKE VENOM

Snake venom is a highly modified form of saliva that enables the snake to 'knock out' its prey and hence to swallow it. Snake venom is usually a cocktail of substances that have different toxic effects. These include neurotoxins that affect nerves and cause paralysis (for example Tiger snakes and Taipans), myotoxins that destroy muscle tissue (for example Rough-scaled, Taipan, Tiger and Mulga snakes) and toxins that act on the clotting system of the blood (for example Copperhead, Mulga, Taipan and Tiger snakes). Snakes can control the amount of venom they inject, and even bites from

Where Dangerous Land Snakes are Found

Australia

Snake	Distribution
Eastern or Mainland Tiger	broad belt across central and southern Australia
Taipan	most northern parts of Australia
Death Adder	most of Australia, except Victoria and Tasmania
Red-bellied black snake	eastern coast of Australia
Brown snakes	seven species, found through out Australia (except Tasmania)
Copperhead	south-eastern Aus, Tasmania
Mulga	most of Australia, except south-eastern Australia and Tasmania

Pacific Islands

Snake	Distribution
Brown snakes	Papua New Guinea
Death Adder	Papua New Guinea
Taipan-like species	Papua New Guinea
Solomons Copperhead	Solomon Islands

venomous snakes don't always result in enough venom being injected to be dangerous.

! Australia is the only country in the world where snake venom detection kits are available in hospitals to identify which snake is responsible and therefore the most appropriate antivenom to use, if necessary.

DANGEROUS SNAKES

Even in Australia, not all snakes that bite are venomous. But unless you are an expert at snake identification, it's best to assume that any snake bite is potentially dangerous. If you've ever tried to identify a snake that has slithered across your path, you'll know that it's hard to do, even with the book open in front of you. Knowing the distribution of snakes helps narrow down the possibilities – see the table on the previous page. Following is a quick guide to some of the main potentially dangerous snakes in Australia and the Pacific islands.

Tiger Snakes

These are widespread in south-east and far south-west Australia, and a common cause of serious snake bite in Australia. About a metre long, tiger snakes vary from light brown to black, and may have light yellow bands. Before striking, tiger snakes usually flatten their neck.

Copperhead

Often active at lower temperatures than most snakes, this one can sometimes be found above the snowline on Mt Kosciuszko.

Brown Snakes

These are the most common cause of death from snake bite in Australia. Brown snakes are often found around barns and farm houses. They're usually a uniform light brown, orange or black, and vary in length but are about 2m in length.

Mulga

This heavily built snake, light-brown or copper-coloured, can be very aggressive if disturbed. It can strike repeatedly, and sometimes chews on its victim.

Death Adder

These have a typically viper-like shape, with a short, stocky body. They tend to ambush their prey, lying half-buried under leaves or sand, luring their prey by twitching their tails. Bushwalkers are at risk of stepping on or near the hidden snake. Their venom is very toxic, as you'd expect from their name, but antivenom is available.

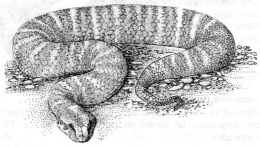

Taipan

This group includes some of the most venomous snakes in Australia. They are the longest venomous snakes in the country, and are common in sugarcane fields in tropical northern Australia. Before antivenom became available, most casualties died. A close relative of the taipan found in Australia is also found in Papua New Guinea. Although usually very shy, if threatened, the taipan can become very aggressive, striking several times.

Solomons Copperhead

This snake reaches over 1m, and is usually reddish brown to almost black above, sometimes with faint darker bands. It's reasonably common throughout the Solomons, especially in forested areas.

Fiji Snake

This venomous (but not known to be fatal) snake is found in Viti Levu and possibly other Fijian islands. It's a small burrowing species, which reaches about 40cm. Not known to give a fatal bite, but venomous.

Loveridge's Snake

This relatively rare snake is found across the Solomons and reaches over 1m in length. It is white with black bands, and sometimes yellow areas along the back. It's not aggressive, but its bite could be potentially dangerous.

SNAKE BITE – EFFECTS

At the time of the bite, you may feel a pinprick, or a sharp burning pain or nothing at all (some snake strikes are lightning fast). Most (90%) bites are on a limb, which is less dangerous than bites to the centre of the body. After a serious bite, you usually get a dull ache around the bite site, extending up the limb. The most common symptom following a snake bite is fear, and sometimes it can be difficult to tell if symptoms are due to the bite itself or to the fear it produces.

Generalised poisoning from bites by Australian and Pacific snakes causes dizziness, headache and nausea, although symptoms may not appear for several hours. In severe envenomation, weakness and paralysis (an early sign is drooping of the eyelids and double vision) appear about 30 minutes after the bite. Without treatment, death may occur after about 24 hours in severe cases, but prompt first aid makes this very unlikely in most situations. In fact, only about one or two people die from snake bite in Australia annually.

PREVENTION

You're quite likely not to see any snakes at all, especially if you are staying in populated urban areas, although children left playing in the garden or on the veranda are at risk through their natural curiosity and, for toddlers at least, lack of fear.

Probably the most likely risk situation for travellers is if you are bushwalking, when you may accidentally step (or sit) on a snake. Snakes hibernate during the winter but they are still capable of biting if they are accidentally disturbed in their place of hibernation (often hollow logs or under branches). Anybody who deliberately tries to catch a snake 'for fun' probably deserves all they get.

Snakes aren't generally aggressive creatures, although some snakes are more easily provoked than others. They will generally only bite in self-defence. You can avoid snake bites with a few basic precautions:

▶ wear socks and closed shoes if you're bushwalking, especially in long grass
▶ give snakes plenty of chance to 'hear' you coming – use a stick to beat the undergrowth before you step, and step firmly
▶ use a torch and don't risk bare feet if you are walking outside on a warm summer night (people have been bitten by tiger snakes on their lawns)
▶ be careful if you're climbing foliage-covered rocks or trees, or swimming in lakes or rivers surrounded by thick vegetation
▶ take care if you're collecting firewood or moving logs, boulders or other debris, as these may shelter resting snakes
▶ always carry a bandage roll with you if you are walking in the bush (don't leave it in your vehicle!)

FIRST AID TREATMENT OF SNAKE BITE

Snake venom gets into the circulation by movement of fluid in tiny channels that is encouraged by muscle activity. This can be effectively prevented by compression bandaging of the bite site and the limb, and by keeping the limb still, which is the basis of first aid treatment of snake bites by Australian and Pacific snakes. Anybody who has been bitten by a snake is going to be very frightened and will need lots of reassurance and morale-boosting from you.

> Immediately apply pressure to the bite by grasping hold of the limb.
> Apply a compression bandage directly over the bite site and then bind up the limb (see p398 in the First Aid appendix).
> Don't bother to wash the venom off the skin, as traces of venom may help doctors identify the species of snake involved.
> Immobilise the limb with a splint.
> Try to ensure the casualty stays still.
> Seek medical help urgently (eg by telephone or radio) for all snake bites.
> Make a note of what the snake looked like but don't endanger yourself and others by trying to catch it.
> Watch for signs of shock and breathing difficulty and be prepared to start emergency resuscitation if necessary.

!*Traditional first aid methods like cutting into the bite and sucking the poison out or applying tourniquets are now known to be less effective and potentially dangerous, and you should avoid them, whatever you may be told locally.*

ANTIVENOMS

Effective antidotes or antivenoms are available for all serious snake bites in Australia and the Pacific, although supplies may be limited outside Australia, and probably only found in major centres. Although they are very effective at preventing the harmful effects of snake venom, antivenoms can cause severe allergic reactions in some people. This means that they should not be given without medical supervision except in extreme emergency. Only about one in 10 people who have a snake bite will need antivenom.

ANIMAL BITES

Rabies, a fatal viral infection transmitted through animal bites, is not reported in Australia, New Zealand or the Pacific islands. A rabies-like virus has been identified in fruit bats (also called flying foxes) in Australia, so it's wise not to touch or pick up any bats, including dead ones.

If you do get bitten by an animal, there's a high risk of the bite getting infected because animal (and human) mouths harbour many bacteria, and animals don't brush their teeth. Bear in mind that dogs in rural areas are not usually kept as pets, and should not be treated as such.

If you are bitten by an animal (or a human), immediately clean the bite thoroughly.

▶ Use lots of soap and water to flush the wound out, then apply an antiseptic solution like povidone-iodine directly to the wound.
▶ Do not attempt to close the wound with stitches.
▶ Get medical help as soon as possible.

You will need a course of antibiotics if it is a deep wound, as well as a tetanus booster if you're not up to date with this.

If no medical help is available, suitable antibiotics are co-amoxiclav or erythromycin if you're allergic to penicillin – see the Medicines appendix for more details on antibiotic treatment.

AFTER YOU GET BACK

If you were on a short trip, some illnesses may not appear until after you get back. Illnesses that started while you were away may persist or get worse after you return, and sometimes it can be difficult to work out if symptoms are related to your trip or not. In some situations a post-travel health check is a good idea:

▶ if you're worried
▶ if you have any new or persistent symptoms (such as diarrhoea, fever, skin lesion, weight loss or just feeling 'not quite right')
▶ if you were on a long trip, in rural areas or living rough
▶ if you were ill when you were away (unless it was just a brief episode of travellers diarrhoea), especially if you needed medical care
▶ if you had unprotected sexual intercourse with a new partner

You may want to spare a thought for one less obvious long-term consequence of travelling – skin cancer, from exposure to the sun.

! *If you had medical or dental treatment while you were away, claim for it as soon as possible on your travel insurance.*

You can go to your usual doctor, a travel health clinic or a doctor specialising in tropical medicine. The advantage of a travel health or tropical medicine specialist is that they may be more alert to symptoms of tropical diseases, if you think this may be relevant. On the other hand, your doctor will be familiar with your medical history.

! *Remember that doctors at home may not consider tropical diseases as a cause for your symptoms unless you tell them you have been travelling; let them know where you went and any risk situations you were in.*

FEVER

This is especially important to look out for if there's any risk of malaria. You should suspect malaria if you develop any fever or flu-like symptoms after you return, especially in the first four weeks. Although the most serious form of malaria (falciparum) is most likely to occur in the first four weeks after you return, malaria can occur several months after you were infected. In some special circumstances you may need to have a course of primaquine, an antimalarial that clears persistent liver forms of the parasite.

Malaria deaths have occurred in returned travellers because the infection was not suspected by doctors at home, so it's important to tell them if you have been to a malarial area, even if you were taking antimalarials.

!Don't forget that you need to continue taking your antimalarials for four weeks after you leave a malarial area or you may be at risk of getting malaria.

There are lots of other causes of fever in returned travellers: dengue fever, hepatitis, typhoid and tuberculosis can all show up in this way.

DIARRHOEA

Gastrointestinal problems can appear for the first time after you get back or, if you had diarrhoea while you were away it may refuse to go away. Bacterial dysenteries, giardiasis and amoebiasis are all possibilities, and even malaria, the great mimic, can cause diarrhoea. However, travellers often find that diarrhoea clears up spontaneously once they get back to their usual routines and lifestyle.

!See your doctor if your symptoms persist for longer than a week after you return or there's blood or mucus in your faeces.

Worms are often symptomless, so it's probably a good idea to get a check for these if you've been on a long trip or you've been travelling rough.

Travelling can make you more likely to develop non-infectious conditions like irritable bowel syndrome or milk intolerance (usually temporary), so bear this in mind if you develop any gut disturbances that are not normal for you. Your problems may turn out not to be related to travelling, but get any symptoms checked out.

!Diarrhoea is contagious; this may affect whether you can go back to work when you return (for example if you work with young children or in the food industry).

SKIN

If you've got any infected cuts, persistent ulcers or rashes, or any weird skin blemish you're not sure about, get these checked out as soon as possible. Mention if tick bites or any other bites or stings were a possibility (some spider bites, for example, can produce persistent skin changes). Fungal infections like athlete's foot are common while you're away, but they may clear up once you get back.

Another thing to look out for is any change in a mole or freckle (see the boxed text 'Skin Cancer' on p156 for more details), especially if you've been scorching yourself in the tropical sunshine.

SEXUAL HEALTH CHECKUP

This is definitely a good idea if you had unprotected intercourse with a new partner while you were away, or you experience any symptoms. Hepatitis B, HIV and other sexually transmitted infections (STIs) are all a possibility. STIs can be symptomless and can have serious consequences on your fertility, so it's worth getting this checked out early if you think it may be a possibility.

OTHER SYMPTOMS

It's worth reporting any unusual symptoms, such as weight loss, night sweats, recurrent fevers or if you're simply not feeling right and don't know why. Tuberculosis (TB) is rare in travellers, but may be a cause of weight loss, fevers and night sweats. Consider this possibility if you spent several months living with members of the host community. Some more exotic diseases may not show up until after you get back.

POST-TRAVEL BLUES

Everyone has to go home eventually. You may be glad to get back to familiar faces, a familiar culture and your old haunts. On the other hand, you may be reluctant to exchange the exciting, challenging, temporary world of travelling for a return to a life that may seem at first less enjoyable and less meaningful.

If you've been away for a while, you may experience reverse culture shock when you return. Have a read of the section on Culture Shock in the Mental Wellbeing chapter, and see if you recognise any of the feelings described.

Added to this is the big change in lifestyle that coming home usually involves – trying to pick up where you left off, maybe trying to find a job, somewhere to live, coping with dreary weather and a (comparatively) dreary environment can be stressful. Friends and family may be surprisingly uninterested in hearing all about the wonderful and not-so-wonderful experiences you had while you were away (can you blame them?).

Be prepared for at least some emotional turmoil after you get back, as you try to match up your expectations of life with the realities. Talking through experiences you have had may help, especially if you had any particularly life-altering or traumatic experiences. Try talking to other travellers to find out how they coped with the transition, to sympathetic friends or to a trained counsellor. Activity and a purpose in life can help enormously. On the other hand, if you feel persistently low and lose interest in life, you may be depressed (see the section on Depression in the Mental Wellbeing chapter for more details) and you should seek medical help.

TRADITIONAL MEDICINE

Illness is an inescapable fact of life, and societies everywhere have developed ways of dealing with it. Most Pacific island, Maori and Aboriginal people have some knowledge of traditional remedies, although traditional healing methods have now been largely superseded by western medicine. Because traditional medical knowledge has been passed down from generation to generation through word of mouth, much of this valuable knowledge has been lost, although attempts are now being made to preserve it in writing.

This chapter provides an overview of the general principles of traditional medicine as practised by people in the Pacific region although you will find there are many local variations.

ILLNESS & SPIRITUAL BELIEFS

Societies view the cause of illness and misfortune in different ways according to their world views. For example, modern medicine looks for disease processes within the body, such as cancerous cells, microorganisms, chemical imbalances etc, because this fits in with the western concept of science. For Maori, Aboriginal and Pacific island people, the spiritual world is a hugely important part of their culture, and this is reflected in how they view illness and the way to ameliorate it. In these societies, people who have the capacity to control spirit influences (for good or bad means) are widely respected – and often greatly feared.

Some illness (such as coughs, colds, sore eyes, earache etc) are seen as caused by body processes, but other illnesses are seen as being caused directly or indirectly by spirits or by magic, for example as a result of displeasing the spirits by breaking a taboo. In addition, there are illnesses that are believed to be caused by sorcerers. Beliefs in spirit involvement are a fundamental part of illness and healing; herbal remedies are thought to work only if the right incantations are said to the spirits.

New Bugs, Old Remedies

Before the arrival of Europeans, there is evidence that the main health problems dealt with by Aboriginal, Maori and Pacific island people were injuries, skin complaints (boils, ulcers and infections), respiratory diseases and eye infections. 'Lifestyle' diseases like heart disease and diabetes were unknown because of the traditionally healthy diet and lifestyle. A variety of mainly plant-based remedies and spiritual healing practices were used to ameliorate illnesses.

With the arrival of Europeans, a whole new set of diseases was introduced. These had a devastating effect on the region's populations, practically wiping out some communities, because people had no immunity against them and there were few effective European or traditional medicines to treat them. Measles, tuberculosis (TB or consumption as it was then known) – already known in the region but re-introduced with drastic results – and sexually transmitted infections (such as syphilis and gonorrhoea) swept through communities. In response, the region's people adapted traditional remedies to deal with the new diseases not always with great success. Later, advances in medical science in the first half of the 20th century, such as the discovery of penicillin, produced more effective means of treatment.

People came to rely more and more on western medicine at the expense of traditional medicine. Medicines were often dispensed by missionaries, and the apparent effectiveness of western medicines at treating diseases compared with traditional healing practices was probably an important factor in the conversion of Pacific islanders to Christianity. The circle has been completed now as traditional remedies are used in both alternative and conventional western medical practice.

TRADITIONAL HEALERS

Most Maori, Aboriginal and Pacific island people have some knowledge of basic plant-based remedies, which are tried as a first strategy for common ailments. Traditionally, some members of society are known for having more specialised knowledge of healing methods, and will be called on for advice and treatment if firstline remedies don't work, or the ailment is more serious. As in western medicine, there are usually 'specialists' for different types of illness. These vary from society to society, but generally include birth attendants, herbalists, bone setters and spiritual healers (responsible for banishing bad spirits or lifting spells).

Herbal remedy specialists are usually women, and often come from a family of healers. They acquire their vast knowledge of local plants through apprenticeship, often learning their craft from early childhood. Herbalists have to learn to recognise several hundreds of species of plants and to know what they are useful for, as poisons or medicines. In recent years, healers have been encouraged to write down this knowledge in an attempt to preserve it for future generations.

In Maori societies, diagnosis and healing were the responsibility of the *tohunga* (expert or learned one). The *tohunga ki*, or seer, used his powers of second sight to determine how the spirits had been offended and therefore why the person had become ill. The *tohunga nana tupapaku*, or medical expert, was responsible for determining what remedies to give and what incantations *(karakia)* to make to the spirits.

In Aboriginal communities in Australia there are usually women whose advice is sought on treatment with herbal remedies. If herbal remedies don't work or the illness is believed to have spiritual causes, people go to spiritual healers for help. Spiritual healers will use charms, magic or witchcraft to treat the illness.

TRADITIONAL REMEDIES

Before the advent of modern medicine and synthetically manufactured drugs, people had to use whatever was available to them from the local environment. Plants were the main sources of remedies, although non-plant-based substances were also used. Remedies were probably discovered in the same way as foods were – by trial and error. People from neighbouring islands shared their medicinal knowledge and brought plants. Later immigrant populations such as Indians and Chinese – who have strong traditions of herbal medicine – introduced other medicinal plants, along with their uses.

Many different plants are used medicinally throughout the region, depending on what grows locally. Plants tend to have multiple uses, with various parts of the plant being used for different purposes (such as food, dyes and medicines). In addition, the same plant may be used to treat a variety of ailments.

The active ingredients in plants vary, but nitrogen-containing chemicals called alkaloids are thought to have the greatest therapeutic importance. Alkaloids usually have a bitter taste, and this was often used as a measure of a plant's potential therapeutic value. Most alkaloids are poisonous in large quantities, but in smaller doses many have therapeutic effects. Several drugs used in western medical practice are derived from plant alkaloids, including morphine (for pain relief), quinine (antimalarial) and reserpine (for blood pressure).

If you break a leaf or stem of some plants, they give off a milky fluid or latex. This fluid is often irritant, but can be used for cleaning ulcers and wounds, and for removing skin lesions like warts and corns. The leaves of some plants (for example eucalyptus species) contain aromatic oils, and if you crush them, the oils are released, giving a characteristic smell. These can be inhaled for colds, sinus pain, coughs and other lung problems. In addition, many have antibacterial properties.

Many plants contain substances called tannins (so called because they were used in tanning hides). These are astringents, causing tissues and blood vessels to contract, and can be useful for treating inflammation or bleeding, for example coughs, colds and intestinal infections, and for bathing wounds. Bark from wattles or eucalyptus contain high levels of tannins, and this is commonly used in tradtional remedies for treating dysentery.

Take Two Crushed Ants ...

Although plant remedies are the most widely used traditional treatments, non-plant-based healing methods are also used. For example, in some areas of Australia, Aboriginal people eat clay (after washing and straining it) as a remedy for coughing or tuberculosis, or for diarrhoea. Another treatment involves using crushed green ants. These are added to other medicines to make a paste that is rubbed on the chest for respiratory problems.

Bathing in hot thermal springs as a treatment for skin diseases, rheumatism and other ailments was a well established practice in New Zealand long before Europeans arrived. Hot mud baths were later used for treating the skin manifestations of syphilis. Mud and clay are commonly used as a treatment for wounds. Because toothache was believed to be caused by the gnawing of the tunga grub as it attacked the root of a tooth, treatment of toothache in Maori societies sometimes involved placing a hollow rush against the tooth to provide the grub with an exit route.

Usually the bark and leaves of a plant are used in medicinal remedies; the seeds and roots are less commonly used. Plants aren't usually taken internally; they are more commonly used as inhalants, lotions or rubbed on the affected part. Plant material is boiled in water, then strained to produce a decoction. Bark and roots can sometimes be crushed or powdered before using. Liniments or ointments are prepared by mixing powdered plant material with coconut oil or a little water to make a paste.

Another way in which plants are used in the region's traditional medicine is by smoking. If a child is to be treated, it is held in the smoke given off when the medicinal plant is put on burning embers. For adults, the procedure is a bit more involved. A pit is dug and a fire is made in the centre and allowed to die down. Green twigs of the medicinal plant are placed on the embers, which produces voluminous amounts of smoke. The patient either lies across the pit or squats over it, depending on the ailment being treated. This way the patient inhales the fumes, is bathed in them and sweats profusely. Australian Aboriginal people often use this method for treating women's problems, for example lack of breast milk or childbirth difficulties.

In Maori societies, an earth oven is used. Hot stones are put in the bottom of a person-sized pit and water is sprinkled over them. A thick layer of leaves and branches from an appropriate medicinal plant is put over the stones. The patient lies or sits on this and is covered with a mat, on top of which a layer of earth is placed. The patient stayed in the oven, sweating profusely and being bathed in aromatic steam for a couple of hours, sometimes longer.

Some plants are believed to be sacred, often because of mythological associations, and are used because of their magical properties. Fijians, for example, eat the leaves of certain sacred trees when they are in a strange district to protect them from sorcery.

MEDICINAL PLANTS

In this section we've listed a few of the many plants used medicinally by societies in the Oceanic region. Traditional healers have a long training so that they can use plants safely – unless you are a medicinal plant expert, you would be wise not to do any experimenting.

Abrus Precatorius

This climbing shrub, with its distinctive seeds, occurs widely in the tropics, often winding round other plants. It's known by a variety of names, including Indian liquorice, crab's eye, jequirity and prayer bean. When ripe, the dark brown pods split open to reveal bright red seeds with a black spot at the base. The seeds are extremely toxic, one seed containing enough of the poison abrin to kill a person. However, the roots and leaves are used medicinally in many areas for treating coughs, colds and diarrhoea. They contain a similar ingredient to liquorice.

Calophyllum Inophyllum

This ornamental tree is widespread around the Pacific and Indian Oceans. It has fragrant white flowers and produces large, round fruits. When broken, the twigs exude a milky sap, which is widely used to treat rheumatism. The oil from the fruit is also used as a liniment for rheumatism, joint pains and bruises. In Australia, Aboriginal people use the liquid obtained from the fruit to induce vomiting and as a purgative. Juice from the crushed leaves is used as an eye wash to treat sore or infected eyes.

Caustic Vine

This plant is leafless, and grows as a tangle of green branches, either alone or on other plants. If you break the stems, they exude large quantities of milky sap. The sap is used by Australian Aboriginal people, applied directly to bleeding wounds, sores and ulcers, and in some areas, used externally to treat diarrhoea. The sap is not taken internally as a medicine, because it is poisonous.

Conkerberry

This prickly shrub *(Carissa lanceolata)* looks very much like a currant bush. It produces small, reddish-black berries. The berries are edible and a good source of vitamin C. Aboriginal people in northern Australia used the plant medicinally, boiling the root in water. The liquid was used as an all-purpose remedy, especially for toothache, and as a wash for scabies.

Cordia Subcordata

This small tree is found near sea beaches and is widely distributed around the Indian and Pacific oceans. It has bright orange flowers and round, pointed fruit that turns yellow when ripe. A decoction of the leaves is used to treat diarrhoea, filariasis and sinusitis. The bark also has a variety of medicinal uses.

Ervatamia Orientalis

This common small tree or shrub is found in the Pacific from Fiji to Samoa and also in northern Australia. It has edible, sweet fruit. All parts of the plant yield a milky sap when broken, which is widely used medicinally. The sap is used like iodine (hence its alternative name, 'iodine plant') to clean wounds. In Tonga, an infusion of the root is used as a mouthwash to treat toothache.

Mangrove

The bark of this common tropical coastal tree *(Avicennia marina)* contains astringent tannins. In Australia, it is used in some areas to produce a traditional Aboriginal remedy for scabies. Twigs and branches are burnt and the collected ash is mixed to a paste with water and applied to the skin. In New Caledonia, small doses are used as a treatment for diarrhoea, although large doses are toxic. The juice obtained from leaves and twigs is used to treat stings from venomous marine creatures. Resin from the bark is also used medicinally, as a contraceptive, aphrodisiac and toothache remedy in some areas.

Pandanus Spiralis

Also known as screw palm, this palm-like tree is common in the north coastal region of Australia and the Pacific islands. The leaves are commonly used for weaving mats. The tree produces striking, large, orange-red fruit, consisting of lots of kernels tightly packed round a central core. The seeds can be eaten and are an important food source in some areas.

Medicinally, it is used to treat diarrhoea, either by drinking an infusion made from the leaves or by eating the inner part of a new stem. A decoction of the inner part of the stem is used to treat soreness of the mouth, tongue and gums. Juice from the aerial roots is used to treat heart attack.

Papaya (Pawpaw)

This plant *(Carica papaya)* is common throughout the tropics. It bears large fruit directly on the stem of the plant. It has extensive medicinal use in traditional remedies and in modern medicine. The papaya tree has been found to contain many active substances, including papain, a protein-digesting enzyme found in all parts of the plant but especially in the fully formed, unripe fruit and carpaine, an alkaloid found in the leaves and seeds. Carpaine has been found to have anti-amoeba and antibacterial properties. Papain is used in meat tenderiser and in indigestion remedies, and papaya ointment or strips of papaya skin are well recognised as aiding the healing of wounds.

Traditionally, the seeds and the milky juice of unripe fruit are used to get rid of intestinal worms. The juice is also used as a remedy for indigestion, and applied to the skin as treatment for sores and ringworm and, in some areas, to treat poisoning by stonefish, jellyfish and other marine creatures. Australian Aboriginal people use the pulp of the fruit to treat prickly heat. The juice of the stem is also used medicinally, applied to sores and boils. In the Solomon Islands, young leaves are applied as a healing dressing to wounds.

Piper Methysticum

The crushed or powdered roots and stem of this common Pacific island shrub are used to prepare kava (yaqona). The shrub is a member of the pepper family. The drink is a mild narcotic, with sedative or soporific (sleep-inducing) effects.

Kava also has a wide variety of medicinal uses, including as treatment for many common ailments such as coughs, colds and sore throat. It's also used to treat kidney and bladder troubles and for filariasis. In some societies, the leaves are chewed and swallowed by women as a contraceptive.

Kava has been extensively studied, and the active constituents have been identified as a series of chemicals called kava lactones. These chemicals are known to have local anaesthetic, antifungal, sleep-inducing, anti-convulsive and anti-muscle spasm properties.

Quinine Tree

Also known as bitter bark, this small tree *(Alstonia constricta)* is found in the Australian states of Queensland and New South Wales. The bark contains several alkaloids, making it taste extremely bitter. European settlers used it as a treatment for fevers and believed it contained the antimalarial quinine, although this was later disproved. It was also used for treating diarrhoea and dysentery. Aboriginal people use sap from the bark directly on sores. One of the alkaloids in the bark is known to be reserpine, which lowers blood pressure and acts as a tranquilliser.

Quinine berry is an unrelated tree of the eucalyptus family. The berry is held in the mouth as a cure for toothache, and an infusion of the bark is used for treating eye complaints.

Sandalwood

Related trees or shrubs of the sandalwood family are widespread in Australia and the Pacific, and include the bush plum and quandong. Sandalwood fruits are reasonably sweet, and were a popular food of Aboriginal people and early settlers, who made them into pies and jams. Sandalwoods are known for their aromatic wood and the aromatic oil has many uses, including medicinal, often blended with other oils such as coconut oil. Aboriginal people use the ground seed kernels as a liniment for a variety of ailments, and the pounded leaves are applied directly to aid healing of boils and sores. A decoction of the leaves and bark is used as a purgative. The leaves are burnt to keep away mosquitoes. In Samoa, a decoction of the leaves is used to treat filariasis.

Snake Vine

This creeping vine *(Tinospora smilacina)* grows up round trees and is found in north-western Australia. It has heart-shaped leaves and produces bright red berries. Snake vine has many uses, including as straps or binding; medicinally, it is used as a painkiller. The stem is pounded and then wrapped around the affected part, for example tied around the head to relieve headache or around the waist for abdominal pain. The milky latex from the stem is applied directly to sores or bites and stings.

Solanum Nigrum

Also called blackberry nightshade or black nightshade, this widespread shrub has white star-shaped flowers with yellow stamens and shiny black peppercorn-sized berries containing many small seeds. It is used medicinally in many countries, including in the oceanic region. The leaves are used as a poultice for sores and other skin diseases. The ripe fruits are edible and are used to treat fevers and diarrhoea. The unripe green fruit causes nausea, vomiting and diarrhoea, hence the plant's reputation for being poisonous.

Sterculia Quadrifida

Also known as peanut tree, this deciduous tree produces red pods that split when ripe to reveal black seeds. The seeds are eaten raw by Australian Aboriginal people in some areas. The inner bark of young trees is mixed with breast milk (used because this is a sterile, nonastringent liquid) or an infusion is made, and the liquid is used as a wash for sore ears and eyes. Heated leaves of the tree are applied to wounds to stop bleeding.

Tamarind

The tamarind tree is found throughout the tropics, and was probably originally introduced to the Pacific islands and northern Australia by fishermen from Indonesia. The fruit of the tree consists of dangling, chocolate-coloured, bean-like pods, which have a brittle outer shell and a dark-brown, sticky pulp. The pulp is very sour and is used widely in the cooking of southern Asia and many of the Pacific islands as a souring ingredient and in chutneys. Native tamarinds are also found in tropical rainforests, with yellowish, orange-brown or red lobed fruit, with orange pulp. The pulp is believed to have a cooling effect, and is valued for its vitamin C (used to combat scurvy) and iron content. It's also used as a mild laxative. A decoction of the leaves is used medicinally to treat skin sores.

Tea Tree

The crushed leaves of this well known Australian medicinal shrub are aromatic, the oil having antibacterial properties. The oil is used externally to treat boils, abscesses, sores and wounds, as well as ringworm.

Witchetty Bush

This shrub *(Acacia kempeana)* is found in north-western and central Australia. It produces dense yellow spikes of flowers and flat, brown seed pods. The seeds are roasted and ground and used as a foodstuff. The roots of the witchetty bush are home to insect larvae called witchetty grubs. The grubs are cooked in ashes or eaten raw and are a good source of protein. In some areas, the leaves are chewed or made into a decoction for treating colds.

FURTHER INFORMATION

If you want to find out more about traditional medicine and remedies in the Pacific region, here's a selection of publications to get you started.

Maori Healing and Herbal by Murdoch Riley – incredibly comprehensive, full of fascinating detail

New Zealand Medicinal Plants by SG Brooker

Koorie Plants, Koorie People by Nelly Zola & Beth Gott – includes a section on traditional medicine

Useful Bush Plants by Peter Binden – illustrated guide to plants found in the Australian bush, organised alphabetically

Bushfires and Bushtucker by Peter Latz – includes details of Aboriginal traditional medicine

Bush Food by Jennifer Isaacs – a classic, sympathetically written text, with a good section on medicinal plants and healing traditions among Australian Aboriginals

Fijian Medicinal Plants by RC Cambie & J Ash – detailed compendium, with plenty of illustrations

Samoan Herbal Medicine by W Arthur Whistler – overview of plants used and herbal treatments by this expert in Pacific flora

Healing Practices in the South Pacific by Claire Parsons

ALTERNATIVE THERAPIES ——————

This chapter was compiled by Elissa Coffman, a Reiki practitioner based in Melbourne, Australia.

Alternative therapies are often described as 'holistic', which means that they aim to improve the health of your entire being, body, mind and soul. Most therapies promote general well-being as well as having specific uses. We've used the term 'alternative therapies' to describe therapies not traditionally included in the practice of conventional medicine. Other terms used include 'natural', 'complementary' or 'holistic' medicine. As a general rule, these therapies are not intended to replace medical consultation and treatment in serious cases.

CHOOSING A PRACTITIONER

There are plenty of practitioners in a variety of disciplines in all the major cities in Australia and New Zealand. Probably the best way to find a practitioner is through a personal recommendation – and your instinct. Otherwise, try any of the national accredited associations, as their members will generally be trained to a high standard, and are answerable to the association. Practitioners are also listed in any telephone directory, or you could try asking for a recommendation at a local health centre. Be wary of anyone who claims to have the ability to 'cure' you, as this misses the point of most therapies, which aim to 'heal' and prevent illness.

Fees

There are no laws in Australia and New Zealand governing the pricing of consultations, but for most therapies, consultations cost between A$25 and A$50, with comparable rates in NZ. For therapies like homoeopathy, naturopathy etc, the consultation fee doesn't generally include the price of treatments, which can make the cost add up.

Many doctors in Australia routinely include complementary therapies like massage, acupuncture or yoga as part of a treatment program, and health care funds now often include alternative therapies in their policies. If you have a Medicare card, you may be entitled to subsidised fees for some alternative therapies – check with the practitioner.

USEFUL ORGANISATIONS

In Australia, some organisations you could try for more information on therapies and therapists include the following.

Australian Complementary Health Association (☎ 03-9650 5327), Ross House, 247-251 Flinders Lane, Melbourne VIC 3000

Australian Holistic Healers Association (☎ 03-5470 5566), 62 Hargreaves St, Castlemaine VIC 3450

Australian Natural Therapists Association Limited (ANTA; ☎ 1800 817 577 toll free in Australia), PO Box 856, Caloundra QLD 4551

Australian Traditional Medicine Society (☎ 02-9809 6800, www.atms.com.au), Unit 12/27 Bank St, Meadowbank NSW 2114

The Australian Alternative Health Directory (www.aahd.com.au)

In New Zealand you could try:

South Pacific Association of Natural Therapists (☎ 9-480 9089), 28 Willow Ave, Birkenhead, Auckland

NZ School of Natural Healing (☎ 9-638 9023), PO Box 56365, Auckland

ACUPUNCTURE

☯ *Just about any disorder can be treated with acupuncture, although it's commonly used for pain relief, asthma, dermatitis (eczema), arthritis, back pain, allergies, digestive disorders (such as irritable bowel syndrome) and emotional problems (depression, anxiety, stress).*

Acupuncture is widely available in Australia. Originating in China, acupuncture is based on a belief that health is directly related to the way in which vital energy (also known as *chi*, or *qi*) flows through our body. Energy flows through pathways in our body (called meridians), and when there are blockages in this flow, caused by external and internal forces, injury or illness can manifest. Acupuncture and acupressure stimulate points in the meridians, which balances your energy flow, restoring and maintaining health and general wellbeing.

A visit to an acupuncturist usually begins with an assessment of your medical history, followed by an examination of your tongue, pulse and abdomen.

When the needle is first inserted, you'll probably feel a slight pricking sensation. Many people report feeling warmth, and some even pleasure. The practitioner may also manoeuvre or heat the needles to help move blocked energy. Needles usually stay inserted for 15 to 30 minutes. When they are removed, you should not feel any discomfort, but there may be some light bleeding.

For more information, you could contact:

Australian Acupuncture & Chinese Medicine Association (AACMA; ☎ 1800 025 334 toll free in Australia), PO Box 5142, West End QLD 4101, Australia

NZ Institute of Chinese Medicine & Acupuncture (☎ 9-309 6945), 402 Windsor House, 58 Queen St, Auckland, New Zealand

ACUPRESSURE

 As a self-treatment, acupressure is generally considered good for arthritic pain, stress-related problems and nausea.

Acupressure uses the same principles as acupuncture, but chi energy is released using the fingertips instead of needles. If you don't like the thought of acupuncture needles but would like to experience the benefits of acupuncture, this is a good option. There are acupressure practitioners, but this is a good self-treatment, and short courses and books are available that give details about the meridians, their locations and functions.

ALEXANDER TECHNIQUE

This technique is commonly used for treating musculoskeletal disorders such as back pain and arthritis, as well as stress-related conditions.

This therapy was developed in Australia by actor FM Alexander, who had trouble with his voice and noticed that he was able to control this by altering the way he used his head and neck muscles. The practitioner-patient relationship is replaced by one of teacher-student. You are taught to be aware of postural bad habits and to restore postural harmony by re-educating your body.

You'll need to have a bit of time on your hands – lessons are usually on a weekly basis, and most teachers recommend students continue for about 30 weeks.

For more information, you could contact:

Australian Society of Teachers of the Alexander Technique (AUS-TAT; ☎ 03-9853 1356), 16 Princess St, Kew VIC 3101

AROMATHERAPY

Good for stress-related conditions (because it encourages relaxation), and digestive problems, aches and pains, premenstrual syndrome and menopausal symptoms.

Aromatherapy uses essential oils extracted from plants to affect your state of mind. Aromatic oils have many uses, and there are several different ways to use them. They can be vaporised in water: add a few drops to hot water, or use a specially designed burner. You can use them topically, as some oils are good as antiseptics or moisturisers (always check the label or ask when you buy it – pure essential oils should not generally be applied neat to the skin). Add a few drops to a bath or to a spray-bottle filled with water. You can also use aromatherapy oils in massage.

You'll find essential oils in some health food stores, natural health and beauty stores, 'New Age' shops and pharmacies, and they usually come with information leaflets. Look for oils labelled as 'pure essential' rather than just 'aromatherapy' as these tend to be of higher quality. There's a wide range of prices depending on the type of oil.

! Essential oils are widely available, but take care – some can cause rashes, burning and nausea, and some oils are best avoided in pregnancy as they can cause miscarriage. Some oils are not appropriate for use on babies or children under 12 years. Never take essential oils internally. Lavender is the only essential oil that can be used neat on the skin.

Although not limited to aromatherapy, you might want to check out *Australian Bush Flower Essences* by Ian White, which has information on preparing and using 50 flower essences.

AYURVEDA

Because Ayurveda is a complete system of medicine, it can be used for any health-related problem, but it is especially good for chronic problems, including migraine, fatigue, arthritis, eczema, irritable bowel syndrome and menstrual problems.

Ayurveda is a traditional form of medicine practised in India and Sri Lanka, and in a variety of forms in throughout southern Asia. It is based on a complex world view, but the basic belief is that you can achieve health and wellbeing through balance and proper energy flow. Ayurvedic treatments include massage, herbal remedies, yoga and diet. It's not easy to find Ayurvedic therapists in Australia, and because of restrictions on importing remedies used in Ayurvedic medicine, you may not be able to receive the treatment prescribed in countries such as India.

A typical consultation involves history taking and physical examination, then the underlying cause of your disorder is diagnosed and a treatment program is recommended.

Australian Institute of Yoga and Ayurveda (AIYA; ☎ 03-9525 6951, www.hotkey.net.au/~yogather/), 7/71 Ormond Rd, Elwood VIC 3184, Australia

COLOUR THERAPY

Each colour has a therapeutic property, and colour therapy can be used to target specific physical or emotional disorders such as high blood pressure (blue), arthritis (yellow) and depression (orange).

Colour therapy involves the application of colour in a number of ways, and is based on the belief that we receive vibrational energies from colours, which we absorb and emit in the form of our aura. By balancing the colours that are displayed in the human aura you can achieve wellbeing. You may be aware of increased aggression or assertiveness when wearing red, or notice that your body relaxes and enters a state of calm when surrounded by blue or green. Colour therapy is about assessing these responses and using them to improve your wellbeing.

A colour therapist will assess your condition in a number of ways: reading your aura, dowsing to read the energies in your spine, or through psychological colour tests. They may then suggest one or more treatments, such as coloured light treatment, solarised water in bottles, coloured oils and scarves, or colour breathing and meditation.

CRYSTAL HEALING

Crystals create general wellbeing rather than treating any specific condition, so put one in your backpack!

This form of healing has a long history, and is based on a belief that crystals release vibrational energies that can affect the body, mind and spirit. As they store the earth's energies, you can draw on them to rejuvenate and harmonise your own energy system. You can buy crystals in New Age, gift and nature shops. These stores will usually have information about the particular crystals, and many stock books on their individual qualities and uses. Prices depend on the size and quality of the crystal. Crystal therapy may be used as part of other therapies, such as Reiki, although specific crystal practitioners are rare.

HERBAL MEDICINE

☯ *You'll find there is a herbal treatment for just about any and every disorder, but they are especially good for skin problems, stress-related conditions, digestive disorders and joint problems.*

The use of plants and plant-based remedies in the treatment of disease is one of the oldest forms of medicine in the world, and every culture has a form of herbalism. Until the end the 19th century, all medicines were derived from herbs.

Herbs are prescribed in a number of forms: as a tea, tincture, in capsule form or as an ointment or cream. If you consult a herbal practitioner, you may also be given advice on diet and lifestyle habits to maximise the effectiveness of the herbal treatments.

Herbal remedies are widely available for self-treatment: drink peppermint tea to aid digestion or chamomile for a calming effect. Echinacea and garlic have become popular treatments for colds and flu, and you can find specifically targeted, ready-to-take mixtures or tablets in health food stores, supermarkets and chemists.

!*A word of warning: herbal remedies contain pharmacologically active substances, and need to be used with care. Take only the recommended dose for the appropriate length of time, and never mix herbal and conventional medicines without getting advice from a doctor or qualified herbal practitioner first. If you are pregnant or breastfeeding, you should get advice from a doctor or qualified herbal practioner before you use any herbal remedies.*

HOMOEOPATHY

 You can call on a homoeopath for almost anything you would see your regular doctor for, but homoeopathy is especially good for hay fever, asthma, eczema, migraine, irritable bowel syndrome and stress-related conditions.

Homoeopathy is based on the principle that medicines that produce symptoms similar to those produced by the disease can relieve the symptoms and counteract the disease. The focus is not on destroying or killing disease, but on improving the body's natural ability to fight it. Homoeopathic remedies are derived from several sources (animal, plant and mineral), and the more dilute they are, the more effective they are believed to be. A visit to a homoeopath is similar to a conventional doctor's consultation, with history-taking and a physical examination.

For more information, you could contact:

Australian Federation of Homoeopaths (☎ 02-9456 3602), 21 Bulah Close, Berowra Heights NSW 2082

IRIDOLOGY

 Used for identifying weaknesses and diagnosing problems, this is not a treatment in itself.

A method of diagnosis rather than treatment, an iridologist examines the iris (the coloured part of the eye) for characteristic signs and colour that indicate the state of your tissues and organs. A thorough analysis takes about an hour, during which the iridologist will examine your eye using a torch (flashlight) and magnifier, or a bioscope. Because this is a form of diagnosis, you'll need to follow this up with a treatment, such as naturopathy.

MASSAGE

Apart from making most people feel good, massage can be used in the treatment of illness, especially stress-related disorders, as well as backache, strains and sprains.

Massage therapies are diverse in their approaches and results, and you'll need to decide which one best suits you. A good massage not only eases muscle tension but aids circulation and muscle condition, and improves your emotional and mental wellbeing. In most cases, a massage treatment will last for an hour (including assessments and any discussion). For most types of massage you will need to undress, so if you think this might bother you, choose a practitioner you are comfortable with. Shiatsu (see later in this section) is rare in that it is performed through clothing. It is important with the tactile therapies that you communicate with your practitioner – if you feel uncomfortable at any stage during the treatment, tell them.

For more information, you could try:

Association of Massage Therapists Australia Inc (☎ 1800 353 930 toll free in Australia), 250 High St, Prahran, VIC 3181, Australia

Institute of Registered Myotherapists of Australia (IRMA; ☎ 0500 50 646), PO Box 646, Carlton South VIC 3053, Australia

New Zealand College of Massage (☎ 9-570 2654), 23 Domain Rd, Panmure, Auckland, New Zealand

Shiatsu Practitioners Association (NZ) Inc (☎ 9-817 6781), PO Box 7008, Wellesley St, Auckland, New Zealand

Massage is generally a safe procedure if carried out by an experienced practitioner, although it's best avoided in some situations: if you have varicose veins, severe back pain or a fever. It's also best avoided in the first three months of pregnancy, or if you've had blood clots in your leg veins.

Sports Massage

This is used to help heal the muscles after extensive or intensive use, and to relieve muscle tension. It also helps to increase flexibility and effectiveness.

Relaxation Massage

This is designed to ease tensions and to promote wellbeing, and is particularly good if your main aim is to improve or maintain general health rather than target problem areas.

Rolfing

This therapy helps to align the parts of the body using deep tissue manipulation, and is based on the idea that the mind and emotions affect this alignment. About 10 sessions are recommended in order to experience the full benefits.

Shiatsu

Similar to acupuncture in its use of the body's meridians to promote health, shiatsu aims to restore the proper flow of energy and therefore to relieve disorders. Unlike acupuncture, the treatment itself has the characteristics of a massage in its use of the hands and its treatment of the body. Reported results include increased energy, release from tension and improved internal health.

MEDITATION

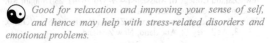

Good for relaxation and improving your sense of self, and hence may help with stress-related disorders and emotional problems.

Direct your mind to a single point of focus, empty and still it. This is the meditative state. There are many different types of meditation, but all promote general relaxation.

Because it can be difficult to control your own mind, many people find it easier to meditate under the guidance of a teacher or in a group. If you're happy to try self-meditation (great for those endless bus or plane journeys), you'll find a selection of meditation tapes and CDs in most music stores. If you want to take a complete break from the tourist trail, try a meditation retreat (usually weekend-long).

NATUROPATHY

Any condition you'd see your family doctor for can be treated by naturopathy, although it's especially good for chronic conditions such as digestive disorders, musculoskeletal problems, allergies, migraine and menstrual disorders.

About a century old, naturopathy is an American development from a European tradition, and is based on the belief that the body has the power to heal itself, given the right circumstances. This is achieved through a variety of methods, including fasting, hydrotherapy and herbal remedies, and contains elements of many natural therapies such as homoeopathy, herbalism and nutritional therapies.

Your first visit to a naturopath will probably be for about one hour; any subsequent appointments will be about 30 minutes. The naturopath will assess your medical history and current condition. There will be questions about diet, lifestyle, relationships and work, followed by a physical examination and a discussion about the most suitable treatment plan. Many naturopaths have studied supplementary therapies or methods of diagnosis, such as massage or iridology.

A typical plan is likely to include natural medicine, plus a recommendation for other forms of therapy, such as massage treatments or nutritional change.

For more information, you could contact:

Australian Naturopathic Practitioners Association (ANPA; ☎ 03-9889 0334), 1st Floor, 609 Camberwell Rd, Camberwell VIC 3124, Australia

ALTERNATIVE THERAPIES

REIKI

 This is good for improving general wellbeing, and for stress-related disorders and musculoskeletal problems.

Reiki is an ancient form of Japanese healing that was rediscovered in the 19th century. Using touch, the practitioner is able to re-balance the flow of energy in the patient. Reiki is a nonintrusive and simple healing method. A treatment lasts anywhere between 45 and 90 minutes, varying from practitioner to practitioner. You lie down, fully clothed, and the practitioner will place the hands on the body in a series of positions. Many practitioners integrate Reiki with other disciplines such as aura diagnosis, pranic healing and massage, so it's important to look around for a practitioner who suits you best.

For more information, you could contact:

Australian Reiki Connection Incorporated (☎ 03-9791 2564), 40 Jarvis Crescent, Dandenong South VIC 3184

Reiki – Usui Reiki Network (☎ 1800 804 525 toll free in Australia), PO Box 1093, Blackburn North VIC 3130

REFLEXOLOGY

 *Because the aim of reflexology is to bring about a general improvement in wellbeing, it has been used to help migraines, asthma, skin disorders and stress-related conditions.*

Believed to have similar origins to acupuncture, reflexology points in the body are found along the energy pathways (the meridians), and imbalance is caused when these pathways become obstructed. By applying pressure to points in the feet and hands, reflexology can release tension, as well as improve your circulation, nervous system, glands and organs. Each point corresponds with a different part of the body. People report an increase in energy, relaxation, the release of tension and an improvement in general health. It is quite often used to accelerate the healing process after surgery.

YOGA

Yoga is good for general wellbeing, fitness and suppleness; because of the breathing focus, it is also good for respiratory disorders such as asthma.

Originating in India, the first record of this discipline dates from between 1000 and 3000 BC. Yoga is a state of mind – where the mind is stilled and directed to a point of focus. It involves movement, both subconscious and physical. There are many different types of yoga – some more physical and some more meditative than others, so it's important you choose your teacher and group with this in mind. Yoga has many similarities to meditation, the main difference being the inclusion of physical movement.

Your yoga instructor will guide you through a series of movements during a session, which usually lasts about an hour. The main focus is the correct breathing method, as this is considered to be the basis for all health.

For more information, you could contact:

Australian Yoga Teachers Network (☎ 03-9592 2949, email yoganet@telstra.easymail.com.au), PO Box 110, Bentleigh VIC 3204, Australia

BUYING & USING MEDICINES——

When you're travelling, expert medical advice may not always be available, especially if you are travelling in remote areas of the Pacific islands. There may be occasions when you need to self-treat with medicines, either ones you have with you or ones you have bought locally. In this chapter we give some general guidelines on using medicines safely.

BUYING MEDICINES

In Australia and New Zealand, as in most developed countries, there are rigorous safety standards governing the sale and use of medicines. So although you will be able to buy basic medicines in pharmacies and supermarkets, for anything more serious (such as antibiotics), you will need a prescription from a doctor. Prescription charges will depend on whether you use the private or public medical sector.

In the Pacific islands, the situation is generally somewhat different, and medicines (such as antibiotics and malaria tablets) are usually available without prescription, often much more cheaply than you may be used to. Medicines and other medical supplies may be in short supply in some areas, especially more remote, rural areas, so you will need to take a well stocked medical kit with you.

If you are buying medicines, here are some basic safety tips:

- buy from a trustworthy doctor or pharmacy
- try to avoid drugs that have been lying in the sun or that should have been kept refrigerated and weren't
- check the expiry date – very few drugs (tetracycline is a notable exception) are actually harmful if they are kept too long, but they may well be ineffective
- if possible, look for drugs made by local branches of international drug companies, and look out for fakes

In the Pacific islands, injections are often seen as the best and most effective way to administer medicines. Unless you are

MEDICINES

Medicines – a Different Outlook

In most parts of the developing world, medicines are seen as a commodity like any other. The majority of local people self-treat with medicines bought from the pharmacy as a matter of course. Often pharmacists are the main source of treatment advice for the majority of people, especially in rural areas. However, bear in mind that pharmacists are not necessarily medically trained, and may recommend inappropriate treatment. Antibiotics tend to be readily used for many ailments, often inappropriately. People often don't complete a full course of treatment, which contributes to the rise in antibacterial resistance worldwide – see the section on Antibiotics later in this chapter for more discussion on this. With less control over medicines, it is easier for counterfeit or substandard drugs to be passed off.

confident that the equipment used is sterile, it's probably best to avoid injections. There's an increased risk of serious side effects from the drug, as well as the risk of an abscess at the injection site or infection with HIV or hepatitis B. Try asking if a tablet form is available instead.

DRUG NAMES

The same medically active substance can have different brand names in different countries, although the generic or chemical name is the same the world over. This is clearly a very unsatisfactory situation for medics and travellers alike, but there is no easy solution in sight. We've used the generic name for drugs throughout this book because these will be understood in any language (although you may need to point this out).

You can consider different brands of drugs as basically interchangeable. Some common drugs that have been around for ages are available under the generic name (for example paracetamol/acetaminophen) as well as various brand names.

To confuse the issue further, some medicines that are made up of a combination of generic substances may be given a new generic name. For example, the painkiller co-codamol is a combination of paracetamol (acetaminophen) and codeine.

MEDICINES TO AVOID

Medicines now considered dangerous in many developed countries because of unacceptable side effects may still be available in some Pacific islands. Remedies containing a combination of drugs are usually best avoided because they may contain unnecessary medications and additional, potentially harmful, ingredients. Some medicines to be wary of include the following (we have used the generic name unless indicated).

- **steroids** – these powerful drugs are used to treat a variety of conditions (such as asthma and dermatitis), usually to suppress inflammation. Combination medications sometimes contain steroids. Never use eyedrops containing steroids except under medical supervision.
- **chloramphenicol** – an antibiotic that may be prescribed for tonsillitis or travellers diarrhoea. Because of potentially serious side effects, it should only be used for life-threatening infections. Note that this does not apply to chloramphenicol eyedrops and eardrops, which are commonly and safely used.
- **clioquinol** – an antidiarrhoeal drug; you should avoid this because it can have serious side effects on the nervous system.
- **opium tincture** – may be available for treatment of diarrhoea and other ailments; best avoided for obvious reasons.
- **phenylbutazone** – an anti-inflammatory painkiller with potentially serious side effects
- **sulphonamide antibiotics** – these will work if no alternatives are available, but are best avoided if possible because of potential side effects.
- **Fansidar** (brand name) – this antimalarial is no longer used for *prevention* in most western countries because of side effects, although it is still used to *treat* malaria; if you are offered it as a preventive, try to find an alternative.

SIDE EFFECTS & ALLERGIES

Any drug can produce unwanted or unexpected effects. Some drugs produce well recognised side effects your doctor or pharmacist will probably warn you about. Familiar drugs that have been around for many years are unlikely to have any unexpected effects, although new drugs may still be capable of causing a few surprises. Sometimes it can be difficult to work out if it's the drug or the actual illness process causing the problems, especially when you're treating diarrhoea, as all antibiotics can cause stomach upsets. If you experience severe or unpleasant side effects with one drug, you may need to stop taking it and try an alternative.

Allergies are one serious type of side effect, but not all side effects are allergies. Mild symptoms of headache, diarrhoea, nausea and vomiting are not signs of allergy. Signs of allergy usually appear soon after taking the medicine and include:

- a red, raised itchy rash (common)
- breathing difficulties and swelling of the face
- fainting or collapsing

!A severe allergic reaction is always a medical emergency – seek medical help urgently.

If you have any drug allergies, record this information and carry it on you.

!Don't take any drugs you know you are allergic to (or related drugs), and always tell anyone treating you of any drug allergies you think you have.

Medicines that commonly cause allergies include aspirin and antibiotics like penicillin and sulpha (sulphonamide) drugs.

DOSES, TIMING & SPECIAL INSTRUCTIONS

Ideally, for any medicine you should be clear about what dose to take at what interval and follow any special instructions on the label. In practice, you may find that the dosage of the brand available locally may differ from the one we've suggested in this book. This is usually because the drug has been formulated slightly differently, or possibly the dose may have been expressed in different units.

If you're not sure what dose to take, either ask a pharmacist or doctor, read the information leaflet carefully or try to find another brand of the drug that causes less confusion. A single extra dose of most drugs is unlikely to cause problems.

COMMONLY USED MEDICINES

We've summarised here details about doses, side effects and cautions for some common medicines you may find you need to use while you're away. Details about other medicines used for specific conditions are described in the relevant sections of this book, and some alternative first aid remedies are detailed in the boxed text 'Alternative First Aid for Travellers' in the Before You Go chapter.

○ preventing (p32) and treating malaria (p128)
○ motion sickness (p59)
○ ear (p167) and eyedrops (p170)
○ vaginal thrush (p213)
○ antifungal creams (p157)

Where the brand name tends to be better known than the generic name, we've listed some common brands, but be aware that these brands may not be available locally.

PAIN & FEVER

Simple painkillers include aspirin and paracetamol (acetaminophen in the USA) and are also good for reducing fever.

Paracetamol has very few side effects, except perhaps nausea, although it can cause liver damage in overdose. Aspirin is more problematic and should be avoided if you are hypersensitive to it, asthmatic or suffer from indigestion or stomach ulcers. It can also cause heartburn and stomach irritation. Aspirin is not suitable for children under 12 years.

drug	dose (adult)	dose (children)
aspirin	one to two tablets every four to six hours when necessary (maximum 4g in 24 hours)	avoid in children under 12 years
para-cetamol (acetamin-ophen)	one to two 500mg tablets every four to six hours (maximum 4g in 24 hours)	three months to one year: 60 to 120mg; one to five years: 120 to 250mg; six to 12 years: 250 to 500mg; over 12 years: adult dose; (maximum four doses in 24 hours)
codeine phosphate	two to four 15mg tablets every four hours, maximum 240mg in 24 hours	one to 12 years: 1mg/kg every six hours
ibuprofen	two 200mg tablets every six hours, as necessary	suspension (100mg/5mL) available for children; six months to one year: 2.5mL; one to two years: 2.5mL; three to seven years: 5mL, eight to 12 years: 10mL; all doses given three to four times daily

Other painkillers include codeine phosphate, which will also stop diarrhoea in an emergency. However, it's no more effective at relieving pain than aspirin or paracetamol (acetaminophen), and side effects include constipation and drowsiness. Codeine can be given to children, but is best avoided if possible.

! Customs officials may be a bit suspicious of codeine because of its potential for abuse, so it's safest to have a letter with you from your doctor explaining what it is and why you need it.

Another popular painkiller is a combination of paracetamol with codeine (for example co-codamol).

Ibuprofen (eg Nurofen and other brand names, also in forms suitable for children) is an anti-inflammatory drug that is good for fever, pain (including period pain) and inflammation (for example a painful joint). Avoid it if you have had stomach ulcers or a hypersensitivity to aspirin. Other anti-inflammatory drugs include naproxen and indomethacin, which are useful for treating strains, sprains, sports injuries and joint pains.

ANTIBIOTICS

Many travel-related illnesses are caused by infections, and you may need to take antibiotics to treat them while you're away. Antibiotics work against bacterial infections but don't have any effect on viral or fungal infections. This means they won't be any good against common viral infections like colds and flu, as well as many throat and gastro infections.

Different antibiotics are effective against different bacteria. We give antibiotic recommendations in this book based on the likeliest cause of infection; however, the best way to find out if an antibiotic will be effective against an infection is to have a laboratory test to identify the bacteria causing it.

Antibiotics should stop most infections within a few days. Because they work to stop the infection and not the symptoms, you may need to treat symptoms (such as pain and fever) with other medications until the antibiotics kick in.

If an antibiotic appears not to be working (it needs at least two days to do its stuff), you may be taking the wrong dose (check) or it's the wrong antibiotic (the bacteria are resistant or they aren't affected by this particular antibiotic), or the illness is not what you think it is. In this case, it's always best to seek medical advice (after you've checked that the dose is correct).

Antibiotics can cause problems, which is why they need to be treated with respect. They often cause nausea and diarrhoea and, because they disrupt the normal balance of organisms in the body, can make women more likely to develop thrush (vaginal candidiasis). Antibiotics (especially penicillins and cephalosporins) can cause allergic reactions, so you should always carry a record of any allergic reactions with you.

! *If rashes and swelling of the throat and face occur, stop taking the drug immediately and seek medical advice. Always carry a record of any allergic reactions with you.*

Resistance

This is a growing problem worldwide, and is one reason why you should always finish the whole course of an antibiotic (unless you experience severe adverse reactions). Antibiotic resistance is more likely to occur if the infection is not quickly and completely eliminated. In some of the Pacific island nations, antibiotics are readily available without prescription and are often taken relatively indiscriminately and perhaps inappropriately. People may not be able to afford to buy a whole course and are often not aware of the importance of doing so anyway. The use of antibiotics in livestock rearing has also been an important factor in increasing antibiotic resistance worldwide.

! *Help prevent the emergence of antibiotic resistance by only using antibiotics if really necessary; use the most effective antibiotic and complete the full course (this way no bacteria are left hanging around, working out ways of fighting back).*

Which One?

Where necessary, suggested lengths of courses of antibiotics are indicated in the relevant sections. All the antibiotics described in this section can cause nausea and stomach upsets. Note that this is not a complete list of all possible antibiotics.

Co-amoxiclav (Augmentin) is a combination of amoxycillin (a penicillin drug) and clavulanic acid (which makes it more effective against some bacteria than plain amoxycillin). It's a useful 'broad spectrum' antibiotic, and is effective against bladder, ear, chest and sinus infections. It's also good for skin infections and animal bites. Although amoxicillin

Which Antibiotic?

Here's a quick guide to which antibiotics are suitable for what. Read the details about the antibiotics to find out if they are suitable for your age group, and avoid any antibiotics (including related antibiotics) you are allergic to.

- Diarrhoea – ciprofloxacin (and related antibiotics), co-trimoxazole, metronidazole, tinidazole
- Chest infection – amoxycillin, co-amoxiclav, co-trimoxazole, erythromycin/clarithromycin
- Throat infection – phenoxymethylpenicillin or co-amoxiclav
- Ear infection – amoxycillin, co-amoxiclav or co-trimoxazole
- Urinary infection (cystitis) – amoxycillin or co-trimoxazole
- Skin infection – phenoxymethylpenicillin, flucloxacillin or co-amoxiclav

Note: clarithromycin/erythromycin can be used if you are allergic to penicillin.

(eg Amoxil) is less reliable generally, it is useful if you can't get co-amoxiclav. Both drugs can sometimes cause skin rashes, and should be avoided if you are allergic to penicillin.

Trimethoprim is useful for treating bladder and ear infections, and for diarrhoea in children. There are concerns over its potential to cause serious but rare side effects, including severe skin rash and blood disorders. It should be avoided in pregnancy. Note that co-trimoxazole is a combination drug that contains a sulphonamide antibiotic plus trimethoprim – it's best avoided if possible, as there is a slightly higher risk of serious side effects.

Ciprofloxacin is effective against most bacterial causes of travellers diarrhoea, cystitis (bladder infection) and chest infection. Ciprofloxacin can occasionally cause kidney problems, which is why you should drink plenty of fluids when you take it. Related drugs that can be used as alternatives include norfloxacin, nalidixic acid and ofloxacin Ciprofloxacin

drug	dose (adult)	dose (children)
ciprofloxacin	500mg twice daily	not recommended in children under 12 years
amoxycillin	250mg three times daily (double dose if infection is severe)	up to 10 years: 125mg three times daily; 10 years and over: adult dose
co-amoxiclav	250mg three times daily	up to 10 years: 125mg three times daily
trimethoprim	200mg twice daily	two to five months: 25mg; six months to five years: 50mg; six to 12 years: 100mg; all doses twice daily
flucloxacillin	250mg four times daily (double dose if infection is severe)	under two years: 75mg; two to 10 years: 125mg; all doses four times daily
erythromycin	500mg to 1g twice daily	up to two years: 125mg; two to eight years: 250mg all doses four times daily
metronidazole	500mg three times daily	7.5mg/kg three times daily

should be avoided in pregnancy and it is not generally recommended for children under the age of 12 years because of potential side effects. Suitable alternatives for children are suggested in the relevant sections.

Flucloxacillin (eg Floxapen) is a penicillin drug that is effective for skin infections, although co-amoxiclav is usually the first choice. It can cause rashes and allergic reactions, and you should avoid it if you are allergic to penicillin.

Erythromycin (eg Erymax) or clarithromycin can be used as an alternative to penicillin drugs if you are allergic to penicillin. Clarithromycin is less likely to cause side effects such as nausea and vomiting.

Metronidazole (eg Flagyl) is effective against infections causing diarrhoea, especially with a fever and abdominal pain, especially giardiasis and amoebic dysentery. It is also effective against bacterial vaginosis.

! *Avoid alcohol if you are taking metronidazole, as it causes a severe reaction (flushing, headache, palpitations).*

Tinidazole (eg Fasigyn) is similar to metronidazole and can be used as an alternative.

ANTIHISTAMINES

These are useful for hay fever, allergies, itchy rashes, insect bites and motion sickness. There are many different ones available, mostly without prescription, and they vary in what side effects they cause (mainly drowsiness).

Antihistamines that are more likely to cause drowsiness include promethazine, chlorpheniramine and cyclizine. Non- (or at least less) sedating ones include cetirizine and loratidine. Ask your pharmacist for guidance on brands available to you, and follow the dosing instructions on the packet. They can be given to children.

Side effects include drowsiness, headache, dry mouth and blurred vision. They're more common in children and older people. You should avoid antihistamines if you have high blood pressure, glaucoma or prostate trouble.

! *Because they can cause drowsiness, you shouldn't drive, dive or drink lots of alcohol after you take antihistamines.*

NAUSEA & VOMITING

○ For details about drugs to prevent and treat motion sickness, see p59.

Metoclopramide (eg Maxolon) is useful for nausea and vomiting associated with diarrhoea or food poisoning. The adult dose is 10mg three times daily. It's best avoided in children – if necessary, try an antihistamine instead. Some are available in suppository form (ie you insert it in the rectum), which might sound uninviting, but it's useful option if you're vomiting; other forms (such as soluble forms or a patch you put against your cheek) are also available.

ANTIDIARRHOEALS

These drugs are best avoided unless it's an emergency and you have to travel. They include loperamide (eg Imodium and other brand names), probably the most useful; diphenoxylate with atropine (eg Lomotil; less useful because of potential side effects); and bismuth subsalicylate (Pepto-Bismol).

The dose of loperamide is two 2mg tablets initially, followed by one 2mg tablet after each bout of diarrhoea, to a maximum of eight tablets in 24 hours. It commonly causes constipation; other possible side effects include abdominal cramps, bloating and, rarely, paralysis of the gut. The dose of diphenoxylate is four tablets initially, followed by two tablets every six hours until the diarrhoea is under control.

Antidiarrhoeals are not recommended for children, and should be avoided if you have a fever, or blood in your faeces.

Bismuth subsalicylate is available in tablet or liquid form, but tablets are more convenient if you're travelling: take two tablets four times daily. It's not suitable for children (as it contains aspirin). It can cause blackening of your tongue and faeces, and ringing in the ears. You shouldn't use it for more than three weeks at these doses.

MEDICAL SERVICES

In an emergency, you'll just have to use whatever services are immediately available, but in less urgent situations, you will have time to look around.

! Although we have done all we can to ensure the accuracy of the information listed, contact details change and places disappear. Note that listing here does not imply any endorsement or recommendation by Lonely Planet of the services provided.

AUSTRALIA & NEW ZEALAND

As you'd expect, medical facilities in both these nations are of high standard and on a par with other developed countries.

AUSTRALIA
Emergency ☎ 000
Poisons Information Centre ☎ 13 11 26; for advice on bites and stings, poisonings

Medical facilities are generally very good to excellent here, and you should have no trouble getting any level of care you need. You will need medical insurance, as medical fees are not subsidised unless you are entitled to a Medicare card, and medical treatment can be very expensive. Medicare is Australia's compulsory national health insurance scheme. Under reciprocal arrangements, residents of the UK, New Zealand, the Netherlands, Finland, Malta and Italy are entitled to a Medicare card. To get this, you need to go to a Medicare office in Australia and present your passport and health insurance card from your country.

If you have a Medicare card, you are entitled to free necessary public hospital treatment and subsidised fees for a doctor's consultation. Depending on the doctor's claim method, you may either have to pay the bill first and then make a claim from Medicare yourself or, if the clinic is advertised as 'bulk billing', the clinic will charge Medicare direct. Find out how much the consultation fee is, as this varies and Medicare only covers you for a certain amount – you will have to pay the balance. For more details, contact Medicare (within Australia) on ☎ 13 2011.

There are public (and some private) hospitals in all major urban centres and general private practitioners throughout the states and territory. If necessary, private practitioners can refer you to the regional specialist centre. In more remote communities, there is generally a community health centre where you could get emergency medical treatment if necessary.

In remote areas, the Royal Flying Doctor Service and the Northern Territory Aerial Medical service can provide emergency treatment and evacuation to the nearest medical facility if necessary. Call ☎ 000 to be connected to the service.

You can find contact details of doctors and hospitals in any telephone book.

NEW ZEALAND
Emergency ☎ 111

High quality medical facilities are available here, but medical treatment is expensive – you will need travel insurance. Doctors, clinics and hospitals are listed in the telephone book.

PACIFIC ISLANDS

Medical facilities are variable in the Pacific islands. Generally, you should be able to find adequate care for routine problems in the main centres, but elsewhere facilities are more limited. There are aid posts and sometimes clinics scattered about in the more remote islands that would be able to provide first aid treatment in an emergency, but some islands will have no facilities at all. Don't expect rapid-response emergency services. Medicines are not likely to be available in more remote areas, so you will need to take a well stocked medical kit with you.

Hotels can often recommend a doctor, or if you have an embassy and the time to contact it, this should be your first call. The services listed here are intended only as a guide to get you started. If you do need treatment, you'll probably find that the service is very different to what you may be used to back home. If you are going to a hospital clinic, you will probably have to queue for some time before you are seen. Different cultures have different views about symptoms, treatments, and the doctor-patient relationship. Patients are often not expected to question or doubt the diagnosis or any treatment the doctor prescribes. Multiple anonymous (and often

Did I see a Good Doctor?

Here are some guidelines for assessing if you have seen a good doctor (but bear in mind these are based on a western cultural perspective).

- Willing to listen and spends a reasonable amount of time asking about your problem; doesn't just jump to a diagnosis. In most cases, the doctor should also examine you for at least the basics like pulse rate and temperature.
- Happy to discuss fully the diagnosis and any treatment with you and any companion accompanying you.
- If blood tests (or other procedures) are needed, the doctor uses good aseptic techniques, ie wears surgical gloves (should put on a new pair for each patient), uses a sterile needle (opens packet in front of you) and a clean dressing.
- Generally, illnesses need one specific treatment (in addition to painkillers, if needed); if you are prescribed multiple treatments, ask what they are for and if they are all necessary. If you are not seriously ill, it's always worth trying a few simple measures first, as outlined in the Help ... chapter earlier.
- Explains what you need to do if your symptoms get worse.
- You feel confident about the way you were treated – if you have any doubts, see a different doctor and get a second opinion.

unnecessary) tablets tend to be prescribed (and expected by patients) for any illness.

! If you do have to take a medicine while you are away, make sure you know what it is and what it has been prescribed for.

If you do have to stay overnight in hospital, be prepared for a very different type of care; standards of nursing and auxiliary care are often very different to what you may be used to, and attitudes towards basic hygiene can be alarmingly casual.

Language may be a problem in some places, although you can communicate much through gestures and miming if you need to. It's a good idea to brush up on a few basic words or phrases before you go.

PAYMENT

Health services are generally not free (for foreigners), and you will be expected to pay up front for consultations and treatment. Credit cards are not usually accepted, so it's best not to rely on these as a method of payment. Even if you are covered by insurance, most clinics and doctors will expect you to put the money down up front, so be prepared. Keep any receipts so you can claim reimbursement later.

MEDICAL EVACUATION

Although you should be able to get adequate treatment for the sort of problems that are most likely to occur, it's usually accepted practice to fly tourists and local people to a neighbouring centre for more specialist treatment, including recompression treatment for diving accidents. This is what you need your medical insurance for!

! Medical evacuation either within a country or to a neighbouring country is always very expensive and costs thousands of dollars – insurance is essential.

Depending on which is nearest or has the most appropriate facilities, you are likely to be evacuated to Guam, Hawai'i,

New Zealand or Australia. If you need to be evacuated to Hawai'i, Australia or New Zealand and you don't have a visa for these countries, generally the immigration authorities will need a referral from a local doctor, proof of acceptance by a doctor at your destination and proof of your ability to pay for the medical treatment. Your insurance company should be able to make the necessary arrangements if needed.

COOK ISLANDS
Emergency (Rarotonga) ambulance and hospital ☎ 998

On Rarotonga there is a hospital and several private doctors. Otherwise, every island has a basic medical clinic. For anything serious, you will need to fly to New Zealand.

▶▶ Rarotonga Hospital (☎ 22664)
▶▶ Outpatient clinic (☎ 20065), main road at Tupapa, about 1km east of Avarua, Rarotonga

FIJI
Emergency ☎ 000

FVB emergency hotline (☎ 0800 721 721 toll free in Fiji)
Fiji Recompression Chamber Emergency (☎ 362 172)

You can get adequate medical care for most common medical problems, although for more serious problems you may need to be evacuated to Australia, New Zealand or Hawai'i. Private and public services are available in the main centres.

▶▶ Boulevard Medical Centre (☎ 313 355, fax 302 423), 33 Ellery St, Suva

▶▶ Fiji Recompression Chamber Facility (☎ 850 630, fax 850 344), Amy St (corner Brewster St), Suva

▶▶ Colonial War Memorial Hospital (☎ 313 444) Waimanu Rd, Suva

▶▶ Dr Ram Raju Surgical Clinic (☎ 700 240 or 976 333), 2 Lodhia St, Nadi

▸▸ Nadi Hospital (☎ 701 128), Market Rd, Nadi

▸▸ Namaka Medical Centre (☎ 722 288), Namaka Lane (off Queens Rd), Namaka

FRENCH POLYNESIA

Emergency (Tahiti) ☎ 15 for a hospital or doctor; or for a doctor, call SOS Médecins on ☎ 42 34 56

Medical facilities (hospitals, clinics, pharmacies) are good on Tahiti and the other major islands, but they are more limited in the more remote or less populated islands. You should be able to find a pharmacy or clinic for basic medical care on most islands, but for anything more serious, you will need to be evacuated to one of the main islands or to a regional centre.

The fee for a medical consultation is about 3000 CFP, although this jumps to 7000 CFP at night or on Sunday; fees are less at Mamao public hospital. French visitors can get the fee refunded when they return home through a reciprocal agreement; citizens of the EU should obtain a form E 111 before leaving home.

▸▸ Mamao Hospital (☎ 46 62 62 or for emergencies 24 hours a day ☎ 42 01 01), Ave Georges Clémenceau – French Polynesia's main hospital, covering all the specialities

▸▸ Clinique Cardella (☎ 42 81 90), Rue Anne-Marie Javouhey, behind the cathedral; private clinic

▸▸ Clinique Paofai (☎ 46 18 18) at the junction of Blvd Pomare and Rue du Lieutenant Varney; private clinic

▸▸ Moorea Hospital (☎ 56 23 23 or 56 24 24), Afareaitu, Moorea

▸▸ Medical Centre (☎ 67 70 77), Vaitape, Bora Bora

GUAM

Emergency ☎ 911

Good medical care is available here, although it is expensive (on a par with the USA).

▶▶Guam Memorial Hospital (☎ 647 2330, emergency room ☎ 647 2489), Tamuning

▶▶Naval Hospital (☎ 344 9232) along Route 7 just above Hagatna; takes civilians in emergencies only

▶▶Seventh Day Adventist Clinic (☎ 636 0894), Ypao Rd, Tamuning; for routine medical problems

Divers requiring recompression therapy are sent to SRF Guam Recompression Chamber (☎ 339 7143) at the naval base, which is staffed 24 hours.

KIRIBATI
Emergency (medical) ☎ 994

Medical facilities are very limited here, and for anything you can't cope with from your medical kit, you will need to be evacuated to Hawai'i, Australia or New Zealand.

▶▶Kiribati Hospital (☎ 28 100), 10 minute ride from the Otintaai Hotel in the airport direction

MARSHALL ISLANDS

The facilities are adequate for routine health problems, but are only available on Majuro and Ebeye. The hospital on Majuro is relatively modern. There's only one private practice on Majuro, opposite the tourist office.

▶▶Hospital (☎ 625 4144 for emergencies, 625 3399 for switchboard), Delap, Majuro; hospital clinic opens daily from 1 pm to 5 pm, and you queue up

MICRONESIA (FEDERATED STATES)
Emergency (medical) ☎ 320 2213

Services are limited but adequate for most routine health problems. Most district centres have small hospitals or health centres built with American aid. For anything more serious, you will need to fly to Guam, Hawai'i, Australia, New Zealand or back home.

» Kolonia Hospital, 2km south-east of Kolonia, on the main road down the east coast; rudimentary and best avoided if you can

» Pohnpei Family Health Clinic (☎ 320 5777, fax 320 2229, email khni@mail.fm); good for non-emergencies, run by Hawai'i-trained general practitioner Dr Bryan Isaac; open weekdays from 9 am to noon and 1.30 to 5 pm, and Saturday from 9 am to noon

» Hospital (☎ 370 3012), Tofol, Kosrae; rudimentary

» Hospital (☎ 330 2216), Weno centre, Chuuk

» Hospital (☎ 350 3446) on the north side of Colonia, Yap

NAURU
Emergency (ambulance) ☎ 118 or 117

Nauru has two hospitals, which are adequate for routine health problems, but for anything more serious you will need to fly elsewhere.

» Nauru Phosphate Corporation Hospital (☎ 555 4155)

» Nauru General Hospital (☎ 555 4302)

NEW CALEDONIA
Emergency (medical) ☎ 15

Medical facilities are good on the main island but are more limited on the outer islands. There are two public hospitals, various private clinics and many pharmacies in Noumea. Outside the main centres, medical supplies may be limited, although each town has a community clinic, or *dispensaire*, where you would be able to get first aid treatment. Health care is expensive in Noumea, but free on the Loyalty Islands.

» Hôpital Gaston Bourret (☎ 25 66 66), Rue Paul Doumer, Noumea; the city's main hospital

» Polyclinique de l'Anse Vata (☎ 26 14 22), 180 Route de l'Anse Vata, Noumea

» Clinique de Baie des Citrons (☎ 26 18 66), 5 Rue Fernand Legras

▶▶ Centre Hospitalier Territorial (☎ 35 62 16), Koumac

The nearest decompression facilities are in Australia (Townsville) or Fiji (Suva).

NORTHERN MARIANAS
Emergency (ambulance) ☎ *911*
Emergency (medical evacuation) ☎ *322 9274*

As for the Federated States of Micronesia, medical services are limited, although you should be able to find a health centre or aid post on most islands. For anything more serious, you will need to fly to Guam, Hawai'i, Australia, New Zealand or back home.

▶▶ Commonwealth Health Center (☎ 234 8950), Middle Rd, Garapan, Saipan

PALAU
Emergency (ambulance) ☎ *488 1411*

You should be able to get adequate care for minor problems, but medical services are limited. You'll need to fly to Guam or Hawai'i for anything more serious.

▶▶ Belau Medical Clinic (☎ 488 2688), Koror centre; good for non-emergency medical attention, and open from 8.30 am to 3 pm Monday, Tuesday, Thursday and Friday, and a gynaecologist comes in these nights from 6 to 9 pm; on Wednesday and Saturday it's open from 8.30 am to 1 pm

▶▶ Belau National Hospital (☎ 488 2558), Arakabesang Island, just over the causeway from Koror; for emergency treatment and has a decompression chamber

PAPUA NEW GUINEA
Emergency (Port Moresby only) ☎ *000*
National Disaster, Surveillance & Emergency Service ☎ *27 6666*

Medical facilities vary here. In Port Moresby and larger towns, there are hospitals, private doctors and pharmacies, and you should be able to get adequate care for routine medical problems. Outside the urban centres, facilities are much more limited, and basically consist of aid posts and missionary-run clinics. The chronic lack of money means that supplies and other medical equipment is often in short supply. For anything serious, including recompression for diving accidents, you will need to be evacuated to Australia, or home. Dentists are mainly limited to Port Moresby, Lae and Rabaul.

▶▶Port Moresby General Hospital (☎ 324 8200), Taurama Rd, Korobosea, Port Moresby

SAMOA (INDEPENDENT)
Emergency (ambulance) ☎ 999

Medical facilities are limited, but adequate for routine medical problems. There are hospitals in Apia and on Savai'i and Up-olu. Health treatment in public hospitals is free for Samoans, but visitors will need to pay a fee. Private practitioners are available in Apia. Medicines are limited.

The Samoa Visitor's Bureau can provide you with a list of local doctors and clinics. For anything serious, you will need to fly to New Zealand or Hawai'i.

▶▶National Hospital (☎ 996), Ifiifi St, Leufisa, Apia

SAMOA (AMERICAN)
Emergency ☎ 911

In American Samoa, basic medical services are available at the LBJ Tropical Medical Center in Faga'alu. You will need to fly to Hawai'i or New Zealand for anything more serious.

SOLOMON ISLANDS
Emergency (ambulance) ☎ 25566

Medical facilities are adequate for routine problems but limited, and consist of hospitals in the main towns plus clinics and aid posts in more remote areas. Medical supplies are limited outside the main centres. Medical treatment is free. The only two pharmacies are in Honiara, where you can get malaria tablets without prescription. Dentists are available only in Honiara, Auki and Gizo. For anything serious, you will need to fly to Australia or New Zealand. There are no recompression facilities available here.

▶▶ Central Hospital (☎ 23600), Kukum (Nambanaen)

TOKELAU

There is a hospital on each atoll, but medical supplies such as drugs are difficult to come by. You will need to go to Apia or New Zealand for more specialist care.

TUVALU

Limited care is at the Princess Margaret Hospital (☎ 20 750), and drugs are often in short supply. There is an ambulance service and specialists visit from time to time. For anything more serious, you will need to fly to Guam, Hawai'i or New Zealand.

TONGA

Medical facilities are limited here, although they are adequate for minor problems. There are hospitals in Vaiola (Tongatapu), Hihifi (Ha'apai) and Neiafu (Vava'u). Consultations cost T$2, and you pay a token fee for medicines. There are also private physicians. You won't be able to get medicines in the more remote islands, so carry all you need with you. For anything more serious, you will need to be evacuated to Hawai'i, New Zealand or Australia.

▶▶ Ha'ateiho Village Mission Clinic (☎ 29 052), Ha'ateiho; Dr Glennis Mafi

▶▶ German Clinic (☎ 22 736), Wellington Rd, Nuku'alofa, Tongatapu

▶▶ National Hospital, Vaiola

▸▸ Italian Clinic & Pharmacy (☎ 70 607, VHF channel 68), Pou'ono Rd, Neiafu, Vava'u

▸▸ Prince Wellington Ngu Hospital (☎ 70 201), Neiafu, Vava'u

VANUATU
Emergency (Port Vila) ☎ 22100

The main medical facilities, including hospitals and well stocked pharmacies, are in Port Vila and Luganville. The only dental surgery is in Port Vila. In total, there are five hospitals, as well as health centres, clinics, dispensaries and aid posts scattered throughout the islands. For anything more serious you will need to fly to Australia or New Zealand.

▸▸ Central Hospital, Seaside District, Port Vila

▸▸ Hospital (☎ 36345), Le Plateau, Luganville

WALLIS & FUTUNA ISLANDS
There is a public hospital in Mata Utu, on Wallis; and in Sigave, on Futuna.

FIRST AID

Although we give guidance on basic first aid procedures here remember that, unless you're an experienced first aider and confident you know what you're doing, it's possible to do more harm than good. Always seek medical help if it is available, but if you are far from any help, follow the guidelines given in this chapter.

! See the inside backcover for guidelines on responding to an emergency situation, dealing with near drowning and how to perform emergency (cardiopulmonary) resuscitation.

CUTS & OTHER WOUNDS

This includes any break in the skin – it could be an insect bite you've scratched, sunburn that's blistered, a raw area that your sandals have rubbed, a small graze or cut or a larger open wound from a fall or coming off a motorbike. If you're travelling in areas with poor environmental cleanliness and lack of clean water, there's a high risk of infection, especially in the hot, humid climates of the tropics and subtropics.

Carry a few antiseptic wipes on you to use as an immediate measure, especially if no water is available. A small wound can be cleaned with an antiseptic wipe (but remember to wipe across the wound just once). Deep or dirty wounds need to be cleaned thoroughly, as follows:

▶ make sure your hands are clean before you start
▶ wear gloves if you are cleaning somebody else's wound
▶ use bottled or boiled water (allowed to cool) or an antiseptic solution like povidone-iodine
▶ use plenty of water – pour it on the wound from a container
▶ embedded dirt and other particles can be removed with tweezers or flushed out using a syringe to squirt water (you can get more pressure if you use a needle as well)
▶ dry wounds heal best, so avoid using antiseptic creams which keep the wound moist, but you could apply antiseptic powder or spray

▶ dry the wound with clean gauze before applying a dressing from your medical kit – alternatively, any clean material will do as long as it's not fluffy (avoid cotton wool) because this will stick

! Any break in the skin makes you vulnerable to tetanus infection – if you didn't have a tetanus injection before you left, you'll need one now.

A dressing will protect the wound from dirt, dust and flies. Alternatively, if the wound is small and you are confident you can keep it clean, leave it uncovered. Change the dressing regularly (once a day to start with), especially if the wound is oozing, and watch for signs of infection (see later in this chapter). Antibiotic powders are best avoided as a rule (although antiseptic powders are fine) because they can give you sensitivity reactions. Alcohol can be used if you have been bitten by an animal in an area with rabies as it can help kill the rabies virus, but otherwise avoid using it on wounds. In general, it's best to avoid poultices and other local remedies if they seem likely to introduce infection.

If you have any swelling around the wound, raising the affected limb can help the swelling settle and the wound to heal (sit with your foot up on your pack, or fashion a sling for your arm – see later in this chapter).

It's best to seek medical advice for any wound that fails to heal after a week or so. If a wound is taking a long time to heal, consider improving your diet, especially your protein intake, to aid healing – see the Diet & Nutrition chapter for more details.

DRESSINGS & BANDAGES
If you're wondering how and when to use all those mysterious-looking packages in your first aid kit, here's a quick rundown:

■ small adhesive dressings (ie sticking plasters or Band-Aids) are useful for small wounds (although they can cause skin irritation in people who are allergic to them, especially in hot climates because they block sweating)

- nonadhesive dressings are usually plain gauze pads or sterile padded dressings; fix in place with tape or a crepe bandage
- use nonstick dressings (eg Melolin or paraffin gauze) for open, oozing wounds

Bear in mind the following if you are putting a bandage on:

▶ remove any rings from fingers (or toes) in case your hand swells

▶ keep fresh bandages rolled and unroll them as you put them on – this makes it easier to put them on smoothly and evenly

▶ start from the extremity and bandage in (ie for an ankle, start bandaging from the toes upward)

▶ don't just bandage the painful bit, you need to bandage from the joint below the injured area to the joint above (ie from toes to knee for an ankle)

▶ make sure the bandage is firm enough to prevent it from slipping, but not tight enough to cut into your flesh or stop the circulation – if your fingers or toes start going numb and cold, it's too tight

PRESSURE IMMOBILISATION BANDAGE

This is used for bites and stings from some venomous creatures: some snakes, blue-ringed octopus, box jellyfish and cone shell. It's not a tourniquet, but applies pressure over a wide area of the limb and delays the rate at which venom enters the circulation. Use a roller bandage, and apply it from the fingers or toes as far up the limb as possible. It should be as firm as for a sprained ankle. Use a splint to immobilise the limb.

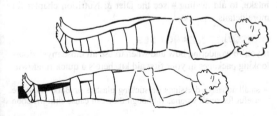

SIGNS OF WOUND INFECTION

Infected wounds take much longer to heal, which is not only a nuisance when you're travelling, it can also be debilitating. When they eventually heal, they're more likely to scar. If a wound gets infected, the infection can spread into your blood to give you blood poisoning, which makes you seriously ill. If you suspect you have an infected wound, it's best to seek medical advice for an appropriate course of antibiotics. However, if medical help is not available, you should self-treat with antibiotics if you have any of the following signs of (mild) infection:

- pain (throbbing)
- redness, heat and swelling in the area around the wound
- pus (thick yellow discharge) in the wound
- red streaks going away from the wound

Any of the following signs indicates a more serious infection:

- swelling of the involved limb
- swelling of the nearest glands eg in the armpit for a wound in the hand, or in the groin for a leg or foot wound
- fever and feeling unwell

Start a course of antibiotics and get medical help as soon as possible. Suitable antibiotics include flucloxacillin 250mg four times daily, co-amoxiclav 250mg three times daily or erythromycin (if you're allergic to penicillin) 250mg four times daily (see the Medicines appendix for more details). Double these doses for serious infections while you're getting to medical help.

Some bacteria in the tropics cause ulcers (sores); treatment is with specific antibiotics.

WOUND CLOSURE

If a wound is deep or gaping, it may need to be closed to help it heal better. If you need stitches, the sooner it is done the better. However, it's probably best not to close them yourself unless you feel confident and able to do so. An alternative to stitching is to close small clean cuts with special sticky strips (such as steristrips) or butterfly dressings. Note that some wounds should never be closed:

- wounds that are dirty and can't be cleaned adequately
- animal or human bites
- infected wounds

For small clean cuts, you can apply wound closure strips or butterfly dressings as follows:

▶ see if the edges of the cut come together easily
  – if not, you won't be able to use this method
    ▶ clean the wound thoroughly, apply antiseptic and dry it with sterile gauze
      ▶ make sure any bleeding has stopped and that the area around the wound is clean and dry so that the dressings can stick
        ▶ put the dressings across the wound (see diagram) so that the edges of the wound are held together, taking care not to touch the side of the dressing that is to go on the wound
      ▶ space the dressings a few millimetres apart, and work from the middle of the wound outwards
  ▶ leave the dressings in place for about seven to 10 days, even if they start to look a bit worse for wear

Wound closure dressings can't be applied to hairy skin like the scalp, but scalp wounds can sometimes be closed by tying hair across them.

BLEEDING WOUNDS

Most cuts will stop bleeding on their own, but if a blood vessel of any size has been cut, it may continue bleeding for some time. Head and hand wounds, also wounds at joint creases, tend to be particularly bloody.

To stop bleeding from a wound:

▶ wear gloves if you are dealing with a wound on another person

- use your fingers or the palm of your hand to apply direct pressure to the wound, preferably over a sterile dressing or clean pad
- apply steady pressure for at least five minutes before looking to see if the bleeding has stopped
- raise the injured limb above the level of your heart
- lie down if possible
- put a sterile dressing over the original pad (don't move this) and bandage it in place
- check the bandage regularly in case bleeding restarts

Get medical help urgently if much blood has been lost.

! Never use a tourniquet to stop bleeding as this may cause gangrene – the only situation in which this may be appropriate is if the limb has been completely amputated.

BOILS & ABSCESSES

Don't try to burst these, however tempting it may seem, because this encourages the infection to spread. Instead:

- wash them with an antiseptic and keep them clean and dry as far as possible
- hot (clean) cloths may be soothing on the boil
- antibiotics don't usually help much with boils unless the infection spreads

SPLINTERS

Treat as follows:

- wash the area thoroughly with soap and water
- sterilise the tips of a pair of tweezers by boiling them for a few seconds
- grasp the splinter as close to the skin as possible and remove it carefully
- squeeze the wound to make it bleed (flushes out any remaining dirt)
- clean the area with antiseptic and cover it with a sticking plaster

If you're not up to date with your tetanus injections, you'll need a booster.

BURNS & SCALDS

There are two main dangers with burns:

- fluid loss through damage to blood vessels leading to shock – the amount of fluid lost from a burn is directly proportional to the area affected by the burn
- infection because of damage to the skin's natural barrier

Burns are classified according to how deep the damage to the skin is:

- painful area of redness – mild or first degree burn, usually heals well
- blisters form later, feels painful – moderate or second degree burn, usually heals well
- white or charred area, feels painless except around the edge – severe or third-degree burn, may result in extensive scarring

You need to seek medical attention for:

- any burn involving the hands, feet, armpits, face, neck or crotch
- any second or third degree burn
- any burn over 1cm to 2cm
- any burn in children

Mild burns or scalds (caused by hot fluid or steam) don't need medical attention unless they are extensive. Treat as follows:

- immediately pour cold water over the burn area for about 10 minutes or immerse it in cold water for about five minutes
- remove any jewellery such as rings, watches or tight clothing from the area before it swells up
- cover with a sterile nonstick dressing or paraffin gauze and bandage loosely in place
- don't burst any blisters, but if they burst anyway, cover with a nonadhesive sterile dressing
- apply antibiotic cream (eg silver sulphadiazine 1%), but avoid any other creams, ointments or greases
- take simple painkillers if necessary

FAINTING

This can occur in many different situations: pain or fright, standing still in the heat, emotional upset, exhaustion or lack of food. It's a brief loss of consciousness due to a temporary reduction in blood flow to the brain. Faints don't usually last long, but you may injure yourself as you fall. If you feel you are about to faint, or you notice someone you are with is about to (usually because they go as white as a sheet and start to sway), lie down before you fall. If someone faints:

- raise their legs (this helps to improve the blood flow to the brain)
- make sure they have plenty of fresh air
- as they recover, allow them to sit up gradually
- check for and treat any injury caused by falling

CONVULSIONS

A convulsion, or fit, is caused by a disturbance in brain function resulting in involuntary contractions of the muscles of the body and leading to loss of consciousness. Fits can occur for lots of reasons, including head injury, diseases affecting the brain, shortage of oxygen to the brain, some poisons and epilepsy. In babies and children, fits can be caused by a high temperature. If someone has a fit:

- ease their fall if possible
- loosen any clothing round the neck and protect their head by placing something soft under their head and shoulders if you can
- remove any sharp objects or other potential hazards from the vicinity
- don't try to restrain them or put anything in their mouth
- once the convulsions have stopped, put them in the recovery position (see inside backcover)
- get medical help

NOSEBLEED

This can be caused by blowing your nose vigorously or after a particularly earth-shattering sneeze. It's more likely when you have a cold. It occurs when blood vessels on the inner surface of your nose burst. Nosebleeds can look very dramatic, but most will stop quite quickly. If you get a nosebleed, do the following:

▸ sit down and put your head forward
▸ pinch your nose firmly just below the bridge (the bony bit) and keep a steady pressure for 10 minutes or until the bleeding has stopped
▸ rest quietly after it has stopped, and don't blow your nose or pick it for at least three hours or the bleeding may start again

An ice pack over the bridge of the nose can help. Putting your head back will allow blood to drip down your throat, which can cause irritation to your stomach and possibly vomiting.

If you can't stop the bleeding after about half an hour OR the bleeding is torrential and you start to feel dizzy, get medical help.

Note that if you get a nosebleed after a head injury, it may indicate a skull fracture, and you need to seek medical help urgently.

SPRAINS & STRAINS

If you're not sure if your injury is a sprain or a broken bone, treat as a broken bone (see Broken Bones later in this chapter).

These soft tissue injuries affect ligaments and muscles and are common if you're doing any sort of vigorous activity like walking over rough terrain. They often occur as a result of a sudden wrench or twist. Sprains are injuries to a ligament near a joint, usually the ankle or knee joint. You get pain and swelling, with bruising often appearing 12 to 24 hours later. Strains are damage to the muscle caused by sudden violent movements, and are felt as a sudden sharp pain within the muscle body.

Treatment of any soft tissue injury is with RICE:

▶ **R**est the injured part
▶ Apply **I**ce/snow or a cold compress (not directly on the skin)
▶ **C**ompress the injury (use a bandage)
▶ **E**levate the injured part

All these measures will help to reduce the swelling, bruising and pain, and are best started as early as possible after the injury. Continue with this for 24 to 48 hours or longer if the injury is more severe.

Use an elastic bandage (or a thick layer of padding kept in place with a crepe bandage) to compress the swelling (see right for how to bandage an ankle). Check the bandage regularly in case further swelling has made it too tight. Simple painkillers should ease any discomfort. If the sprain is mild, you may be able to walk on it; an improvised crutch will help take the weight off it. To prevent further injury, wear boots with good ankle support.

For severe sprains you will need an X-ray to exclude the possibility of a broken bone, but in the meantime treat as for a broken bone and avoid putting weight on it.

PAINFUL JOINTS

If you're doing any sort of strenuous activity, you're at risk of getting overuse injuries of your joints. Signs are painful, sometimes swollen joints, worse after use.

Treat with rest, a cold compress and anti-inflammatory painkillers like ibuprofen (if you don't have a history of stomach ulcers or indigestion). A support bandage may help, although rest is the most effective measure.

Prevention is the best treatment: make sure you are prepared by training well to improve your fitness; remember to warm up and down properly before starting an activity.

MAJOR TRAUMA

INITIAL ASSESSMENT

Accidents can happen anywhere and what you do is determined to some extent by the circumstances you are in and how readily available medical care is. However, remember that emergency services may be very different from what you are used to. They may be very much slower at responding to a call, so you need to be prepared to do at least an initial assessment and to ensure the person comes to no further harm. A basic plan of action is outlined as follows:

▶ keep calm and think through what you need to do
▶ carefully look over the injured person in the position you found them (unless this is hazardous for some reason eg on a cliff edge)
▶ check for a pulse (see the inside back cover), breathing and major blood loss
▶ if necessary, and you know how, start resuscitation – see inside backcover
▶ take immediate steps to control any bleeding by applying direct pressure
▶ check for shock, head injuries, spine and limb injuries, and any other injuries
▶ make the person as comfortable as possible and reassure them
▶ keep the person warm if necessary by insulating them from cold or wet ground (use whatever you have to hand eg a sleeping bag)
▶ don't move the person if a spinal injury is possible
▶ get medical help urgently

HEAD INJURY

Your brain is (obviously) vital to life and you should do everything you can to prevent injury to it – wear a helmet or hard hat if you are going to do any potentially risky activities. You need to seek medical help for any significant head injury.

Scalp wounds need to be treated like any other wound (see earlier). Serious head injury can occur with little or no signs of external injury. If a person has received an injury to the head, you need to assess whether there has been damage to the brain. You can do this by assessing whether they were unconscious at all (how much damage occurred is related to how long unconsciousness lasted), how they are behaving now, and if they show any signs of deterioration in the hours or days following the accident.

- Dazed but didn't lose consciousness – very little risk of brain damage.
- Unconscious (blacked out) for a few minutes, can't remember accident happening – the person is concussed (ie the brain has been shaken and bruised a bit). They may feel dizzy and nauseated, with mild headache, and memory loss can last for a few hours. Concussion generally doesn't cause any permanent damage, but you need to keep an eye on the person for 24 hours in case they deteriorate. Seek medical help.
- Prolonged unconsciousness of more than 10 minutes (coma) – this usually indicates more serious brain damage, and may be associated with a skull fracture. Put the person into the recovery position (see inside backcover) and get medical help immediately. Evacuation may be necessary.

Signs of a skull fracture include:

- blood coming from nose, mouth or throat not due to external injury
- clear, watery fluid dripping from ear or nose
- a depression or dip in the skull

Anyone who has had a head injury causing unconsciousness, however brief, should be observed for signs of deterioration in the 24 to 48 hours following injury. Head injury can sometimes result in compression of the brain because of bleeding from a damaged blood vessel within the head. This causes blood to accumulate gradually within the closed space of the skull, squashing the brain. Signs of brain compression or severe brain damage include:

- disorientation and confusion
- vomiting
- severe headache
- drowsiness
- irritability or change in personality
- noisy, slow breathing
- unequal or dilated pupils that may not react to light
- weakness down one side of the body

If someone has a head injury but is conscious:

- ▶ staunch any bleeding
- ▶ check if they know who and where they are, what the date is etc
- ▶ check they can move all their limbs and don't have any unusual sensations (eg tingling)
- ▶ sit them up gradually and then do a test walk to check balance
- ▶ deal with any external wounds
- ▶ avoid alcohol and sedatives on the first evening
- ▶ rest up for a day or two until you're sure the person is back to normal

If the person is concussed (eg keeps asking the same question), keep a close eye on them for the first 24 hours and be ready to get medical help immediately if there is any deterioration in their condition.

! Note that sometimes a head injury can occur when someone has lost consciousness from another cause (eg a faint).

NECK & SPINE INJURY

The main worry with any spinal or neck injury is damage to your spinal cord. Apart from supporting your trunk and head, your backbone (spine) provides a protective covering for nerve fibres (the spinal cord) carrying messages from your brain to all parts of your body. If these fibres are partly or completely cut, the damage caused may be permanent. The most vulnerable parts of the spine are your neck and lower back. Causes of spinal injury include falling from a height, diving into a shallow pool and hitting the bottom, a head-on crash in a motor vehicle, and being thrown from a motorbike.

Severe persistent neck or back pain indicate that you may have injured your spine. If you have also damaged the spinal cord, you may not be able to move your limbs, or you may have abnormal or no feelings in your body below the level of the injury (for example tingling or a feeling of heaviness). If the injury is at a high level, breathing difficulties may occur if the nerves to the chest muscles are affected.

The main priority in someone with a spinal injury is to prevent new or further damage to the spinal cord by immobilisation of the spine and extremely careful handling during any evacuation procedure.

!If in doubt, eg the person is unconscious, assume there is a spinal injury until proven otherwise.

BROKEN BONES

A break or crack in a bone is called a fracture. Bones are generally tough and you need a pretty forceful injury to break one, although old or diseased bones break more easily. In a simple fracture, the bone breaks in one place and the skin isn't torn. An open fracture is where the broken ends of the bone stick through the skin. You should assume that any fracture associated with a wound near it is an open one, even if you can't see the bone protruding (the broken ends may have come through the skin and gone back).

Any broken bone needs medical attention as it needs to be set properly, and any damage to the surrounding tissues needs to be assessed and treated. Open fractures have the added risk of infection because the bone is exposed, and generally need more urgent treatment.

A broken bone is often obvious because it hurts like hell. Otherwise, indications of a fracture include:

- forceful injury eg a violent blow, a fall or impact with a moving object
- snapping sound as the bone broke
- pain made worse by movement
- tenderness when you press over the bone at the site of injury
- obvious swelling and bruising over the injury site
- pain when you try to use the limb and you can't put your weight on it
- obvious deformity of the limb – twisting, short-ening or bending

What you do next will depend to a certain extent on the circumstances you're in and how readily medical help is available. The aim with any type of fracture is to prevent further dam-age by immobilising the affected part in some way (usually with a splint or sling). Unless the person is in immediate danger where they are, don't move them until the fracture has been sup-ported and immobilised. Painkillers are important but if med-ical help is close at hand, avoid taking anything by mouth in case an operation is needed to fix the fracture.

Some basic guidelines for a simple fracture are as follows:

▶ if the affected limb is bent or angled, straighten it by pulling firmly in the line of the bone, but if this causes too much pain, it's OK to leave it

▶ if you are near medical help, immo-bilise the limb by bandaging it and support the arm in a sling against your body or bandage the uninjured leg to the injured one

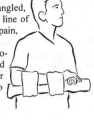

▶ in the field situation, it's worth immobilising the limb in a splint – use plastic air splints or structural aluminium malleable (SAM) splints if you are carrying them, or you can improvise with any piece of equipment you have, but make sure you pad the inside of the splint

Note that simple fractures don't need to be fixed straight away because healing takes several weeks, so if you have a chance to go to a better hospital further away, it would be worthwhile.

With an open fracture, you need to cover the wound and control any bleeding (apply pressure with a clean pad or dressing) before immobilising the limb as for a simple fracture. If no medical help is available within one to two hours, start taking antibiotics (eg cephalexin 500mg four times daily) to prevent infection.

Remember to check that any bandage or splint you've applied is not cutting off the circulation (indicated by numbness, tingling and blue or white colour). Loosen the bandages or splint immediately if necessary.

! In cold conditions, frostbite is a particular risk in this situation, so you need to protect the hand or foot from cold by covering them appropriately.

DISLOCATIONS

This can occur when a bone is wrenched into an abnormal position or because of violent muscle contractions (as in a fit, for example). This displaces the head of a bone from the joint, most commonly the shoulder, thumb, finger and jaw. There can be an associated fracture and there's often damage to the structures surrounding the joint. Don't attempt to replace a dislocation if a fracture is present.

!As a general rule, don't attempt to replace a dislocated joint if medical help is accessible because you can cause permanent damage.

You need to treat dislocations with immobilisation and pain relief as for a simple fracture.

BROKEN RIBS

Flail chest is when a heavy blow fractures several ribs in more than one place. This is an emergency because you will not be able to breathe properly. On inspection, a section of your chest will be moving in the opposite direction to the rest of your chest during breathing. The broken part needs to be splinted immediately by taping a firm bandage over it and supporting your arm in a sling on the injured side.

Otherwise, broken ribs are painful but don't need any specific treatment. Take strong painkillers, such as co-codamol, at the prescribed intervals. If the pain is very severe, or there are multiple fractures, you may need to strap your chest.

!Get help urgently if you experience breathing difficulties or cough up blood.

INTERNAL INJURIES

Some injuries can cause severe internal damage and bleeding without significant external injury. It's easy to control bleeding from external wounds on the skin by applying pressure but you can't do this for internal bleeding.

!Internal injuries are generally caused by considerable violence and always need urgent expert medical care and evacuation if you are in a remote area.

They may not be obvious to begin with, but you need to suspect internal bleeding if there are signs of shock (casualty looks pale, feels dizzy with weak rapid pulse and low blood pressure). Sometimes bleeding in the abdomen can produce a tender, slowly expanding abdomen.

CHOKING

You choke if your airway is completely or partly blocked, for example as a result of swallowing a small bone, eating too quickly or because of vomit, especially if you're drunk. Children often put things in their mouths, and this may result in choking. Small toys, coins and food such as peanuts or boiled sweets are particular risks.

It's usually obvious if a person is choking – they will have difficulty speaking, may gag and usually clutch their throat. A child may make a whistling noise, try to cry but be unable to, or may go blue in the face and collapse.

If an adult or child appears to be choking:

▸ get them to cough – this may bring up the blockage
▸ if this doesn't work, give them four sharp blows between the shoulder blades (ask adults to bend forward; children can be up-ended or bent over your knee)

If this doesn't work, try the following techniques:

▸ child (over one year) – place child on the floor or across your lap and place your hands one on each side of the chest just below the armpits; squeeze the child's chest by giving four sharp thrusts with your hands
▸ adult – lie the casualty down on the floor on their side; place both your hands on the side of their chest, under their armpit, and give four quick downwards thrusts

For babies, you won't be able to get them to cough, so you need to give four sharp slaps between the shoulders to start with – lie the baby face down on your forearm and support their head and shoulders on your hand. If you need to give chest thrusts, lie the baby face down on your lap and give four quick squeezes, as described for a child (but gentler).

Check to see if the blockage is cleared (remove it from the mouth if necessary) if not, get medical help urgently.

GLOSSARY

acetaminophen – US name for *paracetamol*

adrenaline – hormone given by injection to treat severe allergic reactions (such as to bee or ant sting); US term is *epinephrine*

AIDS – acquired immune deficiency syndrome

antibiotic – drug used to treat bacterial infections

antidiarrhoeals – usually refers to drugs used to treat the symptoms of diarrhoea ('blockers' or 'stoppers')

bacteria – microorganisms that can cause diseases; can be treated with *antibiotics*

booster – dose of vaccine given after a full course to bring protection up to optimum level

breakbone fever – old name for dengue fever

CDC – Centers for Disease Control and Prevention (US)

colic – pain that comes and goes in waves

dermatitis – general term for an itchy skin rash

DHF – dengue haemorrhagic fever

diuretic – any substance (such as coffee, alcohol and some therapeutic medicines) that increases the volume of urine lost

drug – in the medical sense, any substance used to alleviate symptoms or treat disease; the term is used interchangeably with medicine and medication

dysentery – any diarrhoeal illness where you get blood in your faeces

enteric fever – another term for typhoid or paratyphoid fever

epidemic – sudden outbreak of an infectious disease that rapidly affects lots of people

epinephrine – see *adrenaline*

fever – when your body temperature is higher than normal (normal is 37°C or 98.6°F)

generic – chemical name as opposed to the brand name of a drug; by convention brand names are always capitalised

haemorrhage – bleeding

HIV – human immunodeficiency virus

immunisation – production of immunity, to protect against disease

infectious – describes a disease caused by a microorganism; something you can 'catch', unlike cancer, for example

jaundice – yellowing of the skin and whites of the eyes

Lariam – brand name of the antimalarial *mefloquine*

mefloquine – a drug used in the prevention and treatment of malaria; brand name is *Lariam*

microorganism – any organism too small to be visible to the naked eye, includes bacteria, viruses, fungi etc

ORS – oral rehydration salts

paracetamol – simple painkiller, also good for lowering fever; US term is *acetaminophen*

pressure bandage – describes a bandage used to apply pressure over a wide area of a limb; used in management of some bites and stings

prophylaxis – prevention of disease

protozoa – single-celled microorganisms (such as the malaria parasites and *Giardia*)

resistance – when antibiotics or other drugs are ineffective against a microorganism

SPF – sun protection factor
STI – sexually transmitted infection
sulpha drugs – a group of antibiotics

TB – tuberculosis
tourniquet – device used to press on an artery to stop blood flow; dangerous if used inappropriately
thrush – common name for vaginal candidiasis

ulcer – break in the skin (or mucous membrane such as the lining of the stomach)

vaccination – not exactly synonomous with immunisation, but in this book we have used the terms interchangeably

WHO – World Health Organization

AFRICA • Africa on a shoestring • Arabic (Egyptian) phrasebook • Arabic (Moroccan) phrasebook • Cairo • Cape Town • Central Africa • East Africa • Egypt • Egypt travel atlas • Ethiopian (Amharic) phrasebook • Ethiopia, Eritrea & Djibouti • Healthy Travel Africa • The Gambia & Senegal • Kenya • Kenya travel atlas • Malawi, Mozambique & Zambia • Morocco • Mozambique • North Africa • Read This First Africa • South Africa, Lesotho & Swaziland • South Africa, Lesotho & Swaziland travel atlas • Southern Africa • Swahili phrasebook • Tanzania • Trekking in East Africa • Tunisia • West Africa • Zimbabwe, Botswana & Namibia • Zimbabwe, Botswana & Namibia travel atlas
Travel Literature: The Rainbird: A Central African Journey • Songs to an African Sunset: A Zimbabwean Story • Mali Blues: Traveling to an African Beat

AUSTRALIA & THE PACIFIC Australia • Australian phrasebook • Bushwalking in Australia • Bushwalking in Papua New Guinea • Fiji • Fijian phrasebook • Healthy Travel Australia, NZ & the Pacific • Islands of Australia's Great Barrier Reef • Melbourne • Micronesia • New Caledonia • New South Wales & the ACT • New Zealand • Northern Territory • Outback Australia • Papua New Guinea • Pidgin phrasebook • Queensland • Rarotonga & the Cook Islands • Samoa • Solomon Islands • South Australia • South Pacific phrasebook • Sydney • Tahiti & French Polynesia • Tasmania • Tonga • Tramping in New Zealand • Vanuatu • Victoria • Western Australia
Travel Literature: Islands in the Clouds • Sean & David's Long Drive

CENTRAL AMERICA & THE CARIBBEAN Bahamas and Turks & Caicos • Barcelona • Bermuda • Central America on a shoestring • Costa Rica • Cuba • Dominican Republic & Haiti • Healthy Travel Central & South America • Eastern Caribbean • Guatemala, Belize & Yucatán: La Ruta Maya • Jamaica • Mexico • Mexico City • Panama • Read This First Central & South America
Travel Literature: Green Dreams: Travels in Central America

EUROPE Amsterdam • Andalucía • Austria • Baltic States phrasebook • Berlin • Britain • British phrasebook • Central Europe • Central Europe phrasebook • Croatia • Czech & Slovak Republics • Denmark • Dublin • Eastern Europe • Eastern Europe phrasebook • Edinburgh • Estonia, Latvia & Lithuania • Europe • Finland • France • French phrasebook • Germany • German phrasebook • Greece • Greek phrasebook • Hungary • Iceland, Greenland & the Faroe Islands • Ireland • Italian phrasebook • Italy • Lisbon • London • Mediterranean Europe • Mediterranean Europe phrasebook • Paris • Poland • Portugal • Portugal travel atlas • Prague • Provence & the Côte D'Azur • Read This First Europe • Romania & Moldova • Russia, Ukraine & Belarus • Russian phrasebook • Scandinavian & Baltic Europe • Scandinavian Europe phrasebook • Scotland • Slovenia • Spain • Spanish phrasebook • St Petersburg • Switzerland • Trekking in Spain • Ukrainian phrasebook • Vienna • Walking in Britain • Walking in Italy • Walking in Ireland • Walking in Switzerland • Western Europe • Western Europe phrasebook
Travel Literature: The Olive Grove: Travels in Greece

INDIAN SUBCONTINENT Bangladesh • Bengali phrasebook • Bhutan • Delhi • Goa • Healthy Travel Asia & India • Hindi/Urdu phrasebook • India • India & Bangladesh travel atlas • Indian Himalaya • Karakoram Highway • Nepal • Nepali phrasebook • Pakistan • Rajasthan • Read This First Asia & India • South India • Sri Lanka • Sri Lanka phrasebook • Trekking in the Indian Himalaya • Trekking in the Karakoram & Hindukush • Trekking in the Nepal Himalaya

Travel Literature: In Rajasthan • Shopping for Buddhas

ISLANDS OF THE INDIAN OCEAN Madagascar & Comoros • Maldives • Mauritius, Réunion & Seychelles

MIDDLE EAST & CENTRAL ASIA Arab Gulf States • Central Asia • Central Asia phrasebook • Iran • Israel & the Palestinian Territories • Israel & the Palestinian Territories travel atlas • Istanbul • Jerusalem • Jordan & Syria • Jordan, Syria & Lebanon travel atlas • Lebanon • Middle East on a shoestring • Turkey • Turkish phrasebook • Turkey travel atlas • Yemen
Travel Literature: The Gates of Damascus • Kingdom of the Film Stars: Journey into Jordan

NORTH AMERICA Alaska • Backpacking in Alaska • Baja California • California & Nevada • Canada • Florida • Hawaii • Honolulu • Los Angeles • Miami • New England USA • New Orleans • New York City • New York, New Jersey & Pennsylvania • Pacific Northwest USA • Rocky Mountain States • San Francisco • Seattle • Southwest USA • USA • USA phrasebook • Vancouver • Washington, DC & the Capital Region
Travel Literature: Drive Thru America

NORTH-EAST ASIA Beijing • Cantonese phrasebook • China • Hong Kong • Hong Kong, Macau & Guangzhou • Japan • Japanese phrasebook • Japanese audio pack • Korea • Korean phrasebook • Kyoto • Mandarin phrasebook • Mongolia • Mongolian phrasebook • North-East Asia on a shoestring • Seoul • South-West China • Taiwan • Tibet • Tibetan phrasebook • Tokyo
Travel Literature: Lost Japan

SOUTH AMERICA Argentina, Uruguay & Paraguay • Bolivia • Brazil • Brazilian phrasebook • Buenos Aires • Chile & Easter Island • Chile & Easter Island travel atlas • Colombia • Healthy Travel Central & South America • Ecuador & the Galapagos Islands • Latin American Spanish phrasebook • Peru • Quechua phrasebook • Read This First Central & South America • Rio de Janeiro • South America on a shoestring • Trekking in the Patagonian Andes • Venezuela
Travel Literature: Full Circle: A South American Journey

SOUTH-EAST ASIA Bali & Lombok • Bangkok • Burmese phrasebook • Cambodia • Healthy Travel Asia & India • Hill Tribes phrasebook • Ho Chi Minh City • Indonesia • Indonesian phrasebook • Indonesian audio pack • Jakarta • Java • Laos • Lao phrasebook • Laos travel atlas • Malay phrasebook • Malaysia, Singapore & Brunei • Myanmar (Burma) • Philippines • Pilipino (Tagalog) phrasebook • Read This First Asia & India • Singapore • South-East Asia on a shoestring • South-East Asia phrasebook • Thailand • Thailand's Islands & Beaches • Thailand travel atlas • Thai phrasebook • Thai audio pack • Vietnam • Vietnamese phrasebook • Vietnam travel atlas

ALSO AVAILABLE: Antarctica • Brief Encounters: Stories of Love, Sex & Travel • Chasing Rickshaws • Not the Only Planet: Travel Stories from Science Fiction • Travel with Children • Traveller's Tales

For ordering information contact your nearest Lonely Planet office.

LONELY PLANET PRODUCTS

TRAVEL GUIDES

Travel Guides explore a destination in depth, with options to suit a range of budgets. With reliable, practical advice on getting around, restaurants and accommodation, these easy-to-use guides also include numerous detailed maps, colour photographs, extensive background material and coverage of sights both on and off the beaten track.

PHRASEBOOKS

Lonely Planet phrasebooks cover essential words and phrases travellers need to effectively communicate. With colour tabs for quick reference, extensive vocabulary lists, use of local scripts and easy to follow pronunciation keys, these handy, pocket size language guides cover most situations a traveller is likely to encounter.

PISCES BOOKS

Beautifully illustrated with full-colour photos, Lonely Planet's Pisces Books explore the world's best diving and snorkelling areas and prepare divers for what to expect when they get there, both topside and underwater. Dive sites are described in detail with specifics on depths, visibility, level of difficulty, special conditions, underwater photography tips and common and unusual marine life present.

WALKING

With detailed descriptions ranging from family walks to hard high-level routes, advice on when to and how to do it, detailed and reliable maps and background information, these informative walking guides are an invaluable resource for both independent walkers and those in an organised group - in fact, for anyone who believes that the best way to see the world is on foot.

CITY MAPS

Lonely Planet's City Map series covers the world's great cities, both on and off the beaten track. This full-colour and easy-to-use product contains downtown and metropolitan maps, transit routes, unique walking tours, and essential information (including phone numbers), plus a complete index of streets and sights. The information is up-to-date and accurate, and the maps are plastic-coated for extra durability.

TRAVEL ATLASES

Lonely Planet's Travel Atlases are thoroughly researched and fact-checked by the guidebook authors to ensure they complement the guidebooks. And the booklet format means none of the holes, wrinkles, tears or constant folding and refolding characteristic of large sheet maps.

PLANET TALK

Our FREE quarterly printed newsletter is full of tips from travellers and anecdotes from Lonely Planet guidebook authors. Every issue is packed with up-to-date travel news and advice, and includes a postcard from Lonely Planet co-founder Tony Wheeler, mail from travellers, a look at life on the road through the eyes of a Lonely Planet author, topical health advice, prizes for the best travel yarn, news about forthcoming Lonely Planet events and a complete list of Lonely Planet books and products.

To join our mailing list, residents of the UK, Europe and Africa can email us at go@lonelyplanet.co.uk; residents of North and South America can email us at info@lonelyplanet.com; the rest of the world can email us at talk2us@lonelyplanet.com.au, or contact any Lonely Planet office.

COMET

Our FREE monthly email newsletter brings you all the latest travel news, features, interviews, competitions, destination ideas, travellers' tips & tales, Q&As, raging debates and related links. Find out what's new on the Lonely Planet Web site and which books are about to hit the shelves. Subscribe from your desktop: www.lonelyplanet.com/comet

LONELY PLANET ONLINE

Lonely Planet's award-winning web site has insider info on hundreds of destinations from Amsterdam to Zimbabwe, complete with interactive maps and colour photographs. You'll also find the latest travel news, recent reports from travellers on the road, guidebook upgrades and a lively bulletin board where you can meet fellow travellers, swap recommendations and seek advice. www.lonelyplanet.com or AOL keyword: lp

UPGRADES

Lonely Planet publishes online Upgrades of some of our most popular guidebooks. Upgrades are regular reports from Lonely Planet authors summarising important information gathered since the book was published. Designed as supplements to current editions of selected Lonely Planet guidebooks, Upgrades can be downloaded for free from the Lonely Planet web site, at: www.lonelyplanet.com/upgrades

INDEX

A

abdominal bloating 110, 120
abdominal pain 102, 120, 121, 126, 144, 151, 152
abscess
    amoebic 121
    tooth 174
accident prevention 69, 233
accidental poisoning 234
acclimatisation
    altitude 288
    cold 283
    heat 60
    sun 64
acupressure 361
acupuncture 360-1
acute mountain sickness, see altitude
AIDS 178-84
    helplines 181-2
air travel
    dehydration and 56
    ear pain 54
    fear of flying 56
    fitness for 54
alcohol withdrawal 201, 203
Alexander technique 362
allergic reaction
    bee sting 323
    medicines 375
    skin 159-62
allergic rhinitis, see hay fever
alternative first aid 50-1
alternative therapies 359-71
    useful organisations 360
alternative travel kits 49
altitude 288-91
amoebic dysentery 121
amoebic meningitis 301

anaemia 101
anal fissure 149
anal itching 150
animal bites 339-40
    first aid 340
antibiotics 378-82
    diarrhoea and 118
    doses 381
    oral contraception and 216
    resistance 379
antidiarrhoeals 116-8, 383
antifungal creams 157, 213
antihistamines 382
anti-inflammatory drugs 378
antimalarials, see malaria prevention drugs
ants 322-3
anxiety 200-2
appendicitis 151
appetite loss 134
Aralen, see chloroquine
aromatherapy 362-3
    travel and 56
arthritis, travel and 245
aspirin 376
athlete's foot 157
Ayurveda 363-4

B

babies, see children
back pain 212
bacterial vaginosis 214
bandages 397-8
    ankle 405
    pressure immobilisation 398
beach safety 67-8
bedbugs 163
bee sting 322-3
bends, see decompression sickness
bismuth subsalicylate 383
bites, see also specific creatures

Colour indicates symptoms

animal 339-40
human 340
insects 69-73
marine creatures 308-17
black widow spider 330
blackflies 320-1
bladder infection 211-2
bleeding, see also illness,
danger signs
dengue fever and 124
hepatitis and 135
trauma and 400-1
vaginal 208
blisters
feet 268-9
skin 159, 160
blood clots 54, 56, 210, 249
blood
coughing up 141
in faeces 110-1
in urine 101
in vomit 101
blood transfusions 82-3
blue-ringed octopus 316
blues, post-travel 344, see also
depression
blurred vision 172
boils 401
books 52-3
box jellyfish 312
breakbone fever, see dengue
fever
breast lumps 210
breathing rate 101
breathlessness 141, 291
broken bones 409-11
broken ribs 412
brucellosis 190
burns 402
portable cookers and 267
bush food 94
bushwalking, see trekking

C
caving 271-2
Centers for Disease Control &
Prevention (CDC) 23
centipedes 332
cerebral malaria, see malaria
chancroid 189
checkup
post-travel 341
pretravel 42
chest infection, see cough
chilblains 286-7
children 224-42
signs of illness 236-7
chlamydia 187-8
chlorine 78
chloroquine 38
choking 413
cholera 190-1
immunisation 30
ciguatera poisoning 146
Citizen's Emergency Center 24
cleanliness 80
clothing
cold climates 285
hot climates 62
insect bites and 70
cold (climate) 283-8
cold (illness) 138-9
cold sores 144
colour therapy 364
concussion 407
condoms 179, 187
cone shell 316-7
confusion 320
conjunctivitis 169-71
constipation 148-9
contact lens wearers 168
contraception (women) 215-20
emergency 218-9
contraception (men) 179
convulsion 102, 283, 403

coral cuts 310
cough 126, 138, 194, 291
cracked heels 64
cramps 111, 294
creeping eruption 165
crocodiles 300
crown of thorns 317
crystal healing 364-5
culture shock 199-200
cuts 396-7
cycling 269-71
cyclones 277-8
cystitis, *see* bladder infection

D

DAN 302
dark urine 134
deafness 168
decompression sickness 306-7
DEET (diethyltoluamide) 71
dehydration 281, 263-4
    children and 235
delirium 203
dengue fever 20 (*map*), 122-4
dengue haemorrhagic fever
    123-4
dental problems 173-7
dentures, repair 248
depression 202-3
dermatitis 159-62
diabetic travellers 251-5
dialysis centres 245
diarrhoea 102, 107-21, 146,
    151, 190, 200, 301
    antibiotics 118
    children and 239-41
    eating and 115-6
    fluid replacement 114-5
    oral contraception and 216
    persistent 119-21

treatment 112-9
types 108-12
diet, *see* nutrition
digestive problems 144-51
diphtheria 194-5
dislocation (joint) 411-2
distress signal 262
diving 301-8
    emergency hotlines 303
    safety tips 304-5
Divers Alert Network (DAN)
    302
dizziness 200, 281, 283, 337
documents 43
donovanosis 189
double vision 337
doxycycline 38
dressings, *see* bandages
drinking water 76-80
    boiling 78
    chemical disinfectants 78-9
    purifiers 79-80
driving safely 264-6
drowning 274
dysentery 110-1

E

ears 166-8
    infection 167-8
earache 166
    eardrum, burst 55
    flying and 54-5
eardrops 167
earthquake 277
eczema 160
elephantiasis, *see* filariasis
emergencies
    allergic reaction 323
    avalanche 276
    bee sting 323
    blizzards 276-7
    bushfire 275-6
    lost 272-3

Colour indicates symptoms

night out 273-4
rescue 260-2
resuscitation 431
sand storm 276
encephalitis 320
EPIRB 260
evacuation, medical 387-8
eyes 168-73
black eye 171
injuries 172
itchy eyes 168
particle in 169
red eye 169-71, 301
wash 169
eyedrops 170

F

facial pain 140
facial swelling 175
fainting 281-2, 403
falciparum malaria, see malaria
Fansidar 131
fatigue 319
febrile convulsion 238
fever 101, 102-5, 111, 121,
    122-33, 134, 138, 140, 141,
    175, 192, 194, 212, 301, 319,
    320, 327
causes 105
children and 237-9
dehydration and 103
how to lower it 103-5
filariasis 191-2
first aid
courses 44
fish stings 316
jellyfish stings 313-4
snake bite 338-9
spider bites 331
fits, see convulsion
fleas 163-4
flies 321-2
flu 138-9

fluid replacement
children and 239-41
diarrhoea and 114-5
heat and 279
food poisoning 111-2
food precautions 73-6
footcare 63-4
footwear 63-4
fracture, see broken bones
frostbite 287-8
fruit bats 339
fungal infections
skin 156-7
vaginal 213
funnel-web spider 328

G

gastrointestinal upset, see
    diarrhoea
genital ulcers 186
genital warts 188-9
German measles, see rubella
giardiasis 120-1, 264
glands, swollen 191, 143, 327
glandular fever 143-4
gonorrhoea 186-7

H

haemorrhoids, see piles
hangover 205
Hansen's disease 192
hay fever 142
head injury 406-8
headache 102-5, 106, 122,
    126, 132, 134, 138, 140, 173,
    192, 200, 281, 283, 289, 301,
    320, 327, 337, 408
healers, traditional 346-7
heart conditions, travel and 245
heartburn 150
heat 279-83
acclimatisation 60-3, 279
fluid replacement 279-81

older travellers and 250
heat exhaustion 282-3
heatstroke 282-3
    first aid treatment 283
hepatitis 133-7
    immunisation (type A) 29
    immunisation (type B) 30
    oral contraceptive pill and
        135
    pregnancy and 134
    prevention 136-7
    symptoms 134-5
    treatment 135-6
herbal medicine 365-6
herpes, genital 188, see also
    cold sores
hiking, see trekking
histoplasmosis 272
HIV, see AIDS
HIV-positive travellers 255-6
homoeopathy 366
hot flushes 209
HRT, travelling and 209-10
hurricanes 277-8
hygiene, personal 80
hypothermia 284-6

I
IAMAT 25
illness
    danger signs 101-2
    general treatment measures
        98
immunisations 26-32
    certificate 27
    children and 225-6
    homoeopathic 31
    older travellers and 247
    side effects 31-2
    timing 26-7

impetigo 158
indigestion 150-1
information sources
    general travel health 21-6
    caving 272
    cycling 270
    diving 303
    wilderness health & safety
        258-60
injections, infection risks 82-3
insect bites 153-4, 319
    prevention 69-73
insects, diseases and 69
insect repellents 71-2
insulin 252
insurance 40-2
    diving and 302
internal injuries 412-3
International Association for
    Medical Assistance to
    Travelers 25
internet resources, see also
    information sources
    travel health 24-5
    wilderness health & safety
        260
intestinal parasites 145
intrauterine devices 218
iodine 78
iridology 366-7
irritable bowel syndrome 120
itching 163, 165
    bites 153-4
    eyes 142
    rash 157, 159

J
Japanese encephalitis 320
    immunisation 30
jaundice 126, 134, 143, 301
    oral contraception and 216
jellyfish 311-4
jet lag 57-8

Colour indicates symptoms

children and 230
jock itch 156
joint pains 122, 319, 405-6

K

katipo spider 330
kava 354
kidney infection 212, see also
  bladder infection
kidney stone 151-2
Kunjin virus 320

L

Lariam, see mefloquine
leeches 323-5
leprosy, see Hansen's disease
leptospirosis 272, 299-301
lice 163
light-coloured faeces 134
lightning 274
lymphogranuloma venereum
  189

M

malaria 20 (map), 125-32, 341
  children and 227, 239
  diagnostic kit 40
  emergency treatment 39-
    40, 128
  information sources 33-4
  prevention 32-40
  symptoms 126
  treatment 127
malaria prevention drugs 34-9
  doses & timing 35-6
  long-haul travellers 38
  scuba diving and 304
  side effects 36-9
malaria treatment drugs 128-32
Malarone 131
marine life 308-17, see also
  specific creatures
massage 367-8

measles 195
medical help 97
medical kit 45-9
  children 228-30
  outdoor activities 262
medical services 384-95
  payment 384, 387
medicinal plants 348-58
medicines 372-83
  buying 372-3
  children and 228-30
  customs and 46
  dangerous 374
  interactions 249
  generic vs brand names 46,
    373-4
  side effects 375
meditation 368-9
mefloquine 36-7, 131
  diving and 304
  mind problems and 203
melatonin 58
meningitis 192-3
menstruation 206-8
  absent periods 208
  heavy periods 208
  preventing periods 206
migraine 173
morning-after pill 218-9
mosquitoes 318-20
  disease and 191
  nets 72-73
motion sickness 59
mouth ulcers 144
mumps 195
Murray Valley Encephalitis 320
muscle strain 404-5

N

nappy rash 242
natural remedies
  bruises 50
  chilblains 287

colds 51, 139
constipation 50
diarrhoea 50, 118
health boosters 61
insect bites 51, 319
jet lag 58
menopausal symptoms 209
motion sickness 50, 59
premenstrual syndrome 207
skin rashes 51
stress 51
sunburn 51, 154
naturopathy 369
nausea, *see* vomiting
neck injury 408
neck stiffness 192
night sweats 194
nitrogen narcosis 307
nosebleed 403-4
nutrition 84-5
    activity and 93-5
    children and 232

O
older travellers 246-51
oral contraception 215-8
    missed pill 216
orienteering 266
outdoor activities, safety rules
    257-8
overbreathing 200
ozone hole 66

P
painkillers 376-8
palpitations 200
panic attacks 201-2
paracetamol 376
paralysis
    shellfish and 147

ticks and 326-7
polio and 196
snake bite and 337
paranoia 204
permethrin 72
piles 149-50
polio 196
pollution, water 295
Portuguese man of war 313
post-travel checkup 341
    children 242
pregnancy, accidental 219
pregnant travellers 220-3
    air travel and 221
    immunisations and 221
premenstrual syndrome 206
pressure immobilisation
    bandage 398
prickly heat 158-9, 242
prostate trouble 152
pubic lice 163
pulse rate 100

Q
quinine 131

R
rabies 339
radio 260
rash 106, 122, 132, 159, 164-5,
    192, 195, 319, 327
    diseases and 164
recompression facilities 303
red-back spider 327
red eye 169-71
reflexology 370
rehydration, see fluid
    replacement
reiki 370
rescue procedure 260-2
respiratory problems 138-44
rigors 103-5
ringworm, *see* fungal skin

Colour indicates symptoms

infections
rip, see sea currents
river crossings 274-5
river hazards 299-301
Ross River Fever 319-20
rubella 195-6

S

sandflies 320-1
sanitary pads 207
scabies 163
scalds 402
scombroid poisoning 147
scorpionfish 315
scorpions 331-2
scuba diving, see diving
sea currents 292-4
sea kayaking 298-9
sea lice 312
sea snakes 311
sea urchins 317
sex
    safer 179-80
    travel and 81-2
sexually transmitted infections
    184-9, 214-5
sharks 308-10
shellfish 147
shiatsu 368
sinusitis 140
skin cancer 156
skin problems 153-65
    infections 157-8
    infestations 162-4
skull fracture 407
sling 410
snakes 332-9
    antivenoms 339
    snake bite 337
snorkelling 295-7
snow blindness 288
sore throat 138, 142-3, 195, 301
spiders 327-31

spine injury 408
splint 410
splinter 401
sprain 404-5
steroid cream 161
stingrays 314
stomach cramps 110, 121, see
    also abdominal pain
stonefish 315
street food 76
stress 197-8
stye 171
sun 64-7
    hypersensitivity 155
    sunburn 154-6
surf 292-4
surfing safety tips 296
sweating 103-5
swimmer's ear 166-7
swimming safety 67-8
syphilis 187

T

tampons 207
TB, see tuberculosis
teeth 173-6
temperature 100
    how to take it 99-100
termination of pregnancy 220
testicle, pain 153
tetanus 196
thermometer 99-100
thrush, see vaginal candidiasis
ticks 325-327
    tick paralysis 326-7
    removal 326
tooth abscess 175
tooth, broken 176
toothache 174-5
trachoma 171
traditional medicine 345-8
    traditional remedies 347-50
trauma 406-13

travel health clinics, *see*
    information sources
travel fatigue 200
travel insurance, *see* insurance
travel sickness, *see* motion
    sickness
travellers diarrhoea, *see*
    diarrhoea
travellers with special needs
    243-56
    flying 243
    general considerations 243-4
    information sources 244-7
    medical conditions 244
trekking 266-9
trichomoniasis 215
tsunami 278
tuberculosis 193-4
    immunisation 30
tummy ache 241, *see also*
    abdominal pain
tunnel vision 173
typhoid fever 132-3
    immunisation 29
typhus 327

U

ulcer, stomach 150
unconsciousness 403, 407-8
urinary problems 151-2
urinary tract infection, *see*
    bladder infection
useful organisations 25, *see also*
    information sources

HIV/AIDS 256
diabetes 251-2

V

vaginal bleeding, heavy 208
vaginal candidiasis 213-4
vaginal discharge 212-5
vaginal infections 212-5
vegetarian diet 90-2
venomous fish 314-6
vision loss 172-3
vitamins 86
vomiting 102, 106, 111-2, 121,
    122, 126, 134, 135, 146, 151,
    192, 283, 290, 301, 320, 337
    oral contraception and 216
    treatment for 382

W

wasp sting 322-3
water purifiers 79-80
web sites, *see* internet resources
weight loss 87, 102, 121, 194
wilderness safety 257-78
worms, intestinal 145-8
wounds 396-7
    cleaning 396
    closure 399-400
    infection 399

Y

yellow fever certificate 27
yellow skin, *see* jaundice
yoga 371

Colour indicates symptoms

THE LONELY PLANET STORY ──

The LP story begins with a classic travel adventure – Tony and Maureen Wheeler's 1972 journey across Europe and Asia to Australia. Useful information about the overland trail did not exist at that time, so Tony and Maureen published the first Lonely Planet guidebook to meet a growing need among the backpacker community.

Written at a kitchen table and hand collated, trimmed and stapled, Asia on the Cheap became an instant local bestseller, inspiring thoughts of another book. A further 18 months in South-East Asia resulted in their second guide, South-East Asia on a shoestring, which they put together in a backstreet Chinese hotel in Singapore in 1975. The 'yellow bible' as it quickly became known to backpackers around the world, soon became the guide to the region. It has now sold almost 750,000 copies, and still retains its familiar yellow cover. A 10th anniversary edition has recently been released and includes a story and photographs by Tony recalling the 1975 trip.

Today Lonely Planet publishes more than 450 titles, including travel guides, city guides, diving guides, city maps, phrasebooks, trekking guides, wildlife guides, travel atlases and travel literature. However, some things haven't changed. Our main aim is still to help make it possible for adventurous travellers to get out there – to explore and better understand the world. At Lonely Planet we believe that travellers can make a positive contribution to the countries they visit – if they respect their host communities and spend their money wisely. Since 1986 a percentage of the income from each book has been donated to aid projects and human rights campaigns across the world.

LONELY PLANET OFFICES

Australia
PO Box 617, Hawthorn, Victoria 3122
☎ 03-9819 1877
fax 03-9819 6459
email:talk2us@lonelyplanet.com.au

USA
150 Linden St, Oakland, CA 94607
☎ 510-893 8555 TOLL FREE: 800 275 8555
fax 510-893 8572
email: info@lonelyplanet.com

UK
10a Spring Place, London NW5 3BH
☎ 020-7428 4800
fax 020-7428 4828
email: go@lonelyplanet.co.uk

France
1 rue du Dahomey, 75011 Paris
☎ 01 55 25 33 00
fax 01 55 25 33 01
email: bip@lonelyplanet.fr
minitel: 3615 lonelyplanet *(1,29 F TTC/min)*

1 Assess the Scene
Is there a danger to yourself, the casualty or others?

- ▶ Yes: if possible remove danger but do not put yourself at risk
- ▶ No: go to step 2.
- ▶ Have you called for medical assistance?

2 Assess the Casualty
Is casualty conscious? Shake gently and shout for response.

- ▶ Yes: go to step 3.
- ▶ No: place casualty in recovery position (see illustration).

3 Clear Airway & Check Breathing.
Clear and open airway. Remove any objects or vomit.
Check for breathing: is the chest rising and falling?
Can you feel the breath on your cheek? (wait for up to 10 seconds)

- ▶ Yes: place casualty in recovery position and examine for injuries.
- ▶ No: you need to breathe for the casualty: see step 4.

4 Perform Expired Air Resuscitation
Turn the casualty on to their back.

- ▶ Use one hand to gently tilt head back.
- ▶ Pinch nose closed using thumb and index finger of other hand.
- ▶ Open mouth, keeping chin raised.
- ▶ Take a full breath and place your lips on the casualty's mouth.
- ▶ Blow steadily into the casualty's mouth for about two seconds.

ADULT
- ▶ Repeat so that you give two effective breaths.

BABY/CHILD
- ▶ Give two effective puffs or light breaths.